Sayyid Abul Hasan Ali Nadwi
Life and Legacy

Dr Yusuf Bamjee Memorial Series

Ahsan Academy of Research
Springs, South Africa

Sayyid Abul Hasan Ali Nadwi Life and Legacy

Abdul Kader Choughley

Tawasul International
Centre for Publishing, Research and Dialogue

© Ahsan Academy of Research

All rights reserved. No part of this publication may be reproduced, stored in a retrieval system, or transmitted in any form or by any means, electronic, mechanical, photocopying, recording or otherwise, without the prior permission of the copyright owner.

First Edition 2023
Second Edition: 2024
ISBN: 9788894948875

Abdul Kader Choughley

Ahsan Academy of Research
(Springs, South Africa)
akchoughley@gmail.com
Mob: 27 72 797 2630

Tawasul Europe
Centre for Publishing, Research and Dialogue
(Rome, Italy)

For

Muhammad Aasif Bamjee

In appreciation of your gracious support

To the multivolume series

CONTENTS

Acknowledgement xv
Transliteration xvii
Sayyid Abul Hasan 'Ali Nadwi: Life and Legacy xix
Introduction xxix

Chapter I: Shaykh Nadwi's Works: A Brief Survey 1
    Sayyid Qutb al-Din Muhammad al-Hasani 3
    Sayyid Shah 'Alamullah 4
    Sayyid Abu Sa'id Hasani 5
    Sayyid Ahmad Shahid 5
    Conclusion 9

Chapter II: Educational Influence: Formative Years 11
    Formative Influences 12
    Maktubāt: Portait of Sayyidah Khairun Nisā' 13
    Arabic Studies: Influence of Shaykh Khalil Yemeni 15
    Urdu Studies: Literary Influence 16
    Tarbiyah: Shaykh Nadwi's Academic and Moral Orientation 17
    Admission to Lucknow University 18
    Lahore: A Historic Visit 19
    Mawlana Husayn Ahmad Madani: An Enduring Mentorship 20
    'Allāmah Taqi al-Dīn Hilālī: Peerless Scholarship 21
    Salafiyyah and Hilālī 22
    Conclusion 23

Chapter III: In Pursuit of Academic Excellence 25
    Snapshot of *Dars i-Nizāmī* 25
    Fiqh in a Changing World 26
    Nadwah and the Arab World 27
    Academic Activities 28
    Arabic Teaching: A New Approach 31
    Quranic Studies 31
    Da'wah: Content and Context 33
    Academic Profile 34
    Shaykh Nadwi as a Historian 36
    Shaykh Nadwi as a Litterateur 37
    Literary Contributions in Arabic 38
    Mukhtārāt min Adab al-Arab 38
    Al-Qirā'at al-Rāshidah 39

Qasas al-Nabiyyīn 49
Salient Feature of Qasas al-Nabiyyīn 40
Conclusion 41

Chapter IV: Contemporary Islamic Movements...................................43
Academic Research: New Opportunities..43
Mawlana Mawdudi and Shaykh Nadwi..44
New Horizons 48
Rise and Fall of Muslims: An Appraisal 50
Salient Features of *Rise and Fall of Muslims* 53
Publication of *Rise and Fall of Muslims* 54
Da'wah Literature: Towards a New Horizon 55
Idārah Ta'limāt i-Islam 56
Conclusion 57

Chapter V: *Da'wah*: Content and Context 59
Tablighi Jamā'at: Mawlana Muhammad Ilyās 59
Shaykh Nadwi's Personal Reminiscences 59
Characteristics of *Da'wah* 63
Da'wah in the Hijaz 64
To the Hijazis: A Message 64
Ikhwān: Islamic Reformist Movement 65
Ikhwān: Personal Reminiscences 68
Ikhwān: A Critique..69
In the Heart of Africa: Sudan 70
Syria, Citadel of Islam: A Eulogy 71
Travelogue Series 72
Kuwait 75
Egypt 75
Sirya 75
Conclusion 76

Chapter VI: *Da'wah*: New Horizons 77
Muslim Hegemony: An Assessment 77
Religio-Political Activism...80
Reform of Muslim Society 82
In the Realms of Spirituality 84
Dimensions of Spirituality 87
In the company of Spiritual Guides 88
Towards New Horizons 89
Invitation from Damascus University 90
Shaykh Ahmad Harun al-Hajjar 91

Two Radio Lectures 92
Visit to Lebanon and Turkey 92
Turkey: Land of Contrast 93
World Muslim Congress 95
Baghdad: Scholars' Paradise 95
Conclusion 96

Chapter VII: Islamic Authenticity 97
Qadianism...100
Academy of Islamic Research and Publication 102
Aims and Objectives 102
Aligarh Muslim University 103
Da'wah Travels...104
Burma: Prediction of Doom 104
Kuwait 106
Demise: Dr 'Abdul 'Ali Hasani 107
Educational System: Muslim Response 108
Dīnī Ta'līmī Council 109
Islamic University of Madinah 111
Relations with Royalty: King Faisal bin 'Abdul 'Aziz 114
Rābitā al-'Ālama al-Islāmī: Muslim World League 117
Towards an Islamic Renaissance 118
Europe: A New Horizon 119
East and West Cultural Encounters 121
Maktubāt: An Overview 122
Geneva: Islamic Centre (n.d.) 122
London: 17 October 1963 123
Paris: October 1963 123
Spain: Andalus Syndrome 124
East and West Encounters 126
Da'wah to the West: Formative Years 127
Lecture: University of London 128
Message to Humanity: Germany 128
Assessment 129
Communal Riots 129
Majlis i-Mushāwarat 130
Conclusion 131

Chapter VIII: Islamic Reformist Thought in Shaykh Nadwi's 133
Literary Initiatives: An Overview 133
The Four Pillars of Islam 133
Hayāt-i Abdul Hayy..134

Nuzhat al-Khawātir 135
India During Muslim Rule 136
Western Civilisation, Islam and Muslims..137
Towards an Independent Islamic Education 138
Pathway to Medina 140
A Personal Loss 141
Strike: An Assessment 142
Turbulence in the Arab World (1967-1971)..................................142
Arab Nationalism: A Reappraisal 145
Assessment 146
The Indian Scenario: Religio-Political Developments 147
Payām-i Insaniyāt (Message of Humanity) 147
Riflections on *Payām* 150
Indo-Pakistan War: 1971 153
Shaykh Nadwi's Assessment 155
Travels 155
Conclusion 158

Chapter IX: East and West: Cultural Encounters 159
Islamic Authenticity: An Overview 160
Personal Loss: Family Members 162
In the Political Arena 164
Hindutva: An Assessment 166
Hindutva: Defenders of Hindu Extremism 167
Muslim Conquests: A Reappraisal 167
Maghreb: Morocco 168
Towards a New World 169
Message to the West 170
Need for an Islamic Environment 172
United Nations: Forum of Muslim Aspirations 173
Lectures in Chicago 174
Farewell Address to American Muslims 175
Daʿwah to the Western Audience 175
Prophetic Mission 176
Prophetic Methodology 176
Sojourn in Pakistan 177
Tuhfah Series..179
Tuhfah-i Kashmir (1981) 179
Tuhfah-i Dakkan (1982) 180
Tuhfah-i Malwa (1983) 180
Hadith-i Pakistan (1984) 181
Tuhfah-i Mashriq: Bangladesh (1984)...182

Signposts of Moral Decadence in Saudi Arabia 182
Sirah Conference 184
King Faisal Award (1980) 185
Centennial Celebration of Dār al-'Ulūm Deoband 186
Towards a New Era 189
Salient Features 190
In the Valley of Kashmir 190
Seminar: Orientalism and Islam 192
Literary Orientalism 195
Seminar in Algeria 195
Sri Lanka 196
Da'wah in Hyderabad 197
Conclusion 197

Chapter X: Trends in Transnational Institutions 199
Hadīth Studies 199
Rābita Adab al-Alam al-Islami 200
Aims and Objectives of Rābita Adab 201
Shaykh Muhammad al-Majzub: Writer and Intellectual Figure 203
Dottor 'Abdul Bāsit: Distinguished Author and Poet 203
Professor Rashid Ahmad Siddiqui 204
Māhir al-Qādiri: Eminent Urdu Poet 204
Shaykh Nadwi's Major Contributions 204
Azamgarh (India), 1995 204
Istanbul (Turchia), 1996 205
Lahore (Pakistan), 1997 205
Oxford Centre for Islamic Studies 205
Islamic Foundation, Leicester 208
Kingdom of Jordan 209
Congress Rule: An Assessment 211
Malaysia: A New Experience 213
Two Conflicting Portraits 215
Conclusion 217

Chapter XI: Revival of Islamic Authenticity 219
Muslim Personal Law 219
Babri Masjid: a Tragedy 223
The Gulf Crisis 226
Tragic Loss 228
Tayyib al-Nisā' 228
Muhammad Asif Kidwai 229
Da'wah Journeys 230
Turchia: a Reappraisal 230

Satanic Verses 232
Seminar: Abul Kalam Azad 235
The Russian Revolution: an Appraisal 236
Conclusion 238

Chapter XII: Da'wah Paradigms: Translocal Trends 239
Letter to King Fahd bin 'Abdul 'Aziz: *Islāhī* Concerns 239
Political Developments in India: Muslim Response 242
Da'wah in England..243
Fundamentalism: An Assessment 245
The Long Journey 247
Divine Intervention 249
Conclusion 250

Chapter XIII: Honours Beyond Borders 251
Aligarh Muslim University 251
Rābita Adab..254
Egypt: Reforms..254
Corporate Islamic Identity: The Road Ahead 255
Police Raid in Nadwah 257
Literary Seminars..258
Honour: Keys to the Ka'bah 259
Sectarianism: An Overview 259
International Conference: Qadianism 261
Onslaught against Islam 262
Conclusion 263

Chapter XIV: Towards Journey's End 265
Dīnī Ta'līmī Council: Challenges and Opportunities 265
Vande Mataram: An Assessment 266
Muslims in a Pluralist Society 268
Honorary Awards 269
Dubai Award..269
Sultan of Brunei Prize: 1999 269
Posthumous Awards 270
Health Concerns 270
Tablighī Ijtimā: 1999 272
Embodiment of Patriotism 273
Last Days 274

Chapter XV: Shaykh Nadwi's Personality: Impressions 277
Salient Features of Shaykh Nadwi's Multifaceted Personality 277
Love for Humanity 278

Embodiment of Generosity 279
Forbearance 279
Towards Moral Regeneration 280
Nobility of Character 281
Perspectives of *Da'wah* 281
Overview of Shaykh Nadwi's Qualities as a *Da'i* 282
Pure *Tawhīd* 282
Purification of the Soul (*tazkiyah*) 283
The Unity and Comprehensiveness of Islam 284
Universality of Islamic Message 284
Challenges of *Da'wah* 285
Tributes to Shaykh Nadwi 286
Shaykh Muhammad bin Abdullah As-Subayyal 286
Dr Abdullāh Sālih 'Ubād 287
Dr Abdul Quddus Abu Sālih 287
Dr Anwar al-Jundi 287
Khalifa Jāsim Al-Kawāri 287
Abdul Rahmān bin Nasir Al-Awhali 288
Dr Zaki Badawi 288
Shaykh Sālih Mahdi Samarai 288
'Abdullāh al-Tantawi 288
Impressions of the Ulama and the Intellectuals 289
Mufti Taqi Uthmānī 289
Mawlana Muhammad Sālim Qāsmi 289
Khurshid Ahmad 290
Khawājah Hasan Thāni Nizāmi 290
Impressions: Islamic Scholars and Associated 290
Mahmud al-Hasan Arif 290
Dr Jameile Shawkat 291
Dr Muhammad Akram Chaudhry 291
Dr Qāri Muhammad Tāhir 291
Mujubur Rahmān Shāmi 292
Dr Sarfaraz Naeemi 292
Impressions: on Contemporary Scholars 292

Chapter XVI: Conversations from the Heart 295
Shaykh Nadwi's Contributions to the *Malfūzāt* Literature 295
Shaykh Nadwi's Reappraisal of the *Malfūzāt* 296
Levels of Preparation for Reciting the Qur'ān 297
In the Company of the *Mashā'ikh* 297
Shaykh Nadwi's Discourse: New Pespectives 299
Rae Bareli: Hub of Spirituality 300
Timeline: 1974-99 300

Heart of the Matter 305
Assessment 308

Chapter XVII: Key Themes in Shaykh Nadwi's Writings 309
Qur'ānic Horizons 309
Islamic Concept of Life 310
Hadīth : A Censor of Morals 311
Islam and the Revival of Humanity 311
Renaissance of Faith 313
Divine Blessings 314
Indo-Islamic Culture 314
Muslim Corporate Identity 315
Islam and the West 316
Challenges of Da'wah 317
Da'wah : Muslim Responsibility 318
Supplication: Evidence of Prophethood 320

Conclusion 323
Glossary 327
Bibliography 329
Book-Review 337

Acknowledgements

THE inspiration to write this book came from my correspondence and meeting with Sayyid Abul Hasan Ali Nadwi. It was almost thirty years ago when I read the first volume of *Kārwān i-Zindagi* in Urdu. Thereafter, my interest intensified and an irrepressible urge to write about his life and works has culminated in this modest attempt.

The present work is a revised edition of *Sayyid Abul Hasan Ali Nadwi: Life and Works* (2011). In recent years there have been scholarly works written in Urdu, Arabic and English from which I have benefited immensely. Likewise, there has been a significant increase in the number or Shaykh Nadwi's writings which have been compiled and edited by competent scholars and institutions. The noteworthy contribution by Abul Hasan Ali Center is a case in point.

Sayyid Muhammad Rabey Nadwi, Rector of Nadwat al-'Ulama (Lucknow) has been exceedingly kind to make available books and manuscripts during my brief stay there in 2005. His keen interest and supportive role are much appreciated. Another scion of the Hasani family is Sayyid Bilal Abdul Hayy who deserves special mention. He has been largely responsible for locating books and articles that have not been easily accessible for my study purposes. He also serves as a patron of our Academy. I also wish to express my appreciation to Muhammad Nu`man Chishti of Iqbal Academy, Pakistan for graciously supplying me translations of selected poems of `Allamah Iqbal.

Two influential figures who have been responsible for the multivolume project on Shaykh Nadwi's life and legacy have sadly passed on. This has been a great loss for the Ahsan Academy of Research. Dr Yusuf Bamjee (d. 2020), was instrumental in setting up the Academy in 2017 to promote the works of Shaykh Nadwi and other pioneering scholars in the field of *tajdīd* (Islamic resurgence). The following comment is reproduced here to highlight his pro-active role to the Shaykh Nadwi Series:

> "I am very much obliged to my colleague, Dr Yusuf Bamjee whose support in every possible way has motivated me to study Islamic scholarship in South Asia. He has given me valuable feedback and encouragement at every stage of the writing process. The multivolume publication of which the present study forms one volume owes its inception to Yusuf. His discerning interest, keen eye for technical production and standards of excellence are reflective of his work ethic and generosity."

Sadly, I have to use the past tense to express my enormous sense of gratitude to the late Mufti Ayoob Moola (d. 2019). A mentor and friend, Mufti Ayoob was always a source of inspiration. His deep interest in the progress of the study and the special $du'\bar{a}s$ for its successful completion are things I now cherish the most. This work, in more than one way, is a tribute to his blessed memory.

To Muniera, her hard work in typing the manuscript meticulously (I can not recall the number of "revised" manuscripts) and her editorial collaboration have enhanced the importance of this study. Finally, I also want to acknowledge many colleagues, donors and well-wishers for their unwavering interest in our multivolume project.

30 June 2022

Abdul Kader Choughley
(Springs, South Africa)
akchoughley@gmail.com

Transliteration

ALL Urdu, Arabic and Persian names have been cited using a simplified transliteration system that eliminates detailed diacritical marks. In the study the *'ayn* and *hamza* as well as *a* have been retained as far as possible. However, variations do arise when these diacritical marks have not been used in English works. Terms such as *sufi* and *tafsīr* appear in their anglicised form. In transliterating personal names and places in Urdu, their particular pronunciation has been adopted for providing some measures of uniformity.

Direct quotations and references whenever possible have been drawn from published translations of the original Arabic and Urdu works. However, when required, original translations have been made from the Urdu source.

Sayyid Abul Hasan 'Ali Nadwi: Life and Legacy

1913 — Born at Takya Kalān, Rae Bareli. (15 December 1913).

1923 — Death of his illustrious father, Sayyid 'Abdul Hayy, author of the multivolume biographical work *Nuzhat al-Khawātir*.

— Commencement of his education in Arabic and Persian.

— Accompanied his brother Dr 'Abdul 'Ali to the annual convocation of Nadwah in Kanpur.

1926 — Met leading Muslim personalities and political activists including Dr Zakir Husain, Mawlana Muhammad Ali Jauhar, Mawlana Zafar Ali Khan and Hakim Ajmal Khan.

1927 — Admission to the advanced Arabic *adab* (literature) course at Lucknow University.

1928 — First acquaintance with Mawlana Husayn Ahmad Madani.

1929 — Obtained first position in the coveted first division: *fādil adab* (literature).

— Met 'Allāmah Iqbal during his visit to Lahore. Presented his translation of Iqbal's poem *Chānd* (Moon) in Arabic.

— Studied *hadīth* at Nadwah under Mawlana Haydar Hasan Khan.

— Commenced study of English.

1930 — Stayed at Medical College on account of mother's eye operation.

Accompanied Moroccan scholar and litterateur, 'Allāmah Taqi al-Dīn Hilāli a Azamgarh.

Debut in writing: A monograph on Sayyid Ahmad Shahid in Arabic.

1931	– Attended *tafsīr* classes of Mawlana Ahmad 'Ali Lahori and his *dars* (lessons) on Shah Waliyullah's *Hujjat-Allah al- Bālighah* in Lahore.
	– Inititated into *tasawwuf* by Shaykh Ghulam Muhammad Dinpuri.
	– Contributed articles to the *Al-Diyā* magazine.
1933	– First meeting with the Grand Mufti of Palestine, Shaykh Amin Al-Husayni.
1934	– Appointed as lecturer in *tafsīr* and Arabic literature at Nadwah.
	– Marriage to Sayyidah Tayyibah al-Nisā.
	– First meeting with Mawlana Ashraf 'Ali Thānawi, illustrious reformer of the subcontinent in Thana Bhawan.
1935	– Tabligh meeting at Mumbai with Dr Ambedkar, leader of the Dalits (Untouchables).
1936	– Participated in Aligarh Muslim Educational Conference.
1937	– Last memorable meeting with 'Allāmah Iqbal.
1938	– Prepared the BA (Islamic Studies) curriculum for Aligarh Muslim University.
1939	– First meeting with Mawlana Sayyid Abul A'la Mawdudi.
	– Publication of his *Sirah Sayyid Ahmad Shahid*.
	– Important meetings with Mawlana 'Abdul Qādir Rāipūrī and Mawlana Muhammad Ilyās (founder of Tablighī Jamā'at).
1940	– Co-editor of *Al-Nadwah*.
	– Preparation of Arabic anthology, *Mukhtārāt*.
1941	– Joined Jamā'at-i Islami under leadership of Mawlana Mawdudi
	– Elected on executive committee of the Jamā'at.
1942	– Presented a paper on *Religion and Civilisation* at Jamia Millia Islamia (New Delhi).

1943	– Resigned from Jamā'at i-Islami.
	– Established Islamic Educational Institute and was responsible for Qur'anic classes.
1944	– Participated in the *sirah* conference in Peshawar (Pakistan).
1945	– Resigned from Nadwah. Letter of resignation withdrawn.
1946	– Obtained *khilāfat* from Mawlana Ahmad 'Ali Lahori.
	– Maintained spiritual (*rūhāni*) ties with Mawlana 'Abdul Qādir Rāipūrī.
1947	– Performed first *hajj* with mother, sister and nephew, Sayyid Muhammad Thāni Hasani.
	– Wrote a letter to King Saud about Islamic rule in the Saudi kingdom.
	– Invited by Jawaharlal Nehru to participate in the Asia Conference alongside Sarojini Naidu and Mohammad Ali Jinnah.
1948	– Appointed editor of *Ta'meer i-Hayāt* magazine.
	– Elected member of the Executive Committee of Nadwah.
	– Obtained *khilāfat* from Mawlana Rāipūrī.
1949	– Appointed director of education at Nadwah.
	– Addressed Muslim-Hindu gatherings in important towns.
1950	– Performed second *hajj*.
	– Honoured to enter the Ka'bah at the invitation of the Shaybi family.
	– First meeting with Sayyid Qutb in Makkah.
1951	–Important *Da'wah* travels to Egypt.
	–Lecturer at Cairo University.
	–Met the father of Hasan al-Banna, founder of Ikhwān movement.

xxi

- Attended reading sessions of his *Rise and Fall of Muslims* at Qutb's home.
- Visited outlying places with the noted Ikhwān member, Shaykh Muhammad al-Ghazali.
- Visited Sudan, Syria and Jordan.
- Spent last ten days of Ramadan in Bayt al-Muqaddas.
- Shared views about the issues concerning Al-Quds.
- Delivered a keynote address on Palestine and its contributions to Islamic culture.

1952 - Following communal riots in India, initiated interfaith dialogue between Muslims and Hindus.

1953 - Established a Tabligh Centre in Lucknow.

1954 - Addressed students at Dār al-'Ulūm Deoband.
- Spent time with noted shaykh Mawlana Wasi-Allah Fatehpuri.

1955 - First volume of *Saviours of Islamic Spirit* published.

1956 - Visiting professor at Damascus University.
- Elected member of the Islamic Conference: head office in Damascus.
- Held a meeting with President Shukri Qawtāli and other dignitaries.
- Visited Lebanon and met influential scholars of various Islamic movements.
- Made a trip to Turkey and also highlighted Kemal Ataturk's un-Islamic policies.
- Visited Iraq and shared views with notable leaders of various Islamic organisations.

1957 - Suffered from cataract and experienced difficulties in writing.

1958 - Wrote editorials for the Arabic magazine *Al-Muslimun*, which was published from Damascus.

1959 - Established the Academy of Islamic Research and Publications in Lucknow.

1960 - Elected President of Dīnī Ta'līmī Council of which he was a founder member.

	–	Visited Burma (Myanmar) to introduce Nadwah to Muslims.
1961	–	Death of elder brother, Dr Sayyid 'Abdul 'Ali, Rector of Nadwah.
	–	Elected Rector of Nadwah.
1962	–	Elected executive member of the Steering Committee of Madinah University.
	–	Meeting with King Saud and Libyan *mujāhid*, Idris Sanusi.
	–	Member of the Rābita 'Ālam al-Islami (World Muslim League).
	–	Delivered a series of lectures published as *Islamic Concept of Prophethood*.
	–	Elected member of the Shura Council in Deoband.
1963	–	Honoured to deliver a public lecture at the Shāfi'ī *musallah* in the *Haram*.
	–	Travel to Europe, including lectures at London and Edinburgh universities.
	–	Two lectures in Arabic broadcast on air by BBC.
	–	Meeting with Sudanese leader, Hasan Turabi.
	–	Visit to Spain which included historic Islamic cities and institutions.
1964	–	Second visit to Europe.
	–	Important lecture at Berlin University of Engineering in Germany.
	–	Participated in mass meetings to restore peace in Jamshedpur after communal riots.
	–	Unsuccessful eye operation in Mumbai.
1965	–	Played a leading role in the establishment of Muslim Majlis Mushāwarāt, a think-tank organisation.
	–	Met King Faisal and discussed Islamic issues of global significance.
1966	–	Confiscation of passport by Indian authorities following his critique of Egyptian President Nasser's policies.
	–	Wrote an Introduction to Hasan al-Banna's autobiography, *Mudhakkirāt*.
1967	–	Visited Hijaz and saved in a car accident in Taif.

1968 - Delivered a series of lectures at Riyadh University.
 - Death of his mother, Sayyidah Khairun Nisā'.
 - Submitted an article to the Education Ministers Meeting (Kuwait).
1969 - Third visit to Europe and delivered lectures at Birmingham and Leeds universities.
1970 - Stayed temporarily in Lucknow following floods in Takya Kalān.
1971 - Eye operation at Sitapur.
1972 - Participated in Delhi conference regarding minority status of Aligarh Muslim University.
1973 - As member of Rābita delegation visited Lebanon, Afghanistan, Iran, Syria and Iraq.
 - Addressed Iranian intellectuals in Tehran.
 - Shared views with Prime Minister of Lebanon and other political members.
 - Met King Hussein of Jordan and addressed military force.

 - Commenced his *Payām i-Insaniyāt* movement.
 - Visited Sharjah at the request of Amir Sultan Muhammad Al-Qasimi.
1975 - Celebration of Nadwah's 75th anniversary.
1976 - Demise of sister, Amatullah Tasnim.
 - Enforcement of State Emergency by government.
 - Meeting with Prime Minister Indira Gandhi and presentation of Islamic view on birth control.
 - Meeting with Mauritanian President, Mukhtar Dildada at Parliament building.
 - Travel to Morocco for the Fourth Federation of Islamic Universities conference.
 - Meeting with King Hasan of Morocco.
1977 - Prime Minister Indira Gandhi made a special trip to visit him at Takya Kalān, Rae Bareli.
 - At the invitation of Muslim Students Association, visited the United States of America.
 - Delivered lectures at several prestigious universities.

- Another eye operation done at Philadelphia (US).
- Meeting with world boxing champion, Muhammad Ali.

1978 - Participated in the Asian conference held in Pakistan.
- Met General Zia-ul-Haq, President of Pakistan, at the State House.
- Reception given by Council of Islamic Ideology in his honour.
- Lectures given at important universities and institutions.
- Meeting with Mawlana Mawdudi and Maryam Jameelah.

1979 - Attended the *sirah* conference in Qatar.
  - Represented Rābita in a meeting with ministers of Awqāf from Arab countries.

1980 - Sultan Al-Qasimi, ruler of Sharjah, paid a courtesy visit to Nadwah.
- Received a special invitation from Iraq's envoy on behalf of Saddam Hussein to participate in an international conference.
- Elected member of the prestigious Scientific Academy (*Majlis 'Ilmi*) in Jordan.
- Awarded the King Faisal Pride. Cash distributed to Tahfiz al-Qur'an (Makkah) and Afghan refugees.
- Delivered a historic address at the centenary function of Dār al-'Ulūm Deoband.

1981 - Conferred a D. Litt by University of Kashmir.

1982 - Organised the seminar on Islam and Orientalism.

1983 - Elected President of Muslim Personal Law Board.
- Met Prince Hasan of Jordan.
- Lectured at the Emirates Gulf-College and Al-'Ain University in Dubai.
- Addressed students and staff at Kuwait University and Jami'at al-Islāh.
- Leading personality in the establishment of Oxford Centre

for Islamic Studies.
- Elected Chairman of OCIS.

1985 - Chairman of World Academy of Islamic Literature.
- Participated in various conferences in Bangladesh.
- Delivered lectures at Sana and Yarmuk universities.
- Met Yemeni President, 'Ali 'Abdullāh Sālih.
- Addressed the Yemeni Airforce.
- Presented General Zia-ul-Haq with a model of Masjid al-Aqsa.
- Cash award for Sayyid Sulayman Nadwi's *Sirat al-Nabi* from Pakistan government. Donated to Shibli Academy (Azamgarh).
- OCIS officially constituted at Oxford University.

1986 - Participated in the Islamic conference on the Algerian
- Interfaith dialogue in Delhi, Nagpur and Pune.
- Pioneering role in the enactment of shari'ah divorce law by government.

1987 - Delivered lectures at several universities in Malaysia.
- Inducted the Abdul Ali Al-Mutawwa lecture series in London.
- Participated in Rābita's Silver Jubilee.

1988 - Presented a series of lectures in Abu Dhabi, Dubai and Sharjah.

1989 - Meeting with the Prime Minister of Turkey, Najmuddin Erbakan.

1990 - Met state officials and religious figures to defuse Babri Masjid crisis.

1991 - Vocal critic of Iraqi invasion of Kuwait.
- Meeting with former Prime Minister of Afghanistan, Abdur Rabb Rasul.
- *Payāmi-Insaniyāt* programs to promote communal harmony.
- Letter to King Fahd of Saudi Arabia about the reform of Muslim society.

	–	Received Abul Kalam Azad Award. Cash distributed for research purposes.
1992	–	Declined the highest civilian honour from Indian government.
	–	Lectured on *Islam and the West* at Islamic Foundation (Leicester).
1993		Participated in the World Conference of Religion in Chicago.
	–	Visited Bukhara, Tashkent and Uzbekistan.
	–	Establishment of Imām Bukhārī Islamic Centre.
1994	–	Lectures to the staff of Aligarh Muslim University.
	–	Police raided hostels at Nadwah.
	–	Compensation from government to injured students.
1995	–	Establishment of *hifz* and *madāris* committees under his supervision.
1996	–	Meeting with the Prime Minister of India.
	–	Seminar hosted in Turkey in his honour.
	–	Presented with keys of Ka'bah to open the holy enclosure.
1997	–	Participated in Rābita Adab's symposium in Lahore.
	–	International Conference on Qadianism at Nadwah.
1998	–	Dīnī Ta'limi Council's opposition to state's education policy.
1998	–	Awarded the *Islamic Personality of the Year*.
	–	Opposition to compulsory introduction of *Vande Mataram* for Muslim students in state-aided schools.
	–	Raid of his home in Zae Bareli followed by protest in town.
	–	Inauguration of media centre in Bengaluru.
1999	–	Severe stroke paralysed him.
	–	Visit by Prime Minister Vajpayee and other notable personalities.
	–	Tabligh address at Nadwah.
	–	Awarded the Sultan of Brunei Prize for his *Saviours of Islamic Spirit*.

- Appealed to hijackers for the release of passengers aboard on Indian Airlines flight.
- Demise on 31 December 1999.

Introduction

The study aims to examine the contributions of Sayyid Abul Hasan Ali Nadwi (1913-99) to contemporary Islamic thought. A long and eventful career spanning over 70 years, Sayyid Nadwi (hereafter Shaykh Nadwi) is considered an important scholar in Islamic resurgence. This term is applied to specific historical settings in our study. It covers the twentieth century during which globalisation and modernity have influenced the Islamic discourse on multiple levels.

The *'ulama* regarded as bastions of traditional Islam have not been immune to the rapid changes taking place across the Muslim world brought about by technological advancement. In his *The Ulama in Contemporary Islam*,[1] Zaman has pointed out the dilemmas facing Muslim societies in grappling with challenges and the *'ulama's* role as custodians of the Islamic traditions. Their constituency is reflected in the institutions they are associated with and their interpretations underpin their respective responses to geopolitical developments.

Shaykh Nadwi is among few Indian *'ulama* to have taken seriously the dynamic role of Islam in multireligious India. The predicament of Indian Muslims who as a minority see themselves increasingly beleaguered and threatened by the rise of Hindu militancy is one of his primary concerns. He insists Muslims must come out of their separatist mentality and search for opportunities that exist and work alongside their religious counterparts to build a viable society.[2] According to Shaykh Nadwi, Islamic authenticity is the ideal to which Indian Muslims should aspire, because they too are connected to the world of Islam at large. This explains his presentation of *islāh* (reform) and *tajdīd* (revival) as tools of Islamic resurgence. It is interesting to note that the scholarly tradition combined with Islamic activism contributed significantly to Shaykh Nadwi's

profile as a spokesman for Indian Muslims and a reformer of international repute. His versatility is best illustrated in his major writings which seek to elaborate the following themes:

- The primacy of the Quran and sunnah as harbingers of world civilisation.
- *Islāh* and *tajdīd* as anchors of Islamic resurgence.

---

[1] Muhammad Qasim Zaman, *The Ulama in Contemporary Islam: Custodians of Change* (Princeton, 2002).
[2] Abul Hasan Ali Nadwi, *Muslims in India* (Lucknow, 1972), 125.

- *Da'wah*: a methodological approach.
- Islam and the West: a critique.
- Islamic order in an Indian setting.

The diversity of themes are embodied in Shaykh Nadwi's multivolume autobiography, *Kārwān i-Zindagi*.[3] Our study focuses on Shaykh Nadwi's salient accounts against the background of sociopolitical developments in both India and the Muslim world. A timeline approach is adopted to give chronological and thematic significance to his contributions to Islamic reformist thought. Shaykh Nadwi is a distinguished *'ālim* whose presentation of Islam is influenced by his *ummatic* concerns which affirm the return to the exemplary lives of the *salaf al-sālih* (early representatives of Islam).[4]

An important element in constructing Shaykh Nadwi's coherent approach to the wide range of issues in the twentieth century is to be found in *Kārwān*. It is to be expected that the autobiography of such a pivotal figure should be an important document. Autobiography as a literary genre was well known in the Muslim world. Examples include al-Ghazali's (d. 1111) justly-famed spiritual autobiography, *Al-Munqidh min al-Dalāl* (Deliverance from Error).[5] The autobiographical tradition established during the medieval Islamic period has been a subject of critical study in the West.[6] Malti-Douglas in *Blindness and Autobiography* has outlined the characteristics of an autobiography that are also relevant to Shaykh Nadwi's *Kārwān*. A text implies a reader, and the reader of the autobiographical text brings certain expectations to it. This genre is more intimate than a biography and the assumption of intimacy provides an identity between the narrator and the subject and helps to create the authenticity in the text.[7]

Shaykh Nadwi's motivation for writing his autobiography is not merely to recount "memorable milestones in his life,"[8] but to provide an all-encompassing spectrum of his activities in respect of his intellectual growth and development.[9] Historical incidents in his life, as Shaykh Nadwi observes, are

---

[3] Nadwi, *Kārwān i-Zindagi*, 7 vols. (Lucknow, 1999).
[4] For an elaboration on the *salaf al-sālih* concept, see Nadwi, *Saviours of Islamic Spirit*] vol. I (Lucknow, 1971), 1-4.
[5] For his life and description of his crisis, see Montgomery Watt, *Muslim Intellectual: A Study of Al-Ghazali* (Edinburgh, 1963).
[6] An excellent study of the autobiography genre can be seen in James Olney, *Autobiography, Essays, Theoretical and Critical* (Princeton, 1980).
[7] Fedwa Malti-Douglas, *Blindness and Autobiography* (Princeton, 1988), 93-4.
[8] Nadwi, *Kārwān*, vol. 1, 12.
[9] Ibid., 12-13.

Introduction

contextualised to provide the reader with an opportunity to critically examine his role in the said events to which he has been an "active participant."[10] Furthermore, his autobiography makes copious reference to his prolific writings to highlight his contributions to contemporary Islamic thought. *Kārwān* also attempts to explore Shaykh Nadwi's vision as represented by Nadwat al-'Ulama (hereafter Nadwah) of Islam's mediating role in contemporary affairs.[11] Nadwah, as Shaykh Nadwi notes in his autobiography, "is a school of thought and learning which believes in steadfastness in its aims, progress in its methods, makes use of everything old which is beneficial, welcomes everything new which is sound, adopts from tradition what is sincere and rejects what is dubious."[12] His personal contributions to producing a number of scholars who could effectively discharge the duty of *da'wah* and who could expound the *shari'ah* as a way of life compatible with modern needs have been critically examined in recent works. Equally important is his broader outlook about pertinent Islamic issues in his interaction with scholars and movements holding divergent viewpoints.[13]

Shaykh Nadwi's *Kārwān* also represents a synopsis of his important works through which his contributions to contemporary Islamic thought are explored.

Shaykh Nadwi's Works: A Brief Survey

The Arabic bibliography on Shaykh Nadwi's works lists 228 publications.[14] Likewise, to date 397 books and monographs in Urdu have been published. These include translations from the Arabic works of Shaykh Nadwi as well as the compilation of his articles and lectures. His writings are wide and varied and deal with the major features of Islamic ideology, history and culture.

- In the *sirah* (biography) of the Prophet Muhammad series, *Muhammad Rasullulah* (1985) is considered an excellent contribution. Written originally in Arabic it has been translated into major European languages.

---

[10] Ibid., 13.
[11] Nadwi, *Western Civilisation, Islam and Muslims* (Lucknow, 1976), 198-9.
[12] Nadwi, *Kārwān*, vol. 3.
[13] *Ta'meer i-Hayāt*, Special Issue (Lucknow, 2000).
[14] 'Abdullah 'Abbās Nadwi, *Mir Kārwān*, (New Delhi, 1999), 367.

- The *tadhkirah* (memoirs) genre has been skillfully crafted in Indo-Islamic culture over the centuries. It has seen a plethora of *sawānih* (biographies) of Muslim scholars, saints and *sufis*. Bruce Lawrence has made a significant comment regarding the concept of *tadhkirah* literature and its impact on the cultural milieu of South Asian Muslims:

> Narratology (*tadhkirah*) is a powerful mimetic strategy that reactualises the past and at the same time compels the narrator in so far as to disappear from the story and let the facts speak for themselves. The lessons of narratives on enduring moral values have greater force and are encoded in self-expression. The historical process of transmission has provided the impetus for biographical accounts, notably of *'ulama* and *mashā'ikh* (sufi-shaykhs), to dominate the South Asian spiritual landscape for the last six centuries. The *tadhkirah* genre continues to wield a strong influence on Muslim masses in their affiliation with *sufi* masters.[15]

Sawānih 'Abdul Qādir Rāipuri (1981) is representative of Shaykh Nadwi's *sufi* orientation.

- Indo-Islamic culture is a dominant theme in Shaykh Nadwi's writings. The motivation for such works is evident in his popular work *Muslims in India* (1976): "It is hoped that the book will be read with interest among the educated circles ... and prove of some value in reducing the ignorance and the attitude of indifference which exists in sister-communities towards the Muslims."[16]
- The projection of the *tajdīd* (revivalist) movements is encapsulated in his widely-acclaimed *Saviours of Islamic Spirit* (1971-93). Written in four volumes, it represents Shaykh Nadwi's interpretation of Islamic history as a history of *'ulama'* and intellectuals instead of a chronicle of sultans and regimes, some noble and some ignoble.[17]
- *Da'wah* in the West. Shaykh Nadwi's involvement with Oxford

---

[15] Bruce Lawrence, *Nizāmuddin Awliya: Morals of the Heart* (New York, 1992), 1-4.
[16] Nadwi, *Muslims in India*, 4.
[17] M.H. Faruqi, Abul Hasan Ali Nadwi in *The Fragrance of the East*, Special Issue (Lucknow), 122-4.

Centre for Islamic Studies (OCIS) and his series of lectures and writings illustrate his vision of *da'wah* in the West. *Muslims in the West* (1983) is illustrative of the challenges for Muslims in the West.
- Arabic literature has been Shaykh Nadwi's fortè and he was the first Indian writer whose distinguished works were prescribed as reference works in a number of Islamic universities. His *Mukhtārāt* (1980) an anthology of prose has enhanced his stature as an Arabic littérateur.[18]
- *Da'wah* literature for the Arab World. Two parallel and often conflicting strands of Islamic authenticity and Arab nationalism, form the basis of Shaykh Nadwi's prolific writings. The books published are monographs, travelogues, compilation of lectures, etc. and, by and large, are impassioned appeals for the Arab world to "shoulder the responsibilities of the mission of Islam." *Bayn al-Suratān wal Haqiqatān* (Between Appearance and Reality) typifies this *da'wah* genre for the Arab audience.[19]
- *Da'wah* for South Asian Muslims. The *tuhfah* genre is a reappraisal of issues affecting Muslims in India, Bangladesh and Pakistan. The reform of Muslim society is a prominent feature of Shaykh Nadwi's writings on this theme.

Major Sources for this Study

The major sources for the study are based on Shaykh Nadwi's original writings in Arabic and Urdu, many of which have been translated into English. The aim of this section is to give a brief introduction and assessment of the sources.

Kārwān (1984-99) is a seven-volume autobiographical account of Shaykh Nadwi. It portrays his versatility in respect of his activities and contribution to the collective identity of Indian Muslims. A distinctive feature of his autobiography is the absence of embellished anecdotes as these tend to mar personal narratives. In contrast, the worldview of Shaykh Nadwi himself should become clear from the text which *Kārwān* seeks to present.

Rise and Fall of Muslims: Its Impact on the World is an English translation of Shaykh Nadwi's prominent work in Arabic, *Mādhā Khasir al-'Ālam bi-Inhitāt*

---

[18] Waris Ahmad Siddiqui, "Ma'ruf Tasānif aur unka Payghām" in *Ta'meer i-Hayāt*, Special Issue, 256-62.
[19] *Mir Kārwān* contains critical reviews of Shaykh Nadwi's writings.

il-Muslimīn. This book does not claim to be a history of the rise and fall of Muslims. It only deals with the effects thereof. The author's main ambition, however, has been to stir the Muslims to an appreciation of Islam's glorious role in the story of human progress. Furthermore, it aims to provide a platform for their self-appraisal in relation to their mission and their duty towards the world. This book has been considered by Von Grunebaum as "a representative self-review of contemporary Islam."[20]

Muslims in the West: The Message and Mission (1983) is an English translation of a collection of Arabic and Urdu speeches delivered in Britain and United States. It offers valuable insights into the predicament of Western civilisation, its strengths and weaknesses, and discusses at some length the role and responsibilities of Muslims living in the West.

The present study is a modest attempt to provide a comprehensive portrait of a scholar associated with a multiple discourse of Islamic resurgence across the Muslim world. It is hoped that future studies will cover in greater depth the multidimensional contributions of Shaykh Nadwi which are inspired by contemporary Islamic thought and are derived from the primary sources of Islam.

---

[20] G.E. von Grunebaum, *Modern Islam: The Search for Cultural Identity*, (London, 1969), 181.

Chapter I

Family Characteristics

Anatomy, psychology, ethics and sociology are all agreed that every man has certain inherited traits in his blood which have a role in shaping his character, aptitude, competence, inclinations and frame of mind. These traits are reflected in the following forms: the beliefs and values held strictly, cherished and revered by a family get in-built in the mind of the people belonging to it. What one hears repeatedly from childhood, as for example, about courage, bravery, generosity, altruism and honesty, get ingrained in one's mindset. These determine the inclinations and disposition and give a measure for judgement of these moral values.[1]

These traits exemplified in the personality of 'Ali, the fourth Caliph of Islam, were embedded in the distinguished family of Shaykh Nadwi. Tracing their lineage to both Hasan and Husayn,[2] the grandsons of the Holy Prophet (SAAS), this illustrious family served as a beacon light in the Indian subcontinent. Their reformatory (islāhī) efforts combined with their admirable piety and virtuous character changed the religious landscape in Muslim India. The true content of tawhīd (Oneness of Allah) illumined the lives of the Muslim ummah, many of whom had previously followed a syncretic form of Islam largely influenced by the shirk-laden (polytheistic) customs, rites and practices of Hinduism.[3] Shaykh Nadwi's forebears led exemplary lives. Their devotion and promotion of the sunnah provided the impetus for Muslims to derive their understanding of the shari'ah from its fundamental sources: the Quran and hadīth literature. Furthermore, the strenuous effort in the way of God in all its manifestations epitomised their pure souls and was generated so extensively that it became "reminiscent of the earliest era of Islam."[4]

Shaykh Nadwi has given a detailed account of his ancestors' major contributions to the islāh of the Muslim society.[5] Reform and revival are twin concepts that are articulated in his prolific writings. The golden chain (silsilat al-dhahab) of reformers and scholars formed the nucleus for presenting the Islamic authenticity ideal in a transnational setting.[6] In

---

[1] Nadwi, *The Life of Caliph 'Ali* (Lucknow, 1991), 11.
[2] Ibid., 237-9.
[3] Nadwi, *Kārwān i-Zindagi*, vol. 1 (Lucknow, 1983), 20-3.
[4] Nadwi, *The Life of Caliph 'Ali*, 251.
[5] The two-volume *Sirat i-Sayyid Ahmad Shahid* reinforces these concepts.
[6] Nadwi, *Kārwān*, vol. 1, 26-7.

tracing the *tajdīdi* contributions of Shaykh Nadwi's ancestors, the following features are discernible:

First, the family did not show exaggerated rigidity in the presentation of their lineage. The *shari'ah* was considered the benchmark in their interaction with other families who considered nobility of birth in the Indian soil as an identity of racial superiority. Second, there has not been a single trace of un-Islamic practices in the family over the last eight centuries. From the arrival of Sayyid Qutb al-Din al-Madani to Shaykh Nadwi's lifetime, the family vision had been embedded on *tawhīd* and the sunnah. In keeping with the spirit of the *shari'ah* there have been no shrines (*mazārs*) built to commemorate the contributions of their *mashā'ikh*. Third, chivalry (*futuwwah*) was an outstanding trait of the family, courage, protection of Islamic virtues and the ennobling passion for the effort in the way of God bore their imprints in the various campaigns these members led. Fourth, the family was, by and large, free from duplicity and their lives were characterised by simplicity and frugal living. On many occasions they were victims of personal intrigues and much maligned by devious elements. Even under these adverse circumstances they were able to maintain their poise and sublimity of character. Fifth, the family produced a number of *'ulama* who promoted a synthesis of *shari'ah* and *tasawwuf*. Prominent members of the family were spiritually affiliated to the revivalist movements of the *mujaddid*, Shaykh Ahmad Sirhindi (d. 1624) and Shah Waliyullah (d. 1762). Last, the family led austere lives and were not inclined to wealth and opulence. Shaykh Nadwi's family believed that their lives were a fulfilment to the Prophet's *du'ā* to grant his descendants sufficient means of livelihood.

The above characteristics were the guiding principles of Shaykh Nadwi's family. During the ebb and flow of their lives they were able to sustain their spirituality and visionary leadership.[7]

A brief overview of the family's success in the domain of *tajdīd* can be attributed to the following factors:

- Their impact was wider in scope in terms of their *Islāhī* contributions. The centrality of *tasawwuf* in their personal lives influenced large segments of the Muslim community.
- Their commitment to the *shari'ah* mirrored the ideals of the *salaf*.

---

[7] Muhiudin Ahmad, *Saiyid Ahmad Shahid* (Lucknow, 1975), 20-1.

Chapter I
Family Characteristics

Sayyid Qutb al-Dīn Muhammad al-Hasani

Sayyid Qutb al-Din, a distinguished descendant of Hasani lineage, was doubly blessed with the amazing spirit of courage and strength in the way of God and the "beauty of holiness." He migrated from Baghdad to Ghazna (Afghanistan) and then moved onwards with a contingent of his *muridin* (spiritual followers) to India in 1211.

He was instructed in a vision by the Holy Prophet (SAAS) to propagate Islam in Kara, situated on the Ganges river in Allahabad. From here he launched a successful campaign against il Raja Jai Chand.[8] Later he was recalled by Sultan Shams al-Din Iltutmish (1211-1236) to assume the role of Shaykh al-Islam in Delhi.

The evolution of the Delhi Sultanate took shape during the Mamluk rule - a dynasty of Turkish slaves. Our focus is on three famous rulers:

Qutb al-Din Aibak (d. 1210) was responsible for structuring the Muslim government on the basis of Islamic principles and traditions.[9] He enforced the *shari'ah* and introduced Islamic reforms along the pattern of the *Khulafā al-Rāshidin* (Righteous Caliphs).

Aibak's successor Shams al-Din Iltutmish (d.1236) was a capable administrator who patronised Islamic learning. His strong leanings towards *tasawwuf* and support for the Chishti order caused a rift between him and the *fuqahā* (jurisprudents).[10]

The accession of Ghiyath al-Din Balban (d.1286) ushered in a period of religious stability. Public morality (*ihtisāb*) and the observance of Islamic values were strongly enforced. A devout ruler, Balban was held in high esteem by both the *'ulama* and the *sufis*.[11]

Several historians have described Sayyid Qutb al-Din as "a prince of the pure-hearted souls"[12] whose descendants propagated the true teachings of Islam. Their ennobling qualities of spirituality and selflessness had a profound influence on the Muslim society. His descendants continued with the great task of shaping Muslim identity according to the *shari'ah*. The Rae Bareli district attracted a considerable number of his descendants which centuries later was to become a focal point for the *tajdīdī* endeavours of

---

[8] Ibid, *Saiyid Ahmad Shahid*, 21.
[9] Khaliq Ahmad Nizami, *Some Aspects of Religion and Politics in India during the Thirteenth Century* (Delhi, 1974), 87-8.
[10] *Ibid.*, 114.
[11] *Ibid.*, 115-9.
[12] Ahmad, *Saiyid Ahmad Shahid*, 21.

mashā'ikh and *mujāhidin* associated with this family.[13]

Sayyid Shah 'Alamullah

Born in 1623, Sayyid 'Alamullah, was guided to the path of *suluk* (spiritual training) by the reputed saint of the time, Sayyid Adam Bannuri, the spiritual successor of Shaykh Ahmad Sirhindi.[14] When Sayyid Bannuri migrated to Arabia, Shah wanted to accompany him, but he instructed him to remain in India.[15] His relocation to a place in Rae Bareli (posthumously named Dā'ira Shah 'Alamullah) on the left bank of river Sa'i was destined to be a haven of scholarly tradition of Sayyid Qutb al-Din's descendants.

Shah 'Alamullah was uniquely endowed with the inner strength to practise the *sunnah* to its minutest details. In his private life he resembled the *Sahābah* (Companions of the Prophet). When he went to perform *hajj*, the inhabitants of Makkah and Madinah who saw him taxing his energies in following the *shari'ah* remarked that he was the Abu Dhar[16] of their times. His devotion to the *sunnah* was so overpowering that he scrupulously avoided any semblance of customary practices. He vigorously opposed *bid'ah* (innovation) both in content and spirit and by his personal example urged Muslims to uphold the sunnah in every facet of their lives. Independence, selflessness and generosity were his personal attributes. He was noted for making *du'a* to Allah to grant sustenance to his progeny only enough to keep their body and soul together lest they should become heedless in His remembrance (*dhikr*).[17]

Shah 'Alamullah was ever mindful of following the *al-uswah al-hasanah* (noble conduct) of the Holy Prophet (SAAS). When he passed away, Aurangzeb (d. 1707) the mighty Mughal emperor, had the vision of the Prophet's demise in a dream. The significance of the dream meant that Shah 'Alamullah had "breathed his last on the very night he had the dream."[18] It was in the early hours of Monday, 26 October 1685, that he passed away at the age of 63.

---

[13] Muhammad Al-Hasani, *Tadhkirah Sayyid Shah 'Alamullah Hasani Rae Bareli* (Karachi, n.d.), 20-2.
[14] For a comprehensive biography of Sirhindi, see Nadwi, *Saviours of Islamic Spirit*, vol. 3 (Lucknow, 1983). Muhammad Abdul Haq Ansari, *Sufism and Shari'ah* (Leicester] 198;)6 is an excellent study about the Mujaddid's reformist vision.
[15] Hasani, *Tadhkirah*, 42.
[16] A *Sahābi* noted for his simple and austere life.
[17] Hasani, *Tadhkirah*, 68-9.
[18] Ahmad, *Saiyid Ahmad*, 25.

Chapter I
Family Characteristics

A prominent feature of Shah 'Alamullah's period was the consolidation of *tajdīd*. During Shaykh Sirhindi's epoch-making era, the doctrinal debate about *wahdat al-wujud* (Unity of Being) dominated the Islamic discourse through which a diluted form of the *sunnah* was emphasised. The Mujaddid through his important writings like the *Maktubāt* and his vast network of *khulafā* (spiritual successors) launched a campaign for restoring the *sunnah* as the prerequisite for the reform of the Muslim society. It was this rejuvenating spirit that was evident in the *tajdīdi* programme of Shah Waliyullah and his descendants. Shah 'Alamullah and his descendants were also influenced by the *tajdīdi* trends and made great strides in removing cumbersome practices that were ingrained in the collective psyche of the Indian Muslims. In a specific sense, Shaykh Nadwi's *Saviours of Islamic Spirit* is an elaboration of his family's strong spiritual ties with the Mujaddid and Shah Waliyullah, and a reinforcement of his own reformist ideas operating in a continuum.

Sayyid Abu Sa'īd Hasani

Another distinguished figure in Shaykh Nadwi's ancestral lineage is Sayyid Abu Sa'īd Hasani (d. 1193 *hijri*). Like Shah 'Alamullah, he scrupulously observed the *sunnah* in his personal life. A contemporary of Shah Waliyullah, Shah Abu Sa'id drew upon much spiritual guidance from him.

The *Maktubāt* (letters) genre which was well-established in the Indian subcontinent, is a treasure trove of *ruhāniyat* (spirituality) and reflects the sublimity of Islamic teachings couched in elegant literary style. Shah Waliyullah paid glowing tributes to Shah Abu Sa'id and his adherence to the *shari'ah* in his *Maktubāt*. *Tawhīd* and strict adherence to the *sunnah* were the hallmarks of the Hasani genealogy. Muhammad Ghazi has referred to the Shah to be one of the most notable disciples of Shah Waliyullah. His *sufi* temperament complemented his study of *tafsīr*, *hadīth* and *fiqh*.[19] Thus, he was able to explain the inner dimensions of *tasawwuf* in the light of the *shari'ah*.

Sayyid Ahmad Shahid

In its comprehensiveness and mass appeal, and the methodology closely following the Prophetic pattern, no contemporary revivalist movement comparable to the powerful movement of Islamic revival headed by Sayyid

---

[19] Nadwi, *Saviours of Islamic Spirit,* vol. 3, 280-2.

Shahid is to be found in the nineteenth century.[20]

The achievements of Sayyid Ahmad Shahid (d.1631) had made a powerful impact in the making of present-day Islam in South Asia. A scion of the illustrious Hasani family in Rae Bareli, the Sayyid established a reformist movement (*Tariqah i-Muhammadi*) based on the *shari'ah*-oriented methodology. Hence, it was free from syncretic practices accumulated both from Hindu rituals and the deviant eclecticism of some *sufi* orders. He wanted to reinstate the *shari'ah* in the Muslim society with the "whole of the practical and conceptual structure of Islam." In a similar vein, Sayyid was critical of scholars and rulers who made the *shari'ah* subservient to their personal interests and political ambitions.

Sayyid's contributions to the reconstruction of Islamic thought were manifold. As a close *murid* (spiritual follower) of Shah 'Abdul 'Aziz Dihlawi, Sayyid was able to enlist eminent scholars like Shah Isma'il Shahid, the grandson of Shah Waliyullah to carry out his visionary program of action, i.e. establishment of an Islamic state based on the pattern of the *Khulafā al-Rāshidin*. Sayyid worked tirelessly to the restoration of the *Imāmat* (central leadership) which apart from its obligatory nature, served as a cohesive force in maintaining the unity of the *ummah*.[21] The religious, social and political awakening of the Muslims in the subcontinent was the result of the *tajdīdī* movement of Sayyid. His call for the strenuous effort in the way of God was a tangible expression of his conviction that this obligation could liberate Muslims from both Sikh rule and English imperialism.[22] His martyrdom at Balakot in 1831 did not stop the *mujāhidin* from their struggle to fight the enemies of Islam. The aftermath of Balakot showed the unwavering spirit of faith "reinforced by selflessness and courage, willingness to die in the way of Allah and the sacrificing zeal for Islam and the unity among Muslims."[23]

Sayyid's movement stressed on *tawhīd*, a simple and unostentatious link to the Prophetic model and *tasawwuf*, which was free from technicalities. It would be no exaggeration to state that Sayyid's movement was responsible for the popularisation of Islamic knowledge and learning translations. In this connection, the use of Urdu as a medium of instruction was one such example to illustrate Sayyid's simple and direct approach to reform the Muslim masses. Among these publications, Isma'il Shahid's *Taqwiyat al-Imān* is

---

[20] Nadwi, *A Misunderstood Reformer* (Lucknow, 1979), 9.
[21] Nadwi, *Tārikh Da'wat wa 'Azimat*, vol. 6 (Karachi, n.d.), 518-20.
[22] *Ibid.*, 358-94.
[23] Nadwi, *A Misunderstood Reformer*, 19.

Chapter I
Family Characteristics

considered an important work reflecting his *islāhī* vision. The work was translated into Arabic by Shaykh Nadwi as *Risālat al-Tawhīd*. It contains valuable notes by him. *Taqwiyat* was widely received by the Arab world for its forceful presentation of *tawhīd* against the background of a syncretic Islam practised by large segments of the Muslim community in the subcontinent. It also served as an icon text for the reformist interpretation of Islam.[24] To a larger extent, it purged Islam of *shirk*-laden beliefs that sadly were built around the shrines of eminent *sufis*.

The reconstruction of Muslim society envisaged by Sayyid was successfully carried out by his followers. A few instances are mentioned to show the far-reaching effects of Sayyid's reformatory endeavors. Shaykh Nadwi observed:

> While Sayyid was staying at Kolkata on his way to the *hajj* pilgrimage, the sale of wine dwindled. Muslims of the town and rural areas were taking *bayʿah* (oath of allegiance) at his hand, promising to desist from drinking liquor and other evils with the result that the wine shops appeared to have a deserted look . . . Muslim ladies took to the observance of *purdah*, un-Islamic practices were given up and the observances commended by Islam were adopted.[25]

These salutary changes did not happen in Kolkata alone, it was replicated in many parts of the country.

Mawlana Mawdudi (d. 1979), the eminent scholar and contemporary of Shaykh Nadwi refers to Sayyid's movement as "a rare phenomenon in our recent history." Sayyid and his followers mirrored the lives of the *Sahābah* in the earliest period of Islam. His call for a return to the ideal past carried with it puritanical ideals and an interpretation of the strenuous effort in the way of God. Likewise, his movement was intended to show its close parallel to the period of the righteous Caliphs and indirectly giving it a religious legitimacy. Shaykh Nadwi, too, showers praise about Sayyid's movement in the

---

[24] Muhammad Ismaʿil Shahid, *Taqwiyat al-Imān* (Lucknow, 1991). The impact of print in South Asia has been extensively covered by Francis Robinson in *Islam and Muslim History in South Asia* (New Delhi, 2001), 66-99. Two of the earliest books to be printed in the early 1820s and 1830s were the *Taqwiyat al-Imān* and *Sirāt i-Mustaqim*, both key works in the Muslim revival of the early nineteenth century.

[25] Nadwi, *A Misunderstood Reformer* (Lucknow, 1979), 33.

following words:

> It was through Sayyid's magnetic personality that the founders of the Deoband school, on the one hand, and a body of selfless workers by the great organisers of Sadiqpur, on the other, were initiated into the Mujaddidi-Naqshbandi *sufi* order. This first group exerted itself to establish educational institutions for religious reform while the second group worked against influences alien to the spirit and teachings of Islam... [This] constituted a marvellous achievement of Sayyid's movement in the history of sufism and religious reforms. It also protected the great Muslim community of this subcontinent against ever reverting back to unsound beliefs and polytheistic practices... [These] achievements assign an honoured place to Sayyid among the galaxy of *mujāhidin* (revivalists) whom we find giving a call to the faithful at every turning point of our history.[26]

The voluminous accounts on Sayyid's revivalist contributions may be analysed on two levels:

- Development of *tasawwuf* in a historical context.
- Emergence of political activism as a trajectory of *tasawwuf*.

Divergent opinions have been expressed about Sayyid's original contributions. It would be worthwhile to examine Shaykh Nadwi's monograph, *A Misunderstood Reformer* to explore the conflicting views regarding Sayyid. The Wahhabi connection, a pejorative term applied to puritanical movements in the subcontinent, had given rise to hostile reactions to Sayyid's movement by a number of groups with different objectives. It is claimed that he was influenced by the Wahhabi movement during his *hajj* journey. However, Sayyid had long before formulated a blueprint for the social, moral and spiritual upliftment of Muslims as elucidated in his *Sirāt i-Mustaqīm*. His discourses were recorded in this work and clearly pointed out to the spiritual reforms, among other issues, he had envisioned to stem the tide of religious deviation. At the same time, he worked out his program of spiritual regeneration based on his understanding of the Quran and *sunnah*. It is,

---

[26] Nadwi, *Saviours of Islamic Spirit*, vol. 4, 333-4.

8

Chapter I
Family Characteristics

therefore, not implausible to draw a conclusion that popular Islam branded his reforms as heretical. No different was the attitude of Western writers who thrived during British colonialism in the subcontinent to denigrate the movement for political expediency. This trend was even perceptible among some Arab scholars whose writings reflected questionable modern scholarship. In sum, no critical evaluation derived from the original historical sources was employed to provide a well-constructed presentation of Sayyid's significant contributions on both societal and spiritual levels.

The thrust of Sayyid's reform was to restore a proper understanding of *tawhīd*. However, in the evolution of Indo-Islamic culture, the primacy of *tawhīd* was compromised at the altar of syncretic religious practices. According to Shaykh Nadwi, Muslims in the subcontinent practised a diluted version of Islam over the centuries that had no semblance to or affinity with the Quranic teachings and *sunnah*. It was, therefore, natural that reforms initiated by Sayyid and decades later by reformist movements would be opposed by practitioners of these *bid'at*. In this strain, this term has multiple meanings and is applied vigorously by reformers to root out un-Islamic rituals and devotional practices.

Shaykh Nadwi deplored the lamentable *bid'ah* tradition in the country that was generally associated with Hinduism. It was almost a parallel religion promoting an accretion of culture formation, peculiar religious norms and standards. Worse, it elevated the *awliyā* (saints) as intermediaries by Muslims for their supplications. It is an irony that the *mazārs* have a tremendous appeal for common people and even educated classes. More concerning is the carnival-like ambience at these sites - a grim reminder of these misguided expressions of Islam.[27]

Conclusion

The rise of Sayyid Ahmad's reformist order consolidated the *tajdīdī* movements in the subcontinent with particular reference to the Wallyullah tradition. Shaykh Nadwi himself strove to uphold the *islāhī* contents of these movements and gave an impetus through his writings and reformatory endeavors for their implementation. It is in this context that Shaykh Nadwi's intellectual contributions must be examined.

---

[27] For a detailed account, see Nadwi, *A Misunderstood Reformer*.

Chapter II

Educational Influence: Formative Years

Shaykh Nadwi was born on 15 December 1913 in Takya Kalan[1] (Rae Bareli) in a family[2] which was distinguished for its proud tradition of selfless service for Muslims in the subcontinent. It was the city of Lucknow, the seat of Muslim culture and learning[3] that had a tremendous impact on his life. Shaykh Nadwi's impressions of Lucknow shed much light about its formative influence on his educational career and provide a snapshot of his family life:

> Bazar Jhaw Lal, one of the suburbs in Lucknow, served as a nucleus for our family's activities. My father's *tibb*[4] practice was situated here and so was our modest home (in which we stayed for many decades). Our family comprised of my parents, four siblings: my elder brother, Dr Hakim Sayyid 'Abdul 'Ali (later to become the Rector of Nadwah), Amat al-`Aziz and Amatullah Tasnim. I was the youngest in the family. Our home saw a regular flow of visitors and was always filled with that special lustre. This was not uncommon as many of our relatives from Rae Bareli visited us often. Among the aristocratic (*ashraf*) families living in Lucknow, I must mention Nawāb Sayyid Nur al-Hasan Khan Bahādur[5] with whom we enjoyed an excellent relationship. My father

---

[1] Also popularly known as Da'ira Shah 'Alam-ullah.
[2] A brief reference may be made to both Sayyid Fakhruddin Khayali, his paternal grandfather and Sayyid Diya al-Nabi, his maternal grandfather both of whose scholarly accomplishments and remarkable spiritual calibre were exemplified in the personality of Shaykh Nadwi, See Nadwi, *Kārwān* (vol. 1) and *Hayāt i-'Abdul Hayy* about their respective biographical accounts.
[3] See Francis Robinson's excellent *The 'Ulama of Farangi Mahal and Islamic Culture in South Asia* (Lucknow, 2001) on the growth and development of Islamic culture in Lucknow. Cf. Barbara Daly Metcalf, *Islamic Revival in British India Deoband, 1860-1900* (Princeton, 1982).
[4] *Tibb* or Greco-Arabic medicine has had an interesting history in the subcontinent. For a brief history of this discipline, refer to the following books: Rashid Bhikha, *Tibb: Traditional Roots of Medicine in Modern Routes to Health* (South Africa, 2001); Sadia Rashid (ed.) *Hakim Mohammed Said: Collection of Essays (1973-1979)* vols. 1-4 (Karachi, 1999).
[5] Sayyid Nur al-Hasan was the son of the prominent scholar, Sayyid Siddiq Hasan Khan, Nawab of Bhopal (India). An illustrious scholar who is credited with widely-acclaimed works both in Arabic and *hadīth* studies, the Nawab is also considered the pioneer of the Ahl-i-Hadīth movement in India. For a detailed account of his

was preoccupied with his writings, his *tibb* practice and his duties as Nāzim of Nadwah. He was naturally inclined to a quiet life, focusing his energies on research and other scholarly pursuits. He was unassuming and always hospitable, especially to eminent scholars. As always, our home was a hub for scholars and writers. In fact, this was a hereditary trait that shaped our family's scholarly temperament. This also explains our deep-seated attachment to Islamic literature and passion to acquire the latest titles in the market. Whatever money we received from our family elders was spent on purchasing new books.[6]

Formative Influences
Hakim Sayyid 'Abdul Hayy Hasani: Exemplar of Scholarship

In the biography of his father, *Hayāt i-'Abdul Hayy,* Shaykh Nadwi describes the sterling qualities of this eminent scholar. A graduate of Nadwah, Sayyid 'Abdul Hayy pursued his studies in *hadīth* and *fiqh* with the illustrious *'ulama.* He gained mastery over *hadīth* studies under the tutelage of the renowned *muhaddith,* Shaykh Husayn bin Muhsin Yemeni[7] who attracted a number of scholars in Bhopal. Sayyid's versatility is evident in his historical and literary contributions. *Nuzhat al-Khawātir,*[8] in this instance, marked out his pioneering contribution as an outstanding historian of Muslim India. Written in Arabic, *Nuzhat* is a remarkable demonstration of the continuity of the Islamic tradition: from the first century of Islam down to the early twentieth century, scholars and saints are shown carrying out similar pursuits in different parts of India, teaching and transmitting the Islamic sciences from one generation (*tabaqah*)[9] to another. The biographical notes in eight volumes represent scholarship of a high calibre. Hakim Sayyid passed away in 1923 when Shaykh Nadwi was nine years old.

---

life and works, see 'Abdul Hayy Hasani, *Nuzhat al-Khawātir*, vol. 8, 202-8.
[6] Nadwi, *Kārwān*, vol. 1, 54-57. Amatullah Tasnim was a prolific writer who translated Imam Nawawi's hadith compendium, *Riyād al-Sālihin* into Urdu entitled *Zād-i-Safar*. Nadwi, *Purāne Charāgh*, vol. 2, 340-69.
[7] See *Nuzhat*, vol. 8, 121-32 for his biographical account and contribution to *hadīth* studies in India.
[8] The motivation for this important work is discussed in detail by Shaykh Nadwi in *Hayāt-i-'Abdul Hayy*, 267-82.
[9] George Makdisi's well-researched article, "Tabaqāt: Biography and Orthodoxy in Classical Islam" in *Islamic Studies*, 1993, 32:4, 371-9 is a useful introduction to the genre of biography.

Chapter II
Educational Influence: Formative Years

Maktubāt: Portrait of Sayyidah Khairun Nisā'

It would be worthwhile to provide a brief comment on the letter writing genre (*Maktūbāt*) with special reference to his mother Sayyidah Khairun Nisā' (d. 1968). Sayyid Wāzih Rashid Nadwi explains:

> The heart is the repository of true feelings and sentiments which are accurately mirrored in letters. Unlike other literature, letter writing focuses on spontaneity and interpretive expression, and parental letters enjoy a distinctive position in this genre. Letters written to children contain an elegant style that are suited to their intellectual and emotional make-up. Subtle pointers, anecdotes, stories and parables adorn this creative style and bring alive the changing fortunes of man's life. Joy, grief and issues affecting our daily lives are poignantly recorded with the least bit of formality. Readers may respond differently to these situations; it may have a positive impact on them or on the contrary, produce a feeling of pessimism and despair. It will not be out of place to state that the biographies of *'ulama, mashā'ikh* and leading luminaries of the Muslim world have as their starting point a mother's influence on their early upbringing and formative development. A mother's affection, love and care have nurtured great figures and enabled them to make their contribution to society. Her heart-rending emotions and tear-filled expressions are succinctly captured in letters containing a literary flair and artistic beauty.[10]

Sayyidah Khairun Nisā's letters to her beloved son Shaykh Nadwi are a treasure trove of wisdom, unbounded enthusiasm and spirituality. These are deftly woven to develop a truly Islamic consciousness. Her letters reveal an inner yearning for Shaykh Nadwi to emulate the illustrious scholars of Islam and pursue the path of righteousness at all times. In one of her letters, she laments at Shaykh Nadwi's strong inclination to English education, which in her estimation is rooted in a culture and civilisation alien to the Islamic ethos. Her intuitive insight strengthened her belief that Shaykh Nadwi's unbridled enthusiasm for the English language would impact negatively his future career as an Islamic scholar. The following extracts illustrate this point clearly:

---

[10] Muhammad Wāzih Rashid Nadwi, "Mawlana Nadwi in the Mirror of his Mother's Supplications and Letters" in *Ta'meer i- Hayāt*, Special Issue, 2000, 282-83.

'Ali, if people hold the belief that position can only be obtained by acquiring English education and maintain that it is important to become a judge or at least a lawyer, then I am totally against this widely-held belief. I consider these English-educated people to be ignoramuses and their knowledge as futile and inconsequential. 'Ali, if you want to earn Divine pleasure and fulfil my obligation then I urge you to focus on the lives of those pure-hearted souls who spent their entire lives in the service of Islam. Shah Waliyullah and other celebrated scholars served as role models and left a powerful influence on the footprints of time. I pray to Allah to endow you with determination and ardour to carry out your religious obligations.[11]

In another letter Sayyidah Khairun Nisā' draws her son's attention to the importance of following the path of virtue as exemplified by the pious predecessors (aslāf).

Wherever possible, develop an awareness of the lofty status of the early scholars of Islam. Acquaint yourself with the shari'ah and avoid those who create mischief by discrediting the status of the 'ulama. It is my ardent desire that you acquire knowledge just like those 'ulama whose powerful personalities were a source of joy and inspiration to the ummah. This is the greatest wish I cherish for you.

Shaykh Nadwi's reminiscences of his mother are beautifully portrayed in the following extracts from his autobiography:

After the demise of my father, it fell upon my mother to assume a greater role. Her maternal affection and concern for my welfare were exemplary. Even so, she maintained a strict code of conduct with regard to salah and the rights of subordinates. Under no circumstances would she condone any mistreatment of servants in our household. Any act of transgression could only be redeemed if we sought forgiveness from the aggrieved person. Thus, I learnt two valuable lessons from such incidents: admit your mistakes and never humiliate others. My mother was an embodiment of righteousness and exemplified in her personal life the quintessence of supplication.[12]

---

[11] Nadwi, Kārwān, vol. 1, 122-23.
[12] Ta'meer i-Hayāt, 284.

Shaykh Nadwi discontinued his English studies; however, in a broader sense, it equipped him sufficiently to undertake extensive research in Islamic studies. It also facilitated his *da'wah* program in the West and enabled him to interact with English scholars of international repute.

Arabic Studies: Influence of Shaykh Khalil Yemeni

Shaykh Nadwi's Arabic education began in the later part of 1924 under the guidance of his uncle Sayyid Khalil al-Din. It was, however, the illustrious Arab scholar, Shaykh Muhammad Khalil Yemeni who initiated him to the intricacies of the Arabic language. His elder brother, Dr 'Abdul 'Ali supervised his educational upbringing and ensured that he was taught by the best teachers. Arab Sahib, as Shaykh Khalil was popularly known, commenced with the basic grammar for Shaykh Nadwi to memorise. He was an Arabic lecturer in Lucknow University and intuitively recognised Shaykh Nadwi's flair for the language. Arab Sahib's innovative method of teaching Arabic generated much interest among students. He included in his curriculum textbooks aimed at developing students' mastery at all levels. Spoken Arabic was compulsory and a fine of two *paisa* was imposed if students spoke Urdu during the lesson. This was a preparatory stage to consolidate their linguistic skills. Arab Sahib was fastidious about the rules he set out for his students. Also, the preparation of lessons in advance by the students was rigidly maintained.

A unique feature of Arab Sahib's teaching method was to contextualise grammar rules. He avoided complex concepts and embellished prosaic works which impeded a student's aesthetic appreciation of Arabic as a dynamic, contemporary language.[13] In this respect, Shaykh Nadwi benefited immensely from Arab Sahib's choice of books. For him classical works could be read without any difficulty:

> To my good fortune, my first teacher (Arab Sahib) was a tender-hearted person. We wished that he would recite for long periods of time, enabling us to listen to him. He also led the *Fajr* prayer at the mosque in our locality. Rarely, however, he could complete a surah. For as he commenced reciting he was overcome with tears and his voice choked. This happened almost every day. He taught me selected *surahs*, especially the ones focusing on *tawhīd*.[14]

---

[13] Nadwi, *Kārwān*, vol. 1, 88-91.
[14] Ibid., 94-5.

Arab Sahib's devotion to and passion for Arabic was exemplary. His eloquence and mastery left indelible imprints on Shaykh Nadwi's appreciation of the language. He was without a peer and gave the opportunity to his students to share in its literary excellence.

Urdu Studies: Literary Influence

It was Shaykh Nadwi's good fortune that his Urdu Studies ran concurrently with the Arabic lessons. He was introduced to a comparatively high standard of Urdu literature and read with unbounded enthusiasm books dealing with the *'ulama's* contributions to *da'wah*. These writings had a direct bearing on his understanding of the Islamic teachings and allowed him to develop an appropriate literary style to present Islam to the new generation of educated Muslims. The voluminous and widely-acclaimed publication of his father's *Gul-i Ra'nā* served as the starting point to his appreciation of Urdu poetry.
Written in an elegant style, *Gul-i Ra'nā* traces the historical development of Urdu poetry and its notable poets.[15]
Urdu has had a fair share of its accomplished writers whose contributions continue to have an impact on the literary scene. Shibli Nu'māni, Hāli and Nazir Ahmad were some of the distinguished writers who influenced Shaykh Nadwi greatly. So was the influential *Al-Hilāl* magazine of Abul Kalam Azad. These writings had a cumulative influence on his career as a writer. He also read *Yād-i Ayyam*,[16] a historical work highlighting Muslim rule in Gujarat (India). Its literary merits lie in its chaste style without compromising historical objectivity. Apart from literary studies, Shaykh Nadwi pursued works of *sirah* with much interest. The following excerpts reveal his unconditional devotion to the personality of the Prophet (SAAS):

> A noteworthy incident that illustrates my passion for reading *sirah* writings is the book entitled *Rahmatanli al-'Ālamin* by Qazi Muhammad Sulayman Mansurpuri. My elder brother, Dr 'Abdul 'Ali[17] who took over as my guardian, on the death of my father, when I was only nine, paid special attention to the books I was to read, and his

---

[15] Nadwi, *Hayāt i-'Abdul Hayy*, 309-12.
[16] Dr. Sayyid 'Abdul 'Ali's mentorship is a recurrent motif in Shaykh Nadwi's writings. In fact, Dr 'Abdul 'Ali was the inspiration behind Shaykh Nadwi's versatility. See *Hayāt i-'Abdul Hayy*, 344-98.
[17] Nadwi, *Guidance from the Holy Qur'an* (Leicester, 2005), 3.

choice was always blessed with Divine grace. He thus gave me *Khair al-Bashar* (*The Best of Men*) to read. He wanted me to concentrate on the biographies of the Prophet (SAAS) as he thought that nothing was more useful for character-building and steadfastness of belief than these works. I consequently developed from my childhood a fondness for books dealing with the life of the sacred Prophet (SAAS).

Within a few days, the postman brought the Value Paid Parcel of the book to our tiny village. This book of Qazi Sulayman made a tremendous impression on me. It shook me to the depths of my being. But it was not in the nature of a hurricane. There was nothing tempestuous about the way it moved me. On the other hand, it was the most soothing and inspiring experience. My heart swayed with joy like a flower-laden branch of a tree, caressed by the morning breeze. That is the difference between the biographies of conquerors and other men of worldly renown and the books relating to the personality of the Holy Prophet (SAAS). The former, too, arouse the heart, but the effect they produce comes from outside and seizes it like an invader while the awakening that takes place as a result of reading the life-accounts of the Prophet (SAAS) spring from within, from the innermost recesses of the believer's heart and sustains it.[18]

Tarbiyah: Shaykh Nadwi's Academic and Moral Orientation

Shaykh Nadwi's upbringing, education and moral instruction were the joint responsibility of his mother and his elder brother. As Shaykh Nadwi noted about his doting brother:

A father to his brother and an obedient son to his mother, with his unbounded affection for me, he extended his patronage to all of us reflecting a role model as he was now before us.[19]

A moving illustration from Shaykh Nadwi's autobiography highlights some sensitive issues on the affectionate relationship between Dr 'Abdul 'Ali and him:

Often on return from medical college he would hasten to verify whether I had offered my *salah* (prayers) at the mosque and detecting the slightest discrepancy in my version insisted that I repeat them in his presence. Soon, I began observing the rules set by him. I was

---

[18] Nadwi, *Pathway to Madina* (Lucknow, 1982), 9-10.
[19] Nadwi, *Kārwān*, vol. 1, 78.

never permitted to read a novel. Rather, my brother urged me to select books from our private collection of books and manuscripts and was my inspiration to my insatiable reading habits.[20]

Admission to Lucknow University

Shaykh Nadwi's versatility was easily recognised by his teacher, Shaykh Khalil. Shaykh Nadwi's comments on this important phase in his educational career are revealing:

The year 1927 marked an important phase in my academic career when Arab Sahib informed my brother that I had obtained admission at the Lucknow University to pursue the Arabic literature course. It must be borne in mind that I was barely fourteen years of age and it was natural for a prospective candidate to feel extremely overjoyed with this honour. Arab Sahib was responsible for the undergraduate and postgraduate classes in Arabic at the university and commanded great respect among the teaching staff... [I] sat for the annual examination in 1928 and was confident that my results would be promising. However, much to my disappointment, I failed and this disturbing news reached Arab Sahib, my brother and my mother who were saddened by the results. In the final analysis, there was a lesson to be learnt about setbacks in life that prepared me for the greater challenges ahead. It did not take me long to realise that apparent failures can be converted into positive goals. I sat again for the examination in 1929 with renewed courage and determination. The results were excellent: I had achieved first position entitling me to a scholarship. By the same token, I was eligible for a gold medal. It was unfortunate that a sponsor was not available for that year and thus I was deprived of this coveted award. It must be borne in mind that the medal was equivalent to a hundred rupees (a considerable amount for that period). Who could have predicted that several decades later (1980 to be precise) the Saudi kingdom would honour me with the prestigious King Faisal Award whose value exceeded all monetary expectations.[21]

---

[20] Nadwi, *Kārwān*, vol. 1, 97.
[21] Nadwi, *Kārwān*, vol. 1, 97.

Chapter II
Educational Influence: Formative Years

Lahore: A Historic Visit

The historic city of Lahore conjured up images of an Islamic centre of culture and learning. It was a city bustling with literary activities and priding itself with renowned scholars and, of course, the poet of the East, 'Allamāh Iqbal. This visit was a milestone in Shaykh Nadwi's life as it ushered him into a new world of academic opportunities from which he was able to draw immense benefit for his future career. According to him, he enjoyed a two-fold advantage: He was equipped through his mastery in Arabic to interact with leading scholars of the day. Also his father's scholarly work, *Gul-i Ra'nā* facilitated his contact with Lahore's academia. Iqbal knew his father well through this work which had just been published and became popular in literary circles throughout the country. Shaykh Nadwi was introduced to Iqbal as a sixteen-year old teenager who was a fervent admirer of his poetry. In that meeting he presented to Iqbal an Arabic translation of his poem *Chānd* (The moon). Iqbal was pleased to read it and then asked him a few questions about some Arab poets probably to assess the extent of his scholarship. Shaykh Nadwi came away greatly impressed by his simplicity, sincerity and humility.[22]

During the course of his visit to Lahore, Shaykh Nadwi was honoured to meet the celebrated interpreter of the Quran Mawlana Ahmad 'Ali Lahori. He possessed a charismatic personality. His devotion to the Quran and *islāhī* activities created an upsurge of religious interest among the masses. According to Mawlana Lahori, faith and practice were twin pillars on which the structure of *da'wah* rested. In a similar vein, he was unsparing in his criticism of pseudo-*sufis* whom he considered to be the bane of the Muslim society.

Mawlana Lahori's bold candour and independence reiterated his detachment to worldly comforts. The Muslim aristocrats and influential entrepreneurs lowered their heads in reverence to his censure of their opulent lifestyle. As much as he acceded to their request for Qur'anic lessons, he politely declined their personal invitations. He firmly believed that intermingling with aristocracy deflected an *'ālim* from expressing *shari'ah* rulings for which there was no compromise.

It is reported that after his passing away, fragrance emitted from his grave. This extraordinary incident was a testimony to his total commitment

---

[22] *Ibid.*, 87.

to the Quran. It was reminiscent of the fragrance that lasted for several days from Imām Bukhārī's grave.

After his return from Lahore, Shaykh Nadwi commenced formally with the study of *hadīth* under the famous scholar, Shaykh Haydar Hasan Khan Tonki. The two-year study program introduced him to the vast corpus of *hadīth* literature and the outstanding scholarship of his teacher. Shaykh Haydar adopted a meticulous approach to the teaching of *hadīth*. He urged students to focus on research, comparative studies and critical evaluation. This was also the method of his teacher, Shaykh Husayn of Yemen. Shaykh Nadwi observed his teacher closely during this period and was impressed by his devotion to *hadīth* studies, his affection for his students and unfailing encouragement for them to achieve excellence on this important source of Islam. He bore in his daily *'ibādah* (worship) unmistakable traces of humility and concern for the Afterlife. These qualities had no doubt a profound influence on his students as well. The certificate of *hadīth* (*ijāzah*) written personally by him is a testimony to his love and caring attitude for Shaykh Nadwi.[23]

Mawlana Husayn Ahmad Madani: An Enduring Mentorship

Shaykh Nadwi's acquaintance with Mawlana Madani was a memorable period in his life. Dr 'Abdul 'Ali made the appropriate arrangements for him to pursue *hadīth* studies in Deoband under the tutelage of this prominent scholar. His personal affection and loving attitude were attributes that endeared students to him. Shaykh Nadwi was very fortunate during his brief stay in Deoband to receive Mawlana Madani's personal attention and to benefit appreciably from his vast learning and experience in *hadīth*. What impressed him greatly was Mawlana Madani's unassuming personality, humility and concern for the welfare of Muslims throughout the world.[24]

---

[23] *Ibid.*, 183-206.
[24] A vast corpus of writings, largely biographical, is available on Mawlana Madani's contribution to *hadīth*, *tasawwuf* and politics. The following books reflect this trend: Sayyid Muhammad Miyan, *Asirān i-Malta* (Karachi, n.d.); Bayazid Pandor, *Biography of Shaikhul Islam Hadrat Mawlana Husain Ahmad Madani* (Azaadville, 2007); D.R. Goyal, *Mawlana Husain Ahmad Madani: A Biographical Study* (Kolkata, 2004).

Chapter II
Educational Influence: Formative Years

'Allāmah Taqi al-Dīn Hilālī: Peerless Scholarship

The arrival of 'Allāmah Taqi al-Dīn Hilālī of Morocco was a historic occasion for Nadwah, which was honoured to have him on its teaching staff. An international scholar who was peerless in his Arabic, 'Allāmah Hilālī drew capable students from across the country and developed their skills. His *sanad* (certificate) was a testimony to his student's thorough familiarity with Arabic. Political circumstances forced him to leave Saudi Arabia during the reign of King 'Abdul 'Aziz Al-Saud. Shaykh Muhammad Yemeni together with other scholars was instrumental in arranging his stay in Lucknow. It eventually paved the way for him to accept the teaching offer at Nadwah. 'Allāmah Hilālī was a prolific scholar whose elegant and chaste Arabic was an inspiration for his students. It was through his tireless efforts that the correct teaching method of Arabic was firmly established on the Indian soil. His approach was innovative and students benefited greatly from his outstanding scholarship.

Shaykh Nadwi had the honour of being one of his students to pursue an extensive study of classical texts under his supervision. He chalked out new methods to the comprehensive understanding of Arabic. Hilālī's influence on his students was profound. As a caring teacher, he would ensure that the environment was conducive to study Arabic. Furthermore, his sterling services served to enhance an appreciation of this dynamic language. The year 1931 was memorable for Shaykh Nadwi because he was selected to accompany Hilālī on an educational journey to neighbouring towns and cities. Having spent days and nights in his company, he was highly impressed by the latter's vast learning and endearing personality. During this period, the urgency of an Arabic journal was felt and a team of young scholars was tasked to study the feasibility of publishing such a journal. It was expected to contain articles of a high standard. In response to this pressing need, *Al-Diyā* was a first in the series of journals devoted to Arabic scholarship brought out by Nadwah.[25]

As a nascent Arabic journal, *Al-Diyā* received accolades from literary critics across the Middle East. The fact that the articles were written by Indian scholars, and in a short period of time established its literary niche, was a tacit endorsement of Nadwah's excellent standards of teaching Arabic. There was no doubt, according to Shaykh Nadwi, that the journals produced by Nadwah blazed the trail of Arabic journalism. More importantly, it stood out against the un-Islamic trends that gaining momentum in the Arab world.[26]

---

[25] Nadwi, *Kārwān*, vol. 1, 115-17.
[26] Shams Tabriz Khan, *Tārikh Nadwat al-'Ulama*, vol.2 (Lucknow, 1984), 423-4.

Shaykh Nadwi had to his academic credentials a monograph in Arabic about Sayyid Ahmad Shahid. Likewise, he contributed articles during this important phase of his career to contemporary issues affecting the Muslim world. The fact that activist scholars, like Sayyid Rashid Ridā were avid readers of the journal underpinned the transnational character of the Islamic resurgence movements.

It has been suggested that Shaykh Nadwi's initial exposure to *Salafiyyah* was largely on account of *Al-Diyā's* popularity and wide recognition in the Arab world. This view is untenable in the light of later developments which clearly marked out Shaykh Nadwi as an independent scholar. He had a clearly-defined mission and strongly advocated *wasatiyyah* (mainstream Islam) in his presentation of Islamic resurgence. His major work *Rise and Fall of Muslims* details his formulation of *wasatiyyah*.

Salafiyyah and Hilālī

A recent study of ʿAllāmah Hilālī's legacy documents his changing orientation towards *Salafiyyah*. During his teaching period at Nadwah he focused on strengthening Arabic literature. His two students, Masʿud ʿAlam and Shaykh Nadwi were representative of the emerging trends of Arabic scholarship in the country. However, his subsequent embrace of *Salafiyyah* drew Masʿud ʿAlam closer to his worldview. The latter's work on Muhammad ibn ʿAbdul Wahhab, eponymous founder of the Wahhabi movement, bears umissable traces of his teacher's influence. If Masʿud ʿAlam absorbed the traits of *Salafiyyah* under Hilālī's training, Shaykh Nadwi was much less enthusiastic of the latter's approach to *islāh*. The exclusivist and rigid interpretation of doctrinal and theological matters did not appeal to him. Needless to add, Shaykh Nadwi's interest connected him to leading intellectuals and *mashāʿikh* advancing the *islāh* cause. Several decades later Hilālī's hardcore Salafi approach crystallised into his critique of theological issues, which he perceived to be a deviance from Islam in its pristine form. Implicit in his trenchant criticism of these 'deviant' interpretations was Shaykh Nadwi's close association with the *tabligh* movement and *tasawwuf*. Notwithstanding these sharp differences, Shaykh Nadwi maintained a cordial relationship with his teacher.[27]

---

[27] Henri Lauziere, *The Making of Salafism: Islamic Reform in the Twentieth Century* (New York, 2015).

Conclusion

The formative influences on Shaykh Nadwi's academic career contributed in later years to his formulation of Islamic resurgence. Notable scholars, like Mawlana Madani shaped his understanding of the Muslim corporate identity (*tashakhkhus*), a recurring theme in Shaykh Nadwi's writings on the Islamic order in India.

Chapter III

In Pursuit of Academic Excellence

The environment of Nadwah was pivotal to Shaykh Nadwi's intellectual development. It was at this institution that his career as a teacher and writer commenced. During this significant phase, his Arabic works reflected the genres which he avidly pursued to develop his *da'wah* framework. Also, the theme of Islamic authenticity assumed greater importance in defining Shaykh Nadwi's multifaceted activities.

Since its establishment, Nadwah's destiny was characterised by two distinct impulses: Challenges and changes. The growth and development of the *madāris* (in this case, institutions of higher Islamic learning) like Dār al-'Ulūm Deoband (hereafter Deoband), played a central role in the dissemination of Islamic sciences, spreading the tenets of Islam and defending the faith against heterodox tendencies.[1] Although the curriculum adopted by Deoband is generally called *Dars i-Nizāmi*, its main emphasis is on Quran, *hadīth* and *fiqh*.[2] However, it adhered strictly to the Hanafi school of thought.

Snapshot of *Dars-i Nizāmi*

Mulla Nizāmuddin (d.1748) is widely credited for crafting the *Dars-i Nizāmi* in the subcontinent. An adept scholar with outstanding expertise in rational sciences and the classical tradition, Nizāmuddin was an intellectual giant who left behind a curriculum that produced "highly skilled scholars, bureaucrats, writers and intellectuals in his day." His goal was to empower graduates to think logically, acquire excellent writing and linguistic skills and have mastery over the classical Islamic tradition to address issues beyond religious practice.

The *Dars-i Nizāmi* enjoyed unrivalled popularity in the subcontinent and beyond for over a century. However, it underwent drastic changes following the establishment of Deoband. The institution laid emphasis on the study of *hadīth*. In fact, considerable changes to the existing curriculum became the distinctive feature of the *madāris* advocating reform. This is not to suggest

---

[1] Barbara Daly Metcalf, *Islamic Revival in British India: Deoband, 1860-1900* (Karachi, 1982), 235.
[2] For a detailed discussion on the *Dars-i Nizāmi*, Francis Robinson's *The 'Ulama of Farangi-Mahal* is a useful introduction to this curriculum.

that the curriculum became obsolete. On the contrary, recent efforts have been undertaken to elevate its status to an intensive postgraduate project.

Shaykh Nadwi explained the scope and function of the *madrasah* in the following words:

> It is the institution of man's upbringing and for channeling his talents. It is a place where those who call towards Islam and defend their faith are prepared. A *madrasah* may be likened, in a manner of speaking, to the powerhouse of the Islamic world, which provides energy not only to Muslims, but also to all of mankind. It is a centre where the heart and soul are purified, and the mind and intellect nourished. A *madrasah* is a place wherein a worldview is cultivated, and humanity is thereby sustained. It leads, and is not led. A *madrasah* is not specific to any particular nation, civilisation, culture, era, language or literature. For it is nourished and sustained directly by the Prophet Muhammad's (SAAS) message, which is universal and timeless. It is inextricably linked with the life force of humanity and with life in its vibrancy and variety. It is independent of the debate about 'classical' and 'modern.' For it is characterised by the eternal and life-giving message of the Prophet (SAAS).[3]

Nadwah's history, both in scope and content, is critically examined in the following pages. It analyses its contribution to the "reformed" curriculum as well as adopting a mission statement. Since its inception its primary focus was on the synthesis of classical Islamic education and the modern sciences. This meant an integration between the everlasting fundamentals of the faith and the everchanging values of human life.

Fiqh in a Changing World

Nadwah represented a change and marked departure from the rigid and fixed interpretation of Islam. This was clearly evident in *fiqh*, which in its evolution in the Indian subcontinent received disproportionate attention. The Hanafi school of thought was deeply rooted in the *madāris* and the *'ulama* resisted any changes to the entrenched position of its *fiqh*. Deoband represented this trend. Nadwah, on the other hand, attempted a rapprochement between the conservative and modernist elements by presenting a balanced position, i.e. a synergy of *fiqh* in a contemporary setting.

---

[3] Mohammad Akram Nadwi, *Madrasah Life* (London, 2007), 3.

Chapter III
In Pursuit of Academic Excellence

The contributions of the *'ulama* of Nadwah have been analysed in several studies on *fiqh*. The emphasis about the unity of the Muslim *ummah* (*ittihād bayna al-Muslimīn*) was of crucial importance to Nadwah, and its phalanx of scholars played a leading role in developing this theme. Shaykh Nadwi's standpoint on *fiqh* issues was balanced and borne out of years of interaction with scholars of various persuasions in the Muslim world. Sectarian prejudice was anathema to him whereas he strove to promote an accommodationist approach, which in his view was the cornerstone of the unity of the Muslim *ummah*.[4] However, Nadwah did not break away from the classical contributions of the *fuqahā*; rather, it focused on the reappraisal of *fiqh* interpretation in a changing society. The institution took the lead in redefining the parameters of *fiqh* as its founding members[5] had envisioned this change several decades earlier. According to Al-Hasani, the changing world in the twentieth century brought about a multitude of problems affecting Muslims at the sociopolitical level. These challenges required realistic solutions:

> New methods and approaches must be presented in the form of simple and reader-friendly books and monographs which are compatible with the psychological make-up of our generation and Muslims in general.[6]

Nadwah and the Arab World

Sayyid 'Abdul Hayy Nadwi, Rector of Nadwah, made pioneering efforts to promote the cause of this nascent institution. It was, however, during the rectorship of Dr 'Abdul 'Ali (1931-61) that Nadwah saw a rapid growth and established international contacts with leading Islamic institutions in the Arab world.[7]

It would be worthwhile to examine Nadwah's emphasis about the Arabic

---

[4] Munawwar Sultan Nadwi, *Nadwat al 'Ulama kā Fiqhi Mizāj* (Hyderabad, 2004), 282-5.

[5] Sayyid Muhammad 'Ali Monghīri (d. 1927), the charismatic founder of Nadwah possessed an enlightened outlook and made an incisive study about the role of *fiqh* in a changing society. See Muhammad Al-Hasani, *Payām-i Nadwat al-'Ulama* (Karachi] n.d.), 64-67. For a biographical account on Mawlana Monghiri, see Sayyid Muhammad al-Hasani, *Sirat Mawlana Muhammad 'Ali Monghīri: Bānī Nadwat al-'Ulama* (Karachi, 1980).

[6] Al-Hasani, *Payām i-Nadwat al-'Ulama*, 121.

[7] *Tārikh Nadwat al-'Ulama*, vol. 2, 418-21.

language in relation to Shaykh Nadwi's literary contributions. The institution's approach was a powerful statement of its cultural orientation and a mark of distinction from other *madāris* in the Indian subcontinent.[8]

Shaykh Nadwi mentions several Arab newspapers and journals[9] to which he was exposed in his early youth and which influenced his thinking about the Arab and Islamic identity, nationalism and secularism. He and his colleagues became intimately acquainted with the intellectual trends in the Arab world, which in turn honed their literary skills for their *da'wah* activities.[10]

Academic Activities

The core subjects of Shaykh Nadwi's teaching career were *tafsīr*, Arabic literature (*adab*) and *hadīth* studies. *Tafsīr* was his forte' and he consulted extensively the works of *tafāsir*, classical and modern, for developing a deeper insight into the meaning and message of the Quran.

Apart from consulting classical *tafāsir* like *Kashshāf*[11] he also drew immense benefit from Mawlana Azad's *Tarjumān al-Qur'an*.[12] For interpretive readings, 'Allāmah Ālūsī's *Rūh al-Ma'ānī*[13] was of great help. With regard to contemporary issues and comparative studies, Shaykh Nadwi sought assistance from Mawlana Abdul Majid Daryabadi[14] through correspondence and personal meetings.[15]

The formative years of Nadwah were, by and large, shaped by the intellectual contributions of 'Allāmah Shibli Nu'māni. His stature as a historian and literary critic was unrivalled; his *magnum opus Sirat al-Nabi*[16]

---

[8] *Ibid.*, vol. 1, 150-52.
[9] Nadwi, *Kārwān*, vol. 1, 125-6.
[10] Nadwi, *Kārwān*, vol. 1, 126-7.
[11] For a brief survey of the classical *tafsīr* literature see, Thameem Uthama, *Methodologies of the Qur'anic Exegesis* (Kuala Lumpur, 1995), 85-106.
[12] Abdur Rahman Doi, *The Sciences of the Qur'an* (Pretoria, 1997), 284-85.
[13] Uthama, *Methodologies.* 85-106.
[14] An eminent commentator of the Quran in English (*Tafsīr-ul-Qur'an*).
[15] Nadwi, *Kārwān*, vol. 1, 147.
[16] Shibli Nu'māni (1857-1914) was an illustrious scholar whose intellectualism bore traces of Muslim glory and its impact on world civilisation combined with the rational spirit which saw the flowering of an Islamic tradition that borrowed liberally from Greek, Indian and Hellenic sources. He was also a proponent of a new *kalām* (scholastic theology) which confronted contemporary challenges. Shibli, despite his major contribution to Islamic thought and culture, remains a

Chapter III
In Pursuit of Academic Excellence

(a posthumous publication and also a collaborative effort by his student, Sayyid Sulayman Nadwi) and works on the early heroes of Islam[17] were a model for students at Nadwah. In fact, Shibli was considered an icon and an inspiration worthy of emulation.[18]

Shaykh Nadwi's personal devotion to his academic pursuits is succinctly described in the revised study[19] concerning his contemporaries' impressions of books and writings that influenced them. As noted in this work, he provides readers with his insightful comments on the writings and literary genres drawn from both classical and contemporary eras.[20] Another useful study *Meri 'Ilmi wa Mutāla'āti Zindagi*,[21] a compilation of articles by Shaykh Nadwi sheds much light about this important phase of his educational career. The influence of Arabic is detailed with special reference to his teacher, Hilālī, an illustrious scholar who made meaningful contributions to the growth and development of the Arabic language at Nadwah.[22] Commenting on the Arabic language, Shaykh Nadwi observed:

In the company of Hilālī, two realities unfolded before me for the first time: The difference between language and literature (*adab*). Language is the foundation of *adab*, which is the gallery of the former and adorns its walls with portraits. *Adab* represents the highest force of literary expression for which progressive thoughts are a vehicle. Culture and ideals are sustained by (this genre).[23]

Language is inextricably linked to literature and both are not mutually exclusive entities. Shaykh Nadwi gives a brief survey of the anomalous situation in India where Arabic had been taught in the *madāris*. According to

---

controversial figure. Murad's analysis suggests that it was his complex personality and enigmatic quality which led people to view him differently (*Intellectual Modernism of Shibli Nu'māni*, 1976). In contrast, Sayyid Sabāhuddin 'Abdur Rahmān echoes the sentiments of his teacher, Sayyid Sulayman Nadwi that Shibli represented the merger of the classical Islamic tradition and modern sciences.

[17] For a biographical account of Sayyid Sulayman Nadwi, see Muhammad Na'im Siddiqui, '*Allāmah Sayyid Sulayman Nadwi: Shakhsiyyat wa Adabi Khidmat* (Lucknow, 1985); Sayyid Sabahuddin 'Abdur Rahmān, *Mawlana Sayyid Sulayman Nadwi ki Tasānif* (Azamgarh, 1988).

[18] Sulayman Nadwi's *Hayāt i-Shibli* (Azamgarh, n.d.). Cf. Nadwi's *Western Civilisation, Islam and Muslims* (1974), 64-65.

[19] Muhammad 'Imrān Khan Nadwi, *Mashāhir-i Ahl-i 'Ilm kī Muhsin Kitāb*. Revised by Faysal Ahmad Bhatkali Nadwi (Lucknow, 2004).

[20] *Ibid.*, 191-98.

[21] Nadwi, *Meri 'Ilmi wa Mutāla'āti Zindagi* (Rae Bareli, n.d.).

[22] Nadwi, *Kārwān*, vol. 1, 119-26.

[23] Nadwi, *Meri 'Ilmi wa Mutāla'ati Zindagi*, 16.

him, Arabic as a dynamic language is marginalised in these institutions and undue emphasis is given to grammar and a few classical works. This approach in no way is expected to build confidence in a student. On the contrary, Nadwah's approach to the teaching of Arabic has been progressive.[24]

The appointment of Hilālī to the Nadwah staff enhanced the standard of Arabic and attracted a considerable number of students whose contributions to the language left a lasting impact both locally and internationally. Special mention may be made of Mawlana Mas'ud 'Ālam,[25] a colleague of Shaykh Nadwi, who worked untiringly with the latter in the production of Arabic journals for Nadwah. The exchange of periodicals between Nadwah and prestigious institutions in the Arab world generated much interest in Arabic journalism. Its own journal *Al-Diyā'*[26] served as a forum for this purpose an opened up new opportunities for Shaykh Nadwi and his colleagues. As Shaykh Nadwi noted:

> During this period our small room and confined environment served as an Arab outpost in the Indian world.[27]

Many of the activities at Nadwah reflected the influence of Arabic journalism in the 1930s. The *Anjuman al-Islāh*, Nadwah's literary society, dealt with current affairs in the Middle East. A debate, sometime in the 1930, on "Who is the greatest personality of the Muslim world" generated much enthusiasm. Significantly, it was Amir Shakib Arsalān (d.1946), an Islamist whose books and articles were avidly read by Shaykh Nadwi and his colleagues, who was chosen for this honour.[28]

The exposure to the Arab world in terms of its literary trends and contemporary thought had a definite impact on Shaykh Nadwi's writings. His acquaintance with Arab littérateurs and scholars broadened his understanding of the cross-currents in the Arab world and gave him first-hand experience to make a critical appraisal of their contributions to Islam. Shaykh Nadwi noted:

During my first visit to Egypt in 1951 I was not overawed by any

---

[24] For an elaborate discussion of Arabic, see Nadwi, *Western Civilisation, Islam and Muslims*, 63-66.
[25] See Shaykh Nadwi's personal reminiscences of Mas'ud 'Alam in *Purāne Charāgh*, vol. 1, 317-57.
[26] The popularity of *Al-Diyā'* journal can be gauged from the critical acclaim by the Lebanese scholar, Amir Nasiruddin. *Ibid.*, 321-22.
[27] Nadwi, *Kārwān*, vol. 1, 148.
[28] *Ibid.*, 149.

personality nor was there an unveiling of new realities. It is, however, important for a *dā'ī* to be acquainted with the critical trends in literature in order to make any real contribution.[29]

Also during his teaching career, Shaykh Nadwi taught for a short period *Hujjat-Allah al-Bālighah,* a celebrated work of Shah Waliyullah. The influence of the *Hujjat* on the writings of Shaykh Nadwi is succinctly expressed by Muhammad Ghazāli:

> We did not find a philosophical explanation of the entire legal system of Islam before Shah Wali-Allah. Therefore, according to our knowledge *Hujjat-Allah al-Bālighah* is the first work dealing with this subject so extensively and comprehensively...[30]

Arabic Teaching: A New Approach

The innovative approach to teaching Arabic was of central concern to Shaykh Nadwi and his colleagues. The direct method of teaching Arabic, a pioneering initiative, produced positive results. Students showed great aptitude for this approach - their fluency and expressive style reinforced its success. During his teaching career, Shaykh Nadwi taught a course on Logic, the history of Arabic literature to senior students and portions of *Sahīh Bukhārī* for several years. In 1934 he married his cousin, Sayyidah Tayyibah al-Nisā'.[31] This was a preparatory period also in view of his diverse activities.

Quranic Studies

Shaykh Nadwi's extensive study of the Quran was reflected in his writings. He was thoroughly grounded in the rich field of Islamic scholarship. In fact, his command over the Arabic language provided him the consummate skills to express the elegance and subtle meanings of the Quran. The following extracts reveal the formative period of his role as a Quranic

---

[29] *Ibid.,* 148-9.
[30] Muhammad Ghazali, *The Socio-Political Thought of Shah Wali Allah* (Islamabad, 2001), 133-34.
[31] She was the granddaughter of the eminent scholar, Sayyid `Abdur Razzaq Kalami, author of the *Samsām al-Islam* (History of the Conquest of Syria) in versified Urdu. This literature, which dealt with the early heroes of Islam, served to sustain the Islamic identity in India. *Kārwān,* 1, 150.

scholar:

> After completing my education, I turned my attention again to a study of the Quran. I made a point of studying other reference works in addition to the texts prescribed in the *madāris*. In pursuance of this objective, I went to Lahore and studied the whole of the Quran at the feet of Mawlana Ahmad 'Ali. His total devotion to the Quran impressed me the most. Whatever he said and did was prompted by the Quran. This cast a spell on my heart. His piety, detachment from the world and meticulous observance of the *sunnah* impressed me much. I then spent some time at Dār al-'Ulūm Deoband. During my stay there, I sought an appointment with Mawlana Husayn Ahmad Madani so as to benefit from his explanation of some difficult Quranic passages. These points were left unresolved in the standard *tafsīr* works. Mawlana Madani was one of the distinguished *'ulama* of the day. Apart from his expertise in *hadīth* studies and other disciplines, he had carried out an intensive study of the Quran. His lifestyle reflected the fruits of his special study. I was fortunate that he granted me time on Fridays to discuss with him such Quranic verses as I found hard to fathom. The Mawlana was a frequent traveler and this was a period of hectic political activity. Yet I managed to draw, to some extent, upon his scholarship.[32]

Shaykh Nadwi's initial exposure, in varying degrees, to the multiple approaches to *tafsīr* studies enabled him to make an independent study of this rich genre. The dynamism of the Quran, he asserted, was perennial and it served as "a true mirror of human nature and a living Book."[33]

In 1934, Shaykh Nadwi was appointed as lecturer at Nadwah. He was entrusted with two subjects: Arabic literature and *tafsīr*. The classical books of *tafāsir* (such as *Jalālayn, Baydāwi and Kashshāf*) were already included in the curriculum. Furthermore, there was a particular emphasis that students should be given a general exposure to the Quran. Thus, the curriculum was arranged according to the standards and abilities of the students in such a manner that no part of it was left out. This system was a speciality of Nadwah compared to other institutions. Shaykh Nadwi's endorsement of this approach is illustrative:

> During this period, I felt that it was necessary to introduce the glorious Quran to students, to acquaint them with the real purpose and central theme and to prepare and enable them to profit from this great Book. It was also

---

[32] Nadwi, *Guidance from the Holy Qur'an* (Leicester, 2005), 2-3.
[33] Nadwi, *Studying the Glorious Qur'an: Principles and Methodology* (Leicester, 2003), 14.

Chapter III
In Pursuit of Academic Excellence

important to warn them about the shortcomings and weaknesses which sometimes prevent one from benefiting fully from the useful effects and blessings which the Quran itself has pointed out. These elements comprise the principles for appreciating and understanding the Glorious Quran.[34]

Da'wah: Content and Context

Dr 'Abdul 'Ali had *da'wah* close to his heart. The decline of Muslim rule culminating in the Partition of India in 1947 was a traumatic period for Muslims. In view of the rising communal tension, the need to chalk out an Islamic identity for the Muslim minority against the emerging Hindu dominance was a harsh reality. Already the political scenario carried the seeds of religious divide between Muslims and Hindus. Moreover, the entrenched social hierarchy remained intact among Hindus. An instance in point was the Dalit community (also known as Untouchables) who continued to suffer under the yoke of the Brahmanical domination. This polarisation brought in its wake a mass protest under the leadership of Dr Bhim Rao Ambedkar, a leading jurist who had announced his community's search for an alternative religion. The Dalits had renounced Hinduism *en masse* and were prepared to embrace a faith that would emancipate them from the blight of religious prejudice. This epoch-making announcement was made in 1935.
Dr 'Abdul 'Ali and Arab Sahib saw this ambivalence as an opportunity to propagate Islam to them. Shaykh Nadwi, barely twenty one years old, was tasked with this responsibility. This was a historic trip to Mumbai and inducted him into *da'wah* and *tabligh* on a practical level. Dr Ambedkar was familiar with the Islamic doctrines as was evident from his study of Pickthall's translation of the Quran. Shaykh Nadwi spoke candidly to him about Islam as the only alternative for his community. In a later development, Dr. Ambedkar's announcement that the Dalits were to embrace Buddhism was an erroneous decision. In fact, it brought no minimal changes to this marginalised community in the years that followed. This disillusionment was articulated by V.T. Rajshekar in his well-documented work *Ambedkar and His Conversion*.[35]
Ambedkar's and his followers' conversion to Buddhism was dictated by the political changes after Partition in 1947. The empowerment of the Dalit community (described by the pejorative "Untouchables") and liberation

---

[34] *Ibid.,* vii.
[35] Nadwi, *Kārwān*, vol.1, 156-60.

from the upper-caste Hindu oppression as Ambedkar had envisioned was only possible in Islam, which would allow the Dalits to merge into the global Muslim community. However, the tide of events in India after 1947 did not provide a happy augury for Ambedkar's decision. In addition, their conversion to Buddhism did not remove the shackles of social oppression perpetuated by the Brahmanical class.[36]

Academic Profile

The maturity of Shaykh Nadwi's teaching experience was a precursor to his intellectual growth. Within a short period his rapid rise as an international scholar, historian and *dā'i* was established. By way of example, Shaykh Nadwi's biographical works take into account the intellectual elements that make up a well-researched study. It is, therefore, appropriate to assess the trends of historical objectivity employed by Shaykh Nadwi. Apart from *Kārwān*, the biographical account *Mir Kārwān* written by Dr 'Abdullāh 'Abbās Nadwi contains valuable information about Shaykh Nadwi's life and thought. His comments on the *Kārwān* are revealing:

> I have been associated with Shaykh Nadwi for fifty three years and have been able to observe him closely under various circumstances: His travels, public and private, times of adversity and prosperity. I have also had the honour of being his student for three years. Therefore, it has not been difficult for me to record from memory and transcribe metaphorically from my heart to the "preserved" pages (about him).
> Biographical accounts concerning *'ulama* and *mashā'ikh* are generally of two types. One genre tends to glorify the shaykh and the exaggerated veneration about his personality gives the impression that his status may be equated to a prophet. This embellished mindset identifies qualities and attributes that implicitly suggests his *'ismāt* (infallibility). The other genre adopted by modern researchers is a scientific approach. The dissertation or field of study is an objective account of the personality. Also, the source material serves as a frame of reference and is distinguished for its contemporary trends as well. Moreover, the bibliography is reflective of

---

[36] For a detailed discussion about the predicament of the Dalit conversion to Buddhism, see Yoginder Sikand, *Muslims in India since 1947: Islamic Perspectives on Inter-Faith Relations* (London, 2004), Chapter 7; "Islamic perspectives on liberation and dialogue: Muslim writings" in *Dalit Voice*, 93-108.

Chapter III
In Pursuit of Academic Excellence

modern critical studies.

It is a matter of coincidence that I have been acquainted with both trends. Belonging to a family with an uninterrupted chain of *mashā'ikh* for over three hundred years, these biographies mirror embellished accounts.

With regard to modern universities, I have been associated with a leading institution in Europe and have over the years been supervising postgraduate studies. Therefore, the modern methods are a familiar terrain for me.[37]

Dr Nadwi is the leading representative of Nadwah's educational philosophy: A synthesis of traditional learning and value-oriented modern knowledge.[38] Shaykh Nadwi translated this philosophy into his prolific writings for steering the destiny of Nadwah to greater educational horizons. According to Habibul Haq Nadvi, the reformers of Nadwah whom he regards as "religio-political positivists"[39] (or `alim-activists) "stimulated contemporary Islamic resurgence" and emerged "triumphant in the reconstruction of Islamic education" through restructuring the curricula from time to time.[40] The concept of a dynamic curriculum is correctly assessed by Nadwi in this well-documented book.[41] This vision is succinctly endorsed by 'Allāmah Yūsuf Qardāwī, a leading scholar based in Qatar and a Trustee of the Oxford Centre for Islamic Studies in an obituary on Shaykh Nadwi:

He (Shaykh Nadwi) headed a school of thought and learning which believes in steadfastness in its aims, progress in its methods, makes use of everything old which is beneficial, welcomes everything new which is sound, adopts from tradition which is sincere and rejects what is dubious.[42]

Shaykh Nadwi's comments on the educational reforms pioneered by Nadwah must be understood in its historical context. He says:

> Having completed my academic studies it was now time for serious decision making. I was initially inclined to devote my energies to research at the prestigious Dār al-Musannifin in

---

[37] 'Abdullāh 'Abbās Nadwi, *Mir Kārwān* (New Delhi, 1999), 16-17.
[38] Ibid., 18.
[39] Syed Habibul Haq Nadvi, *Islamic Resurgent Movements in the Indo-Pak Subcontinent* (Durban, 1987), 65.
[40] Ibid., 72.
[41] Ibid., 74-76.
[42] *OCIS News*, Special Issue, January 2000, 4.

35

Azamgarh. However, the illustrious scholar, Sayyid Sulayman Nadwi strongly urged me to take up a teaching post at Nadwah. His advice was truly reflective of his intuitive insight. I soon realised that if I had opted for research only, it would stifle my creative abilities and confine me to a cloistered environment with no real promise for the future. Moreover, the progressive outlook of Nadwah was in harmony with my intellectual attitude and temperament.

When I joined Nadwah I could not have found a better place for research, studies, *da'wah* and writing. I was entrusted with the responsibility of teaching *tafsīr*. This was a real challenge as I had to study, virtually word for word, classical and modern commentaries on the Quran. Likewise, the teaching of Arabic literature sharpened my writing skills and also enhanced my appreciation of this dynamic language. During this period, Nadwah received most of the widely-acclaimed Arabic journals and magazines, a privilege rarely enjoyed by other Islamic institutions. This was an ideal opportunity to acquaint myself with the writings of celebrated scholars and gain first-hand experience regarding the contemporary events in the Arab world. Fortunately, this exposure had a direct bearing on my first trip to Egypt, because it gave me the opportunity to interact confidently with the literary and intellectual elites of the country.

The general environment of learning, scholarship and piety together with the presence of renowned teachers and scholars was a motivation to work for the cause of Islam.[43]

Literary Debut: An Appraisal Shaykh Nadwi as Historian

Shaykh Nadwi made his debut as a historian through his biographical writings.[44] He invariably treats the topics under study in their historical perspectives. Likewise, his writings are enriched with interesting anecdotes and narratives from world and Islamic history. For example, these are reflected in his biography of Sayyid Ahmad Shahid, written initially as a monograph, and later expanded by him in a two-volume work[45] for the

---

[43] Nadwi, *Kārwān*, vol. 1, 140-47.
[44] Shaykh Nadwi's insightful comments on the rationale and techniques of historiography are summed up in his widely-acclaimed *Saviours of Islamic Spirit*, vol. 1.
[45] See Shaykh Nadwi's *Introduction* to Mohiuddin Ahmed, *Saiyid Ahmad Shahid* (1975).

Chapter III
In Pursuit of Academic Excellence

Saviours of Islamic Spirit series.

Written originally in Arabic, then Urdu, *Sayyid Ahmad Shahid* met with critical acclaim both in India and abroad. It was published at a time (1939) when the intellectual revolution was taking place among the Muslims in India. In a specific sense, it embodied the struggle for independence, and the quest for a normative Islamic identity. This book epitomises through its objective approach and painstaking research the life and times of the Sayyid. Shaykh Nadwi's historical analysis of the Sayyid's leadership qualities combined with his spiritual attainment makes absorbing reading. The anecdotal narrations focus on the fiery zeal and spirit of sacrifice by both Sayyid and his followers. These are reminiscent of the early heroes of Islam.[46] The work was warmly received by both *'ulama* and *mashā'ikh*. Mawlana Ashrāf 'Ali Thānawi, an erudite scholar, wrote in glowing terms about the Sayyid's powerful movement and remarked that he and his followers were "our precursors worthy to be emulated."[47]

Shaykh Nadwi as a litterateur

Shaykh Nadwi's literary output was marked by an original style and the absence of classical embellishments. In the early 1930s evidence of his versatility began to emerge - his close association with the poet of the East, 'Allāmah Iqbal, is one such example. In Shaykh Nadwi's words:

Iqbal was a poet whom Allah had inspired to lend articulation to certain truths and doctrines, in relation to current times, that had not been set forth by any other contemporary poet or thinker. He was a staunch believer in the permanence of the call of Prophet Muhammad (SAAS), in the inherent strength and capacity for leadership of the Muslim community and in the insolvency of modern ideologies and political, social and economic systems. This worldview had imparted lucidity and maturity to his thought and led to the growth and development of his individuality. In this respect, he was even better than the *'ulama* who are ignorant of Western thought and culture and possess little awareness of its real aim and purpose.

I must admit that I find Iqbal a poet of faith, love and deep-heartedness. Whenever I read his works, I am stirred to the depths of my being. His poetry opens a new vista to my imagination and fills me up with an intense ardour and enthusiasm for Islam. This, I think, is the real worth and significance of

---

[46] Nadwi, *Kārwān*, vol. 1, 186-89. See "Mawlana Abul Hasan Ali as an Historian" in *The Fragrance of East,* Special Issue (Lucknow, 2000).
[47] Nadwi, *Kārwān*, vol. 1, 190.

Iqbal's poetry.[48]

Literary Contributions in Arabic

Shaykh Nadwi was a prolific writer in Arabic. His preparation of textbooks in the absence of suitable resource material for the *madāris* students in the subcontinent was a commendable contribution. Shukri has noted that Shaykh Nadwi may be considered as one of foremost pioneers in the field of Islamic literary theory who elaborated his views in *Mukhtārāt min Adab al-'Arab*.[49]

The following three publications are briefly analysed to give an estimation of Shaykh Nadwi's literary contributions:

Mukhtārāt Min Adab al-'Arab

This two-volume book is considered as one of the best Arabic textbooks not only in the *madāris* of India, but also at college and university levels of education in the Muslim world. The book contains the best specimens and treasures of Arabic prose carefully selected from the vast corpus of Arabic literature ranging from the first Islamic century to the present times. This impression has been eloquently expressed by the renowned Arab scholar, Shaykh 'Ali Al-Tantāwī in his *Foreword* to the first volume of the book:

It is clear from the above that this book is not only a rich source of a vast variety of excellent models of expressions in chaste, spontaneous and standard Arabic language, but also it serves as a testimony to the fine literary taste of the author.[50]

It must be remembered that *Mukhtārāt* was published in 1942 against the background of Arab nationalism. It served as an alternative reading to the un-Islamic ideology and works produced by secularists and liberals in the Arab world. There were, however, mixed reactions to the inclusion of *Mukhtārāt* in the *madāris* of the subcontinent. The merits of this work were marginalised largely on account of its non-conformist approach. The rhetoric of Nadwah's 'modernist' leanings was also a contributing factor to its disapproval. It did, however, take several decades to the *madāris* to acknowledge its literary

---

[48] Nadwi, *Glory of Iqbal*, 19.
[49] M.A.M. Shukri, "Towards an Islamic Theory in Literature" in *Islamic Studies* (Islamabad, 1992), 411-12.
[50] Nadwi, *Mukhtārāt*, vol. 1, 5. Cf. *Kārwān*, vol. 1, 205-12.

importance and a suitable text for Arabic.

Al-Qirā'at al-Rāshidah

The next important Arabic textbook prepared by Shaykh Nadwi is titled *Al-Qirā'at al-Rāshidah*. This three-volume series drew upon the resource material from the standard Arabic texts including the *Maqāmāt* of Al-Hariri. The previous efforts to prepare textbooks did not yield the desired results. But, as described by the author himself, it was soon found that these were not found congenial to the taste and temperament for the students of this country. It was obvious that young Indian students shared no interest in these works. For instance, the popular book *Al-Qirā'at al-Rāshidah* of Egypt, introduced in some Arabic institutions of India, contained information on matters that were of little interest to Indian students.

Iqbal Hussain is of the view that *Al-Qirā'at* written by Shaykh Nadwi emphasises the integrated personality ideal, which is based on sound psychological principles. Traits like virtue, justice and beauty are intrinsic to the children's quest for a perfect world. An ideal Islamic society is interwoven with heroes of Islamic history. Therefore, in Shaykh Nadwi's estimation, children possess precocious minds to assimilate positive values. This work is intended to ensure personality development among young Muslims.

Professor Abdul Ali's insightful comments about the *Qira'at* reinforce the importance of Shaykh Nadwi's Arabic works. He says:

The author (Shaykh Nadwi) rightly argues why the Indian students at the primary and secondary levels of education should not be burdened with themes quite alien and dull to them. He, therefore, felt this necessity to prepare easy lessons on *sirah* literature, history of Islam and eminent Islamic personalities. The chief merit of this book is that it contains matters on a vast variety of subjects in the Arabic language and literature, which keeps the interest of the students intact till the end of the book. Another main merit of the book is that it is written in simple, literary and standard Arabic language in a gradually developing style, which is quite congenial to the taste and level of understanding of the young Arabic students in India.[51]

---

[51] See Nadwi's introduction to his *Mukhtārāt* for an incisive analysis on the growth of Arabic literature with a secular orientation. Cf. *The Muslim World League Journal*, May 2000, 43.

Qasas al-Nabiyyīn

Belonging to children literature, *Qasas al-Nabiyyīn* has enjoyed enormous popularity throughout the Muslim world. As mentioned elsewhere in the chapter, Nadwah was constructively engaged in producing standard Islamic textbooks reflecting the Islamic ethos. Obviously, the academic standards were not to be compromised as already a series of Arabic textbooks, authored by Shaykh Nadwi, were prescribed at Nadwah. These were also included in the syllabi of other *madāris*. In the absence of effective Arabic learning material for students in the elementary stages, Kamal Kilani's "Stories for Children" (*Hikāyat lil-Atfāl*) was prescribed. Its secular orientation was glaring: The stories cluttered with copious illustrations tended to focus on issues that were either language-related or dealt with supernatural events. According to the noted littérateur, Abdul Majid Daryabadi there was no "reference to Allah and His Messenger from the start to the end" and he stated in unambiguous terms that the Egyptian textbooks were incompatible with the needs of Nadwah students.[52]

During 1943-44] Shaykh Nadwi began with the *Qasas* series. The lives of the major Prophets were covered and their contributions to human civilisation and culture were briefly dealt with.[53]

Salient Features of the *Qasas al-Nabiyyīn*

- Economical use of vocabulary that is needed for repetition and reinforcement.
- Quranic language and style is employed.
- The Islamic belief system (*tawhīd*, Prophethood, etc.) make up the core content of the book. In contrast, *kufr* and *shirk* are highlighted.[54]

The *Qasas* was duly completed in 1977 with the life of the Prophet (SAAS). The noted scholar of Egypt, Sayyid Qutb made the following comments about the *Qasas*:

I have read many books for children including those about the stories of

---

[52] Nadwi, *Kārwān*, vol. 1, 216.
[53] Mawlana Hifzur Rahmān Seoharwi has also written extensively about the Prophets. *Qasas al-Qur'an* is a two-volume book, which has been well researched by the author.
[54] Nadwi, *Kārwān*, vol. 1, 216-17.

the Prophets. Indeed, I have been closely associated with a series of books drawn from the Holy Quran. Nonetheless, I testify without reservation, that Abul Hasan's present book surpasses all such works. What accounts for its excellence is the inclusion, with elucidation of subtle teachings of the Quran, of explanations that highlight and reinforce the Quranic message through his apt comments that are interwoven into the telling of the story.[55]

The *Qasas* has been translated into major languages of the world and continues to be a must-read in leading *madāris* and institutions of higher Islamic learning. Of interest is the Russian translation, which was completed a few months before Shaykh Nadwi's demise in 1999.

Conclusion

Shaykh Nadwi's literary contributions paved the way for an elaboration of Islamic authenticity. Implicit in his writings is the critique of Arab writers with secular leanings who jealously influenced a generation of Arab readers with themes deemed un-Islamic. According to Shaykh Nadwi, the *turāth* (heritage) is embedded in the *salaf* paradigm and *adab*, too, mirrors the ideals of Islamic thought.

---

[55] Nadwi, *Stories of the Prophets*, 7-8.

Chapter IV

Contemporary Islamic Movements

Shaykh Nadwi's academic profile began to emerge more clearly during the 1940s. His analytical comments about the general apathy of students towards enhancing their study schedule[1] were a compelling reason for him pursuing a literary style that had a lasting impact on his scholarly career. During this period, India was on the threshold of its independence and several Islamic and political movements were actively engaged in a discourse that carried identifiable markers of change. According to Shaykh Nadwi, it was a crucial era that had a decisive influence on all facets of Muslim life.[2]

Academic Research: New Opportunities

The multilayered approach of Shaykh Nadwi's academic career is evident in his study of works that go beyond traditional sources. Among several works, the following books had a significant influence on his prolific writings, especially his important publications that deal with contemporary Islamic issues and are written in a lucid and elegant style.[3]

- Draper's monumental work *Conflict between East and West,*
- Lecky's *History of European Morals,* and
- Gibbon's *Decline and Fall of the Roman Empire.*

The above books are a critique of Western civilisation and were extensively used by Shaykh Nadwi for his *Rise and Fall of Muslims.*

Belonging to this genre is Muhammad Asad's (d.1992) *Islam at the Crossroads.* It is not only a cogent criticism of Western civilisation, but also provides a strong defence of the *sunnah* as the primary source of Islamic civilisation.[4]

---

[1] Nadwi, *Kārwān,* vol. 1, 227-28.
[2] *Ibid.,* 229.
[3] A critique of his writings is to be found by several Egyptian literary Figures, e.g. Sayyid Qutb Shahid.
[4] For a detailed discussion on Asad's contribution to contemporary Islamic thought, see the incisive articles in *Islamic Studies* (Islamabad, 2005) and Abroo Aman Andrabi, *Muhammad Asad and His Contribution to Islamic Learning* (New Delhi, 2007).

Abul Kalam Azad (d.1958), a brilliant intellectual, published his *Al-Balāgh* magazine to awaken Muslims on the intellectual and political levels. His revolutionary fervour[5] had a definite influence on Shaykh Nadwi's writings. The *Tarjumān* journal of Mawlana Mawdudi, founder of Jamā'at-i Islami, broke new grounds in terms of its trenchant criticism of Western civilisation and expounding the supremacy of Islam. Books like *Purdah* and *Tanqihāt* clearly defined his exposition of Islam as a complete way of life (*dīn*). These early writings did not at the time reflect the political influence on Mawdudi's intellectual career. This period also sheds light about Shaykh Nadwi's symbiotic relationship with him. Apart from the *Kārwān*, two important works of Shaykh Nadwi, *Purāne Charāgh* (vol. 2) and *Appreciation and Interpretation of Religion in the Modern Age* provide a more clearer picture of his relationship with the Jamā'at-i Islami.

Mawlana Mawdudi and Shaykh Nadwi: Conflictual Relationship

Mawdudi (1903-79) is widely considered as one of the most influential Islamic thinkers of the twentieth century. His ideas have greatly influenced Islamic movements in the Muslim world. His voluminous translation and interpretation of the Quran is unquestionably a masterpiece of Urdu literature. The author of numerous works and also an accomplished translator, he has articulated his particular views on four major aspects of life: Religion, politics, economy and society. Seen together, his writings constitute a clear and coherent, if at times, a controversial statement of Islam.[6]

This brief comment written by a critic of Mawlana Mawdudi illustrates the challenges of Islamic revival. Furthermore, it offers a glimpse about Shaykh Nadwi's association with Mawdudi. After the formation of Jamā'at-i Islami in 1941, Shaykh Nadwi through a series of meetings with him in Lucknow was impressed by his vision of Islam. The quest for a holy community[7] embodied in the formal implementation of

---

[5] Nadwi, *Purāne Charāgh*, vol. 2. See I.H. Douglas, *Abul Kalam Azad, An Intellectual and Religious Biography* (Chapter 2) and S.S. Hameed, *Islamic Seal on Indian Independence* (Chapter 3) for a critical evaluation of the magazine *Al-Hilāl*.

[6] See Seyyed Vali Reza Nasr, *The Vanguard of the Islamic Revolution: The Jamā'at-i Islami of Pakistan* (Berkeley, 1995). His hostile analysis of Mawdudi's Islamic vision is evident in this work.

[7] *Ibid.*, 23.

the Jamā'at's policies did not go unchallenged.[8] Shaykh Nadwi's vote in support of Mawdudi also revealed the crisis of confidence during the preparatory years of the Jamā'at.[9]

The production of a forceful literature by Mawdudi attracted to its ranks scholars of eminent status. Mas'ud 'Ālam Nadwi, a distinguished scholar in Arabic, was encouraged by Shaykh Nadwi to translate the Jamā'at's literature, which won critical acclaim in the Arab world.[10] Shaykh Nadwi's pro-active association with the Jamā'at in its initial stage turned to scepticism and his disillusionment with the movement became more pronounced. There are several reasons for this shift, and do in no way suggest an irrevocable breakdown or mutual hostility between them. Bearing in mind Shaykh Nadwi's intellectual temperament, his disassociation with Mawdudi and the Jamā'at was understandable. According to Shaykh Nadwi, the personality of Mawdudi had begun to reach levels of exaggeration and members of the Jamā'at as well as the educated class considered him to be the only scholar whose interpretation of Islam was definitive. They argued that the whole gamut of Islamic thought could only be understood through his writings. The *tajdīdī* endeavours of *'ulama* and *mashā'ikh* were considered inconsequential.[11] Another alarming sign of his 'liberal outlook' was his trenchant and often hostile critique of *'ulama* and Islamic institutions.[12]

According to Shaykh Nadwi, the absence of spirituality was glaring in Mawdudi's writings and this was in marked contrast to the former's *tasawwuf*-centred works. Keeping in mind Mawdudi's brilliant exposition of Islam in his earlier writings, his rational approach was in many instances regarded as heretical by the *'ulama* fraternity. However, he did not deviate from mainstream Islam as is wrongly assumed by his detractors. Rather, he infused a new spirit of enquiry, a reappraisal and renewed commitment to Islam as a civilisational force.[13]

This was a period of intellectual crisis for Shaykh Nadwi and the cracks of a widening gulf between him and Mawdudi were discernible. Also, during this period, the emergence of the Tablighi Jamā'at began to make its impact on the local *'ulama* and the masses. Shaykh Nadwi was much influenced by its founder, Mawlana Muhammad Ilyās whose halo of spirituality esemplified

---

[8] *Ibid.*, 24-29 for the disagreement by Mawlana Nu'māni about Mawdudi's election as Amir of the Jamā'at.
[9] Nadwi, *Kārwān*, vol. 1, 242.
[10] Nadwa, *Purāne Charāgh*, vol. 2, 309-11.
[11] Nadwi, *Kārwān*, vol. 1, 244.
[12] See Mawdudi, *A Short History of the Revivalist Movement in Islam* (1972).
[13] See Nadwi's multivolume *Saviours of Islamic Spirit* for a discussion of his views.

"the *sirah* of the Prophet (SAAS) and the true content and spirit of *da'wah*."[14] This association was significant for two reasons:

- It provided the impetus for Shaykh Nadwi to promote the Tablighi Jamā'at in the Arab world.
- Shaykh Nadwi resigned from the Jamā'at-i Islami although no public announcement was made.[15]

The final break with the Jamā'at came with Shaykh Nadwi's publication of *Asr-i Hādir men Dīn kī Tafhīm wa Tashrīh* (*Appreciation and Interpretation of Religion in the Modern Age*) (1978), which was a refutation of Mawdudi's popular and famous book *Qur'ān kī Bunyādi Istilāhāt* (*The Four Basic Qur'anic Terms*). According to Shaykh Nadwi, this work was a new type of *tafsīr* (exegesis) of the Quran and Islam that had a political colouring and revolved around the "Kingdom of Sovereignty" (*hākimiyyah*)[16] in Islam. There was no doubt that Mawdudi advocated an interpretive reading of Islam, "one which aims to mobilise piety and faith for the purpose of political action."[17]

For a repudiation of Mawdudi's book, Abdur Rahmān Doi has referred to this important work of Shaykh Nadwi.[18] His analysis of Mawdudi's controversial work may be summed up as follows:

> Mawlana Mawdudi has not supported his views with adequate authoritative sources. The dilution of respect for *turāth* (Islamic heritage) is much in evidence. Also, a new *taqlīd* had developed which attributed an iconic status to him. Thus, any critique of his views was met with much scepticism and opposition by the followers of Jamā'at-i Islami.[19]

Shortly after the publication of the book, Shaykh Nadwi sent a copy of it along with a personal letter to Mawdudi. The latter replied stating *inter alia*: "I have never considered myself above criticism nor do I take it ill." He invited

---

[14] Nadwi, *Kārwān*, vol. 1, 245.
[15] *Ibid*.
[16] Mawdudi, *The Four Basic Qur'anic Terms* (New Delhi, 1982), 21.
[17] Ali Rahnema, *Pioneers of Islamic Revival* (London, 1994), 104.
[18] Nadwi, *Appreciation and Interpretation of Religion in the Modern Age* (New Delhi, 1982).
[19] Abdur Rahmān I. Doi, *'Ulum al-Qur'an, Sciences of the Qur'an: A Study in Methodology and Approach* (Pretoria, 1997), 332-38.

Chapter IV
Contemporary Islamic Movements

Shaykh Nadwi to analyse and assess his other works in the same detailed manner and to communicate to him his "reaction and doubts."[20] It is significant to observe that Shaykh Nadwi's association with the Jamā'at did not prompt any harsh literature towards Mawdudi. Rather, Shaykh Nadwi maintained a cordial relationship with him and met him on several occasions at conferences hosted by organisations of which both were members.[21] Mawdudi's passing away in 1979 was mourned by Shaykh Nadwi, who paid glowing tributes to his scholarly contributions.

Shaykh Nadwi's critique of *The Four Basic Qur'anic Terms* elicited a robust exchange of views. Shaykh Qardāwī, for example, did not fully agree with Shaykh Nadwi's arguments. The ethics of disagreement were clearly noticeable. By the same token, a number of *'ulama* censured the contents of the book and launched a tirade against Mawdudi's 'heretical' writings. The anti-Mawdudi rhetoric succeeded in creating a hostile reception among the masses. Thus, the term *Mawdūdiyat* conjured up images of a schismatic movement undermining the Islamic *turāth*. It must not be forgotten that identity politics also played an important role in denigrating the personality of Mawdudi. It was, therefore, not surprising that Mawdudi's perceived lack of formal training as an *'ālim* was used by his detractors to brand him a non-conformist. In the light of documents available, his academic pedigree as a traditional *'ālim* has been established. Furthermore, he had to his credit several books of classical Islamic history and philosophy translated into Urdu. These works were commissioned by the prestigious translation unit of Osmania University (Hyderabad) in the 1930s. Like other prominent scholars, Mawdudi also contributed appreciably to the Urdu translation project. His translation of Mulla Sadruddin's philosophical work, *Asfār*, from Arabic into Urdu is a case in point regarding his mastery over Arabic.

Notwithstanding these differences, Shaykh Nadwi's insightful comments about the role of the Jamā'at in the refutation of Western values are instructive:

> Howsoever we may differ in some of the interpretations of religious issues or concepts advanced by Mawlana Abul A'la Mawdudi and other front-rank leaders of the Jamā'at-i Islami, it is impossible to deny the very valuable role they have played in the

---

[20] Nadwi, *Purāne Charāgh*, vol. 2, 309.
[21] Both scholars were founding members of the Shurā: Jami'ah Madinah (University of Madinah).

refutation of the Western cultural and ideological values and ideals. The literature produced by the Jamā'at has rendered indisputable service in counteracting the overwhelming influence of the Western civilisation over the modern educated classes and restoring their faith in the soundness, efficacy and practicability of the Islamic philosophy of life. Mawlana Mawdudi has not followed the apologetic and defensive style of Sir Sayyid Ahmad Khan and his colleagues like Maulwi Chiragh Ali and Syed Ameer Ali in India or Mufti Muhammad Abduh and his disciples in Egypt. Instead, he has boldly attacked the very foundations of the Western cultural and intellectual edifice in the manner of Muhammad Asad and the other writers of the same group, and presented the teachings of Islam with greater confidence and in a positive and convincing style.[22]

New Horizons

New opportunities presented themselves to Shaykh Nadwi and thus, broadened his intellectual horizon. In this regard he was invited by the prestigious university in Delhi, Jamia Millia Islamia in 1942 to deliver a series of lectures. *Religion and Civilisation* originally published in Urdu by the Jamia as *Madhhab wa Tamaddun* is a work of great scholarship. It received positive reviews from the illustrious scholars like Dr Zakir Hussain (former President of India) and the noted historian, Professor Muhammad Mujib. This slim volume shows how revelatory knowledge (*wahy*) provides the perennial sources of peace and success to mankind in contrast to man-made systems that rely on the fallibility of reason and mystical intuition.[23] This work was among Shaykh Nadwi's earlier writings which attracted the interest of academic institutions in the subcontinent.

In the political domain rising tension between Muslims and Hindus was a precursor to the communal riots - a phenomenon orchestrated by the British divide and rule policy. In the years to come (post-1947) it was a spectre that haunted the corporate identity of India after it had cast off its yoke from British rule.[24] According to Azad, the Quit India resolution meant that "the freedom of India must be the symbol and a prelude to the freedom

---

[22] Nadwi, *Western Civilisation, Islam and Muslims* (1974), 90-91.
[23] See the translator's note in *Religion and Civilisation* (1975) for a brief survey on the sources of Western civilisation.
[24] See Ishtiaq Husain Qureshi, *Ulema in Politics* (Karachi, 1974) for a Pakistani perspective about these series of events.

Chapter IV
Contemporary Islamic Movements

of all the Asiatic nations under foreign dominations."[25] Shaykh Nadwi's personal account of these critical events are noteworthy in Indian history. He criticised the Muslims' apathy regarding the political developments in the country.[26] He contended that British rule had spawned an irreligious outlook and advocated a system of life diametrically opposed to the Islamic values. Furthermore, British imperialism was responsible for the dismemberment of the Ottoman Caliphate and the subjugation of Arab and Muslim countries. In the light of these circumstances, Muslims should take the lead in their confrontation and challenge of British rule.[27]

There was a general misperception that Muslims did not actively participate in the struggle for India's freedom. This assumption is untenable, because a large number of Muslims under the leadership of the 'ulama extended full support and co-operation to the national activities and the Indian National Congress. The Jamā'at al-Ulama (Hind) and Majlis-i Ahrār were two powerful organisations mobilising Muslim participation in mainstream political activities.[28] Shaykh Nadwi made an interesting observation about the similarities in the freedom struggle between the 'ulama of India and Algeria. Both were in the forefront of the freedom struggle and made enormous sacrifices to rid their respective countries of foreign rule.[29] Shaykh 'Abdul Hamid ibn Bādis (d.1940) was an Islamic reformer and national leader who together with the Algerian 'ulama laid the foundation for the national identity of the Algerian people.[30] Like the `ulama of India, Shaykh Bādis too, stressed the need for Islamic education to purify Islam of the popular accretions and improve Muslim individual life as a first step towards reconstructing the Muslim society.

This important period also saw the production of Shaykh Nadwi's da'wah

---

[25] Abul Kalam Azad, *India Wins Freedom* (Calcutta, 1962), 240.
[26] Nadwi, *Kārwān*, vol. 1, 250.
[27] Nadwi, *Kārwān*, vol. 1, 250-51.
[28] Nadwi, *Muslims in India* (1976), 114-23.
[29] *Ibid.*, 251-52.
[30] Nadwi, *Kārwān*, vol. I, 252-53. For a critical examination of *Jāhiliyyah* and Shaykh Nadwi's interpretation of this term, see William Shepard, "Sayyid Qutb's doctrine of *Jāhiliyyah*" in *International Journal of Middle Eastern Studies* (2003)] 521-45. Shepard argues that Qutb's interpretation contains political militancy and has been applied by him in a more radical way. Unlike Qutb, Shaykh Nadwi sees the *Jāhiliyyah* of ancient Greece and Rome resurrected in modern Europe and Muslims have become their allies and camp followers without being turned completely into a *Jāhili* community. *Ibid.*, 523.

literature in Arabic. His monograph, *Daʻwatān-i Mutanāfisatān* is an elaboration of *daʻwah* as a model of excellence. Muslim challenge to British imperialism, characteristics of the *Jāhiliyyah* society, etc. were the need of the hour. Shaykh Nadwi contended that Muslim acquiescence to this new form of *Jāhiliyyah* implied a triumph of this ungodly civilisation. The consequences of such complacency would inevitably lead them to the brink of disaster.[31]

Some of Shaykh Nadwi's important works were written during his travels - local and abroad. Self-discipline, time management and consistency were his personal attributes that he carried out uninterruptedly during his long academic career. According to Shaykh Nadwi, he had written several monographs in a third-class compartment teeming with commuters.[32] Their presence and the normal noise and disturbance associated with travelling in no way affected the tempo of his writings. In a similar vein, Shaykh Nadwi's daily routine followed a consistent pattern: Shortly after breakfast he would immerse himself into research work and writing. For almost forty years, he dictated notes to a team of scholars due to his poor eyesight. This routine lasted until noon after which a short recess was taken for the *Dhuhr* (noon) prayer.

Rise and Fall of Muslims: An Appraisal

Rise and Fall of Muslims is the English translation of Shaykh Nadwi's widely-acclaimed book in Arabic, *Mādhā Khasir al- ʻĀlam bi Inhitāt al-Muslimīn*.

The author has identified the factors for this spiritual and material decline and drawn attention to the loss which Muslims themselves had to bear. This was the consequence of having deviated from their faith. They took to neglecting their obligations. This is followed by the account of the world when Muslims were no longer its leader and how the world reverted to its original *Jāhiliyyah*. The author has pointed to the abysmal depths of degeneration in which mankind was steeped. Regrettably, this period of spiritual and moral fall was combined with the era of new knowledge and skills. Mankind did register many advancements in the material domain. In tracing this degeneration the author has not resorted to crude sensationalism or

---

[31] Nadwi, *Meri 'Ilmi wa Mutālaʻati Zindagi* (Rae Bareli, n.d.), 49.
[32] Emad Eldin Shahin, "Ibn Badis, Abdul Hamid" in *The Oxford Encyclopedia of the Modern Islamic World*, ed. John Esposito (OUP, 1995) vol. 2, 161-62.

Chapter IV
Contemporary Islamic Movements

rabble rousing. Rather, he presents cogent arguments and facts. The data cited by him are remarkably free from exaggeration and bias.[33]

The above comment succinctly describes the scope and ambition of Shaykh Nadwi's major work. In fact, the critical reviews[34] over the last seven decades reinforce the popularity of the work, especially in the Arab world.

It would be worthwhile to make a brief survey of the intellectual development in the Arab world to assess Shaykh Nadwi's literary stature in Arabic. This period saw the emergence of literary critics like Taha Husayn,[35] `Abbās ʿAqqād[36] and Dr Ahmad Amin who developed their distinctive schools of literary criticism. Their respective orientations to the Islamic discourse provided ambivalent responses giving rise to a new generation of scholars and intellectuals who shaped the religious landscape of the Arab world.[37]

As discussed elsewhere in the chapter, Shaykh Nadwi's *daʿwah* literature in Arabic made its significant presence. In a broader context, *Rise and Fall of Muslims* established his fame as a distinguished Arabic scholar. The motivation for writing this book, as Shaykh Nadwi observed, was as early as 1943-44 when he gathered information and published monographs which he incorporated as chapters to the book.[38] Unfortunately, the aftermath of the Second World War (1939-45) had caused a disruption of communication with the Arab world and also impacted negatively on the exchange of books and periodicals. This hiatus hampered Shaykh Nadwi's progress on his work; however, it did not deter him from continuing with his research. Under these adverse circumstances he remained resolute. An interesting observation that Shaykh Nadwi makes is the "unseen help"[39] he received in obtaining source material and this accounted for the success of the work.

Shaykh Nadwi's *daʿwah* travels in 1947 to Hijaz assisted him in the publication of the book. The positive comments received from the Imām of the *Haram*, Shaykh Muhammad ʿAbdul Razzāq Hamza after perusing the manuscript, and the acceptance of his *duʿā* in the precincts of the *Haram*[40]

---

[33] Nadwi, *Islam and the World* (1973), 8. The quotation is from the translation by Asif Kidwai.
[34] Nadwi, *Mir Kārwān*, 381-82.
[35] Albert Hourani, *Arabic Thought in the Liberal Age 1798-1939* (Cambridge, 1983), 325.
[36] *Ibid.*, 334-38.
[37] See Nadwi, *Western Civilisation, Islam and Muslims* for a critique on the Arab intellectuals.
[38] Nadwi, *Kārwān*, vol. 1, 257.
[39] Nadwa, *Kārwān*, vol. 1, 259.
[40] *Ibid.*, 264-65.

have been highlighted by him to describe the circumstances and challenges under which it was written.

Rise and Fall of Muslims was published in 1950 by Dr Ahmad Amin in Cairo, Egypt. The popularity that Shaykh Nadwi enjoyed in the country was overwhelming. He observes:

> When I travelled to Egypt in 1951 the book was widely read in academic and religious circles... The Ikhwān movement during this crucial period had been banned (by the state). After the assassination of its leader, Hasan al-Banna (1949), disillusionment set in the hearts of the Ikhwān members. In many ways, this book bore the kindred spirit of the thoughts and objectives of its founder. It instilled self-confidence and courage to the *du'āt* and people desirous to see the triumph of Islam. It was enthusiastically read by thousands of Ikhwān languishing in jail, was studied in *halaqahs* (literary circles) and was also prescribed in their research programs...[41]

---

[41] *Ibid.*, 266-67.

Chapter IV
Contemporary Islamic Movements

It was only in 1951 when Shaykh Nadwi was able to obtain a copy of his book. His personal reaction suggests that he was overwhelmed by its popularity and its acceptance in the Arab world by both the *'ulama* and academia. However, the Foreword by Dr Ahmad Amin, a literary critic and publisher of the book, did not meet the desired expectation of Shaykh Nadwi. In fact, this concern was shared by many scholars[42] who maintained that the Foreword had undermined the merit of *Rise and Fall of Muslims*. Amin remarked: "If the reader notes any *ghumūd* (vagueness) in the book, it should be remembered that the author is of Indian origin."[43] This unfair statement reflected the stereotypical views about Indian scholars and there is no doubt that Shaykh Nadwi's celebrated work changed this perception.

Despite the serious shortcomings highlighted by Dr Amin, the book was widely read by a cross-section of readers in the Arab world. Shaykh Nadwi was fortunate to have another review written by Sayyid Qutb (d. 1966), a pioneer in the Islamic revivalist movement. He commented:

> This work presupposes a cogent view of all the factors which have their bearings on life. In this perspective the author has analysed world history. The work abounds in balanced and sensible suggestions for the Muslim community. In view of these features this book may be acclaimed as a masterpiece of historiography. It illustrates how a Muslim should study history while rejecting the European outlook which lacks balance, objectivity and scholarly integrity.[44]

Salient Features of *Rise and Fall of Muslims*

Habibul Haq Nadvi has given a synopsis of *Rise and Fall of Muslims* in his *The Dynamics of Islam*.

> The work, comprising eight chapters, is an ingenious comparative analysis of the fate and destiny of man before and after the advent of Prophet Muhammad (SAAS). The ever-growing gods in the pre-

---

[42] Notable scholars from Al-Azhar university came out in strong defence of the book. Dr Shukri Faisal, a student of Dr Ahmad Amin, wrote a detailed review on *Rise and Fall of Muslims* and also rebutted the views of Dr. Amin. See Nadwi, *Mir Kārwān*, 3!7-94 for a detailed discussion on Dr Amin's views.
[43] Nadwi, *Kārwān*, vol. 1, 268.
[44] Nadwi *Islam and the World*, 6-7.

Sayyid Abul Hasan Nadwi: Life and Legacy
Chapter IV

Islamic era, the spiritual anarchy, religious strife, social and economic chaos, racial and caste pride, sexual wantonness, tribal prejudices, war and bloodshed, the gulf between the rich and poor, the plight of the women, the worldwide gloom have been examined in the full light of history, primary sources and documents and have been compared with the sudden change, namely the spiritual development of man and his culture in the post-Muhammad (SAAS) period. The blissfulness of the advent of the Prophet of Islam on the destiny of man has also been elaborated upon by the author who in the strain of his predecessors, regards the introduction of monarchy into the Islamic system as one of causes of the fall of Muslims. His main charges against the Western scientific culture have been that the latter has severed man's relation with his Creator, Allah and has buried religion and spiritual consciousness, the essential elements for the development and growth of human personality and his culture. The author is not negative in his approach towards the advancement of human knowledge either in the West or in the East. He generates hope in the future and invites man to the resurgence of spiritual life through the renaissance of faith in Divine Guidance and in the leadership of the Prophet of Islam. Preaching the spiritual well-being of man, the author does not ignore the material progress of man. He emphatically advocates the industrial and military self-sufficiency of the Muslims in addition to educational reorganisation. But faith, being the real strength of the world of Islam, enjoys priority over the rigid materialism.[45]

Publication of *Rise and Fall of Muslims*

The following information shows the popularity of this work in the Arab world. Since its first year of publication (1950) to its latest edition (2020) it has enjoyed unprecedented success and is considered a "bestseller—with an official 170 editions in Arabic alone. This excludes the unofficial editions that have seen innumerable reprints. Apart from Arabic, the book has been translated into major European and Indian languages[46] and has been used as prescribed reading by some Arab universities. In many instances, a print-run of 100,000 copies has not been uncommon for free distribution to

---

[45] Syed Habibul Haq Nadvi, *The Dynamics of Islam* (Durban, 1982), 61.
[46] *Ta'meer-i Hayāt, Mufakkir i-Islam*, Special Issue, 2000, p. 133.

organisations around the world.

It has been suggested that *Rise and Fall of Muslims* became a modern Islamic classic and introduced a new vocabulary to the term *Jāhiliyyah*. This assumption is misleading as it tends to ignore the motivation for writing this book by Shaykh Nadwi. Although written originally in Arabic the thrust of its theme details the effects of Muslim decline within the world civilisation framework.

Western responses to the book reaffirmed its abiding imprint in the larger Islamic resurgence framework. It caused a stir in the Orientalist circles and was regarded as a potential threat to the Western culture. Even the think tanks of Middle Eastern Studies funded by Western countries vehemently opposed its publication. Professor R.B. Serjeant who served as the Director of the Middle East Centre (University of Cambridge) made the following remark: "Had there been any approved custom of banning books in Britain I would have recommended first for banning this book."[47] For many Orientalists the book's contents opened a forum for contemporary Islamic thought. The book had seen several editions in French - a testimony to its global popularity.

The success story of *Rise and Fall* can be gleaned from the following anecdote. The Imām of the *Haram*, Shaykh 'Abdullāh Khayyāt admired Shaykh Nadwi's writings. In his Friday sermons *(khutbas)* the Imām made important reference to Shaykh Nadwi's celebrated work to articulate the core elements of *islāh*. The *salaf* discourse featured prominently in his *khutba* which included the early scholars like Hasan Basri, considered as the archetype of Islamic reform. Therefore, it was a matter of pride for Shaykh Nadwi to be included in the hierarchy of reformers with *salaf* antecedents. It must be remembered that the *khutbas* had a global coverage through television channels and radio broadcasts.[48]

Da'wah Literature: Towards a New Horizon

The steady growth of *da'wah* literature in Arabic by Shaykh Nadwi must be contextualised in the light of shifting political scenarios rapidly taking place in the Muslim world. Special mention may be made of the Arab countries, bastions of Islamic culture and civilisation.[49] These were gradually exposed

---

[47] Nadwi, *The Dynamics of Islam*, 60-1.
[48] Ilyās Bhatkali, *Ta'meer-i Hayāt* (September, 2000), 15-6.
[49] For a detailed discussion about the political changes, see Nadwi's *Western Civilisation, Islam and Muslims*.

to the baneful influence of Western civilisation. Egypt, owing to its geopolitical situation, was the protagonist of a "cultural changeover": The uncritical adoption of Western values and culture. Shaykh Nadwi's critique of the West is based on his personal experience and is also free from the polemics of writers adopting a total rejection of the West. This approach is reflected in his writings.

Likewise, the monograph *Ilā Mumatthilī al-Bilād al- Islāmiyyah* (An Exposition for Muslim Countries) details the shortcomings of the Muslim countries and urges them to reflect on the sacrifices of the Prophet (SAAS) and the *Sahābah* for the establishment of Islam. It was read at an international conference in 1947. Distinguished scholars, *'ulama* and leaders from far-flung countries of the Muslim world participated in this conference.[50]

Idārah Ta'limāt-i Islam

An illustrious scholar of Nadwah, Mawlana 'Abdus Salām Nadwi, was actively involved in the establishment of this institute. Its primary aim was to impart Quranic classes to state officials and professionals with an interest in Islamic Studies. Shaykh Nadwi with his years of experience in *tafsīr* was also instrumental in devising programs for the students. The Quranic lessons based on his mentor's approach (Mawlana Ahmad 'Ali Lahori) served a two-fold purpose: *da'wah* and *islāhī* themes for the reconstruction of the Muslim society. During this period, Nadwah launched its Urdu magazine *Ta'meer-i Hayāt*. Shaykh Nadwi was the co-editor and his collaborative contribution both in terms of the magazine's articles and vision[51] raised its stature among the Muslim readers. However, the *Ta'meer* and the *Idārah* faced budgetary constraints in their early years. As a result, the magazine was published at irregular intervals. Unfortunately, the *Idārah* also faced a similar crisis when Abdus Salam Nadwi was appointed Dean, Faculty of Islamic Studies at Jamia Millia Islamia, New Delhi. Nevertheless, this problem was overcome largely on account of the efforts by individuals with a strong Islamic commitment. The *Idārah* continued to serve an important role for the Muslim society in Lucknow.[52]

---

[50] Nadwi, *Kārwān*, vol. 1, 274.
[51] An article for the *Ta'meer-i Hayāt*, "Our National Character, Weakness and Shortcomings: An Appraisal" is a critical evaluation of the Indian Muslim society. Its publication was met with positive response among Muslims.
[52] Nadwi, *Kārwān*, vol. 1, 276-77.

Conclusion

Two distinct strands of *da'wah* opened up possibilities for Shaykh Nadwi to reach out to a wider audience both in the Indian and Arab worlds. The formulation of *da'wah* also sharpened his focus on *islāh* and *tajdīd*, twin concepts with important ramifications for his vision of Islamic resurgence.

Chapter V

Daʻwah: Content and Context

Before we attempt to discuss Shaykh Nadwi's relationship and contribution to the Tablighi Jamāʻat, some brief comments about this movement will explain its transnational character and phenomenal growth.

The centre of the Tablighi Jamāʻat is in New Delhi, India and the movement currently operates in more than eighty countries. Its annual gathering (*ijtimāʻ*) in India, Pakistan and Bangladesh and meetings in Europe and the US have no doubt built its high profile transnationally. Furthermore, its global spread and the massive number of its participants confirm the Jamāʻat as a phenomenon of *daʻwah*. For over seventy years, it has succeeded in establishing itself as a movement committed to *tajdīd* (renewal) and *islāh* (reform),[1] twin concepts derived largely from the *sunnah*.

Tablighi Jamāʻat: Mawlana Muhammad Ilyās

The founder of the Tablighi Jamāʻat (hereafter TJ), Mawlana Ilyās Kandhlawi began his *daʻwah* activities in Mewāt[2] around 1927. After its establishment, it also reached the *madāris*, Dār al-ʻUlums, educated elite and the *ʻulama* fraternity.[3]

A study on the movement by Sikand examines the TJ in three very different milieus - Mewāt (India), Bangladesh and Britain. From its humble beginnings to its transformation as a global movement, Sikand attempts to show the growing salience of this movement. The reformist trends of the Jamāʻat in relation to other Islamist organisations are discussed to assess its remarkable success in many parts of the world.[4]

Shaykh Nadwi's Personal Reminiscences

Shaykh Nadwi's meeting with Mawlana Ilyās in Nizāmuddin was preceded by his association with Mawlana Manzur Nuʻmāni (d. 1997) who had urged him

---

[1] Muhammad Khalid Masud (ed.), *Travellers in Faith* (Leiden, 2000), xix.
[2] Much has been written about Mewat and its neo-Muslim identity. *Ibid.* xxx-xxxix.
[3] Nadwi, *Life and Mission of Mawlana Mohammad Ilyās* (Lucknow, 1979), 47-65.
[4] Yoginder Sikand, *The Origins and Development of the Tabligh Jamāʻat (1920-2000)*, (New Delhi, 2002).

to accompany him to Mewāt, the hub of the *tabligh* activities. As Mawlana Nu'māni observed,[5] he and Shaykh Nadwi had been influenced by the article about the Jamā'at by Mawdudi in his periodical, *Tarjuman al-Qur'ān*. His personal account expressed a positive opinion[6] of the movement.

Mawlana Ilyās's towering personality had left a lasting impression on Shaykh Nadwi who was touched by the latter's affection and love for him. Ilyās appreciated his seminal work on Sayyid Ahmad Shahid and paid glowing tributes to this illustrious reformer. In Shaykh Nadwi's estimation, Ilyās embodied the Prophetic conduct in his personal life.[7] In a similar vein, Nadwah played a leading role in promoting the mission of the movement. As a result of this rapport with the TJ many misconceptions about its "modern character and inclinations" were dispelled. In a specific sense, Nadwah's prestige as a traditional seat of learning was enhanced.[8]

Shaykh Nadwi's active role in the TJ also introduced him to two illustrious scholars, Mawlana Muhammad Yūsuf (d. 1966),[9] son of Mawlana Ilyās and Shaykh Muhammad Zakariyyah, the noted *hadīth* scholar and author of the *Fadā'il* series[10]. These books were prescribed reading manuals in the TJ's program. Both of these scholars' impact on Shaykh Nadwi's *da'wah* vision was highlighted during his *tabligh* tours to the Arab world.[11]

The affection Shaykh Zakariyyah showed for Shaykh Nadwi is illustrative of the latter's spiritual profile. His mentoring and deep-seated love for Shaykh Nadwi were evident in their decades-long relationship. The Introductions (*muqaddimāt*) of Shaykh Zakariyyah's Arabic commentaries on *hadīth* were penned by Shaykh Nadwi, which again pointed out to his expertise on this primary source of Islam.[12] Shaykh Zakariyyah's

---

[5] Nadwi, *Life and Mission of Mawlana Mohammad Ilyās*, pp. v-vi. See Nu'māni's *Tahdith al-Ni'mat*, 187-90 for his impressions on the movement.
[6] This opinion changed after Mawlana Mawdudi established his Jamā'at-i Islami. He founded the movement "preoccupied with religious concerns" Nasr, *Vanguard of Islamic Revolution*, 16.
[7] Nadwi, *Kārwān*, 280-81.
[8] Masud, *Travellers in Faith*, 123-24.
[9] See Azizur Rahmān Bijnori, *Tadhkirah Mawlana Muhammad Yusuf, Amir i-Tabligh* (Bijnor, 1966) for his contribution to the Jamā'at. An entire chapter of this book (Chapter 5) is devoted to the spread of Islam outside India.
[10] See Masud, *Travellers in Faith*, 82-85 for a critical evaluation of the *Tablighi Nisāb*.
[11] Nadwi, *Kārwān*, vol.1, 312-13.
[12] Muhammad Umayr al-Siddiqi, "Shaykh al-Hadith Hadhrat Mawlana Muhammad Zakariyyah awr Hadhrat Mawlana Sayyid Abul Hasan Ali Nadwi" in *Ta'meer-i Hayāt*

Chapter V
Da'wah: Content and Context

affectionate regard for him bore traces of an inseparable bond in times of both joy and grief, achievements and challenges. In short, it was a bond strengthened by *imān* and *taqwa*. The *Maktūbāt* (letters) written by Shaykh Nadwi demonstrated his great respect for Shaykh Zakariyyah. The following excerpt of a letter written by Shaykh Nadwi attests to their close relationship:

> Every day I am involved in a crisis of hope and despondency. Sometimes this crisis evokes a response from my mind and soul. It is only Allah who gives sanity and security of *imān*. It is important I be present on a regular basis in your company, but distance, pressing work and travel expenses, sadly, are constraints. In this situation I seek your *du'ā* and affection.[13]

The spiritual dimension of the *Maktūbāt* is an integral element of *islāh* and *tajdīd*. In this respect, the Indian subcontinent pioneered and developed this genre and produced a substantial compilation of *Maktūbāt* that is unrivalled in the Muslim world. Shaykh Ahmad Sirhindi's and Yahya Maneri's *Maktūbāt*[14] are representative of this series.

Shaykh Nadwi's correspondence with Mawlana Ilyās is a conspectus of the founder's total commitment to the propagation of this fledgling movement. His great respect for Shaykh Nadwi both in terms of his erudition and his contribution to the spread of the TJ's activities are discussed at length in the *Maktūbāt*.[15] Likewise, the following letter written by Mawlana Yūsuf to Shaykh Nadwi is illustrative of his important role in the TJ.

Respected Shaykh Sayyid Abul Hasan Ali Nadwi:

> It is with great admiration that I mention that you were held in high esteem by Mawlana Ilyās. You were in the forefront of the tabligh movement and devoted all your energies to ensure that it secured a strong foothold in its nascent stages. Your commitment is exemplary and the success it has enjoyed among the learned circles is largely

---

(Lucknow, 2000), 13-17.
[13] Sayyid Muhammad Hamza Nadwi, *Maktūbāt i-Hadhrat Mawlana Sayyid Abul Hasan Ali Nadwi* vol. 2 (Rae Bareli, 2004), 111.
[14] Sharafudeen Maneri, *The Hundred Letters* (New York, 1980), xv-xix.
[15] Nadwi, *Hadhrat Mawlana Shah Muhammad Ilyās* (Karachi, 1993).

through your unrelenting efforts. The fact that even the *'ulama* are active in the Jamā'at work is indicative of your contribution. Moreover, the initial misconceptions harboured by intellectuals about this *da'wah* movement have been dispelled by your charismatic personality. Allah has endowed you with sterling qualities worth emulating and it is my earnest desire that Allah bless us with these noble qualities, which may be harnessed for the benefit of the *da'wah* effort. More importantly, as much as there is a growing interest in the *tabligh* work as is evident from the number of *jamā'ats* working as far afield as Peshawar (Pakistan), the forces of corruption have also made their presence felt. However, the salutary effect of *da'wah* can be felt everywhere as Muslims restore their confidence in Islam and commit themselves to the vision of the tabligh movement. The work has been enthusiastically received in the places visited and this augurs well for the future of *da'wah*.

Yours fraternally,
Muhammad Yūsuf Kandhlawi[16]

The *Life and Mission of Mawlana Muhammad Ilyās*, published originally in Urdu in 1944 is a sympathetic account about the life and character of this pre-eminent scholar, his sterling qualities as well as the development of the tabligh movement.

Shaykh Nadwi's active involvement in the *tabligh* mission also brought about a lasting relationship with Mawlana Manāzir Ahsan Gilāni[17] (d. 1956), a professor of Islamic Studies at the Osmania University in Hyderabad. An erudite author, Gilāni's *Al-Nabiyy al-Khātim* (The Final Messenger) had a profound effect on Shaykh Nadwi. He made several visits to Hyderabad to participate in the esteemed and learned *majalis* (sessions) of Gilāni.[18] During this period his meeting with Mawlana 'Abdul Qadir Rāipūrī marked the beginning of a bond that was to deepen[19] in the years to come.

The noted *'ālim* and *mufassir,* Mawlana Ahmad 'Ali Lahori, whose patronage towards Shaykh Nadwi was proverbial, initiated him into the *Qādiriyyah* sufi order and also conferred on him the mantle of *khilāfah* (spiritual

---

[16] *Al-Ahsan*, vol. 3, 20.
[17] Muhammad Zafiruddin Miftāhi, *Hayāt i-Mawlana Gilāni* (Karachi, 1994) is an excellent biography on this scholar.
[18] Nadwi, *Purāne Charāgh*, vol. 1, 332.
[19] Nadwi, *Kārwān*, vol. 1, 321.

Chapter V
Da'wah: Content and Context

deputyship). Furthermore, his letters to Shaykh Nadwi reaffirmed his high regard for the latter.[20]

Shaykh Nadwi saw the TJ as a "faith revivalist movement" which consciously eschewed political activities, refraining from communal controversy and conflict. It rooted itself among the poor and lower middle-class Muslims, emerging as a truly mass movement, with its simple message of faith in Allah, knowledge and performance of basic Islamic rituals and abandoning of un-Islamic customs. The movement probably suggested itself to Shaykh Nadwi as the most pragmatic strategy for Muslims in India, living as a marginalised community.[21]

Notwithstanding his admiration of the movement's forceful *da'wah* activities, Shaykh Nadwi expressed his candour about its restrictive vision. Of particular concern was its fixation on the six points outlined by its founder. According to Shaykh Nadwi, the TJ did not consider the challenges Muslims faced in their respective social milieus and ignored the need to adapt its *da'wah* accordingly. For him the TJ "ought to have some openness and familiarity with the temperament of modern educated youth, their outlook and values and their ways of thinking." His letter to the elders of the TJ was intended to highlight the dilemmas facing Muslims and the constructive role it could play in Muslim affairs. The response of the elders was muted and no positive exchange of ideas could as such be discussed. Shaykh Nadwi, however, continued supporting the TJ and did not publicly express his dissenting view concerning this crucial matter.

Characteristics of *Da'wah*

During its formative period, the program of action envisaged by the TJ did not hinder Shaykh Nadwi's *da'wah*. His *tabligh* travels to Hijaz and the other Arab countries sharpened his intellectual outlook and broadened his *da'wah* horizon. In this perspective, he employed the Quranic paradigm, *sirah* of the Prophet (SAAS), critique of materialism and Western civilization, the reconstruction of Muslim society and finally his *islāhī* guidelines.[22] These critical tools enabled him to interact with Islamic movements of divergent affiliations, Islamic scholars, *'ulama*, royalty and elite.[23]

---

[20] Nadwi, *Purāne Charāgh*, vol. 1, 160-61.
[21] Nadwi, *Kārwān*, vol. 1, 342-47.
[22] *Al-Qāsim*, Special Issue, 157-74.
[23] Nadwi, *Mir Kārwān,* 177-86.

Da'wah in the Hijaz

Shaykh Nadwi's travels to the Arab world took place in 1947. It may be considered an important milestone to his *da'wah* mission. His Arabic publications, though still not widely read, marked him out as a scholar with immense potential. Mawlana Muhammad Yūsuf, the then *Amir* of the TJ, recognising his talents in Arabic, was instrumental in arranging his travels to the Hijaz. He was eager to see Tabligh making inroads into the Hijaz which was the "fountainhead of this work."[24] For the successful implementation of *da'wah*, an articulate scholar was required to reach out to other scholars, *'ulama* and the educated class. Shaykh Nadwi was the perfect choice for this mission as he possessed the required expertise. Moreover, his oratorial skills[25] were widely acknowledged. As he had not performed *hajj* before, it was resolved that he would be accompanied by his family members, as well.

The profound influence of the *Haramayn* (Makkah and Madinah) on Shaykh Nadwi is described in his personal account of his *hajj* experience. The indescribable joy he experienced as he proceeded to Madinah is captured in these words:

> *Durūd* (salutations) on the Prophet (SAAS) constantly on the lips, the heart pounding with a passion and the Arab driver perplexed at (my) spontaneous recitation and uncontrollable tears.[26]

This succinct description revealed his soul-enriching impression of the sacred city. According to Shaykh Nadwi, this was also a defining moment in his life.

To the Hijazis: A Message

As discussed elsewhere in the previous chapter, Shaykh Nadwi had already prepared a monograph, *Ilā Mumatthilī* for the Arab audience. The message, couched in elegant style, is a candid assessment of the issues affecting the Arabs. Interestingly, its impact penetrated through the rank and file of the

---

[24] Mamshad 'Ali Qasimi, *Sayyid Abul Hasan Ali Nadwi, Akābir wa Mashāhir Ummat ki Nazar Mein* (Phulat, 1998), 48-51.
[25] Shaykh Nadwi's views are succinctly discussed in his monograph, *Qur'anic Paradigm: Da'wah in the West*.
[26] Nadwi, *Apne Ghar se Baytullah tak* (Lucknow, 1989), 32.

Chapter V
Da'wah: Content and Context

'*ulama* fraternity. Shaykh 'Ali Harakān,[27] lecturer of *hadīth*, (later the secretary general of Rābitā) paid glowing tributes to his erudition. So did Shaykh 'Umar bin Hasan Al-Shaykh through whose personal interest the *tabligh* work was able to establish itself in the *Haramayn*.[28] His affectionate regard for Shaykh Nadwi was proverbial. In fact, he was largely instrumental in promoting the writings of Shaykh Nadwi. King Saud revered Shaykh 'Umar and the Islamic orientation displayed by the Saud royalty was the result of his influence. He was also responsible for introducing Shaykh Nadwi to King Saud. The historic letter written by Shaykh Nadwi to the king expressed his candour about the realities and challenges facing the Arabs. It also alluded to the dangers looming ahead on account of the changing political fortunes affecting the kingdom.[29] There was no doubt that the baneful influence of Western civilisation was making inroads into the heartland of Islam. Shaykh Nadwi's sensitive personality and Islamic conscience could not tolerate the intrusive presence of a foreign culture that conspired to subjugate the Arab world, politically and culturally. Hence, his impassioned *da'wah* message contained in his writings.[30]

Shaykh Nadwi's contact with the leading scholars and '*ulama* enhanced his popularity in the Arab world. He was able to articulate his views to the Arabs through his public lectures and writings, reminding them about their responsibilities to Islam. His radio lectures broadcast on Saudi Radio reinforced this message for a larger audience.

Da'wah: New Perspectives

Shaykh Nadwi's second *hajj* in 1950 added new dimensions to his *da'wah* mission. Between 1948 and 1950 the political developments in India provided him with new perspectives and maturity of experience. The events (which are discussed in the following chapter) also deepened his understanding of issues affecting the Muslim *ummah*. Therefore, it is important to contextualise the second *hajj* in relation to his wider *da'wah* contributions.[31] Additionally, the publication of *Rise and Fall of Muslims*

---

[27] Nadwi, *Purāne Charāgh* vol. 3 for his appreciation of Shaykh Harakan's contribution.
[28] *Sawanih Mufakkir-i Islam*, 229.
[29] *Ibid.*, 230-31.
[30] For an exposition on this theme, Nadwi's *Bayn al-Jibāyat wa al-Hidāyat* is an excellent introduction of his intellectual response to Western civilisation.
[31] Nadwi, *Kārwān*, vol. 1, 326-29.

profiled his stature as a renowned scholar in both the Arab and Islamic world.

Shaykh Nadwi wrote several monographs reminding the Arab nations of their commitment to Islam. His second *hajj* illustrated the grim realities facing the Saudi kingdom. In a letter written to his brother, Dr 'Abdul 'Ali, he presented the following facts:

> I had visited Saudi Arabia first in 1947. Now in 1950 within three years, I can see a marked change. Westernisation has made its inroads into the market, economy and even thought patterns. One senses it on landing in Jeddah. The more one learns about the local life, the more the above bitter reality is affirmed. It is hard to say how many persons in their Arab garb have turned Western in their outlook. Arabic, the language of the Quran, is now the vehicle of Western thought and patently materialistic psyche. The Arab devotion to money, desire for more and more wealth and seeking worldly glory have reached serious proportions. It is hard to think of leading a prosperous life and achieving progress without turning to the United States.[32]

In the intellectual domain the *majālis* (sessions) of scholars epitomised a distinctive feature, and pointed out to the tempo of Islamic learning. In view of the political developments in Egypt, the upsurge of contemporary Islamic thought was very much present. There was no doubt that the intellectual trends that were drawn from the Egyptian intelligentsia had a major impact on both the Arab and Islamic world. Moreover, the cutting edge scholarship in Egypt, hardly much evident in other parts of the Muslim world, served as a locus on which the major points of Islamic disciplines converged. Shaykh Nadwi observed:

> During this period, the Nasserist regime did not make its full appearance on the political stage. (Its influence) dried out the branches of literature, politics and morality of their freshness and vitality. It swept the whole country with its revolutionary ideas, leaving behind nothing but a trail of dust in the lives of people.[33]

---

[32] Bilal Hasani, *Sayyid Abul Hasan Ali Nadwi: His Thought and Mission* (Springs, 2019), 42.
[33] Nadwi, *Kārwān*, vol. 1 p. 367. For a fuller appreciation of the Nasserist regime and its ideological content, see Nadwi, *Western Civilisation, Islam and Muslims*.

Chapter V
Da'wah: Content and Context

Another important development was the role of intellectuals in formulating new approaches to Islamic reformist thought. The pantheon of scholars/intellectuals who blazed innovative trails in their respective fields of learning must be mentioned to appreciate Shaykh Nadwi's literary contribution in the Arab world. European influence shared and created new impulses for a critical approach to the classical Islamic heritage.[34] This movement rose rapidly and was inextricably linked to the European domination of the Muslim lands. It was, however, the French occupation of Egypt[35] in 1798 that paved the way for a gradual assimilation of foreign values in the intellectual and cultural domains. These contours gradually took shape in the Egyptian society as a sizeable segment of the Muslim intellectuals trained in France wielded a strong influence on its Islamic character. Francophile trends were best represented by Dr Taha Husayn.[36] His long-standing and controversial impact has been widely covered in major studies about his contribution to contemporary Islamic thought. Other leading scholars included the literary critic 'Abbās 'Aqqād,[37] historian and critic, Dr Ahmad Amin, the eminent *hadīth* scholar, Dr Mahmud Shakir and the Al-Azhar *'ālim*, Shaykh Mahmud Shaltut.[38] They were associated with a distinctive school of thought and were widely praised for their pioneering contributions. Thus, the proliferation of their publications shaped public opinion and it is against this background that Shaykh Nadwi's interactive role must be examined.

A brief survey of the reformist school in Egypt merits special mention to assess the role of the Ikhwān movement. Badawi's study[39] of Jamāluddin Afghāni, Muhammad 'Abduh and Sayyid Rashid Ridā, the triad of the reformist tradition, strongly advocated a return to the *salafi* ways. Their incisive analysis of *tajdīd* and *islāh* continues to hold sway in the Muslim world. Whatever patterns of revivalism are discernible in the contemporary Islamic movements

---

[34] Albert Hourani, *Arabic Thought in the Liberal Age, 1798-1939* (Oxford: OUP, 1983). Cf. S.M. Yunus Gilani, *The Socio-Political Role of 'Ulama in Egypt: 1798-1870* (New Delhi, 2007)
[35] Nadwi, *Western Civilisation, Islam and Muslims*, 91-93 for Egypt's role in promoting Western thought and culture.
[36] Hourani, *Arabic Thought in the Liberal Age* details Taha Husayn's major role in the modernisation of Islamic thought in Egypt.
[37] Noted literary critic and author of important critical texts.
[38] Zaki Badawi, *The Reformers of Egypt* (London, 1978). Cf. Hourani, *Arabic Thought in the Liberal Age.*
[39] Isma'il Abu Rabi, *Intellectual Origins of Islamic Resurgence in the Modern Arab World,* 62-84.

owe their source of inspiration to these reformers who wielded tremendous influence on Egyptian society, which was a transmitter of these trends to the Muslim world.[40] Shaykh Nadwi's critique of these reformist movements with special reference to Egypt[41] shares a commonality with Badawi as they both discuss "a form of synthesis of trends within the *ummah*."[42]

Ikhwān: Islamic Reformist Movement

Shaykh Nadwi's association with the Ikhwān cannot be underestimated. His important writings[43] had a direct bearing on the Ikhwān's vision of Islam. It would be correct to state that Shaykh Nadwi's contributions to its vast corpus of Islamic literature[44] energised it as a full-fledged Islamic movement. One thing that clearly emerges from Shaykh Nadwi's association with the Ikhwān is his balanced approach and sympathetic understanding of the movement during its early years. His appreciation of its influence in the Arab world and the salutary changes among the disaffected generation of educated Arabs who would have otherwise easily succumbed to atheism, is touching. According to Shaykh Nadwi, their return to Islam was a direct result of the powerful personality of Imam Hasan al-Banna and his *da'wah* activities in all spheres of Egyptian society.[45]

Apart from its intellectual initiatives, the growth and development of the Ikhwān movement as a social and political force must also be kept in mind. Its phenomenal success followed by a turbulent phase which resulted in the martyrdom of its founder did not prevent the movement from its vision of *islāh*.[46] Among its major achievements was the reform of the Muslim society that had not only fallen prey to vice, immorality, but had adopted a European culture. Therefore, a clarion call for reform was given by Imām al- Banna to stem the rising tide of its intrusive presence. His personality was a symbol of "those extraordinary figures in history who were selected by Allah to lead a movement of *da'wah* and produce an Islamic

---

[40] Cf. Nadwi, *Western Civilisation, Islam and Muslims*, 91-122.
[41] Badawi, *The Reformers of Egypt*, 16.
[42] For example, Shaykh Nadwi's *Rise and Fall* was read in the *halaqah* of the Ikhwān.
[43] For a list of the Ikhwān's literature which provided the nucleus for its *islāhī* mission. See Muhammad Shawqi Zaki, *Tāhrik al-Ikhwān al-Muslimīn* translated into Urdu by Sayyid Ridwān 'Ali Nadwi (Lucknow] 1999), 223-33.
[44] *Tāhrik al-Ikhwān al-Muslimīn*, 41.
[45] Reform and revival (*islāh* and *tajdīd*) are twin concepts which form a thematic unity and dimension in Shaykh Nadwi's multivolume *Saviours of Islamic Spirit*.
[46] Nadwi, *Kārwān*, vol. 1, 377.

Chapter V
Da'wah: Content and Context

revolution during this epoch-making period."[47] He possessed multifaceted qualities: leadership, an enlightened mind, a profusely loving heart, oratorial skills and an endearing personality of a strong moral fiber. These personal traits were the hallmark of Al-Banna's character and resonated in his comprehensive *da'wah*.

Ikhwān: A Critique

Shaykh Nadwi's autobiography *Kārwān* (vol.1) must be read together with *Mir Kārwān* for a contextualised reading of his relation with the Ikhwān. In addition to these sources, his article on Al-Banna in the *Purāne Charāgh* - an Introduction (*muqqadimah*) in Arabic to the Imām's memoirs[48] provides a synoptic impression of this charismatic personality. Shaykh Nadwi's association with the Ikhwān was a productive period of his intellectual life as the spectrum of activities and literary output reveals. The inner circle of the Ikhwān brought him into close contact with luminaries like Shaykh Muhammad al-Ghazali[49] with whom he developed a lasting friendship. He was instrumental in disseminating Shaykh Nadwi's writings and through the lecture tours introduced the latter to the Egyptian audience. Similarly, the internationally renowned Scholar, 'Allāmah Yūsuf Qardāwī,[50] maintained a close affinity with Shaykh Nadwi.

The Ikhwān's enthusiastic support of Shaykh Nadwi's *da'wah* can best be gauged from the monographs he penned to reach a wider audience. Apart from *Rise and Fall of Muslims*, a must-read for Ikhwān members,[51] the hierarchy in the Ikhwān was responsive to Shaykh Nadwi's fair exhortations (*mawā'iz*). His honest assessment about the Ikhwān's political ambitions to effect strategic changes in the Egyptian society was ungrudgingly accepted by the movement to re-assess its "plan of action." Overall, the groundswell of interest in Shaykh Nadwi's prolific writings and rapport he enjoyed with a cross-section of Egyptians are discussed in detail in the *Kārwān*.[52] Among his other writings, the following monographs focus on the thematic message of *da'wah* and a recommitment to Islam:

---

[47] Nadwi, *Purāne Charāgh*, vol. 3, 13-22.
[48] Hasan Bannā, *Mudhakkirāt al-Da'wat wa al-Dā'iyāt* (Beirut, 1984).
[49] See the obituary on Ghazāli in *Impact International* (1995).
[50] Qardāwī was the Director: *Sirah* and *Sunnah* Centre, University of Qatar.
[51] Nadwi, *Kārwān*, vol. 1, 368-72.
[52] *Ibid*.

- *Isma'i Yā Misr* (For the Egyptians)
- *Bayna al 'Ālam wal Jazirat al-'Arab* (Between the world and the Arabian peninsula)
- *Al-Madd wa al-Jazr fi-Tārikh Al-Islam* (Ebb and flow in Islamic history)

These writings are characterised by an admirable fluency, spontaneity and direct approach. The contents are largely drawn from the Quran and *sunnah*. Another feature of these monographs is the notable absence of polemics and sectarian bias. It would be worthwhile to reproduce a few pertinent excerpts from Shaykh Nadwi's writings regarding the Ikhwān for a correct appraisal of its activities:

Notwithstanding all this, the need remained for a sustained and concentrated effort against the mounting influence of Western civilisation. A crusading campaign was called for and mere emotional allegiance to Islam was not enough.

A deeper and stronger faith and a more solid conviction in Islamic values and teachings, as against the concepts floated by the West, was required. A struggle of this nature could, of necessity, neither be confined to politics, as Jamāluddin Afghani had sought, nor conceived in a purely defensive manner, as Muhammad 'Abduh had done.

Had the Ikhwān movement of Egypt developed at a steady pace and the leaders of Islamic thought in the countries of the Middle East given to it their unqualified support, it could have fulfilled the mission of Afghani and 'Abduh by working out an Islamic renaissance in West Asia.[53]

Ikhwān: Personal Reminiscences

In retrospect, the relationship between Shaykh Nadwi and the Ikhwān was based on mutual respect. According to Shaykh Nadwi, the Ikhwān had a profound effect on him for the following reasons:

It infused the Egyptian society, which had succumbed to influence of Western civilization, with renewed hope and faith in the dynamic message of Islam. This changed religious atmosphere had no parallel in the Egyptian society. The spirit of brotherhood dominated the lives of the members of the Ikhwān. Their moral conduct was above reproach; their vision of *da'wah*

---

[53] Nadwi, *Western Civilisation, Islam and Muslims*, 110-11.

Chapter V
Da'wah: Content and Context

was guided by the bond of brotherhood that rejected all forms of prejudice. The Ikhwān was actively involved in the affairs of the Egyptian society and made realistic efforts to remedy the malaise, which, by and large, had weakened its moral fiber. In its pursuit of *da'wah*, it shunned sectarian bias and expended its energy and time in building the moral foundation of an ideal Muslim society.

The pan-Islamic vision of the Ikhwān cut across territorial barriers. In contrast, the scenario of the Egyptian society was a dismal picture of rising atheism and Francophile tendencies. Unsurprisingly, the phalanx of intellectuals and journalists made unashamed efforts to undermine Islam. Worse still, academic and research writings with a satirical character were promoted as an alternative to the perennial sources of Islam. Even the renowned institution of al-Azhar was powerless to counter these grave dangers. It was the Ikhwān which not only challenged the atheistic onslaught, but also created a formidable cadre of Islamically-oriented youth and Islamists who reasserted the supremacy of Islam. In fact, the Ikhwān dealt a death blow to the un-Islamic elements by producing a number of intellectuals whose impressive scholarship was the ideal to be followed.[54]

In the Heart of Africa: Sudan

Sudan's Arabo-Islamic links have been extensively published, as has its historic importance as an Islamic heartland.

Shaykh Nadwi was accompanied by Mawlana 'Ubaydullah Balyāwī, a Nadwi scholar whose stay in Egypt facilitated the latter's *da'wah* activities to Sudan. Notable scholars like Ustādh Ismā'il Bek (later the Prime Minister of Sudan) and Shaykh Muhammad Musa Sulayman of the Jami'at al-Shubbān al-Muslimīn (Muslim Youth Society) developed a special affinity towards him. In fact, Shaykh Nadwi's presence echoed strong *da'wah* sentiments of Brotherhood. Dr 'Abdul 'Ali maintained an abiding interest in the affairs of the Muslim *ummah*, particularly Africa. In one of his letters he writes:

May your efforts (of *da'wah*) be accepted by Allah. Egypt is the door to Africa. If only the Egyptians can realise their responsibility and derive every benefit from the *hujjaj* (pilgrims) travelling through their country by disseminating the teachings of Islam. Their *tabligh* efforts should also reach non-Muslim countries, so that, Insha- Allah, one day the whole of Africa will

---

[54] Nadwi, *Kārwān*, vol. 1, 378-82.

shine with the *nūr* (light) of Islam.[55]

Syria, Citadel of Islam: A Eulogy

Syria, the land of Islam, the land of the *Sahābah* who lay buried in her sacred soil, the land of innumerable scholars and saints who carved out a niche for themselves in the pages of Islamic history - in short, Syria has preserved the best treasures of Islamic culture.

According to Shaykh Nadwi, Syria had over the centuries evoked an aura of spirituality and captured in frozen time the splendid images of the grandeur of Islam. Transcending territorial and racial barriers, the passionate attachment to Syria is encapsulated in a versified compilation *Samsām al-Islam*, a translation of the Arabic *Futūh al-Shām*, and religiously read by Shaykh Nadwi's family members.[56] The *Samsām* recounted in majestic verses the conquest of Syria as well as the valour and courage of the luminaries of Islam. This eulogy was not meant merely to re-enact the history of Syria. Shaykh Nadwi explains:

> The poignant descriptions of the battles would excite one's sensibilities and the accounts of martyrdom were so moving as to make the listener restless to live for Allah. Also, the tribulations of the *Sahābah* (Companions) and the early warriors for the faith made the listener forget his personal loss completely.[57]

This identification, as Zaman notes, was necessary to articulate the cultural identity of Indian Muslims in a Hindu- dominated society.[58]

There was no doubt that the Shaykh Nadwi's *da'wah* activities in Syria was an unforgettable experience. Eminent scholars, *mashā'ikh* and professors were his ardent admirers and he, in turn, benefitted from them. Damascus, once the bastion of the Umayyad dynasty, continued with its prestigious tradition of scholarship. As a reservoir of Islamic learning, it boasted an uninterrupted and enviable scholarly tradition that left indelible imprints across the Muslim world. Here we will mention a few names to illustrate Shaykh

---

[55] Nadwi, *Hayāt i-'Abdul Hayy*, 396-97.
[56] Comprising 25,000 couplets this compilation used to be recited by the Hasani family on occasion of grief and tribulation.
[57] Nadwi, *Kārwān*, vol.1, 82.
[58] For a detailed discussion of Nadwah's intellectual tradition, see Muhammad Qasim Zaman, "Muslim Identity in Twentieth Century India" in *The Muslim World* (1997), pp. 277-78.

Chapter V
Da'wah: Content and Context

Nadwi's stature among his Arab contemporaries. Shaykh Bahjat al-Baytar, a prominent *'ālim*,[59] Dr Mustafa Sibā'i,[60] a distinguished Ikhwān member, Dr 'Umar Bahā al-Amirī,[61] the noted poet, Professor Muhammad al-Mubārak, an eminent litterateur and critic[62] were profoundly influenced by him. The *da'wah* literature in the form of lectures and radio broadcasts was inspirational both in content and style. Also of interest were the *ismā'ī* series, which added a new dimension to Shaykh Nadwi's literary output and also brought out his charismatic personality. His writings were widely read amid much critical acclaim.[63]

During his prolonged stay in Damascus, Shaykh Nadwi's *da'wah* schedule also gave him the opportunity to travel to Palestine, and personally assess the plight of the Palestinians. His monographs[64] published during this important period also speaks of his global concern for the *ummah*. At the same time, he made serious efforts to mobilise the Arab consciousness on Palestine. His meeting with King Abdullah of Jordan recounts the importance of asserting the supremacy of Islam in this newly established kingdom. The king had a reverential regard for Shaykh Nadwi as he had already read the latter's *Rise and Fall of Muslims*. He was greatly impressed by Shaykh Nadwi's thoughtful analysis about the issues affecting the Muslim world. King 'Abdullāh's untimely assassination in the sacred precincts of Masjid al-Aqsā also thwarted any concrete steps to address the refugee problem in Palestine.[65]

Shaykh Nadwi returned to India after performing his third *hajj* in 1951. Approximately fourteen months were spent abroad and devoted to *da'wah*. This was also a productive phase in terms of his intellectual and *da'wah* career.

---

[59] See *Kārwān*, vol. 1, p. 388 for Shaykh Nadwi's impressions of Shaykh Baytar.
[60] Accomplished scholar whose literary contribution is marked by academic scholarship.
[61] An obituary appeared in the *Al-Ba'ath al-Islami Monthly* (Lucknow) which describes his erudition.
[62] *Ta'meer-i Hayāt* (2000), 19-27. Cf. Mamshād 'Ali Qāsimi, *Sayyid Abul Hasan Ali Nadwi: Akābir wa Mashāhir Ummat ki Nazar Mein*, 129-30.
[63] 'Abdullah Nadwi, *Mir Kārwān*, 298-99.
[64] For Shaykh Nadwi's soul-stirring lectures on the Palestinian issue, see Muhammad Asjad Qāsimi, *Mufakkir i-Islam, Mawlana Sayyid Abul Hasan Ali Nadwi* (Deoband, 2000), 219-24.
[65] Nadwi, *Mir Kārwān*, 301.

Sayyid Abul Hasan Nadwi: Life and Legacy
Chapter V

Travelogue Series: An Overview

It is important to shed light on the "travelogue" genre which Shaykh Nadwi employed as an extension to his *da'wah*. His travels to the Middle East - Hijaz, Egypt, Lebanon and Jordan - is a trajectory of his broad vision of reawakening the Arabs and their responsibility to Islam. In this connection, his *Middle East Travelogue*[66] highlights his personal observations of the turning tides of Islamic activism in these countries. A parallel development is the rise of nationalism and atheism through which the concerted efforts to undermine the Islamic *Turāth* (legacy) in several Arab countries are critically examined by the author. By the same token, this work also offers readers a glimpse of the political and religious scenarios in the countries under discussion. Personal reminiscence combined with critical appraisal are the distinctive features of Shaykh Nadwi's travelogue writings. As 'Abbās Nadwi observes in his *Mir Kārwān*, Shaykh Nadwi consistent with his unassuming personality, has not included anecdotal accounts in his autobiography or his other writings.[67] These incidents are gleaned from either his contemporaries or close associates. For this reason, *Mir Kārwān* stands out as an important document highlighting the defining moments of Shaykh Nadwi's long and eventful career. In fact, it may be considered a supplement to his multivolume *Kārwān*.

The travelogue series of Shaykh Nadwi is important for a better understanding of his *da'wah* with particular reference to the Arab world. An early work written in 1951, *Mudhākarāt* is a pen portrait of Shaykh Nadwi's interaction with accomplished scholars and leading Islamic movements in the Arab world. Although it does not provide details of historical places visited, it covers issues within the framework of *da'wah*. In sum, it is a reminder to the Arab world of their commitment to Islamic ideals. Shaykh Nadwi's perceptive impressions of his visits and his soul-stirring speeches and addresses are themes dealing with the universal revolution brought by Islam.[68] Apart from its historical value, the travelogue also reveals Shaykh Nadwi's personality framed through the lens of interviews and incidents that he describes.

---

[66] Originally written in Arabic *Mudhākarāt-al-Sāih fi-al-Sharq-al-'Arabi* is the first of series of travelogues in Shaykh Nadwi's intellectual career.
[67] 'Abbās Nadwi, *Mir Kārwān*, 295-97.
[68] Wasi Ahmad Siddiqui, "Sharq i-Awsat ki Diary" in *Kārwān i-Adab* (Lucknow, 2001), 417.

Chapter V
Da'wah: Content and Context

Brief mention was made of the *ismā'ī* series elsewhere in the chapter. Apart from its *islāhī* character, its literary style is couched in an impassioned appeal for the Arab nations not to abdicate their Islamic responsibilities. These monographs contain critiques of western civilisation that had left its imprints on the Arab soil. Equally disturbing was the proliferation of a consumerist society that was indifferent to the core values of compassion and justice - hallmarks of the Islamic society.

We reproduce selected extracts from the *ismā'ī* series which are intended to bring into bold relief the menace of materialism, vices of the self and the Islamic solution to these problems. It must be remembered that the historical developments in the Arab world prompted the forceful critical appraisal by Shaykh Nadwi.

Kuwait:

You have advanced much in culture, built skyscrapers and towering buildings. However, your task is far nobler than this. You must be proud of your faith. You have lost your identity by engrossing yourself into worldliness. You have withdrawn from the leadership of mankind. Do regain your lost position and gain self-knowledge.

Syria:

When your messengers (read as *du'āt*) came to us, we had a nationality of our own, in which we took pride. We were proud of our language. We were willing to lay down our lives for these. Yet we forsook all these and joined the wider community of Islam. We learnt Arabic and severed all our ties with nationalism and all other *Jāhiliyyah* notions. You had rescued us from these and the narrow confines of nationalism. For Allah's sake, keep away from nationalism. Do not fall into the very morass from which you had freed us.

Egypt:

You represent a convergence of two civilisations. On the one hand, you are the seat of Islamic culture, and on the other, of Western civilisation. You owe your responsibilities to two continents, Asia and Europe in that you are the bearer of message for both. You should transmit the knowledge and experience of Europe to Asia and Arab countries. Your other main task is to convey the message of the Arabian Peninsula (Islam) to Europe.[69]

Conclusion

One of the salient features of Shaykh Nadwi's *da'wah* writings is the articulation of the Islamic ideals with a clearly-defined goal: Spirituality nurtured in the Islamic ethos. It is this line of approach that shaped his understanding of Islamic resurgence. His personal meetings with distinguished scholars and the *'ulama*, together with the publication of his forceful literature with a strong *da'wah* orientation, paved the way for his pioneering role in the Arab world.

---

[69] Bilal Nadwi, *Sayyid Abul Hasan Ali Nadwi*, 54-7.

Chapter VI

Da'wah: New Horizons

This chapter attempts to explore the significant factors that influenced Shaykh Nadwi's involvement in Indian mainstream activities. Also noteworthy are the contributions of the eminent Shaykh Mawlana 'Abdul Qādir Rāipūrī to Shaykh Nadwi's quest for spirituality. The Arab audience, central to his *da'wah* vision, is addressed on an intellectual level through a series of university lectures in Damascus on influential personalities of Islam. It may also be noted that his multivolume *Saviours of Islamic Spirit* has a specific revivalist setting. It is discussed elsewhere in the chapter.

Muslim Hegemony: An Assessment

Muslim rule in India, which spanned over 800 years, had seen a symbiotic relationship between Muslims and members of the other faiths. The Hindu majority who were ruled in the past by the Muslim dynasties of different ethnic backgrounds had responded differently to the set of political situations in the subcontinent. Their conflicting loyalties combined with sporadic uprisings against the Muslim rule have been a subject of extensive study.[1] Despite the political vagaries that represented centuries of Muslim rule, it was unavoidable that the synthesis of Indo-Islamic culture would evolve.[2] Such an integrated culture flourished for several centuries under the Mughal dynasty[3] and began to gradually decline after the British occupation of India. The consolidation of British control was dramatically challenged in 1857 when a series of uprisings spread across northern India.[4] Muslims in this region actively participated in the uprising against British rule. After the abortive effort of 1857 to overthrow the foreign yoke, Muslims were so dejected that they could not even think of planning a further massive uprising against the British government.[5]

The repressive policies against the *mujahidin* by the British and its deliberate policy of alienating the Hindus from the Muslims resulted in the

---

[1] Nadwi, *Muslims in India* (Lucknow, 1976), 125.
[2] *Ibid.*
[3] Nadwi, *Reconstruction of Indian Society* (Lucknow, 1972), 10.
[4] Barbara Daly Metcalf, *Islamic Revival in British India: Deoband, 1860-1900* (Karachi, 1989), 10-11.
[5] Ishtiaq Husain Qureshi, *Ulema in Politics* (Kararchi, 1974), 182.

latter advancing in terms of educational and employment opportunities.[6]

It is widely accepted that the 1857 political response to British rule marks a watershed in the development of the ideas and attitudes of Muslims, especially in northern India in the nineteenth century. Robinson's historical assessment of the "gestation period" of the Indian Muslims' ideological vision is revealing:

> After it (the uprising) they were increasingly concerned to discover how best they could be Muslim under the new dispensation, whether it meant building ideological and institutional bridges between Islam and the West, or developing systems which could enable them largely to ignore Western civilisation and the colonial state, or making a point of defending Islam whenever it was threatened in India and the world.[7]

Furthermore, the uprising was a prelude to the "parting of ways" between Muslims and Hindus fomented by the manipulative propaganda tactics of the British Empire.[8]

Muslim hegemony represented by principalities and fragmented dynasties soon disappeared from the political scene when the Partition of India took place in 1947.[9] The wave of mutual distrust between Muslims and Hindus escalated into a genocide and millions lost their lives following the Partition.[10] Even under the tragic circumstances *da'wah* gained momentum through the declining days of Muslim rule in India right up to the termination of British rule. Politics dictated the religious landscape; and it was inevitable that the Hindu-Muslim conflict exacerbated the dynamism of *da'wah*. This turbulent period also saw the rise of Hindu revivalist activities, which under the name of the Shuddhi movement spread all over India.[11] The TJ was established as a reaction to these Hindu revivalist movements. Thus, *da'wah* faced a formidable challenge in an atmosphere of religious polemics and debates, culminating in violent communal disturbances.[12]

Shaykh Nadwi was not oblivious to the issues affecting the Indian Muslims. Therefore, he was not prepared to relegate the harsh realities facing them as

---

[6] *Ibid.*, 183-85.
[7] Francis Robinson, *Islam and Muslim History in South Asia* (Delhi, 2001), 139.
[8] *Ibid.*, 11-12.
[9] Nadwi, *Muslims in India*, 128.
[10] *Ibid.*, 11-12.
[11] *Ibid.*, 119.
[12] *Ibid.*, 127.

Chapter VI
Da'wah: New Horizons

political dilemmas. The challenges were not only unleashed by parochial interests of the emergent Hindutva, but also by an orchestrated campaign to obliterate the Islamic identity of Indian Muslims. His anguished soul witnessed the carnage; the senseless loss of human lives took its toll on his sensitive personality. In his *Muslims in India* he raised the concerns of the Indian Muslims both in terms of their religious and political rights that were enshrined in the Indian Constitution. Secularism, a Gandhian ideal meant to remove religious prejudice was now a theoretical construction. In fact, the *Andalus Syndrome*[13] was used by the noted anthropologist Akbar Ahmed as a metaphor for the Muslim decline in countries which they formerly ruled. One such example was Hyderabad, the metropolis of Muslim culture. The parallels between Muslim rule in Andalusia (Spain) and Hyderabad (India) reveal a synthesis of culture - Muslim and non-Muslim - and paradoxically points out to its abrupt ending, leaving the marginalised Muslim community traumatised and forlorn. It is in the context of these conditions that Shaykh Nadwi's analysis of Muslim predicament in India must be understood. He says:

[Islam] enjoyed a superiority over other faiths because of its rationalistic teachings, its solidly monotheistic creed (*tawhīd*) and its enlightened concepts of universal brotherhood and social justice. There was no room in its social order for things like casteism and untouchability. The glorious message of the Quran, the glittering life-example of the Prophet (SAAS) and the simple, impeccable teachings of the faith never ceased to conquer new minds and captivate new hearts. And, if circumstances had not undergone a change, it was quite possible that Islam would eventually have emerged as the strongest religious force not only of the subcontinent, but the whole of Asia. But, as ill-luck would have it, a dismal and uninspiring political tussle ensued between the Hindus and Muslims. It rapidly assumed such awful proportions that it filled the two communities with repugnance and anger against each other, and resulted, finally, in the division of the country into two independent states of India and Pakistan.

The Indian Constitution has guaranteed the freedom of religion and cultural development to all individuals and communities and

---

[13] Akbar Ahmed, *Discovering Islam: Making Sense of Muslim History and Society* (London, 1988), 158-71.

bestowed a status of complete equality on all citizens, irrespective of their religious affiliations. This Constitution is most ideally suited to the conditions of our country which has a diverse population and where a number of religious and linguistic groups live side by side with each other.[14]

The crisis of identity has also been critically examined by other writers. Habibul Haq Nadwi remarks that as a corollary of the anti-Muslim violence and communal riots, the *'ulama-* activists launched a two-pronged effort to:

- preserve the corporate identity of Muslims.
- establish interfaith dialogue in order to maintain mutual respect and harmony between Muslims and Hindus.[15]

Religio-political Activism

The religio-political activism of the *'ulama* has been critically examined in several studies.[16] Shaykh Nadwi's contribution has been highlighted to illustrate "[his] long intellectual and political career which offers a fascinating glimpse both into efforts to preserve Muslim identity in the framework of a secular nation-state as well as into the often conflicting base of the *'ulama's* leadership of the community."[17] An extension to the activism of the *'ulama* is embodied in Shaykh Nadwi's perspective of *da'wah* on a different level: A communal audience (*makhlūt*) of both Muslims and non-Muslims. However, this form of *da'wah* must not be confused with the TJ to which Shaykh Nadwi was actively associated or the *wahdat al-adyān* (unity of faiths) theory with its syncretic peculiarities.[18] To dispel these misperceptions, Shaykh Nadwi was conscious of the sensitivity of the task ahead and the need to address the audience keeping in mind their temperament and worldview. The vexing issue was to remove from the

---

[14] Nadwi, *Muslims in India*, 127-29.
[15] Syed Habibul Haq Nadvi, *The Dynamics of Islam* (Durban, 1982), 60-64. Although reference is made to Shaykh Nadwi, the contributions of Mawlana Abul Kalam Azad in this regard cannot be ignored. See Azad's *India Wins Freedom* for his role in promoting a patriotism transcending religious barriers.
[16] See Zaman, *The 'Ulama in Contemporary Islam* (Princeton, 2002).
[17] *Ibid.*, 161.
[18] Nadwi, *Kārwān*, vol. 1, 396.

Chapter VI
Da'wah: New Horizons

Hindus' psyche their hostility towards Muslims and their culture. To exorcise the demon of the distorted interpretation of Muslim history in India, Shaykh Nadwi envisioned this forum in the hope of bringing these two communities closer to pursue goals of national interest.[19] According to Shaykh Nadwi, the Muslims' destiny was irrevocably linked to the Indian scenario and their contribution was equally significant as any other community. He proposed to show in his writings that Muslims are part of, and as loyal to India as are the Hindus:

> [Muslim] culture which has taken centuries to evolve itself, is a combination of both Islamic and Indian influences. This two-fold aspect has, on the one hand, endowed it with a beauty and richness which is characteristically its own. On the other, it strengthens the assurance that this culture will operate here not like an alien or a traveller, but as a permanent citizen who has built his home in the light of his peculiar needs and circumstances and past traditions. To seek to deprive a person or to make him revolt against transcendental values and ethical ideals which are common between him and large portions of mankind spread all over the globe will mean an attempt to freeze his spiritual fountainheads and destroy the universality of his outlook. In the same way, it will be utterly futile and unjust to expect him to cut himself aloof from his environment and lead a life of complete immunity from the local influences.[20]

Over a relatively short period of time the initiatives undertaken to bring closer the two major communities yielded positive results. In fact, a series of speeches[21] was warmly received by both common people and intellectuals and eventually became the forerunner to the *Payāmi-Insāniyat* (Message of Humanity). It would be worthwhile to examine the thematic significance contained in these speeches in relation to Shaykh Nadwi's pursuit of a new social order. The following points deserve special mention:

- An incorrigible growth of anarchy in the country.
- Widespread corruption and cronyism in the society.
- Selfish interests and disintegration of moral values.

---

[19] *Ibid.*
[20] Nadwi, *Muslims in India*, 67-68.
[21] Nadwi, *Kārwān*, vol. 1, 397-99.

As a remedy to the above malaise, society should reassess its role as an agent of change. This can only be possible if the starting point is linked to the heart. It is the repository of moral values and consciousness. Unless moral regeneration is fully implemented, no society will be free from the vices that mirror a peculiar form of *Jāhiliyyah*. Moreover, it was also the temperament of the Prophets to remove the vices of the heart in order to reconstruct an ideal society.[22]

A brief overview about the interfaith initiative is intended to clarify the mission of the *Payām* (discussed elsewhere in the volume). Needless to add, the proliferation of faith- based groups had indirectly challenged Islam about its *tawhīd* doctrine and comprehensive code of life. In other words, these groups sought to synthesise religious expressions of all faiths as universal truths. By contrast, any attempt to reconcile the irreconcilable truth clearly violated the mission of Islam. South Asia had witnessed the syncretic Islam called *Dīn-i Ilāhī* promulgated by the Mughal Emperor Akbar, which if it had gone unchecked would have had grave consequences for Muslims in this populous region. Akbar attempted to combine elements of different religions and culture to evolve a new eclectic system where Islam no longer enjoyed a pivotal role as the only faith of salvation.

Shaykh Nadwi proposed an alternative model to the interfaith discourse. The bedrock of the *Payām* was its recurrent theme of the moral regeneration of humanity. It also suggested the possibility that people from different faiths could articulate and promote the core values that serve as a thread to bind humanity to a common cause. Shaykh Nadwi was not averse to this form of conversation which reflected the message of the Prophets. Social upliftment and meaningful changes in the lives of communities, in his estimation, also pointed out the unity of purpose with clearly-defined goals. In respect of a social order, his formulation stood apart from several Muslim organisations pursuing a utopian Islamic state in South Asia.

Reform of Muslim Society

It is an undeniable fact that Muslims were not immune from the influence of syncretic practices which were deemed un-Islamic by the *'ulama*. Shaykh Nadwi too deplored the fact that *shirk*-laden (polytheistic) practices had

---

[22] Nadwi, *Ta'meer-i-Insāniyat* (Karachi, n.d.), 19-21.

Chapter VI
Da'wah: New Horizons

crept into the very fabric of Muslim society. He was uncompromising in his criticism of these harmful beliefs and practices. However, he adopted a balanced approach to issues of secondary importance (*furu'*) and avoided theological hairsplitting, which in his view was detrimental to the unity of the *ummah*.

In Shaykh Nadwi's estimation, Muslims have been facing a crisis of confidence and the challenges confronting them do not allow them to be trapped in argumentation and controversy. Difference of opinion in *fiqh* and other related issues have continued over the centuries and so have the intellectual debates, which by and large, are peripheral in nature. As a practical measure, Muslims could serve Islam the best by concentrating on matters of fundamental importance. Shaykh Nadwi reiterated that the moral decadence in Muslim society and adoption of un-Islamic practices were real concerns for effective remedial action.

In the domain of public affairs Shaykh Nadwi chose a course that was best suited for the occasion. The following excerpt from his writings reflect his incisive assessment of Muslim society:

> It is against the spirit of the *shari'ah* and a gross violation of morality to condone extravagance in weddings and other social functions. The lavish spending and overindulgence displayed by the wealthy class is in stark contrast to the economic plight faced by a large segment of the Muslim *ummah*. The impoverished and disadvantaged Muslims have to eke out an existence. They do not possess the basic resources to lead a decent life. Their children do not possess the means to purchase textbooks and pay for their school fees. Their lives and security hang in the balance - in short, they lead dismal lives.[23]

Mention may be made of Shaykh Nadwi's *islāhī* lectures in the magazine *Ta'mir-i Insāniyat*. By and large, these focus on the maladies plaguing the Indian society. According to Shaykh Nadwi, egoism has evolved into a religious phenomenon with the result that worldly success is measured by the fulfilment of carnal desires and selfish interest. No religion is free from its baneful influence. It is a scourge which has caused indescribable misery and affliction to mankind.[24]

---

[23] *Ta'meer-i-Hayāt*, Special Number, 91-96.
[24] Nadwi, *Ta'meer-i-Insāniyat*, 145-46.

In his pursuit of a new social order for both Muslims and Hindus, Shaykh Nadwi could not escape the scathing criticism of dissenting Muslim voices. Their motives were clear: No co-existence was possible with the other faith groups. However, he remained steadfast in his resolve and undeterred by hostile comments pursued a course that he believed would foster better relations between Muslims and other faith groups.

In the Realms of Spirituality

As mentioned in previous chapters, Shaykh Nadwi maintained a spiritual affinity with a number of *mashā'ikh* who were the embodiment of *sharī'ah* and *tasawwuf*. As a result, the fusion between these two dimensions of Islam produced a spate of reformist literature. For example, the *Maktiūbāt*[25] of the Mujaddid as well as writings of the illustrious sufi scholars reinforced this fusion. In the South Asian setting, this reformist vision was pivotal to the establishment of *madāris*[26] whose teachers were also distinguished spiritual guides.

During the early twentieth century the fissure between these two complementary Islamic dimensions began to alienate *mashā'ikh* and intellectuals on grounds of irreconcilable ideological differences. In reaction to this schism, the *Salafiyyah* vigorously launched an anti-*tasawwuf* tirade in the name of the *salaf* authenticity. Unsurprisingly, the battle of ideologies blurred a proper assessment of *tasawwuf*. In all fairness *tasawwuf* did not always present a pristine notion of Islam. Quite often, its arbitrary interpretation of Islamic doctrines and convoluted views compromised the *sharī'ah*. As a result of this laxity, the gulf widened between the Islamists represented by a spectrum of scholars and intellectuals on the one hand and the *'ulama* who typified the sufi hierarchy on the other.[27]

Shaykh Nadwi's comments about the semantic usage of the term *tasawwuf* merits attention. According to him, critics of the sufi movement find it

---

[25] For a discussion on the Mujaddid's thought and reformatory effort, see Fazlur Rahman, *Selected Letters of Shaykh Ahmad Sirhindi* (Lahore, 1984).

[26] The following books cover a detailed account of the *Shari'ah-tasawwuf* nexus: Muhammad Abdul Haq Ansari, *Sufism and Shari'ah* (Leicester, 1986); Mahmood Ahmad Ghazi, *Islamic Renaissance in South Asia 1707-1867* (Islamabad, 2002); Barbara Metcalf, *Islamic Revival in British India: Deoband 1860-1900* (Princeton, 1982).

[27] The Ahl-i Hadīth movement with sectarian orientation vehemently opposed the integration of *tasawwuf* into the *sharī'ah* paradigm. See Zaman, *The 'Ulama in Contemporary Islam*, 23-24.

acceptable if it falls under the rubric of the *shari'ah* terminology. For example, if the term *tasawwuf* is replaced by the Quranic term *tazkiyah* (self-purification) then it will be endorsed by certain segments of scholarly tradition. However, it would be an oversimplification to suggest that the whole gamut of sufi practice and tradition would be palatable to them. In several of his biographical accounts (*tadhkirah*), Shaykh Nadwi was able to demonstrate that the *shari'ah* and *tasawwuf* merged seamlessly over the centuries and was the confluence of Islamic spirituality. His *Rabbāniyyah lā Rahbāniyyah*[28] is a forceful presentation of *tasawwuf* rooted in the *shari'ah* setting. In another place, he succinctly remarks:

> Their (sufi) concept of the actual purpose of *tasawwuf* is that it is essentially the sincerity of desiring Allah's pleasure. This entails reformation of character, honest dealings, development of a balanced personality, self-control, giving preference to others, etc. If these are not achieved then all this effort is synonymous to a person who works all day long trying to move a mountain with a piece of straw.[29]

This view is supported by the prominent intellectual, Professor Syed Naquib Al-Attas that *tasawwuf* is the practice of the *shari'ah* at the level of *ihsān*.[30] Shaykh Zakariyyah also remarks that even if the term *tasawwuf* poses a problem to critics then it would be naïve to discredit it on the basis of semantics. He argues that other sciences were developed and incorporated into the primary sources of Islam in the early centuries of its history. One may refer to the vast corpus of ancillary sciences associated with *'ulūm al-hadīth* to appreciate its systematic formulation. Likewise, *tasawwuf* has not essentially strayed from the path of *tazkiyah* and *ihsān*.[31]

An alternative interpretation of *tasawwuf* is illustrated by the Quranic term *tazkiyah*. Several scholars have advanced their views that this term is the cornerstone to the Islamic path of self-development. In his work *Tazkiyah-i Nafs*, Mawlana Amin Ahsan Islāhī states:

> If one is not fully committed to self-reform, even the best guidance

---

[28] Nadwi, *Rabbāniyyah la Rahbāniyyah* (Karachi, n.d.).
[29] Muhammad Iqbal, *The Achievement of Love: The Spiritual Dimension of Islam* (Vermont, 1987), 10.
[30] Wan Mohammad Nor Wan Daud, *The Educational Philosophy and Practice of Syed Muhammad Naquib Al-Attas* (Kuala Lumpur, 1998), 394.
[31] A detailed discussion on *tasawwuf* appears in Muhammad Zakariyyah, *Aap Beti (Autobiography)*, vol. 6 (Lenasia, 2007), 420-73.

cannot avail him. There is no better guidebook than the Quran. However, it benefits only those who resolve to act upon its guidance. It does not do any good to those who praise its eloquence or other literary excellence, but are not prepared to act upon its guidance.[32]

Thus, *tazkiyah* and *tasawwuf* are interchangeable terms and it is the different perspectives that give rise to the multitude of doubts and reactions.

Shaykh Zakariyyah, a contemporary of Shaykh Nadwi and also his mentor, had some interesting observations about the nature of *sulūk* (spiritual journey). He writes:

It is the prescription of the spiritual guides that the *murīd* (novice) will not be able to infuse his action with fervour or cleanse his heart of spiritual malaise unless he devotes his time and energy to the company of luminaries of Islam.[33]

Shaykh Nadwi expressed a similar view: "Our activities and actions - in fact, our daily routine must be imbued with the correct intention *(niyyah).*"[34] He lamented the fact that a spiritual personality like Shaykh Zakariyyah as "a speaking picture, and a living, breathing image" is of an age now past.

Shaykh Nadwi's own spiritual profile reaffirms the primacy of authentic *tasawwuf*. Mawlana 'Abdul Qādir Rāipūrī, according to Shaykh Nadwi, was an enlightened personality and whose versatility and spiritual stature was a source of inspiration for the *ummah*. These sentiments were echoed by Shaykh Zakariyyah and Mawlana Nu'māni in their respective writings.[35] Shaykh Nadwi was pprofoundly influenced by Mawlana Rāipūrī whom he regarded as his Rumi.[36] The poignant description of the Mawlana's towering

---

[32] Cited in Abdur Rashid Siddique, *Tazkiyah: The Path to Self-Development* (Leicester, 2004), 66-67.
[33] For a comprehensive biography of Mawlana 'Abdul Qadir Rāipūrī, see Nadwi, *Sawanih Hazrat Mawlana 'Abdul Qādir Rāipūrī* (Lahore, 1977), Muhammad Husayn Ansari, *Hayāt-i Tayyibah* (Lahore, 1984).
[34] Nadwi, *Hadhrat Shaikh al-Hadīth Mawlana Muhammad Zakariyyah* (Lucknow, 1982), p. 106.
[35] See Muhammad Zakariyyah, *Aap Beti* (Karachi, 1988); Muhammad Manzur Nu'māni, *Tahdith-i Ni'mat* (Lucknow, 1997).
[36] The symbolism of Rumi is accentuated in the writings of poets like Iqbal. Shaykh Nadwi as a literary critic employs this symbol to convey the influence of *Mathnawi* in shaping his intellectual and spiritual worldview. For details on the archetypal symbol of Rumi, see Afzal Iqbal, *Life and Works of Rumi* (Lahore, 1978).

Chapter VI
Da'wah: New Horizons

personality and his spiritual perfection are recounted in the *Kārwān*. He was inducted as a *khalifah* in the four spiritual orders[37] by Mawlana Rāipūrī in 1948. In addition, his guidance and supervision had a lasting impact on Shaykh Nadwi's works.

Several scholars from the Arab world paid glowing tributes to Shaykh Nadwi's unassuming personality and his tireless efforts to impart the lessons of spiritual reformation. Shaykh Qardāwī, for example, described him as a *Rabbani*, who detached from worldly comforts and was an activist striving relentlessly to serve humanity. His articulation of *tasawwuf* or *tazkiyah* received tacit endorsement from Islamist figures like the Ikhwān in Syria. Shaykh Nadwi argued that technicalities linked to this discipline should not be an obstacle to appreciate its positive contributions to the Islamic resurgence. He observes:

> Had these genuine sufis not been there the Muslim society would have collapsed long ago. Materialism would have struck a fatal blow to faith and conviction. Hearts would have been devoid of any link with Allah, life with spirituality and society with morals. Sincerity and sense of accountability would have been forgotten, giving rise to numerous spiritual ailments afflicting the heart and self. Worse, there would have been no cure to these. People would have been prompted all along by greed and lust.

Dimensions of Spirituality

It is generally agreed that *tasawwuf* works within the ambit of the *shari'ah*. Over the centuries the sufi orders developed their own hierarchy for the purpose of guiding a *murīd* to the desired level of *ihsān* (spiritual perfection). A closer study of Shaykh Nadwi's *Rabbāniyyah* offers interesting insights into his elaboration of *tasawwuf*. The *mashā'ikh* and scholars with different temperaments and affiliations to their respective sufi orders have made sterling contributions to the spread of teachings of Islam.

---

[37] The unitary representation of *tasawwuf* as envisaged by the *'ulama* in the Wali-Allah tradition is found in the merger of the four *silsilah*s: Qādiri, Chishti, Suhrāwardi and Naqshbandi.

Sayyid Abul Hasan Nadwi: Life and Legacy
Chapter VI

In the Company of Spiritual Guides

In the realms of spirituality Shaykh 'Abdul Qādir Rāipūrī features prominently. It was in his company and charismatic personality that Shaykh Nadwi drew immense benefit. He seldom spoke in the assemblies of his spiritual guide and made passing remarks to the topics under discussion when prompted to share his thoughts. Of course, there was a remarkable degree of spiritual progress for Shaykh Nadwi on account of his total obedience to his spiritual mentor. This is evident in his interaction with his *murīds*. There was no ceremonial display when he was deputed to initiate would-be aspirants in the Naqshbandi order. He, however, focused on the importance of *tawhīd* and the *sharī'ah-tarīqah* amalgam. At the same time, he also cautioned them against technicalities which tended to give cold comfort to the warm embrace of *tasawwuf*.

In his personal life Shaykh Nadwi was loath to attribute his rising success to his own efforts. Instead, the nurturing elements of family members and the mentoring of his spiritual guide were given credit for his global profile. His personal motto: ' I am nothing' was cogently expressed in his interaction with the leading figures of the day. If someone related a dream or glad tidings given to him by the Holy Prophet (SAAS) there was a muted silence followed by a reverential pause. Drops of tears crystallised into the unexpressed ecstasy of Shaykh Nadwi in response to the glad tidings received. Shaykh Nadwi's autobiography barely makes any reference to particular incidents highlighting his spiritual stature. After his demise in 1999, books and articles were written about his charismatic personality. Although Shaykh Nadwi downplayed incidents that were likely to reveal his levels of spirituality, these incidents inform readers about his *islāhī* efforts. The following incident illustrates the power of spiritual energy (*tasarruf*) which had a life - transforming experience for Sayyid Zahur al-Hasan.

A scion of an aristocratic family, Sayyid Zahur was a government official who took bribes to facilitate the work of the enderpreneurs. During an annual gathering of *tabligh* (*ijtimā*) his gaze inadvertently fell on the presence of Shaykh Nadwi who at the time was deeply engrossed in writing. Sayyid Zahur was instinctively drawn to the gracious presence of Shaykh Nadwi. At the same time, he could not fathom his agitated condition resulting from this momentary gaze. Thereafter, he mustered sufficient courage and approached Shaykh Nadwi to accept him in his spiritual fold. Shaykh Nadwi's reluctance was characteristic of his humility. After much persuasion, he acceded to Sayyid Zahur's insistence. Contrary to the prescribed *dhikr* schedule offered to aspirants, Sayyid Zahur was asked to focus on *du'ā*.

Chapter VI
Da'wah: New Horizons

Sayyid Zahur was overwhelmed with remorse over his past life that unfolded before him. He resolved to make amends by returning his unlawful wealth to its rightful owners even if it meant travelling long distances. Indeed, his Allah- consciousness *(taqwā)* induced him to settle paltry sums of money notwithstanding the inconvenience it caused him. Apart from his impeccable personal life, Sayyid Zahur's prolonged *du'ās* were proverbial. And so were his *islāhī* efforts to root out un-Islamic practices in his community.

In sufi parlance Shaykh Nadwi possessed an aura of spiritual grace which he transferred to Sayyid Zahur that had an enduring effect.

Towards New Horizons

Director of Education: Nadwah

Sayyid Sulayman Nadwi, the illustrious scholar whose lasting fame rests on the *Sirat al-Nabi*, a comprehensive biography of the Prophet (SAAS), was responsible for expanding the academic horizons at Nadwah. Shaykh Nadwi who was appointed as executive member in 1948, served as an assistant director of Nadwah's academic unit. After the demise of Sayyid Sulayman Nadwi in 1953, Shaykh Nadwi was promoted to the position of director, a duty which he carried out with admirable efficiency.[38]

Visits to Islamic Institutions

The students union at Dār al-'Ulūm Deoband invited Shaykh Nadwi in 1954 to address them. His lecture, which later was published as a monograph, dealt with the responsibility of students in the Islamic institutions.

The two journeys to Lahore during the period (1955-56) also reconnected Shaykh Nadwi to his early links with the historic city.[39] At the Jami'ah Salafiyyah, an Ahl-i Hadīth institution of higher Islamic learning, Shaykh Nadwi received a meritorious certificate, which recognised his *dīnī* contribution. The Ahl-i-Hadīth movement had in its initial years extended their support to Sayyid Ahmad Shahid during his mission and their contributions were lauded by Shaykh Nadwi in his historical writings.[40] This tribute also showed Shaykh Nadwi's balanced outlook and unbiased approach that accommodated

---

[38] Nadwi, *Kārwān*, vol. 1, 352.
[39] *Ibid.*, vol. 1, 407-9.
[40] See Nadwi, *Purāne Charāgh*, vol. 2, 280-82 on Shaykh Nadwi's impressions of this distinguished family.

divergent religious viewpoints.[41]

Invitation from Damascus University

Shaykh Nadwi's second visit to Damascus was of importance for two reasons:

- It broadened his intellectual horizon and created opportunities to interact with the leading scholars and *'ulama'* of the day.
- It established his stature as an eminent scholar whose writings were appreciated in the Arab world.

Thus, the invitation by Dr Mustafa Siba'ī,[42] Principal of the *Shari'ah* Faculty in Damascus University, to deliver a series of lectures as a visiting professor confirmed his growing popularity. For Shaykh Nadwi, this invitation from a premier institution was a "singular academic honour." In a similar vein, the letter by Sayyid Manazir Ahsan Gilānī,[43] reaffirmed his scholarly contributions:

> You are leaving for the abode of Ibn Taimiyyah and Ibn Qayyim. Imagine the *'ilmī* gifts you could be sharing with the Indian *'ulama'*. Over the years the celebrated works on *fiqh* by 'Allāmah Shāmī had already reached India. How a great opportunity lies ahead for you to reciprocate this gratitude by presenting your contributions to the Syrians.[44]

The series of lectures delivered in April 1956 at the Damascus University was based on the theme: "The Revivalist Movements in Islamic Thought." Already, *Saviours of Islamic Spirit* (vol.1) facilitated his preparation for this lecture series. In keeping with the theme of the lectures, the reformist spirit of these distinguished luminaries was the focal point of Shaykh Nadwi's lectures. Reform of morals envisioned by Hasan al-Basri for the reconstruction of Muslim society, vigorously championed by Ghazali were the *islāhī* ethos

---

[41] Nadwi, *Kārwān*, vol. 1, 410.
[42] An influential member of the Ikhwān, Dr Sibā'ī was a distinguished scholar. His celebrated work *Al-Sunnah wa Makānatuhā fī al-Islam* (The Position of Sunnah in Islam) has established him as an important scholar in *hadīth* studies.
[43] See Miftahi, Muhammad Zafiruddin, *Hayāt i-Mawlāna Gilānī* (Karachi, 1994).
[44] Nadwi, *Kārwān*, vol. 1, 422.

Chapter VI
Da'wah: New Horizons

of Shaykh Nadwi's lectures. Illustrious scholars like Ustādh Muhammad al-Mubārak and Shaykh Mustafa Ahmad Zarqā' attended these lectures regularly and their unwavering interest was a tribute to Shaykh Nadwi's intellectual status. During his three-month stay in Damascus, Shaykh Nadwi met his old acquaintance, Dr Sa'īd Ramadān,[45] a jurist and editor of *Al-Muslimin* in Geneva, Switzerland.

Shaykh Ahmad Harun al-Hajjār: Sufi Par Excellence

Shaykh Harun al-Hajjār, a devout shaykh who was acknowledged as an authority on the mystical doctrines of the Great Master Shaykh Muhyi al-Dīn ibn 'Arabi,[46] conducted his *majlis* (session) in the month of Ramadān. The atmosphere possessed eclectic elements of spirituality and joviality displayed by the attendees. This was a "discernible departure from the *majālis* (sessions) conducted by our *mashā'ikh* in the subcontinent."[47] Shaykh Nadwi's personal assessment of Shaykh al-Hajjār is revealing:

[After] the *majlis* the shaykh established a close affinity with me. Although he socialised very little, he used to call at my home quite regularly. On many occasions he made personal arrangements for me, his disciples and close associates to visit Damascus' famous recreational facilities. The more intimate I became with him the greater was my awareness of his strong bond with Allah. As a matter of fact, he did not possess any formal qualification and was presumably familiar with elementary knowledge of Arabic, yet he would elaborate with relative ease about the complex doctrines with particular reference to Ibn 'Arabi's interpretation of mystical doctrines. Even after my departure from Damascus we maintained regular correspondence. His disciples continued mailing me his spiritual pearls of wisdom (*malfuzāt*) culled from the various *majālis*. A happy augury was that my close association with the shaykh paved the way for many enlightened persons to be spiritually affiliated to him. Special mention must be made of Dr Mustafa Siba'i who entered into

---

[45] Tariq Ramadān's brief reference to his father's contribution in exile is discussed in his book, *Islam, the West and the Challenges of Modernity* (Leicester, 2001), vii-xiv.
[46] For an understanding of Ibn Arabi's mystical doctrines, the following works may be consulted: M.M. Sharif, *A History of Muslim Philosophy*, vol. I (Karachi, 1980). Claudia Addas, *Quest for the Red Sulphur* (Cambridge, 1993).
[47] Nadwi, *Kārwān*, vol. 1, 426.

his spiritual fold. The devotion that he bore for the shaykh is evident from his will requesting that he be buried beside him.[48]

Two Radio Lectures

The multifarious activities during Shaykh Nadwi's stay in Damascus included a request by the Damascus radio station to present two lectures. He chose to speak on the topic: "To the Syrians." The issues highlighted were his personal impressions as well as the emotional, religious and spiritual connection that Syria has held for the Muslims. At the same time, he referred to his childhood recollections of Syria and their formative influence on his life. Reference was then made to the great personalities among whom were the leading *Sahābah* and great leaders of Islam whose sacred presence in Syria had made it an important Islamic city. These were the factors that motivated the Muslim world to recount the glorious heritage of Syria. The Syrians were reminded that the revival of their immemorial past could not be achieved by irrelevant emphasis on nationalism or exaggerated veneration of linguistic and cultural chauvinism. Instead, this position could only be secured by setting unspecific goals and objectives and contributing selfless services to mankind. In this strain, Syria could progress by cooperating with the West in diffusing the message of *imān* and then assimilating the expertise and technical sciences the West had to offer. This relationship of reciprocity would be beneficial to both Syria and the West.

The second lecture revolved around the theme: "Muhammad Iqbal in Madinah." Shaykh Nadwi quoted extensively from Iqbal's famous *Armaghān i-Hijāz* (Gift from Hijaz). This soul-stirring and rapturous ecstasy couched in these verses of Iqbal's imaginative journey to Madinah are also expressive of his unrestrained love for Muhammad bin- Qasim Thaqafī, through whose efforts Islam reached India. He was a capable General of the Umayyad Caliph, Walid bin 'Abdul Mālik whose seat of authority was firmly established in Damascus. In sum, the message highlighted the age-long services rendered by this historic city for which Muslims could be justly proud.[49]

Visit to Lebanon and Turkey

During his short break from his public lectures in Damascus, Shaykh Nadwi made a brief visit to Lebanon and Turkey. He was honoured to meet

---

[48] *Ibid.*, vol. 1, 427-28.
[49] See Nadwi, *Pathway to Medina* (Lucknow, 1982).

Chapter VI
Da'wah: New Horizons

the influential *mashā'ikh* and scholars in Beirut, among whom was the famous scholar, Muhammad Asad whose masterpiece *Road to Mecca*[50] was due to be published. En route to Turkey, Shaykh Nadwi spent a night in Aleppo and at the request of Ikhwān delivered an inspirational address. The theme focused on the growing menace of Arab nationalism and its tragic consequences on Muslim unity. Shaykh Nadwi's critique of Arab nationalism was contrasted with the Indian Muslims' contributions to *da'wah* in a country dominated by *shirk*. According to him, it would be "one of the ironies of history that the Arabs who had given India the message of Islam were now plunging headlong into the culture of *Jāhiliyyah* (Ignorance)."[51]

Zaman, in his analysis of Shaykh Nadwi's rhetoric of Indian Islam as being autonomous, does not deny the Arab factor. However, it was a bold assertion that the Arabs are clearly culpable for their loss of faith: It has led to their own decline in the world. Although others will continue to persevere in their devotion to Islam, the Arabs have nevertheless let them down.[52]

Turkey: Land of Contrast

Shaykh Nadwi's evocative description of Turkey and its glorious past was contrasted with the political realities the country was facing. He commented:

This was Turkey which conjured up splendid images of its enduring history: The sacred blood that flowed to establish its hegemony; the defenders of the honour of the Muslim world; the protectors against the onslaught of the menacing Crusaders; the custodian of the *Haramayn*, the bastion for Arab countries; protector of all sacred precincts - in short, all these attributes were representative of Turkey's magnificence. We also saw the stately castles and regal paraphernalia of this majestic country. By contrast, there were ominous signs of Ataturk's modernising campaign through his relentless efforts to obliterate all traces of the Islamic and Arabic influences that were firmly impressed in the culture of

---

[50] For a biographical account on Muhammad Asad and his autobiography *Road to Mecca*, see Chughta'ī Ikram, *Muhammad Asad: Europe's Gift to Islam* 2 vols. (Lahore, 2006). The obituary of Asad by Shaykh Nadwi in *Al-Minbar Monthly* (Lahore, 2003) provides concise details on the translation of *Road to Mecca* into Urdu.

[51] Nadwi, *Kārwān*, vol. 1, 432.

[52] Muhammad Qasim Zaman, *The 'Ulama in Contemporary Islam*, 165.

the Turkish nation. Furthermore, his shameful action of changing the alphabet paved the way for the Turks to be alienated from the mainstream of Islamic civilisation and consequently be deprived of the rich treasures of Islamic learning.[53]

The splendid past to which Shaykh Nadwi refers is the Ottoman Caliphate. It was Muhammad the Conqueror who was honoured to conquer Constantinople at a relatively young age of twenty four years. His military feats saw Islam's penetration into the heartland of Europe for the purpose of da'wah. The Caliphate also witnessed turbulent periods during its prolonged rule over Muslim and non-Muslim countries. However, it always prized the independence of Palestine largely, because Al-Quds was considered the third holiest site in Islam. Even during its political decline the Caliphate under Abdul Hamid Khan II did not yield to the Zionist notorious campaign of wrestling control of Palestine.

Shaykh Nadwi refers to the following incident to illustrate the Caliphate's total devotion to the Palestinian cause:

Mufti Amin Al-Husayni mentioned to Shaykh Nadwi that a Zionist delegation called on Abdul Hamid Khan with the sole intention of persuading him to relinquish the Palestinian cause. Turkey at the time experienced financial crisis on account of several political factors. The delegation offered to alleviate its financial plight on the condition that Palestine became a Zionist state. The Sultan seething with anger retorted:

I will not give an inch of land!

He reproached his advisers for accommodating the 'despicable' delegation.

Shaykh Nadwi's critique of Ataturk's policies provoked mixed response when he returned to India. Muslim sentiments in support of Ataturk's policies, particularly by several intellectuals and organisations, were prompted by the entrenched presence of colonialism. In this respect they regarded Ataturk as the saviour of the Turkish nation and the defender of Islam. By contrast, Shaykh Nadwi was able to show that the policies Ataturk pursued were ominous signs of intellectual and spiritual genocide. He referred to the pertinent remark of the philosopher-historian, Arnold Toynbee regarding the change of alphabet in respect of the Turkish nation:

---

[53] Nadwi, *Do Hafte Turkey Men* (Karachi, 1992).

Chapter VI
Da'wah: New Horizons

Nowadays there is no need to burn books or huge libraries. The change of alphabet of a nation is sufficient to put the storehouse of knowledge out of currency.[54]

World Muslim Congress

The establishment of the *Mu'tamar al-'Ālam al-Islāmī* (World Muslim Congress)[55] in 1956 proposed the mobilisation of a united "Muslim front" to collectively address issues confronting the Muslim *ummah*. Notable scholars like Shaykh Nadwi, Mufti Muhammad Shafi (Pakistan), Dr Muhammad Natsir (Indonesia), Mufti Muhammad Amin al-Husayni (Palestine) were delegates at the conference. Shaykh Nadwi delivered an inspiring lecture on the Palestinian issue. For him "[it] required a fresh reappraisal of the Muslims' indifference and lethargic response to the plight of the Palestinians. Now there was a greater need to galvanise the Muslims to display a genuine concern, which is the only solution to this growing problem."[56]

A positive development during Shaykh Nadwi's stay in Damascus was the publication of his father's Arabic work, *Al-Thaqāfat al-Islāmiyyah fi al-Hind*[57] by the premier academic institution *Lajnat al-'Ilmi*. Its membership was exclusively limited to personalities with exceptional intellectual credentials. Shaykh Nadwi was appointed as an executive member in recognition of his impressive literary contribution.

Baghdad: Scholars' Paradise

Shaykh Nadwi's itinerary to Baghdad included his first spiritual journey to the mausoleum of Shaykh 'Abdul Qādir Jilānī eponymous founder of the Qādiriyyah order. Mausoleums of other luminaries to which he paid respect

---

[54] For a detailed discussion on Ataturk's un-Islamic policies, see Nadwi, *Western Civilisation, Islam and Muslims*, pp. 49-60.
[55] Dr. Inamullah Khan of Pakistan was a leading figure of the Mu'tamar who took an active part in mobilising Muslim responses to issues affecting Muslims worldwide.
[56] Details of the article are contained in Nadwi's *Al-Muslimūn wa Qadiyat al-Filistin* (Lucknow, n.d), 158-94.
[57] This publication was translated into English as *India during Muslim Rule* (Lucknow, 1977).

were the famous saint, Maʿrūf Karkhi, Imām Abu Hanifa and the famous *Sahābi*, Salmān al-Farisī.

This journey also reunited Shaykh Nadwi with his teacher, 'Allāmah al-Hilālī after a prolonged absence of twenty three years.

Conclusion

The *islāhī* concept is evident in Shaykh Nadwi's analysis of issues affecting the Muslim world. In fact, his series of lectures in Damascus University allowed him to give fuller expression to his presentation of the Islamic resurgence and develop his own style of writing for a wider audience of different intellectual backgrounds.

Chapter VII

Islamic Authenticity: Challenges and Opportunities

The hiatus in Shaykh Nadwi's teaching period at Nadwah as a result of his prolonged da'wah in the Middle East was a temporary phase. He returned to his academic pursuit - teaching - and resumed his Sahīh Bukhārī classes.[1] Teaching hadīth was a formidable challenge for him especially when he had to consult the commentaries on Sahīh Bukhārī. The interlinear translation (Arabic to Urdu/Persian) followed by a sharh (commentary) or hāshiyah (notes) were peculiarities to these sources of hadīth studies.[2] Furthermore, the "fine print created a serious difficulty for Shaykh Nadwi following his deteriorating eyesight[3] to have direct access to reading and research. Dictation was the only alternative for his writing purpose. It was in a particular sense a paradox for Shaykh Nadwi that all his major works were written by dictation (imlā).[4] Although no comprehensive works were written by him on hadīth, nevertheless, his attachment to Sahīh Bukhārī is evident from his daily routine of listening to approximately three pages[5] from this celebrated hadīth work. Abu Subhan Nadwi has correctly observed that Shaykh Nadwi's Introductions (muqaddimāt) in Arabic to major works on hadīth are illustrative of his mastery over this discipline.[6]

The hadīth specialists had devoted their lives to the meticulous preservation of the life and actions of the Holy Prophet (SAAS). The evolution of hadīth disciplines shows clearly that it was not developed in a vacuum; rather its structured and rigorous analysis was an unprecedented undertaking. At the core of hadīth studies is the unconditional commitment of Muslims to mould their lives according to the exemplary conduct of the Holy Prophet (SAAS). Shaykh Nadwi's assessment of the reformatory role of

---

[1] For a brief survey on the hadīth literature, especially Bukharī, see M.M. Azami, Studies in Hadīth Methodology and Literature (Indiana, 1977), 87-93.
[2] Islam and the Impact of Print in South Asia is a synoptic overview about the nature of print and its effects on religious change. See Francis Robinson, Islam and Muslim History in South Asia (New Delhi, 2001), 66-103.
[3] Shaykh Nadwi's family's health concerns and the several operations he underwent both locally and abroad have been discussed in Kārwān, vols. 1-2.
[4] Nadwi, Kārwān, vol. 1, 518.
[5] Bilāl 'Abdul Hayy Hasani, Sawanih Mufakkir-i-Islam, 503-4.
[6] Abu Suhbān Zuh al-Quds Nadwi, "Mawlana Shaykh Nadwi aur 'Ilm-i Hadīth" in Al-Qāsim, 327-46. A list of Shaykh Nadwi's Introductions (muqaddimāt) to the hadīth commentaries is provided in this article.

ḥadīth is indicative of his deep study of this foundational source of Islam. He observes:

> The Prophet's *aḥadīth* constitute a source of strength that is full of life, motivating reform and renewal. It has always urged the need to fight corruption and deviation, providing social checks and balances in all Muslim generations and communities. It is the standard by which all deviation, superstition and un-Islamic customs are rejected. It shows the way to maintaining the true path of Islam. Hence, the Prophet's *aḥadīth* represent a basic need of the Muslim community; and they must be verified, recorded and published.[7]

To the critics of *ḥadīth*, Shaykh Nadwi makes a pertinent remark:

> Those who continue to cast doubt on the authenticity of the *ḥadīth* and reject the sunnah fit the image of the old Arab poet in which a deer tries to remove a solid rock by repeatedly hitting it with his horns. The rock remains solidly in place but all that the deer achieves is to injure himself.[8]

In a similar vein, Shaykh Nadwi's *rūḥānī* (spiritual) eminence[9] has not been correctly appreciated, largely because of his scholarly preoccupation. His association with leading *mashā'ikh* like Shaykh Zakariyyah and Mawlana Rāipūrī have already been discussed in the previous chapters.

We now focus on two leading spiritual personalities who had left lasting impressions on Shaykh Nadwi's spiritual growth. The charismatic *'ālim*, Mawlana Wasiyullah Fatehpuri[10] was an accomplished shaykh whose letters to Shaykh Nadwi epitomised his reverence for him. Similarly, Shaykh Muhammad Ya'qub Mujaddidi of Bhopal had unbounded love for Shaykh Nadwi. An important work *Suhbate ba Ahl-i Dil* belonging to the *malfūẓāt*

---

[7] Nadwi, *Ḥadīth Studies and Role: An Introduction* (London, 2005), 64-5.
[8] Ibid., 77
[9] Shaykh Nadwi's contemporary, Mawlana Muhammad Ahmad Phulpuri, expressed his profound love for the former. He once remarked: "Shaykh Nadwi is the beloved of Allah. Therefore, Allah has concealed him (his spiritual attainment) under the cloak of academic pursuits (*'ilm*)."
[10] See Nadwi, *Purāne Charāgh*, vol. 1, 164-81. Shah Wasiyullah's *rūḥānī* (spiritual) rapport with Shaykh Nadwi is summed up in the following statement: "Look at everyone's heart. But look at the pure heart of Shaykh Nadwi. It is a heart that I have never seen in anyone else." See *Qāsimi*, 219.

Chapter VII
Islamic Authenticity: Challenges and Opportunities

genre is marked by its "simplicity and informality, affection and correct diagnosis of the general malady [of the masses] and its appropriate remedy administered by the *mashā'ikh*."[11] To a large extent it is the *malfūzāt* literature that played a pivotal role in the *islāhī* traditions and their writings reflect this reformist spirit. Schimmel notes that through the *malfūzāt*:

[The] Indian sufis, however, carefully collected the dicta of their masters from day to day. These "diaries" constitute a valuable source for our knowledge of life outside the court circles[12].

According to Khalid Ahmad Nizami (d. 1997) the first work on this literary form was Nizāmuddin Awliyā's *Fawā'id al-Fu'ād*, which was "epoch-making as it laid down the foundation of a new genre of mystic literature..."[13]

Shaykh Nadwi sought to realign *tasawwuf* as a lived experience rather than a motley collection of abstract concepts that created a barrier to the essential message of Islam. An instance in point is his emphasis about the twin concept of correct intention and introspection embodied in *ihsān*. According to Shaykh Nadwi, *tasawwuf* devoid of morality tarnished Quranic terms like *tazkiyah* and gave space for deviant sects to speak in its name. The consequences hardly need elaboration as we witness the proliferation of pseudo-sufis presenting a distorted image and incredulous account of its inner dimensions.

In Shaykh Nadwi's personal life, social interaction and righteous conduct were given prominence. Even on matters in which disagreement was unavoidable, he ensured that the family ties or friendship were not compromised. There was the proverbial envelope containing cash which Shaykh Nadwi presented as a gesture of goodwill and camaraderie. For him, enmity bred unproductive traits that alienated a believer from making the self-evaluation of his actions. In Shaykh Nadwi's hierarchy of priorities, earning Allah's pleasure was the path to perfection.

---

[11] Nadwi, *Suhbate ba-Ahl-i-Dil* (Karachi, 1982), 54. Belonging to the Mujaddidi lineage, Shah Ya'qub was a paragon of virtue whose *islāhī* endeavours attracted an array of *murīdīn* from diverse academic and social backgrounds. For a detailed account on the Mujaddidiyyah movement, see Nadwi, *Saviours of Islamic Spirit*, vol. 3.
[12] Annemarie Schimmel, *Mystical Dimensions of Islam* (Chapel Hill, 1975), 356.
[13] For a detailed discussion, see Bruce Lawrence, *Nizam Ad-Din Awliya: Morals for the Heart* (New York, 1992), 3 -60.

Qadianism

A brief survey of Shaykh Nadwi's writings (1939-58) reveals a strong and inseparable link with *da'wah* and *islāh*. Polemical writings (*munāzarah*)[14] were absent in his literary works; instead, he undertook comparative studies regarding un-Islamic sects by employing tools of critical objectivity.

Qadianism: A Critical Study[15] was his first critique about a deviant religious movement. As a marked departure from his writings in which the theme of *da'wah* was emphasised, Shaykh Nadwi gave the rationale for writing this important work:

> Towards the end of December 1957, and in the beginning of January 1958, an International Islamic Conference was held in Lahore under the auspices of the Punjab University. A large number of distinguished and noted scholars of the Muslim world and Western countries took part. The scholars who had come from Egypt, Syria and Iraq to participate in the conference showed considerable keenness to collect correct information about the fundamental beliefs and doctrines of Qadianism, the well-known religious movement of India and Pakistan.
>
> As the writer's mental framework was that of a student of history, he undertook this intellectual journey by meticulously studying the movement's evolution. His observations, therefore, moved along the lines through which Qadianism had passed during its course of development. This approach helped him to grasp the real nature of the Qadiani movement, its gradual growth, and its motivating factors.
>
> He delved deep into the writings of the founder of this movement, Mirza Ghulam Ahmad Qadiani. It is through the primary sources that he has tried to arrive at unprejudiced conclusions in respect of the message, the movement and the practical achievements of Qadianism. The result of this study has been published in the form of *Al- Qādiyānī wa al-Qādiyāniyat* in Arabic.[16]

---

[14] The rhetorical writings and lectures are analysed by Zaman in the chapter, "Refashioning Identities", *The 'Ulama in Contemporary Islam*, 111-43.

[15] Originally written in Arabic *al-Qadiyānī wa al-Qadiyāniyat* was translated into English by Zafar Ishaq Ansari, *Qadianism: A Critical Study* (Lucknow, 1974).

[16] Nadwi, *Qadianism: A Critical Study* (Lucknow, 1974), iii-iv. For a concise discussion on *Qadianism*, see Abul A'la Mawdudi. *The Qadiani Problem* (Lahore, n.d.).

Chapter VII
Islamic Authenticity: Challenges and Opportunities

Apart from its heterodox beliefs, Qadianism employed ambiguous terms to re-define the Finality of Prophethood, which is the cornerstone of Islamic belief (*'aqīdah*). Its motive was unambiguous: To invest its founder, Mirza Ghulam Ahmad with the mantle of Prophethood. Iqbal, who was a poet of rare insight and had also studied the Qadiani movement, remarked about its deviant beliefs as explained by Shaykh Nadwi:

> I consider Iqbal's defence of Islam as a grace of Allah - a manifestation of the Quranic verse: "Allah's are the hosts of the heavens and the earth." Had Iqbal been in two minds at that time or hesitated in countering Qadianism, it would have become extremely difficult to redeem the younger generation from the snare of Qadianism. It was a blessing from Allah that Iqbal was very clear in his mind about this menace and he made a valuable contribution in combatting it at the intellectual level.[17]

In another work, Iqbal describes the motives of imposters like the Qadiani founder as:

> A class of "apostles" whose sole ministry is to glorify, by the force of seductive language at large, all that is ignoble and ugly in the life of their people. These "apostles" clothe despair in the glaring garments of hope, undermine the traditional values of conduct and thus destroy the spiritual virility of those who happen to be their victims.[18]

A month after the publication of *Qadianism*, the leadership of the movement responded vehemently to its contents. The polemical tone and disparaging remarks against Shaykh Nadwi were a propaganda ploy to undermine his critique about this deviant movement. Against this volatile background, the book was widely received in the Arab world and within a few years was translated into several major languages. There was no doubt that Qadianism

---

[17] Muhammad Iqbal, *Six Lectures on the Reconstruction of Religious Thought in Islam* (Lahore, 1978), 176-77. Cf. Nadwi, *Islamic Concept of Prophethood* (Lucknow, 1976), 151-88. The chapter is an exposition on the Finality of Prophethood and its significant role in preserving Islam in its pristine form.
[18] Nadwi, *The Final Prophet and the Perfect Religion* (Lucknow, n.d), 21.

received a huge setback in its dubious outreach project of spreading its mission in the Middle East and other Muslim countries. Its base remains in Pakistan while it continues to operate in certain countries under the patronage of governments harbouring Islamophobic agendas.[19]

A satirical expose on the Mirza's creed and sinister plots is graphically examined in *The Disciple of Dajjāl*. The author describes the Qadianis as crafty salesmen who deviously offer ludicrous explanations to their defender's claims of being a Prophet. The variations of Prophethood are a futile attempt by his followers to invest him with an aura of divinity. Moreover, the hardcore disciples like Hakim Nuruddin and Khwājah Kamāluddīn unreservedly supported his "sublime" status. In response to the grave dangers posed by the sect to the Finality of Prophethood, resolutions were passed by Muslim countries declaring them as non-Muslims.

Academy of Islamic Research and Publications

The lacuna of forceful Islamic literature written in literary idiom and compatible with the needs and aspirations of the modern world was an issue of pressing urgency for Shaykh Nadwi. As early as 1958 he had edited the esteemed Arabic journal *Al-Muslimīn* while Sa'īd Ramadān had gone to Germany to complete his doctorate in Islamic law.[20] An important monograph *The New Menace and its Answer*[21] was serialised in the journal and was widely distributed in the Arab world.

In 1959 the Academy of Islamic Research and Publications was established.

Aims and Objectives

- To produce healthy and forceful literature which may adequately convey the message of Islam.
- To strengthen the roots of faith in the minds and hearts of the Muslims.
- To provide a fitting answer to the moral unrest, spiritual frustration and scepticism that are sweeping the world as a natural consequence of the grossly materialistic thought and civilisation

---

[19] Nasrullah Khan, *Qādianiyat: Mutāla'at wa Jā'izāt* (Islamabad, 2002), 156- 60.
[20] Ramadan's dissertation was published as *Islamic Law: Its Scope and Equity* (1970) which is an important contribution to Islamic law.
[21] This monograph was originally written in Arabic *Riddatu'n wa lā Abā Bakr lahā* (Lucknow, 1959).

Chapter VII
Islamic Authenticity: Challenges and Opportunities

of the West.
- To stem the tide of apostasy and atheism which constitute a menace to the Islamic faith, ideology and way of life.[22]

Since its establishment the Academy's literature has maintained an impressive record of intellectual standards and has published Shaykh Nadwi's works in Arabic, Urdu, English and Hindi.

Aligarh Muslim University

The history of Aligarh Muslim University (AMU) has been extensively examined in the context of its position as the premier institution of Muslim learning.

The British rule had inflicted atrocities against Muslims whom they saw as principal conspirators to the abortive 1857 uprising. Sayyid Ahmad Khan, founder of the AMU, witnessed the tragic turn of events against Muslims. He believed that education had a redemptive role in extricating Muslims from their socioeconomic plight. To this end, the AMU (formerly Oriental Anglo College) was established.

According to Sayyid Ahmad, the intellectual and social upliftment of Muslims was only possible if ignorance was removed through a structured and pragmatic system of education. His proposed vision of educational reforms was initially met with scepticism by Islamic institutions on account of his perceived modernist leanings. Amid the storm of criticism and *kufr* bashing, he vigorously pushed ahead with his visionary educational policy and even endured financial hardship and budgetary constraints. Of course, there was always a chorus of dissenting voices that opposed his sincere intentions of relieving the Muslim *ummah* from the heavy burden of their dismal lives under the British colonialism.

The evolution of the AMU was synonymous with Sayyid Ahmad's spirit of self-sacrifice. According to Nawab Muhsin al Mulk who collaborated with Syed Ahmad in collecting funds for the nascent institution, the latter had dedicated his life to serve the cause of Indian Muslims by promoting their distinct Islamic identity. The institution was, therefore, a symbol of his unwavering commitment for generations to come.[23]

---

[22] http://www.nadwatululama.org/academy1.htm (accessed on 4 July 2017).
[23] On the history of the AMU and its founder, Sir Sayyid Ahmed Khan, the following books may be consulted: Khaliq Ahmad Nizami, *Secular Tradition at Aligarh Muslim University* (Delhi, 1991); J.M. Baljon, *The Reform and Religious Ideas of*

Shaykh Nadwi representing the Nadwah's standpoint on the AMU, consistently maintained a balanced outlook towards this institution in its efforts to retain its Muslim character. He noted:

> The great Aligarh movement whose destiny Sir Syed guided with conspicuous sincerity and ability for about half a century was successful in a considerable way in filling the educational and economic void created in Indian Muslim society with the collapse of the Mughal Empire and the establishment of the British rule.... The movement gave to the community a fair number of highly accomplished young men, writers, thinkers, journalists and politicians who spearheaded the Khilafat movement and played a role worthy of their glorious past in the national struggle for independence.[24]

In the aftermath of the Partition in 1947 and in a relatively short period, the AMU was relegated to a minority status. This arbitrary move posed a danger to the very ideals for which it was established. As a result of this transformation the AMU became vulnerable to secular influences, which again threatened to erode its objectives. Therefore, Shaykh Nadwi's participative role and his public lectures to protect its identity and also promote its cause must be examined in this historical context.

Da'wah Travels: New Horizons

We now turn to Shaykh Nadwi's *da'wah* activities in two countries, Burma (Myanmar) and Kuwait. The maturity of his intellectual experience and inner intuition (*basīrat*) come to the fore in his series of lectures.

Burma: Prediction of Doom

Nadwah as a nascent institution had experienced severe budgetary constraints and began to look abroad to solicit financial assistance. Burma (Myanmar) had over the decades attracted a large contingent of Indian Muslim merchants from the state of Gujarat. A prosperous merchant elite class, they financially supported Muslim institutions in India. Shaykh Nadwi's itinerary was

---

Sir Sayyid Ah- mad Khan (Lahore, 1970).
[24] Nadwi, *Western Civilization, Islam and Muslims*, 74-75.

Chapter VII
Islamic Authenticity: Challenges and Opportunities

primarily *da'wah*-based. His lectures revolved around Muslim responsibilities as *du'āt* (missionaries) and imparting the message of Islam in the Burmese language. One major concern was the volatile political climate in the country. He alerted the Burmese Muslims to the consequences of neglecting *da'wah* among the predominantly Buddhist population.

In this present era, the most important and prime duty is to involve oneself in the effort of *dīn*. This is the great wisdom and strategy for this era. Make a firm resolution to spread the message of Islam for the next ten, twenty years and to safeguard the beliefs of the Muslims. If this country has to come under Buddhist rule, your responsibilities will increase. It is a favour (of Allah) that this country is still not a Buddhist state, but (May Allah forbid) if this country has to turn into a Buddhist state and you do not pay attention and have concern for the well-being of your religion, then nobody will come to your rescue. You will be left neither here nor there. Right now, the government is neither inclined, nor favouring Buddhism; therefore, acquiring knowledge of religion are all your duties. The obligation of the time - if Allah has granted you intelligence, even the slightest of intelligence, is to open your eyes, comprehend and understand that you cannot survive in this country without Islam.[25]

The events in Burma after 1960 presaged the bleak prospects that Shaykh Nadwi highlighted in his lectures. A military revolution and Communist takeover dealt a severe blow to the fate of the minority Muslims. More alarming was the state's intolerance to the viable religious presence. It did not discriminate between Muslims and Buddhists and made every effort to obliterate everything associated with Islam. Another disturbing trend was the opulent lifestyle by the marginalised Muslims. Their indifference to the Quranic dictum and history had a direct bearing on the traumatic happenings in Burma.

In sum, there is a thematic pattern of *da'wah* envisaged by Shaykh Nadwi in countries where Muslims constituted a minority. The Muslims of Burma (Myanmar) were reminded that their greatest asset was *imān* without which their presence in the country was of no consequence. The acquisition of wealth and building of palatial homes were not the index of a vibrant Muslim community. Addressing the Burmese Muslims about the vices that

---

[25] Cited in *Sayyid Abul Hasan Ali Nadwi in Burma* (Azadville, 2009), 24.

had crept in their lives, Shaykh Nadwi's message had a timeless relevance. If Muslims did not invest their energies into building solid foundations of Islamic learning then the prospects of future generations remaining steadfast in *dīn* were bleak. Also, if there was no scholarly temperament or inclination to produce *'ulama'* and *Imāms* then the consequences for Muslims of living as a minority community were extremely grave.

Shaykh Nadwi reiterated the Andalusian tragic history that is applicable to Muslim countries, as well. Muslim rule in Spain inaugurated a period of unprecedented achievement. The towering presence of Islamic landmarks were expressed in architectural beauty, exquisite garden landscapes, magnificent cities and Islamic institutions of symmetrical design. These also symbolised the unmatched progress of Muslims in arts and culture. Notwithstanding their contributions, it did not deter the Christian majority from expelling them from Spain. Muslims had to abandon their paradise and flee from Christian persecution in the form of the Inquisition. Their cherished longing of return drifted away like floating clouds. There was a palpable reason for this traumatic chapter in Muslim history: Muslims had abdicated their duty to impart the message of Islam to non-Muslims. On a sombre note, Shaykh Nadwi expressed his foreboding that the Burmese Muslims were likely to share the Andalusian fate if *da'wah* was not sincerely pursued.

Kuwait

Although Shaykh Nadwi's *da'wah* in Kuwait does not strictly follow the chronological sequence of his eventful life, it is intended to show its overall thematic significance. It must also be noted that it was undertaken after the demise of his brother Dr 'Abdul 'Ali in 1961. Shaykh Nadwi was subsequently appointed Dector of Nadwah. During his term of office, Nadwah built academic relations with international Islamic institutions that were a testimony to its high-profile image.

During his *da'wah* in Kuwait, Shaykh Nadwi focused on the nation's obligation to disseminate the message of Islam. His independent spirit and indifference to royal formalities endeared him to notable scholars of the country. On many occasions his lectures produced rapturous applause from the audience. It was, however, the Quranic message that permeated:

If the disbelieving Quraysh observed the conditions of the present-day Muslims they would lament at the fact that they (Muslims) have hankered after the trappings of the world. We (Quraysh) waged a war

Chapter VII
Islamic Authenticity: Challenges and Opportunities

against Muslims who represented a unique *da'wah*, faith, a way of life. If we had only known their (innermost) desires we would have presented it to them.[26]

The frank assessment in Shaykh Nadwi's speeches and writings extended to royalty, as well. In a letter to Shaykh 'Abdul Salām al-Sālim, Amir of Kuwait, he discussed the issues of progress, leadership and unity of the Arab and Muslim world. Another aspect that was of concern to Shaykh Nadwi in Kuwait was the erection of churches, a move that militated against the *shari'ah*. The letters to Arab leaders served as an indispensable source of information to analyse Shaykh Nadwi's *islāhī* endeavours.

Demise: Dr 'Abdul 'Ali Hasani

Against the background of Shaykh Nadwi's busy *da'wah* schedule mention must be made of his personal tragedy. The poignant details of Dr 'Abdul 'Ali's demise reveals his personal loss and indescribable anguish. "[It] was a tragic event that affected my mature life. The tragedy was compounded by the fact I had been to Raipur and Saharanpur. As a result [of my absence from home], I was not present when he passed away nor could I participate in his *janāzah* (funeral) service."[27] The news of his demise was mourned in South Asia and the Arab world.

Habibul Haq Nadvi has succinctly presented the contributions of Dr 'Abdul 'Ali to the growth and development of Nadwah. He says:

> He [Dr 'Ali] was unanimously appointed as the fifth Rector of Nadwah, on 9 June 1931. He served the institution for about three decades until his death on 7 May 1961. Some of the new features that occurred during his period in the academic field, however, merit brief mention. A new Arabic monthly *Al-Diyā*, edited by Mawlana Mas'ud 'Alam Nadwi, was issued in 1932 and *Al-Nadwah* was re-issued for the third time in 1940 by 'Allāmah Sulayman Nadwi. The stature of the Arabic language and literature was raised when al-Hilāli joined the teaching staff of Nadwah. It was during the splendid period of Dr 'Abdul 'Ali that Nadwah prepared its independent syllabus and its own textbooks, almost on every possible subject. Many of them are taught in Arab and Western universities. It created a new era in the

---

[26] Nadwi, *Kārwān*, vol. 1, 470-71.
[27] See Shams-i Tabriz Khan, *Tārikh Nadwat al-'Ulama*, vol. 2, 454-55.

history of Arabic journalism when the Arabic monthly entitled *Al-Ba'th* and a bi-weekly in Arabic entitled *Al-Rā'id*, were published in addition to *Ta'mir-i Hayāt*, an Urdu fortnightly.[28]

According to Shaykh Nadwi, his brother represented the synthesis of Islamic and modern learning. A medical doctor by profession, Dr 'Abdul 'Ali bore the hallmarks of an enlightened *'ālim* with a strong interest in *da'wah* trends in the Muslim world. Under his mentorship, Shaykh Nadwi honed his *da'wah* skills that enabled him to interact confidently with Muslims of different intellectual temperaments. Again, it was Dr 'Abdul 'Ali who encouraged him to read works on Ibn Taimiyyah and his scholarly contributions in the *tajdīd* domain.

Dr 'Abdul 'Ali possessed a self-effacing and unassuming personality. He followed a rigorous schedule in terms of his position as Rector of Nadwah while also attending to his medical practice. His study of Arabic literature was extensive and he ensured that Shaykh Nadwi had an excellent training in the language. Uncompromising on the essentials of faith, Dr 'Abdul 'Ali maintained a balanced approach to *tasawwuf*, modern education and Western civilisation. To a large extent, Shaykh Nadwi was psychologically prepared by his brother to broaden his *da'wah* horizons.[29]

Educational System: Muslim Response

The Indian Constitution in its efforts to promote communal harmony saw secularism as a neutral leverage to its largely diverse population. However, the educational system which was expected to reflect this secular orientation did not measure up to the marginalised Muslim expectations, because the curriculum was designed to articulate the Hindu- ideology ethos. Therefore, it was no surprise that the rapid rise of aggressive Hindu revivalism spared no efforts to give the curriculum a communal bias.[30] Shaykh Nadwi argued:

[The] basic reader incorporated material that was inundated with Hindu mythology and polytheistic (*shirk*-laden) stories. This [step], if it gained momentum, would negatively impact on the faith,

---

[28] Habibul Haq Nadwi, *Dynamics of Islam* (Durban, 1982), 68-69.
[29] Nadwi, *Hayāt i-'Abdul Hayy*, 387-95.
[30] On the problems of discrimination faced by Indian Muslims, see Barbara Metcalf, "Madrasas in Secular India", in Hefner (ed.), *Schooling Islam*, 87-106.

Chapter VII
Islamic Authenticity: Challenges and Opportunities

practice and pristine *tawhīd* of the corporate Islamic identity of the new Muslim generation. The ignorance and unfamiliarity of their own Islamic faith would make them vulnerable to the polytheistic and syncretic practices of Hinduism.[31]

The climate of uncertainty in schools provoked a definite response from concerned Muslim individuals to redress this imbalance. Under these circumstances, *makātib* (primary Muslim schools) were urged to incorporate secular subjects to their curriculum. This scenario of state prescription assumed alarming proportions in Uttar Pradesh (North India) and for this reason educational reforms commenced in this state.

Dīnī Ta'līmī Council (Religious Education Council)

To meet the challenges of this new threat, the Dīnī Ta'līmī Council was established in 1959. Influential members, like Qādi Muhammad 'Adil 'Abbāsī,[32] a visionary of this movement, Mawlana Manzur Nu'māni and Shaykh Nadwi who was elected President played a pivotal role in the Council. It was committed to expose and refute the harmful impact of the educational policies of the state. For the next forty years under Shaykh Nadwi's inspirational leadership, the Council remained steadfast in steering the destiny of the educational needs of Muslims, particularly in the Uttar Pradesh regions.

The essence of the Council is summed up in the Presidential address of Shaykh Nadwi. Religious education, according to Shaykh Nadwi, has a specific goal and noble purpose that gives orientation to it. In other words, Islamic consciousness is collectively derived from its primary sources: Quran and *sunnah*. The Muslim community in India owes its existence to the enduring legacy of the Prophet Ibrahim which was perpetuated by the timeless message of the Prophet (SAAS). Thus, Islamic teachings are informed by a clearly defined spirit that filters through the daily lives of Muslims.

Shaykh Nadwi clarifies this point further. The council can only achieve its objectives if the stakeholders align the *da'wah* mission to character development. A movement that has conflicting impulses in word and deed cannot succeed in its noble pursuits. Similarly, the Council cannot survive

---

[31] Nadwi, *Kārwān*, vol. 1, 460 (adapted).
[32] For 'Abbāsī's contribution, see Masud al-Hasan 'Uthmāni, *Takbir-i Musalsal* (Lucknow, 2002), pp. 17-54.

on idealism. Practical measures and strategies are needed to redress the biased educational policies imposed by government structures that discriminate against Muslim history and the Urdu language. In respect of the Council's objectives, Shaykh Nadwi remarks:

> We regard the movement (Dīnī Council) as a means for the revival of Islam and the awakening of Islamic consciousness in the peculiar circumstances existing in India.

The articulation of religious and cultural self-expression was a long-term project undertaken by Shaykh Nadwi and other leading figures associated with the Council. This period was marked by political instability and religious volatility. Therefore, it was not surprising that the promotion of ideological teachings was entrenched by the state-driven policies. As a result, Muslim families were exposed to un-Islamic practices that bordered on *shirk*. In fact, the *'ulama* organisations and *da'wah* movements were alarmed by the toxic effects following the arbitrary implementation of the state educational system. Shaykh Nadwi noted:

> The fear of the Muslims that the new educational system is rapidly throwing Muslim children in the lap of religious and intellectual apostasy is not imaginary. The writing has already appeared on the wall. The lethal effects of the system can only be seen in Muslim families who, for one reason or another, could not take special care to keep alive in their midst the basic ideals of Islamic civilisation. The children of these families are progressively accepting the influence of un-Islamic and polytheistic teachings and practices. This obviously is a highly distressing situation for Muslims.

For Shaykh Nadwi the main concern was Muslim non-committal to Islamic education. Qādi 'Abbāsī shared his impressions regarding Shaykh Nadwi's Presidential address at one of the annual educational conferences:

> Shaykh Nadwi read out his Presidential address of which every word struck a chord in the listeners' hearts. He critically examined the prevailing situation of educating the common people and the elite. Also, he emphasised the importance of imparting education for boys and girls. When he finished the address, it had a spell-binding effect on listeners. Everyone realised that they had wasted the precious opportunity of not imparting religious education to their children. They resolved to take up remedial steps in this

Chapter VII
Islamic Authenticity: Challenges and Opportunities

regard.[33]

Islamic University of Madinah

The establishment of the Islamic University in 1961 represented a watershed in the transnational Islamic vision of which Shaykh Nadwi was a vocal supporter. In 1962 Shaykh Nadwi was elected member of the Supreme Executive Council, a position which he held up to 1997.[34]

Shaykh 'Abdullāh bin Bāz, vice-chancellor of the university,[35] extended an invitation to Shaykh Nadwi to deliver a series of lectures as the visiting professor. A collection of eight lectures based on the theme: "Prophethood and Prophets in the Light of the Quran" was later published as *Islamic Concept of Prophethood* in English.

The rationale of these lectures as Shaykh Nadwi wrote was the failure of the Western educated young men "to comprehend the true significance of Prophethood" and their ignorance of the "Godly favours conferred by the Prophets of Allah - on man, his life and intellect, culture and civilisation."[36]

The monetary incentives associated with the academic position Shaykh Nadwi held were the most rewarding. However, Shaykh Nadwi declined any financial considerations in keeping with his independent spirit and unassuming personality. Neeedless to say, the Saudi patronage has over the years shaped the orientation of many religious leaders and organisations advancing its vision of Islam. In other words, monetary incentives imply an unconditional endorsement of the Saudi agenda. There have been subtle insinuations or blatant accusations that Shaykh Nadwi's appointment to several Islamic organisations was intended to promote the interests of the monarchy.[37] This perception is hardly reflected in the series of speeches/lectures delivered by Shaykh Nadwi during the crucial period of Saudi Arabia's transformation. Contrary to this assumption, Shaykh Nadwi's

---

[33] See *Takbir-i Musalsal* for a conspectus of Shaykh Nadwi's Presidential addresses.
[34] According to 'Abbās Nadwi, Shaykh Nadwi's membership of the Executive Council was permanent. It was only after 1997 when the Executive Committee was dissolved that Shaykh Nadwi's membership terminated. *Mir Kārwān*, 334.
[35] A leading scholar of Saudi Arabia who became Chief Mufti and an important ideologue of the *Salafiyyah* movement. Obituary on the *shaykh* in *Al-Ahsan* (Springs, 2000), 1:2.
[36] Nadwi, *Islamic Concept of the Prophethood* (Lucknow, 1996).
[37] Saudi Arabia and other Arab states changed the religious environment in the Muslim world. Funding of an organisation implied a tacit approval and promotion of the Wahhabi interpretation of Islam.

critique[38] of the Arabs' abandonment of their religious duties, their subservience to the pervasive influence of the Westernisation and their abysmal failure to address the plight of the Palestinians reinforced his ability to express his independent views.

On several occasions, a bag containing gold coins was sent to Shaykh Nadwi by the Arab aristocracy, but he would politely return the gift. In keeping with the *sunnah* he would accept one gold coin as a token of appreciation to the donor or well-wisher.

During his *da'wah* travels to the Arab countries, donations intended for Nadwah were presented to Shaykh Nadwi. He politely declined such donations and instead informed them to transfer the said amount to the banking account of the institution. He was averse to receiving monetary gifts as he believed these devalued the importance of *da'wah*. Quite often, the visits by Arab royalty to his guest house at Nadwah seemed to suggest the clandestine offering of gifts to him. On the contrary, Shaykh Nadwi respected the protocol; he would welcome them with the following pithy message:

It is a blessing for the amīr (aristocrat) to reach the door of the faqīr (humble).

This attitude was not confined to the Arab elite only; he applied this rule to well-wishers, as well. His sense of independence permeated his outlook to wealth. To cite one example: A car was given to him for his personal use. After much insistence, Shaykh Nadwi reluctantly accepted the gift on the condition that he would use it at his discretion. The well-wisher agreed. Immediately Shaykh Nadwi donated the car to Nadwah for its daily use.

In his interaction with royalty and laity, Shaykh Nadwi was guided by the exemplary conduct of the *salaf*.

Apart from these writings, Shaykh Nadwi also delivered several lectures on the multifaceted personality of the Prophet (SAAS) and his message to the Arab world. Shaykh Nadwi pointed out that the "attachment of a large number of men belonging to the educated classes in the Arab countries, particularly those who had come under the influence of Arab nationalism, to the Prophet (SAAS) was weakening and getting reduced to a soulless

---

[38] Qasim Zaman's comment on Saudi patronage to Shaykh Nadwi is debatable. A close associate of Shaykh Nadwi, Dr 'Abbās Nadwi referred to several incidents in his *Mir Kārwān* to demonstrate Shaykh Nadwi's admirable independence and his refusal to accept gifts from either Saudi royalty or from influential members of the Arab world. Nadwi, *Mir Kārwān*, 320-25.

Chapter VII
Islamic Authenticity: Challenges and Opportunities

formality."[39] In a similar vein, Shaykh Nadwi lamented the ineffectual leadership of the Arab world that not only suffered dismal defeat at the hands of the Zionist regime in 1967, but possessed no singular qualities to lead the Muslim world in periods of crises. He says:

> The Arab-Islamic comity of nations does not need a new call, religion or philosophy of life to fill itself with an ardent zeal and courage. There has been, in fact, no diminishing spirit, and the *ummah* is prepared, as ever, to undergo the greatest sacrifice for its faith. Regrettably, its leadership is like a tidal wave which often rises sky high only to make its presence felt by all. It sometimes encloses a ship to submerge it beneath the sea, and then loses its own mooring in the surging ocean, which remains where it was, unchanged, unperturbed.

Shaykh 'Ali Tantāwi, a distinguished Arabic litterateur was critical of the polarised attitude of the Arab intellectuals towards the personality of the Prophet (SAAS). Even their literary production was unimpressive because of its lacklustre contents. By contrast, *The Pathway to Medina* was a refreshing work of unequalled merit and a repository of life-enriching accounts about the life and mission of the Prophet (SAAS). These lectures are informed by an impassioned appeal for Muslims to realign their lives according to the Prophetic ideal. In fact, humanity at large owes a permanent debt to the revolutionary message brought by the Prophet (SAAS). Shaykh Nadwi says:

> A new dawn was heralded. A new dawn was ushered in. As man changed, the world too changed with him. The earth and the sky changed. The family of Adam is not indebted to anyone more than him. He is the greatest benefactor of humanity. The clock of civilisation would be put back by thousands of years if what the Prophet (SAAS) gave to the world was taken away.[40]

---

[39] The following writings serve as a contextualised reading of the Arabs, shortcomings: Nadwi, *'Alam-i 'Arabi ka Almiyah* (Karachi, 1980). A collection of lectures (translated in Urdu) of Shaykh Nadwi's assessment of the issues affecting the Arab world. The monograph *Al-Arab wa al-Islam*. The Arab responsibility to Islam is elaborated. *Rise and Fall of Muslims*. The chapter, "The Arabs must Win" may also be consulted for Shaykh Nadwi's objective appraisal of the Arab world.
[40] Nadwi, *Pathway to Medina* (Lucknow, 1982), p. 1. These are a compilation of lectures written at different times and published as *Al- Tariqa ilā al-Madinah*. The noted littérateur, Shaykh 'Ali al-Tantawi penned an inspiring foreword to the book.

Sayyid Abul Hasan Nadwi: Life and Legacy
Chapter VII

Relations with Royalti: King Faisal bin 'Abdul 'Aziz

The role of King Faisal bin 'Abdul 'Aziz (d. 1975) in the promotion of the transnational Islamic vision has been examined by his biographers.[41] Faisal also attempted to overcome the influences of Nasser's socialist policies[42] in the Arabic-speaking world and beyond by emphasising the religious element as the foundation of the Saudi Arabian kingdom. The Wahhabi[43] influence, which welded the Al-Saud power with the Al-Shaykh interpretation of Islam, served as the nexus for defining the contours of da'wah. Additionally, the milieu in which these developments were taking place also had far-reaching effects in the Muslim world. Also, the Saudi patronage included an endorsement of a stricter and rigid interpretation of Islam as envisioned by the 'ulama' associated with the Al-Shaykh fraternity. The alliance did, to some extent, compromise the autonomy and authority of scholars who were perceived to be "religious functionaries." They, too, were exposed to the wave of modernity sweeping across the kingdom and directly affecting the entrenched Islamic heritage. Shaykh Nadwi had correctly observed that it was only the Saḥābah who were immune from the trappings of wealth and power and, instead, wielded a powerful influence on the civilisations of the day.

During this crucial period nationalism was gaining momentum in the Arab world. Academics and media were vigorously promoting the systems of

---

[41] Willard Beling (ed), *King Faisal and the Modernisation of Saudi Arabia* (Boulder, 1980). Thirteen essays cover the creation of the Saudi State, its modernisation programme, currents of social change and the role of Islam in the conduct of its foreign policy. Gerald De Gaury, *Faisal, King of Saudi Arabia* (New York, 1967) is a thought-provoking essay about Faisal;s achievements.
[42] See Z. Schulze, *A Modern History of the Islamic World*, 148-52 on the Nasserist policies.
[43] Shaykh Muhammad 'Abdul Wahhab (d. 1792), eponymous founder of the Wahhabiyyah movement was a strict follower of the Hanbali school of thought (*fiqh*). His source of inspiration was the eminent *mujaddid* Ibn Taimiyyah to whom is attributed the evolution of the *Salafiyyah* which emphasises the restoration of Islamic doctrines to their pure form, adherence to the Quran and *sunnah*, rejection of accretions (*bid'ah*) and the unity of the *ummah*. For a biographical account on Shaykh 'Abdul Wahhab, see Ahmad Abdol Ghafour Attar, *Muhammad Ibn Abdel Wahhab* (Makkah, 1982). Cf. Jamal-al-din Zarabozo, *The Life, Teachings and Influence of Muhammad Ibn Abdul Wahhab* (Madinah, 2003).

Chapter VII
Islamic Authenticity: Challenges and Opportunities

nationalism and socialism as alternatives to Islam. Leading academicians succumbed to the charisma of Nasser's ideology. They relentlessly employed political slogans to propagate his brand of socialism. A few *'ulama'* unashamedly relegated the position of the Prophet (SAAS) to the domain of intellectual discourse that bordered on *kufr* and apostasy. The Arab version of Communism promoted by the iconic status of President Nasser of Egypt spared no effort to undermine the status of the Prophet (SAAS). In fact, the forces of atheism were arrayed against the immutable message of Islam. It was in the context of this historical setting that Shaykh Nadwi launched a vigorous campaign against Nasser and his policies.

King Faisal was vehemently opposed to Nasser's ambitious designs of representing the collective voice of the Arab world. An alarming development was the erosion of Islamic values that were under threat as a result of new- fangled interpretations by some scholars and *'ulama'* in the Arab world.

Shaykh Nadwi's role was aimed at stemming the tide of irreligiousness. His meeting with King Faisal (then Prime Minister) in 1963 focused on the modernising trends affecting the *Haramayn* (Makkah and Madinah). Shaykh Nadwi raised his concerns about the adverse effects of mapping out new grids of planning for the *Haramayn* as they were incompatible with its sacred heritage. His subsequent meetings and correspondence with King Faisal reiterated his appeal to preserve the unique character and sanctity of Hijaz. The proliferation of wealth in the kingdom, according to Shaykh Nadwi, generated a slothful lifestyle and indulgence in material comforts, predictable tendencies that continue to erode the social fabric of the Arab nation. King Faisal's reply to Shaykh Nadwi in one of his letters pledged his commitment to the preservation of the kingdom's heritage. However, political circumstances changed their course of direction and created a complex set of problems that continue to affect the kingdom.

King Faisal was an outspoken critic of Communism and Zionism. He viewed these ideologies as sources of danger to Islam. Furthermore, he opposed all radical and irreligious trends in the Arab world, such as nationalism and Arab socialism. In these trends he saw a threat not only to the kingdom he ruled, but to the eternal message of Islam. His advocacy of an Islamic solidarity alliance was probably the most effective weapon he used in combatting radicalism and secularism in the Arab world.[44]

In his assessment of King Faisal's reform program Al-Osaimi remarks:

---

[44] See Nadwi, *Mir Kārwān*, 336-50.

He was a conservative reformer who was cautious not to upset the traditional foundations of his society, because his legitimacy as a ruler was directly dependent on the observance of these traditional values. So, he gradually pushed the country towards modernisation without cutting traditional ties to the past, especially the Islamic connections.[45]

The following account reveals King Faisal's profound respect for Shaykh Nadwi. Shaykh Nadwi was invited to meet King Faisal at the royal palace. The guards showed Shaykh Nadwi in, and he entered the reception area in the palace to meet the king. Shaykh Nadwi looked around, not cursorily, but closely, as if in wonderment. The king enquired as to why he looked around in such amazement. Shaykh Nadwi answered:

We, too, once had a king who ruled over the (present) India, Pakistan, Sri Lanka, Burma, Nepal and other places, and out of the fifty two years of his rule he spent twenty on horseback. Muslims, in his time, enjoyed freedom and happiness. Life was easy for them. Yet, the king was such that that he wore patched clothes. He scribed the Quran and knitted caps to earn his living and used to cry before his Lord in night vigils (*tahajjud*). Those were the times when simplicity and poverty characterised the lives of rulers, and contentment and fulfilment was the masses share. Today on seeing the palace of yours I wonder how times have changed. Today, our kings and rulers enjoy the riches of this world when the Muslims are rendered homeless in Palestine, their blood having lost all worth in Kashmir, and stripped of their identity in the Middle East. Today, when I stepped into your palace, I got lost in the bewildering comparison.

Shaykh Nadwi fell silent. Tears were streaming down the King Faisal's face. It was his turn now. Soon the streaming tears turned into profuse weeping. The guards were all worried and rushed in to see what was happening. He gestured them to leave. King Faisal now addressed Shaykh Nadwi: "Those kings were thus, because they had advisers like you. (I wish) you keep coming here and advising us, the weaker ones!"[46]

---

[45] Mohammed Al-Osaimi, *The Politics of Persuasion: The Islamic Oratory of King Faisal ibn 'Abdul Aziz* (Riyadh, 2000), 39.
[46] *Kārwān-i Adab* (2000, 174-5).

Chapter VII
Islamic Authenticity: Challenges and Opportunities

Rābitā al-'Ālam al-Islāmī: Muslim World League

After the establishment of the Islamic University of Madinah, the political crisis in the Arab world (discussed elsewhere in the chapter) affected the unity of the Muslim world. Parochialism and factionalism were spawned by nationalism, a neo-*jāhiliyyah* that sapped the vital arteries of the Muslim *ummah*. In response to these alarming developments the Rābitā was established in 1962 to mobilise global Muslim support and establish a viable link to issues affecting Muslims. Its first secretary-general, Shaykh Muhammad Sarwar al-Sabban saw the organisation as a forum to garner the collective Muslim opinion against Nasserism. The nature and scope of Rābitā's activities were later expanded during the tenure of its second secretary-general, Shaykh Muhammad Sālih al-Qazzāz.

Prominent leaders were enlisted from the Muslim world as members serving on the executive committee of Rābitā. Shaykh Nadwi's high-profile position and growing popularity in the Arab world made him a natural choice. An estimation of the respect he enjoyed is supported by the portfolio that was assigned to him. He served as chairman of Rābitā's sessions and guided its policies within the framework of *islāh*.

A critical appraisal of Shaykh Nadwi's relationship with *Salafiyyah* in the Arab world sheds interesting insights into his views concerning the movement. The Saudi monarchy, for example, advocated a strict and scriptural interpretation of the *shari'ah* in line with the mission of *Salafiyyah*. Hence, there was no scope for *tasawwuf* as it was considered a deviation (*bid'ah*). As opposed to this presumptuous claim, Shaykh Nadwi supported *tasawwuf* as an authentic expression of the Islamic tradition. It implied a rejection of custom-laden practices and exaggerated veneration of saints invested with a halo of divinity. The unwary masses were exposed to a distorted version of Islam where superstition and incredulous beliefs supplanted the original teachings of Islam. Shaykh Nadwi was a vocal critic of the syncretic beliefs and their corrosive effects on *tawhīd*. In sum, his exposition about the inner dimensions of Islam is a trajectory of *islāh*.

Qardāwī maintained that Shaykh Nadwi mirrored the true essence of *ihsān* (spiritual excellence) and steered clearly away from any semblance associated with innovations condoned by certain *mashā'ikh* of the spiritual orders.

Recent studies about the specific facets of *Salafi* thought point out to the complexities and realities it represents. The term *kufr* (disbelief) is loosely used against Muslims who purport to maintain social relations with non-Muslims. Quoting Quranic verses to support their *fatwās*, the *Salafi* establishment has not spared non-*Salafis* in its censure of their peaceful co-existence with non-Muslims. This has resulted in the justification of violence against individuals and organisations who advocate dialogue in a multireligious world. The *Salafis* have expanded their footprints in countries where Muslim minorities are exposed to greater challenges that impact their Islamic identity. Instead, the *Salafis*' extremist understanding of Islamic doctrines has widened the gulf for Muslims seeking to find new pathways of *da'wah*.

Shaykh Nadwi was cognisant of the raging debates about *takfir* (excommunication of Muslims) in the Arab world and its growing influence in Europe. For Shaykh Nadwi, a culture of *da'wah*-driven initiatives was the alternative for saving the Muslim minorities from isolation and suspicion against the dominant culture of their respective countries.

Shaykh Nadwi's perceptive observation of the Muslim dilemmas in the West is a positive reminder that *da'wah* is a Quran-inspired ideal that takes into account factors like individual temperament, societal aspiration and circumstantial setting. In Shaykh 'Ali Tantawi's estimation, Shaykh Nadwi built forts in the hearts of students. Like the proverbial rock, his firm faith and conviction had a solid impact on students seeking to serve Islam selflessly in all facets of *da'wah*. In this strain, *tarbiyyah* or moral instruction was integral to a sound and efficient educational system. According to Shaykh Nadwi, its goal was to foster a culture of consciousness and serve as a buffer zone against the currents of corruption and moral deviance. He reiterated the view that the government policies cannot turn the tide of positive reform which is anchored on *tarbiyyah*.[47]

Towards an Islamic Renaissance

The geopolitical developments of the twentieth century in the Muslim world saw the emergence of movements advocating key elements like awakening (*sahwah*) and renaissance (*nahdah*). In a positive sense, the Islamic renewal project witnessed a new discourse about the intellectual reform and sustaining a robust scholarly tradition. For Shaykh Nadwi Islamic awakening expressed a pragmatic approach that worked within the ambit of Quranic norms and standards. These included the following points:

- The Islamic belief system (*'aqīdah*) was not compromised for political opportunism.

---

[47] For an elaboration of these key points, see Nadwi, *Tarshid al-Sah- wah al-Islāmiyyah* (2004).

Chapter VII
Islamic Authenticity: Challenges and Opportunities

- A profound knowledge of the Quran and *sunnah* is required to understand contemporary trends and movements.
- Confrontation must be eschewed in non-conflict arenas with wisdom (*hikmah*) and fair exhortation (*maw'izah*) given precedence.
- High profile figures associated with Islamic awakening movements must maintain a respectable distance from the corridors of power and authority.
- Islamic awakening must be infused with the spirit of self-sacrifice, courage and unconditional reliance on Allah (*tawakkul*).[48]

Europe: A New Horizon

Before we attempt to discuss Shaykh Nadwi's *da'wah* activities in Europe, a few preliminary remarks about his acquaintance with the West shed much light regarding his contributions to the Islam and West discourse.

Two towering figures, Mawlana Daryabadi and Mawlana Mawdudi had a formative influence on his understanding of the Western civilisation. Muhammad Asad's *Islam at the Crossroads* deepened his critique of the West. Likewise, Shaykh Nadwi had access to the primary sources which he consulted in the preparation of his *Rise and Fall of Muslims*. Against this background, Shaykh Nadwi's *da'wah* activities in Europe in 1963 and 1964 enhanced his understanding of the psyche and spirit that moulded the character of the Western civilisation and culture. From London to Lausanne and Berlin to Paris, Shaykh Nadwi's message was consistent with his *da'wah* vision: The West needs to reassess its obsession with its materialistic culture. By the same token, the values of Islam allow for the development of an integrated personality. He addressed his audience in London University on the topic, "Between East and West", gave interviews on BBC Channel, met distinguished scholars, like Professor Arberry of Cambridge University and Professor Hamidullah of Paris. The collection of lectures including his address to the German nation in Munich was translated into English as *Speaking Plainly to the West*.[49] Shaykh Nadwi also visited the prestigious British Museum Library and the Indian Office Library to gather material for his *Western Civilisation, Islam and Muslims*.

---

[48] *Ibid.*, 35.
[49] These letters are contained in Nadwi's *Maktūbāt* writings.

Rabey Nadwi who accompanied Shaykh Nadwi during his *da'wah* travels to Europe echoed a similar sentiment. Shaykh Nadwi's message was clear:

> Don't forsake your Islamic and cultural values. Don't be influenced by the moral and religious weaknesses of the local population. Educate and raise your children in such a way that their connection to Islam is not compromised. Learn the language of the land as best as you can so that you can do the work of *da'wah* effectively. Live a life that becomes a means of introduction of Islam to non-Muslims. Look at your surrounding environment in such a way that you see an evil as an evil. And if you find something good, appreciate and value it as is mentioned in the Prophetic advice: "Wisdom is the lost treasure of a believer and he is the most deserving to acquire it when it is found."

Shaykh Nadwi's primary focus was on the collective Islamic identity in Europe. Muslims faced a number of challenges of which assimilation and integration were advocated as state policies. In the public domain Muslims who refused to be governed by these policies were not treated as equal citizens of the country and labelled as counter- productive elements to progress. In other words, diversity as an expression of cultural pluralism was only acceptable if Muslims integrated into the ideals and ethos of the mainstream life of the country. A clash of civilisational values comes to the fore regarding such interaction.

Mohiuddin Ahmad, translator of Shaykh Nadwi's works into English, has made some thoughtful comments about Shaykh Nadwi's assessment of the West. He says:

> [Shaykh Nadwi] reviews the situation in comprehensive terms in its true perspective and advocates that the vitality and skill of the West should be appropriated rather than accepted. He wants the East to be enlightened rather than to be intoxicated by the West. At the same time, he urges the Muslim East to maintain its distinctive individuality, its faith, its moral integrity and the fervour of heart and spirit. He wants the Muslim East to understand the real cause of material prosperity and worldly success of the West, accept only what is worthwhile, and, in return, help the West in overcoming its follies and shortcomings, aberrations and excesses for their mutual benefit. He asks the East to guard and conserve its own latent energies of faith and righteousness, intellectual integrity and moral strength, and build a new bridge across which humanity may walk along to mutual

understanding, progress and prosperity and material advancement as well as spiritual enrichment to create a brave new world - a world that would be worth living for all, for the White and the Black, for the great and the small, for the powerful and the weak.[50]

East and West: Cultural Encounters

By 1950 Shaykh Nadwi made noteworthy contributions to the Islam and West discourse. His iconic work *Rise and Fall of Muslims* received critical acclaim in the Arab world and also by Muslim organisations in Europe. A critique of Western civilisation was one of the themes explored in the formative period (1950-53) of his academic career. His association with Saʻīd Ramadān, the illustrious Ikhwān member and son-in-law of Hasan al-Bannā broadened his horizon about the evolution of Western thought and culture. As an executive member of the Islamic Centre in Geneva (Switzerland), Shaykh Nadwi was able to interact with other Muslim intellectuals who resided in Europe. He contributed a series of articles to the prestigious magazine *Al-Muslimīn* and also served as its editor during Saʻīd Ramadān's sabbatical leave to complete his doctoral dissertation on Islamic law at the University of Cologne in Germany.

During this period, Shaykh Nadwi met Muhammad Hamidullah, a polyglot whose contribution to Quranic and *hadīth* studies earned him international fame in academic circles. His research on the extant manuscripts of the *hadīth* literature deposited in the libraries of Europe and other Muslim countries proved beyond doubt its authenticity in the early years of Islam. The *daʻwah* lectures delivered by Shaykh Nadwi in Europe commenced from 1963 and developed into a more systematic study of the West's worldview. Amid the growing presence of Muslim communities, the challenges they faced were not only confined to immigration issues, economic opportunities or religious discrimination. It was inevitable that the fault lines between Islam and the West would reappear in the clash of civilisation discourse. Decades later the specter of Islamophobia confirmed this historical reality.

---

[50] For a detailed account of Nadwi's impressions about the West, see Nadwi, *Muslims in the West*.

Maktūbāt: An Overview

Before we attempt to explore Shaykh Nadwi's da'wah formulation in the West, his letters to his colleagues are a useful guide in this regard. It must also be remembered that it was his first visit to the citadels of Christian/European culture. The relevant chapters of *Rise and Fall* written in the late 1940s signposted his critical examination of the Western civilisation. Also, several monographs written during this period (1960s) reflect his mature outlook in respect of its intellectual influence on the European thought.

Shaykh Nadwi was among the pioneering Muslim scholars who steered away from polemical writings about the West. Instead, his critique of the West was based on primary sources. By tracing its genealogy, Shaykh Nadwi explained how the armoury of Western intellectual thought held sway in the colonised Muslim countries. Fifty years later the decolonisation of knowledge campaign framed from the political lens assumed greater importance in institutions of higher learning. This mindset also extended to the rising presence of progressive Muslims advocating new approaches to the Quranic studies.

Here we will examine selected excerpts of Sayyid Nadwi's *Maktūbāt* in the light of his experience in several cities of Europe.

Geneva: Islamic Centre (n.d.)

> Muhammad Asad came to meet us at the Centre. His warmth and animated conversation were touching. In the course of our conversation the question of translation arose. Asad referred to the progress of his Quranic commentary in English. Muhammad Hamidullah who was also present gave his impressions about the Quranic translations in European languages. Semantics and linguistic competence were key issues that dominated the conversation. Hamidullah had already translated the Quran into French.
>
> Zafar Ishaq Ansari referred to Asad's monumental work *Road to Mecca* which was being translated into Urdu. Asad countered the claim that he had granted permission to other publishers for the Urdu translation except Nadwah.

Two points emerge from the above excerpts. First, Shaykh Nadwi's familiarity with contemporary Islamic thought comes to the fore. Asad's *Islam at the Crossroads* created space for the contextual reading of the Islamic faith and

Chapter VII
Islamic Authenticity: Challenges and Opportunities

practice. Second, trends in the Quranic studies were gaining momentum and programs were devised to teach this discipline at prestigious Western universities. Shaykh Nadwi's contribution, albeit briefly, was acknowledged by the Orientalists.

London: 17 October 1963

I met the renowned scholar of Islamic and Oriental Studies, Professor A. J. Arberry at Cambridge University. He has to his credit many published translations of classical works on *tasawwuf* and Persian poetry. His translation of the Quran written largely for a non-Muslim audience has been widely received. According to Arberry, he was commissioned by an Islamic organisation to work on the translation project. It was difficult to make a generalisation about the Orientalists' areas of specialisation in the field of Islamic studies. They did not leave any profound impression on me, simply because theirs was a time-bound project and in many instances non-committal. It must be remembered that Arberry spent several years in Cairo studying classical Arabic.

A noteworthy monograph on Orientalism reveals Shaykh Nadwi's balanced and unbiased assessment about its contributions to Islamic Studies. Works on *hadīth,* for example, displayed "genuine scholarship and research which attested to their exhaustive study and unflagging efforts." Without typecasting all Orientalist writings as inimical to Islamic culture, Shaykh Nadwi makes a candid observation regarding the majority of Orientalists who have adopted a censorious attitude: It is "no different from the drain inspector who can only see sewers, drains and heaps of rubbish in an otherwise exquisite and beautiful landscape."

Paris: October 1963

We visited Sorbonne University which has an interesting history. Like al-Azhar University, it, too, was established and patronised by religious figures and endowments. Religion played a central role in the establishment of institutions of learning in Europe and the Muslim world. (The leading patron of Islamic learning, Fatima al-Fihri founded the Qarawiyyin university in 859 C.E in Fez, Morocco.

The Bibliothèque Nationale is a rare phenomenon. It has a library holding seven million books and four thousand journals and magazines. One section of the library is dedicated to all published works in French and contains six million books.

The French nation is an amalgam of conflicting attributes. Passionate about their language, they are amicable and easy going. In reality, their natural disposition betrays their laxity towards important matters like ritual purity (*tahārat*). They appear to have inherited this trait from the Roman Catholic priests who frowned upon physical cleanliness in general. Likewise, gender equality slogans have not improved the lot of women. They continue to work in menial positions while their femininity is sacrificed at the altar of the male domination.

Shaykh Nadwi draws readers' attention to the European attitude to life. Unlike Islam which possesses a *shari'ah* that dictates norms and standards for a successful living, Europe promotes a culture that is deprived of spiritual values. While acknowledging the great strides made by the French nation in higher learning, their free-spirited lives are marred by the flawed understanding pertaining to freedom of expression and gender equality. These conflicting strands are woven into their everyday life and cultural orientation. Therefore, a willing acceptance of the Islamic code of life for the French nation is a formidable challenge in view of their other-worldly outlook.

Apart from the *Maktūbāt* genre, Shaykh Nadwi was interviewed by the British Broadcasting Corporation to give his impressions of his visit to London. Additionally, his lecture in Arabic in the London University Hall on the theme "Between East and West" received appreciable interest from Arab students residing in London. The lecture was translated into English by Zafar Ishaq Ansari (d.2016), a leading scholar in Islamic Studies and translator of Mawdudi's *Tahfim al- Qur'ān* into English. Several of Shaykh Nadwi's books were also translated by him. Mention may be made of *Qadianism: A Critical Study* which by all accounts is praised for its fluency, objectivity and clear presentation about this deviant sect.

Shaykh Nadwi was able to access information from the British Museum and the Indian Office libraries for his important book *Western Civilisation, Islam and Muslims*. The Introduction was completed in London. This book originally written in Arabic (1963) focuses on the attitude of the world of Islam towards Western civilisation. It was later expanded in the English translation in view of the changed sociopolitical situations in the Muslim countries.

Spain: Andalus Syndrome

Islam's footprint in Europe was discernible in Spain formerly known as Andalus, and the powerful Ottoman Caliphate. The flowering of Islamic

Chapter VII
Islamic Authenticity: Challenges and Opportunities

civilisation was a remarkable achievement in Spain. Cities like Cordova and Granada epitomised the glorious past of Muslim rule that set the pace of unprecedented success in various fields of learning. Tragically, the political factors gradually led to its terminal decline. It was the Inquisition in 1492 that sealed the fate of the Muslim rule and the Muslim populace who were persecuted by Christians. They either fled the country or were coerced to embrace Christianity.

The visit to the immortal legacy of Islamic history was a painful reminder to Shaykh Nadwi of Spain's unrivalled past. Granada, a model city of architectural brilliance, could now only be captured in frozen time. In a similar way, Alhambra Palace lost its soul and typified the 'Paradise lost' syndrome. In essence, the profound effect of an irredeemable loss is the best told in Shaykh Nadwi's own words:

> We boarded the bus that took us to these historic sites. A guide was assigned to the English-speaking tourists. Whenever the guide pointed to the historical landmarks, he often made the following remark: "When we expelled the Arabs..." I could not endure it any longer and politely asked him to refrain from making this remark. He did stop...

It was not only the splendour of Islamic history, which created a new world in Europe; it was also a cultural encounter between Islam and the West. Paradoxically, the tell-tale signs of Muslim decline were interlinked to *da'wah*. Muslim rule spanning over eight hundred years did not win over the hearts of the indigenous people to Islam. Nor was there a sustained and tangible expression of *da'wah* in action. In the course of time this neglect turned the tide against Muslims with grave consequences. Again, this grim reminder of Muslims' indifference to *da'wah* is reflective of Shaykh Nadwi's reformist vision. For a Western audience his lectures have a recurrent theme: It is Islam only that can redraw the lines between material gains and eternal success.

To return to Cordova. Time stood still at the majestic beauty of the breathtaking landscape. It was, however, the Mosque of Cordova that attracted the attention of great scholars and poets. Shaykh Nadwi was no exception. Iqbal, too, wrote a poem immortalising the grandeur of the mosque and is considered a masterpiece of poetic inspiration and artistic expression. According to Iqbal, love transcends time and space. In a similar vein, the mosque itself represents the universal qualities of love. Art, beauty and architecture are the motifs that are reminiscent of Islam's unrivalled past. For Iqbal, the *'adhān* (call to prayer) is symbolic of Islam's timeless mission. According to Shaykh Nadwi, the regeneration of Islam has shown steady signs in Muslim Spain and this augurs well for its future.

However, the encounter between Spain and Islam whose ties had been severed following the Reconquista in 1492 have now assumed different dimensions. Even if Muslim families held keys to their ancestral homes, their dispossession remained sentimental. On a positive note, the immigration patterns of Muslim settlement in recent decades illustrate the potential of Islam establishing its footprints once more in Spain. This development underscores the importance of da'wah. By the same token, the prospects of 'Paradise regained' for Muslims in the country are illusory.[51]

East and West Encounters

The opening decades of the nineteenth century saw the overarching presence of the West in Muslim countries largely due to colonial expansion. Not only was the firepower of the West the primary cause for its success in Muslim lands; its intellectual superiority created a passive resistance particularly from 'ulama'.

The Western encroachment produced two opposite responses from 'ulama' and intellectuals, respectively. The 'ulama' in particular saw the West as something to be rejected and protested against its corrupting influence on the conquered Muslim countries. This condemnatory attitude assumed that the West was soaked in evil in every facet of life. By then Muslim countries had lost their self-confidence and, as such, built a wall of insularity against the rapid incursion of the West. This attitude did not take into account the internal decadence that had set in not only in the political sphere, but in other fields like economics, literature as well as science, politics and even culture.

The emergence of the modernist Muslims was a phenomenon spawned by the intellectual superiority of the West. They attributed Muslims' deterioration to their internal structure that could not face the challenges of the West. Accordingly, they sought to harmonise the East (read as Islam) with the West. This implied that Muslim success lay in discarding the shari'ah and embracing the pervasive values of the West as progressive ideals. No doubt, this was an apologetic stance adopted by the emerging intellectual group to reinterpret Islamic teachings and traditions. They were supported by state institutions which at the behest of the West consolidated the modernist project in their

---

[51] Nadwi, *Maktūbāt*.

Chapter VII
Islamic Authenticity: Challenges and Opportunities

respective countries.

Shaykh Nadwi's analysis of the two responses is a testimony to his balanced and unbiased approach. He offers a third course which in his view can reconcile the conflicting trends that have had a negative impact in understanding the dynamics of the West. According to Habibul Haq Nadwi:

> Shaykh Nadwi [reviews] the situation in its true perspective and advocates that the vitality and skills of the West should be appropriated rather than accepted. He wants the Muslims to be enlightened rather than intoxicated by the West. At the same time, he urges the Muslim East to maintain its distinctive identity, its faith, its moral integrity (which) will play a useful role for itself, the West and the rest of humanity.

As much as Shaykh Nadwi critiques the West for deriving its sources from the ancient Greek civilisation, he adopts a positive approach which is free from polemics and destructive tendencies.

Da'wah to the West: Formative Years

We now present a thematic exposition of Shaykh Nadwi's lectures in London and Berlin. Shaykh Nadwi deplores the conflict that has set apart Islam and the West. The gulf has widened over the decades and has thwarted serious attempts to reconcile the two civilisations. The term East is applied to Islam. It has a comprehensive code of conduct and values cast in the Prophetic mould. By contrast, the West is inextricably linked to the Crusade mentality, colonialism and Orientalism. These have wreaked socio-political and intellectual upheavals in Muslim countries. Notwithstanding these cleavages, Shaykh Nadwi makes the following observation:

> [It] is clear that East and West remain isolated from one another. Whenever these two came together it was in an atmosphere of mutual suspicion, even hatred. Seldom have they joined hands for the greater good of humanity and with a view to build an ideal civilisation. A readiness to exchange the natural capabilities and knowledge acquired through generations has always been absent. If there has been any exchange, it has taken place in a very restricted area.

Lecture: University of London

As this lecture was delivered at the University of London, Shaykh Nadwi referred to the remarkable accomplishments of the institution in the fields of science and technology. He asserted that these strides are a blessing of Allah, which should not be underrated. However, Shaykh Nadwi strikes a pessimistic note when he says that the separation of faith and science has been disastrous for mankind. The outlook is bleak as "[faith] continues to wait for the companionship of science, while science stands lost in need of guidance of faith. Therefore, humanity is waiting for the two to come together so that peace and true happiness can be achieved."

Faith, according to Shaykh Nadwi, is the special key for unlocking the secrets of the heart to guide humanity. To this end, the West needs to remove the crust of materialism so that the key gifted to humanity by the Prophets can unlock its inner potential and thus, restore the true contents of faith.

Message to Humanity: Germany

Shaykh Nadwi addressed students, staff and people from diverse backgrounds in Germany. Originally delivered in Arabic at the University of Berlin, the lecture was translated into German. As the title suggests, Shaykh Nadwi reminded the German nation that it occupied a special place among the nations of Europe on account of its outstanding qualities and intellectual contributions made to European civilisation. Its revolutionary ideas brought about winds of change in Europe and recast the continent's intellectual identity to which the West is greatly indebted.

Shaykh Nadwi laments the fact that Germany's natural capabilities did not adopt a constructive approach to a civilisation that reduced man to a soulless entity. As a result, the civilisation was devoid of noble attributes - faith, sincerity, purity of thought and love for humanity. Germany had the opportunity, given its history of producing revolutionary leaders, to open a new chapter in world history by adapting the strides made in science and technology to the service of mankind. Regrettably, the course of action undertaken by Germany did not change the destiny of Europe. In a similar vein, the Church did not reconcile faith and science; instead, it alienated them to the extent that a contradiction remains the essential feature of European thought to religious matters.

Shaykh Nadwi clearly states that Europe has not been fortunate enough to embrace the message of Islam. Although the Ottoman Caliphate did in many ways give a new life and impulse to a decadent Europe, its success was limited due to a number of historical factors. Even under these circumstances Germany could have taken the lead by virtue of its revolutionary fervour to bring about a transformation in Europe. The idealism that Shaykh Nadwi expressed about the German nation has not been realised.

Assessment

Shaykh Nadwi brings into full light the clash between materialism embodied in the attitude of the West to the spiritual dimensions of Islamic civilisation. He argues that technological progress does not guarantee any measure of real success. Ironically, it develops an insatiable lust for illusory materialistic prosperity and stability. Hedonistic pleasures or instant gratification are thus the outcomes of materialism. The US, Europe and Russia are "at war with spirituality, religious ethics and divine accountability." According to Shaykh Nadwi, the logical climax of this mindset is the prelude to the appearance of Dajjāl as described in the *hadīth* literature. It is also "the culminating point of this godless civilization which is being brewed in the crucible of Europe for the past few centuries."

Shaykh Nadwi cautions the Muslim world not to fall into the trappings of materialism, which has brought in its wake untold misery and suffering to millions of people languishing in grinding poverty and leading meaningless existence. For example, promises of success in a consumerist society are elusive, because capitalism serves the interests of the huge conglomerates. Likewise, teeming millions are victims of politicians who regard them as vote banks during elections. It is, therefore, not surprising that intrinsic values like social justice, equality and brotherhood do not exist in the lexicon of materialism.

Communal Riots

Communal riots between Muslims and Hindus were a phenomenon even before the Partition of India in 1947. Muslim persecution was committed by Hindutva, an ideological movement with its rapid anti-Muslim rhetoric. It saw the Muslim community as peripheral to the mainstream Hindu majority and, therefore, launched a relentless campaign to destabilise Muslims at both economic and religious levels. Also, the politicians' ambitions to boost their own vote banks had by and large fanned the fires of communal violence.

Shaykh Nadwi's return to India in 1964 after an extensive visit to Europe drew him into the critical phase of Muslim crisis. The eruption of communal riots in Kolkata, Jamshedpur, Ranchi and other towns had a searing effect on Shaykh Nadwi's vision of communal harmony. Worse, the conflagration was reminiscent of Partition days: Blood patches splashed on walls and human skulls strewn all over the fields. A gruesome picture was palpable. The litany of woes and trauma was unbearable for Shaykh Nadwi. Together with his colleagues they mobilised Muslim support to collectively voice their grievances to the state authorities. Shaykh Nadwi was not unmindful of the need for national reconstruction and articulated this message to both the Muslim and non-Muslim audience. His famous address at the Tata Steel Company reflected his concern for communal harmony:

[If] steel was given voice it would say : "I have not been created so that man may cut man's throat. If that happened then it is not I, the steel, that needs to be blamed. The blame is on those educated people who use me not for constructive but, for destructive purpose."

Majlis i- Mushāwarat

The growing communal polarisation put the quest for public representation of Muslim interests on the agenda. As early as 1964 the All-India Majlis i-Mushāwarat (AIMM) was founded in Lucknow, when communal riots in West Bengal and Uttar Pradesh called for effective political representation on a broad base. Its main constituencies were prominent Muslim organisations and distinguished Muslim individuals. Shaykh Nadwi was a driving force behind the constitution of the AIMM. Dr Sayyid Mahmud (d. 1972) gave birth to the idea to fill the vacuum of moral leadership. The AIMM outlined its aims: To overcome the traumatic experience of the Partition in 1947 and to integrate all parts of society into the Indian Union. In a similar vein, the Uttar Pradesh branch of the organisation transformed itself, under the charismatic leadership of Dr 'Abdul Jalil Faridi (d. 1974) into a coordinated political party that managed to contest State Assembly elections in 1969. After this split, the AIMM under the leadership of the Deobandi Mufti 'Atiq al-Rahmān 'Uthmani (d. 1984) adopted new statutes, which saw the body as an amalgam of different Muslim organisations with no intention to participate in parliamentary policies.

In the wake of the escalating communal tension the All- Indian Muslim Personal Law Board (AIMPLB) was established in December 1972 in Mumbai. This body gained momentum in response to the radicalisation of Hindu extremist groups (Hindutva) as well as certain secularist forces calling for the abolition

Chapter VII
Islamic Authenticity: Challenges and Opportunities

of the religious personal laws and the unconditional adoption of a Uniform Civil Code. These developments were perceived by both Muslim intellectuals and *'ulama'* as a threat to Indo-Muslim identity and a violation of the constitutional article of the freedom to individually profess any religious faith.

However, disparate elements which made up the AIMPLB did not take unilateral decisions concerning issues of crucial importance to Muslims. The period of conflict had a negative impact on the effective management of this important organisation as later events turned out to confirm the problems Muslims faced.

Conclusion

The transnational character of Shaykh Nadwi's *da'wah* pointed out to the prevalent challenges faced by Muslims locally and in the Arab world. Political activism on issues affecting Indian Muslims became more pronounced as was his engagement with important stakeholders, whose efforts to maintain a cohesive Islamic identity provided a commonality of concerns to which Shaykh Nadwi focused his undivided attention.

Chapter VIII

Islamic Reformist Thought in Shaykh Nadwi's Writings

This chapter examines some of Shaykh Nadwi's important writings which are interlinked with specific historical developments, both locally and abroad. The social milieu is also explored to interpret his growing involvement in mainstream politics. During this crucial period the *Payām-i Insāniyat* was established. It must be noted (as discussed in the previous chapter) that his critique of Arab nationalism associated with Nasserist regime is discussed here to show its ramifications in the Muslim world.

Literary Initiatives: An Overview

Shaykh Nadwi's failing eyesight had hampered his writing routine. His reliance on dictation was acutely felt by him. Undeterred by this impediment, this period was a productive phase in his literary career. His several books covering a gamut of Islamic themes, widely appreciated in the Muslim world, were written under different circumstances. Shaykh Nadwi's eye operation in Sitapur (1966) and London (1969) provided temporary relief only. For Shaykh Nadwi, the pain and the distress experienced was like hovering between life and death,[1] both in terms of his health and the bleak prospects of leading a life of dependence. Later, in 1978, it was his *da'wah* visit to the US[2] that gave him renewed hope of recovering from his deteriorating eyesight. (There was no laser implant technology during that period to alleviate his recurring ailment).

The Four Pillars of Islam[3] [Arkān-i Arba'ab]

A series of articles on *hajj* were written for the Arabic journal *al-Muslimīn* in Geneva (Switzerland). The impressive style employed by Shaykh Nadwi was aimed at dispelling misconceptions that this pillar of Islam had political connotations. For example, it was widely held by individuals and organisations with modernist tendencies that *hajj* was an international political conference while completely ignoring its aims, objectives and spiritual dimensions.

---

[1] Nadwi, *Kārwān*, vol. 1, 516-18.
[2] *Ibid.*
[3] Nadwi, *The Four Pillars* (Lucknow, 1976).

In writing this volume, Shaykh Nadwi studied afresh the Quran and *hadīth* literature and other relevant sources, both classical and contemporary. Also, a comparative study of other faiths was examined to present in an unbiased manner their existing forms of worship. The rational interpretation in the *Four Pillars of Islam* was earlier elucidated by Shah Waliyullah (d. 1762) in his well-known *Hujjat Allah al-Bāligha.* This work, considered a masterpiece, helps one understand Islam's presentation of man's material, moral and spiritual aspirations.[4]

Another consideration for writing this volume was a kind of confusion and waywardness that had been noticed in the presentation of these pillars of Islam. In fact, if these approaches went unchecked, they could have posed a "grave threat to the *millat* (community of Islam)" and could be "a prelude to the perversion of the understanding of the basic truths and realities of the faith and aims and objectives of the *shari'ah*."[5]

The *Four Pillars of Islam* was based on admirable scholarship in respect of the importance of the *shari'ah*. However, a vacuum was felt in many intellectual circles that *tawhīd*,[6] an important pillar (*rukn*) of Islam was not discussed. It was in 1982 that *A Guidebook for Muslim*[7] was written to conclude this publication. It contained a synoptic overview of the beliefs and practices of the *Ahl al-Sunnah* and was a timeous sequel to earlier manuals[8] and compendia dealing with similar themes. Another noteworthy book *Islam: Three Core Beliefs* (published in 2016) provides a detailed explanation of *tawhīd*.

Hayāt-i 'Abdul Hayy

Before we attempt to discuss Shaykh Nadwi's editorial involvement in

---

[4] Marcia K. Hermansen, *The Conclusive Argument of God* (Islamabad, 2003).
[5] Nadwi, *The Four Pillars of Islam*, x-xi.
[6] In fact, the Shaykh-al Azhar (Cairo) Shaykh 'Abdul Halim Mahmud (d. 1978) urged Shaykh Nadwi to co-write a work on *tawhīd* so that the volume on the *Four Pillars* could be completed. Nadwi, *Kārwān*, vol. 2, 20-21. Cf. Nadwi, *A Guidebook for Muslims*, 10-11.
[7] Written originally in Arabic, entitled *Al-'Aqidah wa-al 'Ibādah wa-al Suluk*.
[8] The following books belong to this genre of *islāhī* series:
- Imām Ghazāli (d. 1111), *Ihya 'Ulūm al- Dīn*;
- Sayyid Ahmad Shahid, *Sirāt al-Mustaqīm*;
- Ashraf 'Ali Thānawi, *Ta'lim al-Dīn*.

The reformist spirit in this book has shaped the temperament and orientation of the large sections of Muslims over the century in the subcontinent.

Chapter VIII
Islamic Reformist Thought in Shaykh Nadwi's Writings

publishing his father's writings, his *Hayāt-i 'Abdul Hayy* is a benchmark for assessing the latter's scholarly achievements. Written in an objective yet lucid style, Shaykh Nadwi avoids the trodden path of the *manqabah* (eulogy) style. It invariably presents an embellished account of its subject; the narrative generally makes hyperbolic claims about the religious personalities under discussion; and more often than not, a halo of infallibility is invested in them. According to Shaykh Nadwi, his reason for writing the biographical account of his father was to record his contributions as one of the eminent and authoritative historians who rendered sterling series in preserving "the lives and works of thousands of scholars" in the subcontinent.[9]

Nuzhat al-Khawātir

Another form of biography was the biographical dictionary (*tabaqah*), a highly developed discipline providing a composite picture of the literary and intellectual accomplishment of Muslims living in a particular era and social milieu. It was through the lens of this genre that the Muslim cultural heritage could be portrayed. The *tabaqah* saw its emergence in the early period of Islam[10] and preserved as collective memory the outstanding achievements of *'ulama'*, *mashā'ikh* and scholars representative of Islamic thought. *Nuzhat al-Khawātir*,[11] published in seven volumes, could not be completed owing to the author's (Sayyid 'Abdul Hayy's) death in 1923. Thus, the eighth volume was in a manuscript form and did not cover a comprehensive spectrum of scholars who were either his contemporaries, or decades later made lasting contributions to Islamic thought.

At the insistence of well-wishers Shaykh Nadwi undertook the responsibility of completing the eighth volume of *Nuzhat*, a task which was a daunting challenge for him. The simplicity of style and the historical sobriety were hallmarks of this volume and he had to follow closely its stylistic usage keeping in mind the diction employed by his father.[12] *Nuzhat* was published by the D ā'irat al-

---

[9] Nadwi, *Kārwān*, vol. 2, 42-43.
[10] Mention may be made of ibn Khalliqān's multivolume *Wafayāt al- A'yān* - a biographical dictionary dealing with the early scholars of Islam.
[11] The multivolume *Nuzhat al-Khawātir* was published under a new title, *Al-I'lām* by Dār al-Arafat (Rae Bareli, 1991). It is a monumental encyclopaedic work of unsurpassed merit which covers Islamic activities during the last fourteen centuries.
[12] Nadwi, *Kārwān*, vol. 2, 24-25.

Ma'ārif Uthmāniya in Hyderabad.
In terms of its scholarly excellence, *Nuzhat* was an original contribution that matched the *tabaqat* written during different periods in Islamic history across the Muslim world. Shaykh Nadwi noted:

> What India needed was a biographer like Ibn Khallikān, an analyst like Haji Khalifa and a word painter like Al-Maqrizi who could have portrayed the great cultural attainments of this ancient land, a perennial source of civilisation in truthful and vivid colours. 'Abdul Hayy was gifted with all these qualities, who, being a historian, biographer and writer, could adequately represent all the three above-mentioned writers of the past. His accomplishment was nothing unusual, since many an industrious encyclopaedist had to their credit such a prolific output as could be produced only by a literary academy.[13]

India During Muslim Rule[14]

This excellent work has preserved the cultural heritage of Muslim rule in India. It examines not only the different dynasties that ruled India, but offers an overview of major cities, places of learning and also the infrastructural features of the country. The medieval spirit is blended with the early twentieth century and one can discern the achievements of Muslim dynasties despite the sporadic tumultuous period that marked their respective rule. Viewed from another angle, this work is intended to show the salutary influences of the various Muslim dynasties in India. It was in this country that the valour of the Turks, the perseverance of the Mughals and the stately pride of the Afghans mingled with the Islamic ideals of justice and compassion. And the culture thus coming into being by this blending of ideas and ideals could justifiably be called Indo-Islamic. Its administrative set-up was an amalgam of Turkish, Indian and Islamic systems, generally known as the Mughal system of administration; and its design of construction as Indo-Islamic architecture.[15]

---

[13] Syed 'Abdul Hayy, *India During Muslim Rule* (Lucknow, 1977), 15-6.
[14] The Arabic version was published by the prestigious Arabic Academy (Damascus).
[15] Syed 'Abdul Hayy, *India During Muslim Rule*, 7.

Chapter VIII
Islamic Reformist Thought in Shaykh Nadwi's Writings

Western Civilisation, Islam and Muslims[16]

The approaches adopted by Shaykh Nadwi towards Western civilisation require elaboration. He maintains that a blending of modern sciences with the fundamental teachings of Islam is possible. Its impact can be revolutionary for humanity who are the beneficiaries of the integration of knowledge. This plan of action, Shaykh Nadwi reiterates, can be implemented if Muslims take the lead in bringing about a genuine transformation in their respective countries. According to him, the integration process or the fusion of knowledge and faith resides only with Islam, because it has a universal message:

> Islam stands for a faith, a *shari'ah* and a law for which the term 'ancient' and 'modern' has no meaning. It is a civilisation whose roots are implanted in imperishable truths. Like an evergreen tree, it is always young and ready to send forth new blossoms.[17]

Shaykh Nadwi's critique of the Western civilisation must be contextualised to examine his major contributions in this field. In fact, his balanced approach, free from the polemics of both extremism and modernism, has set him apart as an independent intellectual who has chalked out new paths for understanding the Western mind. Already, his masterpiece, *Rise and Fall of Muslims* signposted his critical assessment of the West. This equally famous volume *Western Civilisation, Islam and Muslims* delineates the trends of Westernisation and their negative impact on Muslim countries. Shaykh Nadwi surveys several Muslim countries which had either been colonised by Western imperialism or independent Muslim countries owing to their peculiar political circumstances had succumbed to the arsenal of Western thought and ideals. As a result of polarisation, its baneful effect was inevitable. Tragically, the Islamic identity and character were lost to an alien system that was incompatible with the ideals of Islam.[18]

At the same time, the changing political landscapes are brought in full by Shaykh Nadwi in this work. The solution he offers is pragmatic: Islam alone offers a balanced outlook for mankind's progress. By the same token,

---

[16] Nadwi, *Western Civilisation, Islam and Muslims* (Lucknow, 1974).
[17] Nadwi, *Western Civilisation, Islam and Muslims*, 213.
[18] *Ibid.*, 10-14.

Shaykh Nadwi argues that the practical course for Muslims lies in making the fullest use of the physical sciences and technology of the West. These are then adapted to the lofty purposes which the Prophet (SAAS) had bequeathed to Muslims.

Shaykh Nadwi's treatment of the West can be summarised as follows:

> Western civilisation derives its sources from Greek and Roman cultures. The excessive dependence on rational thought with an obsession for materialism has moulded its character as a "worldly-oriented" system. Devoid of the spiritual resources the West has spawned a culture that seeks comfort in the burgeoning of material pleasure and a plethora of man-made religious institutions that merely provide temporary, if not illusory, spiritual peace.[19]

Towards an Independent Islamic Education[20]

The cataclysmic changes which were visible in the Arab world largely by its embrace of Arab nationalism and socialism, had a direct influence on its educational system. With the erosion of firmly rooted beliefs (*'aqā'id*), intellectual confusion and moral decline were grafted into the Arab Muslim culture. There was no critical evaluation of the educational system's compatibility with the Muslim mind and spirit. As a result, more emphasis was given to its political expediency rather than its effective outcomes. This anomaly had a direct bearing for the new generation of Muslim youth both in terms of their Islamic outlook and their approach to Western values. Against this background, Shaykh Nadwi delivered a series of lectures urging Muslim intellectuals to reassess the existing educational system. He warned them against wearing the "borrowed robes" of alien systems[21], because these would deprive them of their Islamic and cultural identity. Again, the theme of these lectures reminded the Arab world that their sources of inspiration were perennial and infallible. Moreover, the *sirah* of the Prophet (SAAS) served as a model of excellence for mankind. Therefore, the message he conveyed needed to be translated into tangible forms in the educational sphere. No dichotomy, Shaykh Nadwi asserted, existed between worldly pursuit and religious acquisition. This vision pursued by him was further

---

[19] For an elaboration on this theme, see Nadwi, *Rise and Fall of Muslims*, 113-56.
[20] A collection of lectures delivered in Riyadh, Kuwait and other Arab countries. Published in Arabic, *Nahw al-Tarbiyyat al-Islamiyyat al-Hirrat* (Riyadh, 1976).
[21] Nadwi, *Kārwān*, vol. 2.

Chapter VIII
Islamic Reformist Thought in Shaykh Nadwi's Writings

elaborated in a paper read at the International Muslim Educational Conference (Lucknow)[22] in 1975. For him, the conflict between intellectual leadership and the masses in Muslim countries created an imbalance in the educational system that was devoid of Islamic ideas. Extensive studies by leading educationists[23] had been carried out in the West and their findings had relevance to Muslim countries. An apt parable by Shaykh Nadwi illustrated the slavish mentality of Muslims towards the prevailing educational systems.

There is an old oriental story that accurately depicts the pitfalls of an unwary foreign educational system: Once upon a time there was a great flood, and involved in this flood were two creatures, a monkey and a fish. The monkey being agile and experienced was lucky enough to scramble up to a tree and escape the raging waters. As he looked down from his safe perch, he saw the poor fish struggling against the soft current. With the very best of the intentions he reached down and lifted the fish from the water. The result was inevitable.[24]

Shaykh Rabey Nadwi makes a pertinent point about Shaykh Nadwi's assessment of the Western educational system:

[Shaykh Nadwi] was convinced that the Western nations did not progress, because they were genetically superior to other nations. Rather, it was the result of their hard work and advancement in education. He was fully convinced that Islam is the divine religion and the practices of the Prophet (SAAS) are most suited for mankind. He believed Muslims could accomplish higher levels of success than the Western nations if they combined Islamic principles with the know-how of the West.[25]

Knowledge sustained by the Islamic higher objectives can save mankind from the perils of moral and spiritual ruin. By the same token, core values like *taqwa* and love for humanity will channelise our thoughts and actions into

---

[22] Nadwi, "System of Education in Muslim Countries" in *Al-Furqan English Digest* (1976).
[23] Don Adams, *Educational Patterns in Contemporary Societies* (London, n.d).
[24] Nadwi, *System of Education*, 62.
[25] Rabey Nadwi, *An Eminent Scholar*, 108.

constructive strategies. On a serious note, a rebellious spirit that seeks to undermine the worldview of Islam must be exorcised so that the *ummah* may redeem itself from its past failures. Muslims need to reassess Western civilisation from a different perspective. The challenges posed by it are not cast into iron moulds. The *ummah* on the other hand can reframe its own destiny by benefitting from the technological gains of the West without compromising its noble pursuits.

Pathway to Medina[26]

The following extract from *Pathway to Medina* is reproduced here to give the readers an overview of Shaykh Nadwi's deep-seated affection for the Prophet (SAAS). At the same time, his *da'wah* to the Arab audience was a bold reminder of their earlier role as ambassadors of Islam through whom the world was illumined with the exemplary teaching of the Prophet (SAAS). Nowadays, Shaykh Nadwi lamented, the Arab elite and educated classes have reduced their attachment to the Prophet (SAAS) to a soulless formality:

> The warmth and earnestness of love had gone out of it, although it was very clear that the love for the Prophet (SAAS) should be stronger than the love one had for one's dearest relatives or worldly possessions. Keeping these considerations in mind, I decided to bring out a collection of these speeches and writings which had proved beneficial and were widely acclaimed in the literary circles of the Arab world. I was encouraged by the hope that it might be of some use in rekindling the fire of love in the frozen hearts and mitigating the alarming effects of exaggerated nationalism. It, indeed, was all that a non-Arab and distantly placed Muslim could aspire to do.[27]

Madinah has its glorious history and its landmarks are a testimony to the epoch-making events that Shaykh Nadwi immortalised in the these words:

> Today you visit Uhud. It is only three kilometres from Madinah. This

---

[26] Originally written in Arabic, *Al-Tariqah ilā al-Madinah* and translated into English as *Pathway to Medina* (Lucknow, 1982).
[27] Ibid., 1-3.

Chapter VIII
Islamic Reformist Thought in Shaykh Nadwi's Writings

is the place that was saturated with the most precious blood of Islam and where exemplary feats of love and loyalty were performed. It was here that the limbs of Hamza were chopped off and his liver eaten. And 'Ammār bin Ziyād had breathed his last rubbing his eyes on the Prophet's (SAAS) face. It was from this side of the mountain that Anas bin al-Nadr had felt the sweet fragrance of Paradise and died with eighty wounds on his body. Here it was that the blessed teeth of the Prophet (SAAS) were broken and he had received a wound on his head also. His devoted *Sahābah* used their arms and backs as a shield to protect his body...The lions of Allah are asleep. The whole of its land is covered with the ashes of the moths of the candle of *Nubuwwat*. It is the home of the ardent love of the sacred Prophet and the valiant sons of Islam.

A Personal Loss

Shaykh Nadwi's meteoric rise to fame can also be traced to his mother's major influence on his life. Her death on 14 September 1968 brought to a sad end a relationship that had lasted over forty-seven years. Khairun-Nisā' Bahtar personified a saintly figure immersed in divine absorption, a paragon of virtue and an accomplished scholar.[28]

Khairun-Nisā' was an outstanding poet who described in poignant verses her innermost thoughts about the meaning and message of Islam. A widow for more than forty years she maintained high standards of decorum and ensured that her family members adhered to the code of conduct set out by her. Her love for Shaykh Nadwi was profound and her daily *du'ās* for his success was an indicator of her spiritual stature.

Khairun-Nisā' lived to an advanced age of ninety-three years. According to Shaykh Nadwi, his own tender disposition could not reconcile to the reality that she too was susceptible to the chronic ailments usually associated with old age. There was a gnawing fear in him that her passing away would make him an orphan. Such sensitivities left an indelible impression on his personality, and it was not un-often that he would visualise the void in his life if the inevitable happened.

Khairun-Nisā' suffered a hip fracture in 1968 and was confined to bed for several days. Her restless soul awaited the arrival of Shaykh Nadwi who had

---

[28] Her devotional anthology of poems, *Kalid-i Bāb i-Rahmat* (Key to the Door of Mercy) was published from Lucknow.

to travel to Bhopal for *da'wah* matters. His presence at home relieved her excruciating pain. Indeed, there was also a painful foreboding that Shaykh Nadwi dreaded most-death.[29]

Strike: An Assessment

The mounting workload as Rector of Nadwah combined with his extensive *da'wah* travels took its toll on Shaykh Nadwi's frail health. His deteriorating eyesight taxed his energies on his writing output. In profiling his multifaceted activities, it would be useful to keep in mind the twin issues he passionately pursued: *da'wah* and dialogue.

During this crucial period (1969) Shaykh Nadwi submitted his resignation to the executive committee of Nadwah. His reasons were based on his busy schedule of *da'wah* that did not allow him to carry out fully his duties as Rector. His association with the prestigious institution by now had already consolidated his popularity both locally and abroad. However, the executive committee declined to accept his resignation and urged him to reconsider his decision. Barely ten months later he had to face another crisis at Nadwah: The strike by students. Shaykh Nadwi was devastated; it was if the strike had literally paralysed him. Luckily, his close associates rallied around him during his period of ordeal. Steps were instituted to avert the strike from spreading to its other branches.

In sum, the phenomenon of strikes in the *madāris* has not been objectively studied. Leading *madāris* like Dār al-'Ulūm (Deoband) and Mazāhir al-'Ulūm (Saharanpur) had been similarly affected by student strikes. These were sometimes provoked by teachers with parochial interests in the form of hereditary claims, kinship demands and clannish loyalty.[30]

Turbulence in the Arab World (1967-1971)

The Arab-Israeli War of 1967 was a humiliating defeat for the Arab world, particularly the Egyptians who had taken an active lead in trying to obliterate the illegal occupation by the Israeli regime. Slogans of nationalism, however, produced the opposite result: Loss of territory, humiliation and capricious changes in the Middle East. Israel occupied Gaza, West Bank, Al-Quds and

---

[29] Nadwi, *Kārwān*, vol.1, 47-50.
[30] See Masih-Allah Khan, *Strike* (Port Elizabeth, n.d) for the madrasah perspective on student strikes.

Chapter VIII
Islamic Reformist Thought in Shaykh Nadwi's Writings

the Palestinians were subjected to a life of misery and suffering. During this period of Palestinian political upheaval, the war of attrition against refugees was intensified. This was also illustrated by the superpowers' (US and UK) preferential treatment of Israel. Their support and collaboration with Israel was unwavering just as much as their guarded criticism of its policy was ineffectual.

No different was the Arab defeat under the leadership of Nasser, which gave a somewhat incongruous picture of the war. According to Shaykh Nadwi, Arab goals were misdirected. Under the veneer of Arab nationalism, they disregarded the Islamic cause and frittered away their energies to support a neo-*jāhiliyyah*. Paradoxically, their numerical superiority was no match to the military firepower of the Israeli army. As the tragic turn of events unfolded, the power and capability of the Arab world diminished rapidly making them mere pawns and vulnerable to a new world order led by US and its allies.

About the American foreign policy, Shaykh Nadwi was vocal in his criticism:

> The tragically immobile or rather irresponsible policy of the US in regard to the Arabs is dictated by the traditional dislike of the Arabs and Islam by the West and has hardly anything to do with an intelligent assessment of the situation. The formulation of a realistic foreign policy requires wisdom, moral courage and ability in order to take correct decisions. Devoid of all values of justice and equality of mankind, American diplomacy is controlled by the Jews and a bureaucracy which is absolutely blind to the factual position. Such a policy reinforces the mental bankruptcy of a nation exposed to gradual decay.[31]

Likewise, he was unapologetic about the prevalent Arab leadership. He says:

> [And] it is a misfortune of the Arabs that their leadership has been unable to do justice to them and to their history. Their leaders have pushed them between the devil and the deep sea, and now they can neither retreat nor go ahead.[32]

---

[31] Nadwi, *The Arabs must Win* (Lucknow, n.d.), 24.
[32] *Ibid.*, 25.

Ethnic cleansing of Palestine continued unabated despite the UN Security Council Resolution 242 passed on 22 November 1967 which ordered Israel to withdraw from the occupied territories. Zionist terrorism ensured the displacement of Arab villagers followed by the illegal settlement of Jewish families from several parts of the world. The aggressive policies of Zionism saw the disfigurement of the collective Arab identity on its own soil.[33]

The crisis in Palestine brought into focus the role of the Palestinian Liberation Organisation (PLO) as the sole representative of its liberation from the Zionist regime. Under the charismatic leadership of Yasser 'Arafat, the demand for a Palestinian state changed from an armed struggle to a strategic policy. Political pressure from countries engaged in the thorny issue of independence narrowed down its future as an Arab problem. As early as 1973, Shaykh Nadwi had an opportunity to address the Arab leaders at a meeting convened by Rābitā. 'Arafat was also present. Shaykh Nadwi's message about the Palestinian issue was clear: It was a Muslim issue that required the moral support of the Muslim world. Furthermore, it had to be tackled with the Islamic spirit as was displayed in the past by the Muslim predecessors. Shaykh Nadwi noted:

> If you take this approach, you will be remembered in the same way as Salāhuddin Ayyubi (d.1193) is remembered. Otherwise, it will become a game of imperialist powers and many innocent lives will be lost for no reason. So, treat it as an Islamic issue and try to resolve it in the light of Islamic principles.

In his thought-provoking articles about the Palestinian problem, Shaykh Nadwi highlighted the tragic consequences of the Nasserist ideology which had caused political instability in the Arab world. Nasser advanced the cause of Arab socialism as a modified version of communism and vehemently promoted it to undermine the timeless Islamic values. In many instances, the unwary Muslim masses in the Arab world and the 'ulama' in the subcontinent did not fully grasp the existential threat it posed to Islam.

Shaykh Nadwi recognising the dangerous trends that emerged from Nasserism took bold steps to expose its claims of liberating the Arab world from Islamic conservatism. Egypt was the epicentre of importing

---

[33] See Suraya Dadoo and Firoz Osman, *Why Israel?* (Melville, 2013), 37-42.

Chapter VIII
Islamic Reformist Thought in Shaykh Nadwi's Writings

intellectual apostasy to the Arab world and launched "an intensive campaign of doubt and disbelief against the accepted tenets of Islam and its social and cultural ideals and practices." To this end, Islamic institutions like the mosques were reined in to give these a socialist slant. Likewise, the nationalisation of the prestigious al-Azhar university was a veneer to dismantle its autonomous character. In sum, Islam was under siege by Arab nationalism under the notorious leadership of Nasser.[34]

Arab Nationalism: A Reappraisal

In retrospect, Arab nationalism was a vigorous campaign to undermine the universal message of Islam. Its leading protagonist dominating the political stage was the Eyptian President Jamal Nasser, whose charisma and authoritarian rule developed a socialist ideology. An alarming trend was the unquestioning support given by the media to lend legitimacy to the Nasserist vision. Three extracts gleaned from newspapers and journals reveal the aura of sanctity (*taqaddus*) that was built around Nasser's personality:

> Abdul Nasser did not pass away, but he travelled on a heavenly journey just like the Messengers and holy men ascended to heaven...
> Jamal 'Abdul Nasser, prophet of patriotism, messenger of freedom: Your name and body ascended the heavens during your night of *mi'rāj* (heavenly ascent)...
> Nasserist vision is anchored on three principles: Socialism, freedom of expression and democracy. These three elements perpetuate the unity expressed by Nasser...[35]

There was no doubt that the descriptions of *mi'rāj* exclusively associated to the Prophet (SAAS) were given a carte blanche. Thus, Nasser's sanctity was elevated from a political figure to a prophetic status. To counter these exaggerated claims, Shaykh Nadwi's trenchant criticism of Nasser provoked a series of debates within India and Egypt. Sayyid Muhammad al-Hasani, editor of *al-Ba'th al-Islami*, the Arabic journal of Nadwah, collaborated with Shaykh Nadwi in exposing the Nasserist ideology. The strong diplomatic ties

---

[34] A critique of the Nasserist ideology is comprehensively covered in Nadwi, *'Ālam-i Arabi ka Almiya* (Karachi, 1980), 147-68.

[35] Nadwi, *Purāne Charāgh*, vol. 2, 391-95. For an overview of the audacious claims made by journalists and academics, see Nadwi, *Kārwān*, vol. 2, 67-69.

between India and Egypt were used to pressurise Shaykh Nadwi to stop with his critique of Arab nationalism, euphemistically called Nasserist ideology.[36] However, Shaykh Nadwi was unrelenting and continued with his mission of alerting the Muslim world of the Nasserist menace.

The complexities and realities facing the Arab world were closely followed by Shaykh Nadwi. For him the personality of the Prophet (SAAS) epitomised the success of the Arab world over the centuries. On many occasions he reiterated the timeless message contained in the following verse:

Their existence does not rest at all: On borders long and deserts vast
The Arab world exists because of Muhammad (SAAS)

These immortal lines of Iqbal served as the frame of reference for Shaykh Nadwi's vision of Islam. He was unequivocal in linking the Arab world's destiny to Islam.

I am no stranger to the Arab world. My knowledge (of the Arab) is not derived from second hand sources. I have not started my critique of Arab leadership or the shortcomings and crises facing the Arab world after the Arab-Israeli War. My presence on the Arab scene has not been sudden or arbitrary. Rather, I consider myself as a member of this big family that stretches from Morocco to Baghdad on the basis of my Islamic identity and cultural link. I share in their grief and consider my destiny to be inextricably linked with theirs. I do not regard myself any inferior from [the towering figures] of Taha Husayn, Mahmūd 'Aqqād in appropriating the cultural heritage established in Egypt (and other parts of the Arab world).[37]

Assessment

A noteworthy feature of Shaykh Nadwi's prolific writings is the absence of despondency and pessimism with regard to the Muslim *ummah*'s shortcomings. It is an indisputable fact that the "doom and gloom" syndrome tends to weaken the inherent dynamism of Islam. By contrast, Shaykh Nadwi's critique was tempered with a positive outlook as he believed

---

[36] Shaykh Nadwi's passport was confiscated by the Indian authorities in 1969, a subtle coercive measure against his uncompromising attitude towards Nasser.
[37] Nadwi, *Kārwān*, vol. 2, 73.

Chapter VIII
Islamic Reformist Thought in Shaykh Nadwi's Writings

that the beleaguered Muslim nations (in this case, the Arab world) could rise from the ashes of humiliation and soar above its present predicament. At the same time, he reminded Muslims that success was based on following the universal message of Islam. This message is in stark contrast to the parochial mission of the Jews, whose success is transitory, and to a large extent, illusory. To this end, *The Arabs must Win*[38] is a thought - provoking monograph that evokes a powerful picture of the future of the Arabs in the world of Islam.

The Indian Scenario: Religio-Political Developments

Shaykh Nadwi's multifarious involvement in the mainstream activities gave his critics the opportunity to insinuate that he did not focus fully on matters affecting the Indian Muslims. However, Shaykh Nadwi dispelled these misconceptions by citing one of his forebears Sayyid Ahmad Shahid's untiring efforts in the reconstruction of Muslim society. Thus, the reformist spirit was again articulated about the challenges facing the Muslim *ummah* both on the Indian soil and around the Muslim world.

Payām-i Insāniyat (Message of Humanity)

The circumstances and rationale for the establishment of the *Payām-i Insāniyat* have already been discussed in Chapter VI. An attempt is made here to assess its historic importance and its policy of rapprochement between Hindus and Muslims. It must also be noted that the *Payām* was not an extension of the Tabligh movement nor did it envisage the syncretic unity of religions. The reconstruction of society based on tolerance, harmony and morality were buzzwords of a stable India. In his public lectures, Shaykh Nadwi made reference to the sinking ship analogy employed by the Prophet (SAAS) to highlight the destiny of both Muslims and Hindus:

It has been reported by Nu'mān ibn Bashīr that the Prophet (SAAS) said: "There are people who do not transgress the limits of Allah, and there are others who do so. They are like two groups who boarded a ship; one of them settled on the upper deck, and the other, on the lower deck. So, when the people of the lower deck needed water, they said: "Why should we cause trouble to the people of the upper

---

[38] The Arabic version *Al-Fath al-'Arab al-Muslimin* was widely read in the Arab world.

deck when we can easily have plenty of water by making a hole in our deck?" Now, if the people of the upper deck do not prevent this group from such foolishness, all of them will perish.[39]

The origins of the *Payām* go back to the early 1950s when, in the wake of growing attacks on Muslims by Hindu extremist groups, Shaykh Nadwi began addressing joint Hindu-Muslim public rallies, calling for communal harmony and peace.[40] In the course of his interaction with Hindus in various parts of India he discovered that many of them had doubts and misunderstanding about Islam, which, he recognised, further widened the gulf between them. This led him, in 1974, to formally launch the *Payām-i Insāniyat*.

The activities of the *Payām* consisted, largely, of organising public rallies addressed by Shaykh Nadwi, his deputy Mawlana 'Abdul Karim Parekh of Nagpur, as well as other Muslim and Hindu leaders. It was also responsible for publishing literature in various languages on communal harmony, largely from the writings of Shaykh Nadwi. His speeches generally focused on moral values, communal hatred, violence and oppression of marginalised groups, social vices and corruption in public life. He, however, strongly believed that India could progress only in a climate of peace, free from inter-communal violence. For Muslims, this message was clear: They were enjoined by Islam to build friendly relations with faith communities rather than alienating them.

According to Shaykh Nadwi, the essence of *Payām* was to exemplify the teachings of Islam through Muslim interaction with others.[41] Not only was this their religious duty, it was also imperative if they were to live in security and peace as a minority group.

In advocating peace with others Muslims, Shaykh Nadwi insisted, would not be betraying their religion. Rather, he pointed out, Islam is clear that human beings, irrespective of religion, race, caste and class, are "the most precious" of Allah's creation, and an "expression of Divine mercy." This being the case, Muslims should strive for peace and must also raise their voices against all forms of oppression. In this way, they would show others that they are an integral segment of the country rather than a burden. But peace, he pointed out, could not be achieved if one community sought to impose its beliefs or culture on the others.

As much as religious tolerance had the potential to promote communal

---

[39] The *hadīth* appears in *Sahīh Bukhārī* and *Sahīh Sunan Tirmidhi*.
[40] Muhammad Rabey Nadwi, "The Philosopher of Islam: A Close Up" in *The Fragrance of the East*, 2000, 17-20.
[41] Nadwi, *Kārwān*, vol. 4, 55-57.

Chapter VIII
Islamic Reformist Thought in Shaykh Nadwi's Writings

harmony, Shaykh Nadwi also believed that democracy and secularism were mechanisms through which the *Payām* could achieve its aims.[42]

The core message of the movement was based on the unconditional love for humanity. Shaykh Nadwi observed:

> The excellence of man lies in his love and mercy for others: One person is pricked with a thorn, but another feels the pain. Man is gifted with tears which fall from his eyes when he sees a widow's head uncovered in helplessness, a poor man's kitchen unlit and a sick man in distress.[43]

According to Shaykh Nadwi, religion fosters faith and love for the Creator in the hearts and removes deception from the eyes. It was the work of Prophets to remove the curtain of darkness from the eyes and bring peace and tranquility to the hearts. He observed:

> We tell Muslims that you have devalued the message and work of the Prophets. You are guilty of being negligent. You have abandoned the treasure and have become an agent of the greedy people of the world. You have become a mere bargainer and developed a mentality of a selfish businessman. You were not supposed to be a mere trader. You had come here as a *dā'ī*, but you forgot your position and purpose for which you had come.
>
> Political parties and other outfits, instead of fighting for power and control, should strive to mend the broken structure of humanity. Likewise, they should refrain from working only for their own interests and of their own friends and relatives. Overall, they should work for the welfare of the entire mankind. Without this reform, no one can achieve peace and success.[44]

---

[42] See, Nadwi, *Kārwān*, vol. 2, 109-27. The *Islāhiyāt* writings provide useful insights into the importance of *Payām*.

[43] Nadwi, *Islam: An Introduction* (Lucknow, 1979), 152.

[44] A similar theme appears in the *islāhiyāt* series. See Nadwi, *Message of Humanity* (Springs, 2019).

Reflections on *Payām*

The subcontinent had witnessed over the centuries a plethora of religious activities that focused on the sanctity of human life, quest for righteous living, social upliftment, and most importantly, the interiorisation of spirituality. Alongside the evolution of Indo-Islamic culture, there was a blending of religio-mystical traits resulting from the convergence of faiths in the subcontinent. Framed from the lens of a cosmopolitan outlook, the rich tapestry of the evolving nation woven into the universal expression of love, compassion and brotherhood became more pronounced. These forms may have differed in the multicultural nation, but the imprint was permanent and significant. And it was in the subcontinent that the *insāniyat* (humanity) theme was raised and nurtured on the indigenous soil.

Muslim-Hindu co-existence existed from the early years of Muslim rule. It was, however, the British imperialist policies that caused a rift between the two communities. It was evident that the simmering tensions that surfaced from the late nineteenth century were politically motivated. In response to these rising tensions, the principles of secularism and non-violence were enshrined in the Constitution after the Partition in 1947 to safeguard the rights of its citizens. These constitutionally protective measures, however, did not deter Hindu extremists from accusing Muslims of supporting the nascent Pakistan cause. In the years that followed communal tensions flared up with a vengeance. Muslims were victims of a deliberate campaign by the Hindutva outfit to obliterate their collective Islamic identity. Thousands of lives were lost during the communal riots, and in its aftermath, the slogan of universal peace turned into a fragile truce negotiated by influential leaders of both communities.

The *Payām* movement must be understood in the context of the volatile situations existing in the country. Shaykh Nadwi's call had a two-fold purpose: First, to create a climate of mutual harmony so that faith-based communities might not harbour suspicions on the basis of patriotic loyalty. In this instance, Muslims were on the receiving end of hostility largely on account of ignorance by other communities. They were held culpable for the perceived excesses against the Hindu majority in the past Muslim rule. More perturbing was the notion that Muslims of India wholeheartedly supported the Pakistan state.

Second, Shaykh Nadwi believed that the reconstruction of the Indian society was only possible if the process of moral regeneration was set into motion. This approach was in response to the scourge of corruption, cronyism, nepotism and other vices that had sapped the dynamism of a great country.

Chapter VIII
Islamic Reformist Thought in Shaykh Nadwi's Writings

Instead, political parties and the bureaucratic system worked in cahoots to deepen the social inequality that was rampant over the decades. Shaykh Nadwi's *Payām* was unequivocal:
Communities would inevitably live in isolation and tear apart the fabric of a stable society. Needless to add, moral anarchy, social greed and political instability delinked the citizens from constructive ideals. As a result, mutual respect, empathy and humanitarian initiatives became hollow expressions, which impeded the implementation of universal values. In keeping with the tradition of Nizāmuddin Awliyā, the great saint of Delhi, Shaykh Nadwi echoed a similar sentiment:

Thorns spread on the pathway will be a thorny issue. Plant flowers instead so that the pathway may be lush with flowers and flowers only.

On the contrary, if moral vices eroded the collective life and outlook of society then divine punishment was inevitable. Shaykh Nadwi was forthright in this regard:

I am a man of religious convictions. My study of history tells me that sins and wrongdoings invite the wrath of Allah in the form of natural calamities. Allah warns us through these disasters. He tells us that He has greater power to destroy us than we have. When I hear of any cruelty and oppression, I shudder at the thought of divine punishment visiting people. I make no exception for anybody in this matter. Whenever acts of savagery and brutality occur, Allah's punishment is sure to visit upon the wrongdoers in a way unimaginable and unpredictable by the most learned astrologer. The problems relating to economic and social reconstruction get complicated, law and order situation deteriorates, administrative apparatus becomes loose and ineffective, intellectual and political leadership is rendered incapable of solving myriad issues facing the country which becomes weak internally and loses prestige in the international forums.[45]

Shaykh Nadwi stressed the awakening of the human spirit, as is evident from his speech on 2 December 1990:

What has sustained man throughout, from the earliest phase of

---

[45] Nadwi, *For Every Patriot to Read* (Rae Bareli, n.d.), 12-3.

history is that good persons have never lost faith in fellow human beings. They did not dismiss others as incorrigible animals or terminally ill patients. They did not harbour revulsion towards them. Nor did they deny their rights to existence.

The light of humanity can always be kindled. It survives under all hostile conditions. History testifies that Messengers of Allah always protected this light. They bore personal hardships, hunger, roamed in forests and deserts in inclement weather for serving humanity. No discomfort demoralised them or dissuaded them from their noble mission. What lay behind their inexhaustible energy and their ceaseless efforts was their belief that man is Nature's masterpiece.[46]

The need for divine guidance is articulated by Shaykh Nadwi:

The Messengers of Allah placed restraint on desires and urged man to be moderate in gratifying his desires. Far from stoking base desires they infused into man a strong desire for pleasing Allah and developing sympathy for fellow human beings.

We are keen on instilling the above quest for truth. Life does not stand for eating or drinking. Man should not lead a materialistic or animal life. We wish to infuse a new thirst which may sound novel today. However, our message is the one which was brought by all Messengers to their respective communities. The same message was most forcefully and clearly presented by Prophet Muhammad (SAAS) as the final word. This truth should be reiterated everywhere. Man is attracted only to his animal instincts, ignoring his true self. Mankind is in serious loss. We raise the call to truth with which the world might be unfamiliar. Yet we have not despaired of mankind. Man is gifted with conscience which is not dead. It is only clouded. Once it is cleansed of pollution, man is likely to greet truth and develop faith.[47]

In order to avoid the subtle trappings of the unity of religions approach, Shaykh Nadwi reminded his audience that the divine guidance serves as the common platform to articulate the concerns of the Indian society. The *Payām* was a pioneering movement with no formal structures and yet had a sobering impact on society. By and large, Shaykh Nadwi generally spoke at these meetings to ensure that there was no semblance of integrated faiths. More

---

[46] Hasani, *Nadwi: Thought and Mission*, 180.
[47] Ibid., 175-6.

Chapter VIII
Islamic Reformist Thought in Shaykh Nadwi's Writings

often than not speakers were inclined to overstep the boundaries of the *Payām* that inadvertently created the climate for religious debates. In Shaykh Nadwi's estimation, these were counterproductive to the goals set out by him for establishing the movement.

Indo-Pakistan War: 1971

Tension between India and Pakistan was not inherently religious. However, the hostile political climate in the subcontinent after the 1947 Partition did not show any signs of abating. Rather, the prospects of a war escalating were looming over the horizon. In response to the volatile climate, the marginalised Muslim community in India had to be wary about expressing their sentiments on the imminent war between India and Pakistan. Shaykh Nadwi recalled the swing of political events "as a critical and enduring period of his life."[48] He had hoped that mature and conscientious individuals from both countries would make constructive efforts to pursue peace and security. This reciprocal approach could enable both countries to make strides in technology and create a viable economy for the benefit of their respective citizens. Muslim leaders like Mawlana Azad who had vociferously opposed Partition had reassessed their previous stance and supported Pakistan as a neighbouring country. Azad's vision of an undivided India was used as the propaganda tool to vilify his status as an erudite scholar to the extent that questions were raised about his religious credentials. His argument was based on the premise that religious affinity cannot unite areas which are geographically, economically, linguistically and culturally different. This allusion was to East Pakistan (Bangladesh). However, after Partition, Azad was pragmatic enough to accept the creation of Pakistan.

> It is to the interest of India and Pakistan that they should develop friendly relations and act in co-operation with one another. Any other course of action can lead only to greater trouble, suffering and misfortune.[49]

Political expediency dictated the bloody course of events in 1971 and brought in its wake a deepened sense of insecurity among Indian Muslims. What was

---

[48] Nadwi, *Kārwān*, vol. 2, 128.
[49] Abul Kalam Azad, *India Wins Freedom* (Calcutta, 1964), 227.

more disturbing were the political implications for Muslims. These were looked upon with suspicion and their patriotism was challenged by militant Hindu groups. The war of 1971 ironically also saw the dismemberment of Pakistan. East Pakistan, which was geographically and culturally cut-off from West Pakistan, was in the throes of a national uprising. Also, West Pakistan's political supremacy, inequitable distribution of state resources and discriminatory policies were contributing factors to the break-up of Pakistan. A tenuous link existed between the two wings of Pakistan and Islam. However, nationalist and cultural aspirations dominated the independence discourse. The Pakistani occupation of East Pakistan had terrible consequences and eventually led to the establishment of Bangladesh. It was, therefore, not surprising to see nationalism rooted in a culture alien to Islamic values gaining momentum. For Shaykh Nadwi these alarming trends were reminiscent of *Jāhiliyyah* and posed a challenge to the spirit of brotherhood envisaged by Islam. His monograph *Calamity of Linguistic and Cultural Chauvinism* was in direct response to this growing menace, which he argued violated the universal teachings of the Prophet (SAAS).

The following extracts reveal Shaykh Nadwi's incisive analysis about the vices entrenched in the Bangladeshi society and their grave implications for the broader community of Islam.

[When] the languages are excessively praised and raised to the level of divinity, these become a curse rather than a blessing. These again serve as a vehicle of destruction instead of a means of goodwill and harmony. Then human beings are sacrificed at their altars like the living sacrifices offered to the deities. Languages are meant to unite rather than divide; they are to communicate and not to separate. Likewise, languages bring the people together, make them share each other's cares and worries and act as mentors.

[It] is a dangerous precedent to keep any language deprived of the Islamic thought and spirit, and vocabulary connected with the faith. Languages are closely in touch with inner recesses of the heart and mind. If the language of any people is stamped with its pagan (read as *Jāhiliyyah*) tradition and mindset then, be careful, that nation is always susceptible to intellectual and cultural apostasy.[50]

---

[50] Nadwi, *Calamity of Linguistic and Cultural Chauvinism* (Lucknow, n.d), 14-21.

Chapter VIII
Islamic Reformist Thought in Shaykh Nadwi's Writings

Shaykh Nadwi's Assessment

Shaykh Nadwi's assessment of cultural and linguistic tolerance had far-reaching implications for Muslims in South Asia. For Indian Muslims, this approach not only promotes the Prophetic dictum of human dignity, but it also strikes at the root of *Jāhiliyyah*. Shaykh Nadwi refers to the period of the *salaf* where merit took precedence over racial and cultural affiliation. Any deviation from this path resurrected the *Jāhiliyyah* past of chauvinism in its various forms. The Prophetic model was a criterion for Shaykh Nadwi's presentation of an Islamic order. In contrast, he was critical of Muslim societies in Pakistan and Bangladesh, which had not removed the shackles of cultural and linguistic chauvinism. He was equally critical of these Muslim countries which were separated after the civil war in 1971. The cause was attributed to linguistic and cultural prejudice. "The idol of language prevailed over the faith in the unity of Allah (*tawhīd*) and universal human brotherhood. National and racial fanaticism smashed the brotherhood of Islam and *Jāhiliyyah* overcame the unifying bonds of the Islamic faith." The image of *Jāhiliyyah* permeating Muslim countries, Pakistan and Bangladesh, is employed to compare and contrast the positive effects of cultural and linguistic tolerance among Indian Muslims.[51]

Travels

As an executive member of Rābitā, Shaykh Nadwi led a delegation to six Muslim countries on a fact-finding mission. The countries' cultural importance was a reason among other things for their visit. Shaykh Nadwi's diarised account of these countries sheds much light on the changing geostrategic situations as well as the ebb and flow of religious activities. His account also gives an overview of the political developments in these countries. Shaykh Nadwi says:

> This book *Min Nahr Kābul ila Nahr Yarmuk* (From Kabul to Yarmuk) records my thoughts and impressions and is also based on my specialised research and experience. The views reflected here do not represent Rābitā's standpoint.

---

[51] The book was published from Ankara, Turkey by Dār al-Hilāl.

It was a lens through which Shaykh Nadwi's spectrum of activities and insightful comments were depicted. The following countries were covered: Afghanistan, Iran, Lebanon, Syria, Iraq and Jordan.

Shaykh Nadwi's reflections on and objective analysis of these countries are accurately recorded in his travelogue. The shortcomings in Afghanistan, which once carried the legendary tradition of Mahmud Ghaznawi are highlighted. Similarly, Iran's cultural heritage, a source of inspiration, is positively portrayed by Shaykh Nadwi. However, its sectarian orientation with specific reference to the concept of *Imāmat* is critically examined. Iraq's changed political environment as a result of the military coup is also discussed in detail. In sum, Shaykh Nadwi's thoughtful comments are tempered with a graceful style, and is an attempt to illustrate his personal reminiscences of these countries.

Not all the countries visited by the Rābitā delegation provided a cordial reception. Syria is a case in point. In fact, the course of events did not run smoothly as the delegation anticipated in this country. In Shaykh Nadwi's words:

> [Our] brief stay in Syria was meant to interact with leading religious and public figures and organisations. The programs were already organised in our honour. However, the following incident in Damascus unfolded in a dramatic way: We were unceremoniously expelled from the city and driven to the Syrian-Lebanese border. The intelligence agency entered the room in the Umayyad hotel where we stayed, ordered us to pack our bags and bundled us into a car.
>
> When the news of our abrupt departure from Damascus reached our acquaintances in Beirut, there was a huge outcry from the local and Arab media concerning this eventful experience.[52]

About his impressions of Iran, Shaykh Nadwi followed a balanced approach. The Rābitā delegation which undertook a fact-finding mission in 1973 visited Iran. This was a pre- Iranian revolution visit with no rhetoric of the Sunni-Shiah divide. Shaykh Nadwi's impressions of its glorious past illustrates his unbiased approach to the conflicting portraits of Islam in the country. He appreciated the Iranian Islamic temperament, their gentle disposition and their efforts to unite Muslims of different sectarian

---

[52] Nadwi, *Kārwān*, vol.1, 161-2 (paraphrased).

persuasions. Iranians' unconditional love for Islam and the *Ahl al-Bayt* (family of the Prophet) was proverbial as is evident from the number of shrines dedicated in memory to them. Even the mosques possessed unrivalled architectural designs and were filled with worshippers at the time. More importantly, the Quran was printed in illuminated fonts and considered the best publication in the world for its high- quality standards.

Notwithstanding these remarkable achievements of the Iranian nation, Shaykh Nadwi lamented the *'aqīdah* dilemma that set the Iranians apart from mainstream Islam. Although Shi'ite Islam was the country's official interpretation, the paradoxical nature and complexities of its cardinal beliefs diluted the original spirit of the Islamic faith and practice. For example, The Imāms whose lineage is traced to the Prophet (SAAS) were elevated to the status of infallibility. This belief militated against the *Ahl al-Sunnah's* formulation of the *'ismat* (infallibility) doctrine. According to Shaykh Nadwi, the prospects of reconciliation on this count were virtually impossible.

By the same token, Shaykh Nadwi critiqued the disproportionate construction of mausoleums, a trend that had a massive appeal to the Iranian populace. He drew a parallel with shrine worship in the subcontinent, Egypt and Iran and expressed his dismay at the carnival atmosphere that marked these assemblies and events. It was regrettable that that the teachings and contributions of the Imāms and *mashā'ikhs* were de-sacralised at the altar of un-Islamic pursuits.

According to Shaykh Nadwi, the attachment to the Quran requires total dedication and reverence. The soul of the Quran is correct pronunciation (*tajwīd*), memorisation and interpretation based on authoritative sources. For a transformation to take place Shaykh Nadwi advised the *'ulama'* and intellectuals that *tawhīd* in its true sense needed to be embedded in the hearts of people. Rigidity of religious beliefs based on exaggerated claims cannot revive the creative spirit of Islam. If sterile thoughts led to the intellectual decline of the Iranian society, then introspection was essential to remedy the situation.

Shaykh Nadwi's wise counsel and reappraisal of the prevailing conditions in Iran did not bring about any changes on account of the political upheavals and entrenched ideology that formed the basis of Shi'ite Islam. Six years later, the Iranian Revolution of 1979 overthrew the dictatorial rule of the Shah. What followed thereafter was a Cold War between the Islamic Republic of Iran and its neighbouring Arab countries. The rhetoric of Islamic unity assumed sectarian forms and shattered any hope for Sunni-Shiah reconciliation

amid threats of war and political rivalry.[53]
In sum, Shaykh Nadwi directed his energies to constructive engagement with countries embracing doctrinal differences. His important book *Conflicting Portraits* may be regarded as the sequel to his travelogue.

Conclusion

In response to the challenges facing the Muslim world, self-introspection and the courage to initiate meaningful changes are priorities. Shaykh Nadwi says:

> Islam can again help the country in rooting out the religious, linguistic and racial prejudices, and sectarian leanings. It can help to instill tolerance, sense of justice and equality of mankind. If you are a patriot, your primary concern should be to ensure that the country remains united and strong. And it should be of little importance to you as to who provides the remedy. Therefore, one need not reject the principles that can save the country, simply because these have been outlined by the Quran or from the teachings of the Prophet (SAAS).[54]

---

[53] Details of the Rābitā delegation are gleaned from Nadwi, *Daryā Kabul,* 77-126.
[54] Nadwi, *Reconstruction of Indian Society: What Muslims Can Do?* (Lucknow, n.d.), 23.

Chapter IX

East and West: Cultural Encounters

A study of the history of Nadwah suggests its crucial role in shaping the future of Islam in India. Like other *madāris*, it also emphasised the shared goal of spreading the Islamic teachings and defending Islam against the deviant sects.[1] Its progressive ideas both in terms of the curriculum development and *da'wah* were consolidated during the rectorship of Shaykh Nadwi (1961-99). Nadwah's international recognition was also due to his fame as an accomplished writer. The annual convocations pointed out to Nadwah's profile as an academic institution with impressive credentials.[2]

A significant development took place when Nadwah passed a resolution to celebrate the eighty-fifth anniversary of its existence in 1975. By all accounts, the convocation was regarded as the turning-point in defining the transnational character of the institution. Dignitaries from the Arab world as well as other countries attended its elaborate celebration. Mention may be made of the Shaykh al-Azhar Dr 'Abdul Halim Mahmud, who presided over the sessions. Apart from his literary works, the Shaykh was also known for his outstanding publications on the early sufi orders whose contributions shaped the Muslim society in Egypt. Schleifer has noted that the Shaykh's efforts "bridged the artificial gap that had been developing since the nineteenth century separating *'ilm* (knowledge) from *ma'rifah* (cognition), sobriety from ecstasy, *shari'ah* from *haqīqah* (truth) and Azhar from sufi life and thought.—[3]

As this occasion was considered a milestone in Nadwah's history, the mammoth task of planning was a symbolic expression of its role as the premier Islamic institution in the subcontinent. In his *Rudād-i Chaman*, Muhammad al-Hasani has captured in emotive language the spirit of the proceedings:

> The Convocation was the first historic event in the subcontinent where knowledge and excellence, beauty and perfection converged. Representatives from the Islamic universities arrived in huge

---

[1] For a historical account of Nadwah, see Barbara Metcalf, *Islamic Revival in British India*, 336-42.
[2] Refer to *Tārikh Nadwat al- 'Ulama'*, vol. 2 for details about Nadwah's growth and development.
[3] Abdullah Schleifer, "Sufism in Egypt and the Arab World" in *Islamic Spirituality*, vol. 2 (New York, 1991), 204.

numbers. This captivating scene could not be ignored by any historian or chronicler.[4]

In his inaugural address Shaykh Nadwi reiterated the Indian Muslims' commitment to Islam derived from the primary sources of the faith:

By the Grace of Allah, the Muslims of India are to a large extent autonomous as regards Islam. They draw guidance from the earliest and the most authoritative sources of Islam - the Quran, *sunnah* and from the lives of Islam's earliest representatives... Their faith and their life are tied to the radiance of Islam, not to the ephemeral glimmerings of the Muslim nations and Arab states.[5]

'Abdus Salām Kidwai in his review of Nadwah's achievements paid glowing tributes to the prestige of the institution in the Islamic world. He observed:

First, the aims and ideals of the earlier leaders of the Nadwah, during its first two stages, clearly indicate that they did not intend to establish merely an Arabic *madrasah* imparting religious education with a bit different curriculum from the traditional institutions. Their primary aim was to save the Islamic branches of learning from the danger of gradual decay and ultimate extinction hovering over its head. Their second objective was to redeem the Muslim community from the growing menace of irreligiousness, scepticism and apostasy which was spreading like a torrent with the advancing materialism of the West.[6]

Islamic Authenticity: An Overview

Shaykh Nadwi reiterated the Indian Muslims' unique role in preserving their Islamic identity. Notwithstanding the crosscurrents of history after the First War of Independence in 1857, the sacrifices of the *'ulama'* and Islamic activists contributed immensely to the Indian struggle of liberation from the colonial rule. In fact, the role of the *'ulama'* was two-fold:

---

[4] Muhammad al-Hasani, *Rudād-i Chaman* (Lucknow, 1976), 79-80.
[5] *Ibid.*, 117.
[6] 'Abdus Salām Kidwai, *85 Years of Nadwat al-'Ulama'* (Lucknow, 1976).

Chapter IX
East and West: Cultural Encounters

- Guiding the community (*millat*) by zealously safeguarding their Islamic presence in the Hindu-dominated country.
- Making the legacy of Islam accessible to the masses by promoting the Urdu language.

According to Shaykh Nadwi, the Indian Muslims can justly be proud of being self-sufficient in the matters of faith. They draw their guidance from the noble characters, ambitions, trials and sufferings of the *salaf*. They have 'hitched their ideals and ambitions not to any setting or rising star' of the Muslim countries, but to the pristine teachings of Islam. Needless to add, their attachment to the Prophet (SAAS) "[has] helped them to steer their way clear from the troubled waters of many a social and cultural crisis and has thus saved them from losing their identity like several other peoples entering India to make it their homeland."

The Islamic authenticity (examined in Chapter 3) is cogently expressed by Shaykh Nadwi in these words:

> Indian Muslims as torchbearers of Islamic faith and culture are not subservient to other Muslim countries which might have forsaken their religious ideals. Alternatively, they deem it improper to be enamoured by their bygone culture or civilisation that of course has no link to Islam.

Shaykh Nadwi categorically shares the Indian Muslims' commitment to the authentic interpretation of Islam. Their common vision with the other Muslim countries or nations is derived primarily from the Qur'an and *sunnah*. Again, he vociferously maintains that they will not surrender their Ibrahimi culture which has been nurtured on the Indian soil for over a millennium. Shaykh Nadwi explains:

> [We] are confident that if we are successful in living up to our resolve, translate our decision into action with the best of our talents and abilities and our Allah will not be displeased with us, we shall not be a loser in the end. For we are convinced that the whole of the universe along with its physical law of causation is by the Will of Allah.[7]

---

[7] See Nadwi, *Kārwān*, vol.2, 192-4.

Personal Loss: Family Members

Several months after the successful Convocation, Shaykh Nadwi suffered a personal loss; the death of his sister, Amatullah Tasnim. He recounted the years of kindred spirit expressed in their unparalleled love for each other and the joys of reading and research. Amatullah's outstanding publications were a marked departure from the confined learning environment for Muslim females. The early twentieth century saw the emergence of Islamic education for them from different strands of Islamic reformist thought. Of course, the aristocratic or religious minded families were exception to the rule. Private tutors or educated family members offered in-house Islamic education. The pedigree of Islamic learning, classical and literary, was in many ways singularly associated to Shaykh Nadwi's family. Amatullah was a beneficiary to the rich repository of Islamic knowledge.

A scholar of repute, Amatullah had the singular honour of translating Imam Nawawi's *hadīth* collection, *Riyād al- Sālihīn* into Urdu. The *Zād al-Safar* earned critical acclaim from the '*ulama*' and scholars alike for its brevity of expression and fluency. This work saw several reprints from leading publishers and continues to be a must-read in the subcontinent.

To date a Hindi translation has been published which has elicited positive response from both Muslim and non-Muslim readers. The motivation for this work has an interesting background. Amatullah's brother, Dr 'Abdul 'Ali urged her to do the translation as an effective remedy for her sickness. A work of significance like the *Riyād* entailed total devotion and preoccupation. For Amatullah, the translation project brought indescribable tranquility to her life.

Subsequent to its publication, her fame reached many religious and literary circles. In Saudi Arabia, for example, the work was serialised and broadcast on several radio stations. There were other books written by her for children's literature that were equally recognised for their innovative style.

Amatullah was an embodiment of perseverance and humility. She accompanied Shaykh Nadwi on his first *hajj* in 1947. Her spiritual yearnings crystallised into a form of supplications known as *Munājāt*. These stir emotions and are spontaneous expressions of heart-throbbing experiences.[8]

Another personal tragedy affected Shaykh Nadwi in 1979. Muhammad al-Hasani's untimely death dealt another blow to his family. He was a rare

---

[8] For a detailed obituary, see *Purāne Charāgh*, vol. 2, 340-69.

Chapter IX
East and West: Cultural Encounters

prodigy; a remarkable scholar whose mastery over Arabic was unrivalled. An adept translator of Shaykh Nadwi's writings in both Urdu and Arabic, Muhammad al-Hasani was the founder and editor until his death of Nadwah's Arabic journal, *Al-Ba'th al-Islami*. His trenchant criticism of Arab nationalism and his reformist ideals were articulated in his own writings and to a large extent he replicated the missionary zeal of Shaykh Nadwi. His sad demise at the relatively young age of forty four deprived the *ummah* of a versatile genius, a prolific writer and an outstanding *dā 'i*.[9]

The visionary spirit of Muhammad al-Hasani transcended territorial boundaries, and like Shaykh Nadwi he focused on the renewal of Islamic faith and practice. The following extract reveals his perceptive observations about the challenges facing the country:

> Our country (India) enjoys unprecedented success and there is no paucity of resources, because Allah has blessed it with manifold favours. Take education for example: It is accessible in many states. Excellent standards permeate our tertiary institutions and this is evident from the burgeoning admission of students. Our country has excelled in many sectors like agriculture and technology and has surpassed neighbouring countries in these fields. It has joined the ranks of countries possessing nuclear capacity. Notwithstanding its great strides and phenomenal progress, there is a pointed decline in the collective life of Indians. What are the factors that have contributed to this decline? There is no accountability linked to the fear of Allah (*taqwa*). This is the only key that can unlock the potential of mankind. It is the only panacea for the ills plaguing society. Clearly, a restoration of ethical values like accountability, transparency and equity are essential for the nation's real progress.[10]

Muhammad al-Hasani had a distinguished academic career. Although he did not strictly follow the traditional *madrasah* curriculum, he was guided in his wide-ranging studies by his father, Dr 'Abdul 'Ali and Shaykh Nadwi. He rose to prominence in Arabic writing which showed a mature and reflective style. His editorials in Arabic and Urdu journals were remarkable for their originality and lucidity. In many respects his writings were a mirror image

---

[9] See Muhammad Thāni Hasani, *Sawānih Sayyid Muhammad Hasani* (Rae Bareli, 2013).
[10] These views have resonance in Shaykh Nadwi's overall concern about the amelioration of the Indian society.

of the *ummatic* concerns articulated by Shaykh Nadwi. His critique of Arab nationalism is a case in point.

Translations of contemporary works was no easy task as these required mastery of languages combined with a nuanced understanding regarding the dynamics of effective communication. For example, Muhammad Asad's The Road to Mecca is a classic work of unequalled merit. Muhammad al- Hasani translated this work into Urdu by consulting eminent scholars like Daryabadi and at the same time developing his own literary style that did not compromise the charm and beauty of the English text.[11]

In the Political Arena

During the turbulent period of India's struggle for independence the Indian National Congress was in the forefront against British rule in India. It succeeded in enlisting a number of Muslim and Hindu leaders of various political persuasions who made exemplary sacrifices in the freedom struggle. In the wake of the communal tensions, it formulated three principles which were enshrined in the Constitution to protect the basic human rights of its citizens: Democracy, secularism and non-violence. These measures were necessary, because under the guise of Hindutva punitive actions were perpetrated against the marginalised communities, especially Muslims who suffered much in terms of loss of life and property.

There existed a predictable pattern of leadership in the Congress; the Nehru dynastic rule (i.e. Jawaharlal Nehru, the first Prime Minister of post-Partition India followed by Indira Gandhi who brought charisma to the party). No doubt, the ideals of the Gandhian philosophy were the cornerstone of its success story. Another factor in garnering support was the Muslim vote bank. The Congress acknowledging the Muslim factor for their political success exploited it with the assurance of political stability and religious protection. However, during Indira Gandhi's tenure of office political instability became more pronounced. A set of draconian laws was imposed during the State of Emergency in 1975 together with her notorious family-planning schemes which consolidated her authoritarian rule. This was more evident in the repressive policies of her son, Sanjay Gandhi who by all accounts was considered the *de facto* ruler of India. The political fortunes of the Congress Party in 1977 changed dramatically after it was

---

[11] Reference to the Urdu translation entitled *Tūfān se Sāhil tak*.

Chapter IX
East and West: Cultural Encounters

defeated by the Janata (People's) Party. Ironically, this period was the tilting-point of the Hindu-dominated rule in India.[12]

In retrospect, the Emergency period brought a rude awakening to the masses about insecurity, the state's political ploys and nepotism. These gnawed into the social fabric of India. More ominous trends in the political arena gave way to pessimism and despondency. The civic sense (*sha'ūr*) and the moral high ground of Indian politics were jettisoned for the more blatant form of rule by compromising the ideals promoted by its founders. Shaykh Nadwi's sensitive soul balked at this disturbing turn of events. The conflagration caused by the state of emergency and other unconstitutional policies had engulfed the country into a state of turmoil. Against this background, his important meeting with Indira Gandhi and her subsequent visit to his home at Rae Bareli focused on the issues of national interest. Also, his correspondence with Indira Gandhi revealed his patriotism and expectations of a moral society:

> The [emergency] has produced a tragic aspect which has deprived its (citizens) from the sense of independence and confidence. India is a free democratic country which is saved from all forms of aggression and extremism and its struggle for the ideal has no parallel in other countries... It is important to appraise the situation in the country. If any nation chooses cowardly and subservient roles (it is natural) the qualities of self-sufficiency, valour and morality will be removed from their lives...[13]

Shaykh Nadwi's larger-than-life personality dealt with matters that affected Indian citizens in general. However, the specific issues concerning Muslims were taken up by him through his association with Muslim organisations. He reiterated that the framework of the constitutional principles of equality and freedom of religion were the benchmark for safeguarding Muslim identity. In stark contrast was the proposed implementation of the Uniform Civil Code. It was a brazen attempt to undermine the Muslim Personal Law and also Muslims' inalienable rights enshrined in the Constitution. (This debate was to resurface during Rajiv Gandhi's premiership - the Shah Bano case.) Indira Gandhi's second legislative

---

[12] Shaykh Nadwi's detailed discussion about the period of emergency sheds much light on the tense atmosphere that gripped the country. Detention without trial, gagging of the press and suppression of oppositional voices characterised this turbulent period. Nadwi, *Kārwān*, vol. 2, 201-30.

[13] *Ibid*, 220.

period from 1979 to 1984, indirectly sparked off the fire of communalism. Hindu national movements were emboldened to "work out strategies for the cultural and political genocide of Muslims so that they would no longer survive as a culturally distinct community within this society."

In sum, Shaykh Nadwi's patriotic spirit was illustrated in a letter to the Prime Minister, Narasimha Rao (1991). He writes:

I will not draw on your precious time by referring to peripheral issues or only the grievances and requirements of the largest minority group (Muslims) of India. Whatever I am going to say is only in the overall interest and welfare of India and by way of matters of principles[14].

The rest of the letter details the deepening concerns about the fast-deteriorating morale and sad plight of the people of the country that Shaykh Nadwi had at heart.

Hindutva: An Assessment

The rise of Hindutva during Congress rule coincided with the political ferment in the country. Religious outfits like the RSS had a two-pronged plan to incite violence against the Muslim minority: Employ agitational politics to stir up communal violence and challenge Muslim patriotism in the backdrop of Indo-Pakistan conflicts.

The militancy of its campaigns unfolded in many ways and were designed to blame Muslims for their belligerent attitude. The *madāris* and Islamic institutions were singled out as the dens of terrorism and preaching hate speech against other faith groups. These extremist organisations distorted Indian history to malign the Muslim contributions to the multireligious and multicultural India. For them, the Muslim conquests of India implied forced conversion to Islam and the demolition of temples. Centuries later after Partition, the blame game was amplified by Hindutva. Historic mosques like the Babri Masjid were demolished in the name of the historical redress process. At the heart of this campaign was the obliteration of the Muslim culture which was nurtured on the indigenous soil.

---

[14] Nadwi, *Kārwān*, vol. 3, 81.

Chapter IX
East and West: Cultural Encounters

Hindutva: Defenders of Hindu Extremism

Hindutva or Hindu extremism opposed the social reforms of progressive organisations like the Arya Samaj which condemned the caste system as a blight to Hinduism. In the nineteenth century, reactions to these social reforms resulted in the vigorous Hindu revivalist consciousness.

Muslims, in particular, were perceived as enemies of Hindutva who demanded their expulsion from India or else be forcibly converted to Aryanism. Leaders of these extremist movements adopted an aggressive policy of recasting Muslim rulers like Mahmud of Ghazna as plunderers and their invasions as a calculated campaign to wipe out Hinduism. Not surprisingly, therefore, the rhetoric of foreignness against Muslims became a contributing factor in communal riots that characterised the deepening crisis between Muslims and Hindus. It was not un-often that Urdu, despite its Indian rootage, was looked upon with suspicion and, for political reasons, was identified as a conspiracy against Hindu revivalism. In sum, Muslim-bashing or Islamophobia in its incubation stages developed virulently in the country.

Muslim Conquests: A Reappraisal

The stereotypical representations of the Muslim conquests in the subcontinent have hampered a broader understanding of the important role of *da'wah* during these epoch-making periods. It is generally assumed that *da'wah* operated in a social milieu detached from the flux of political events. By contrast, the Muslim rulers strengthened the cause of *da'wah* and institutionalised the ideals of social justice. Many of them left a lasting legacy towards building a viable and stable society that was free from religious bigotry and the blight of racial discrimination.

Shaykh Nadwi provided anecdotal evidence to prove that social justice was extended to the non-Muslim communities. Muslims diffused the most valuable treasure they had with them - the wealth of faith in Allah *(tawhīd)*, equality and Prophethood. There was no coercion or massacres against those who did not accept Islam. Instead, the Muslim rulers imparted the values of human dignity and equality in a climate of co-existence. At the same time, Muslims introduced intellectual, social and cultural changes, adding richness to the cosmopolitan nation. Arts and literature and new branches of learning created a "renewed zest and vigour in a new and brighter world in these lands." The Indo-Muslim culture exemplified the seamless fusion of different cultures and streams of thought that did not compromise the essential belief system of Islam.[15]

Maghreb: Morocco

Rābitā's *da'wah* was aimed at bringing closer the Muslim world and establishing networks of shared Islamic interest. Shaykh Nadwi's participation in the conference, organised by Rābitā in Morocco in 1976, was an opportunity to visit this rich historic region of the Muslim world. Libya, Tunisia, Algeria and Morocco formed the area called Maghreb and played a pivotal role in the consolidation of Islamic culture and civilisation. A proud legacy, the Qarawiyyin University stood as an example of classical Islamic learning. The *Futūhāt* (Conquests) of Maghreb, especially Morocco, was an integral link to the Muslim rule in Andalusia (Spain). Ismail Faruqi has aptly summed up the Islamic spirit of conquest by the immortal statement of the Muslim general, 'Uqbah ibn Nafi who overran the whole of North Africa and reached the shore of Atlantic Ocean: "If I know of a land beyond this sea, I would cross it on horseback and conquer the land for Islam."[16]

As a member of the Federation of Islamic Universities with its headquarters in Morocco, Shaykh Nadwi had been invited on a regular basis by King Hasan. However, circumstances did not provide him the opportunity to visit the country. As Shaykh Nadwi noted in his travelogue,[17] the conference in Rabat was an appropriate forum to express his thoughts about the real crisis engulfing the world of Islam. For him, the true spirit of Islamic values was embodied by the exemplary conduct of the *Sahābah*. Their *imān* blazed a trail of spirituality and imparted a warmth to the world with their qualities of unshakable resolve and principles - attributes that gave a distinctive Islamic identity to the Muslim *ummah*.

Shaykh Nadwi also visited Casablanca to pay tribute to 'Allāmah 'Allāl Al-Fāsi (d. 1973), the leading Moroccan *'ālim* who combined in his personality *'ilm* (knowledge) and strenuous effort in the way of God. The scholar-activist kept abreast of contemporary political systems. He was the leader of the Istiqlāl party and also an admirer of Shah Waliyullah, the reformist scholar of India whose celebrated work *Hujjat* was avidly read by

---

[15] Shaykh Nadwi's *Muslims in India* is a conspectus of the the changing religious landscape brought about by the Muslim rule over the centuries.

[16] Ismā'il Rajī' Al-Faruqi and Lois Lamya Al-Faruqi, *The Cultural Atlas of Islam* (New York, 1986), 216.

[17] Nadwi, *Do Hafte Maghrib Men* (Lucknow, n.d.)

Chapter IX
East and West: Cultural Encounters

him. Moreover, he was among the few Arab scholars who were familiar with the contributions of the Indian *'ulama'*.[18]

At the invitation of King Hasan, Shaykh Nadwi used the opportunity to deliver a persuasive speech to both royalty and dignitaries at a *majlis* organised in his honour. Shaykh Nadwi while maintaining the rules of protocol did not deflect from his mission of engaging the attendees on the importance of *da'wah*. In the words of Sayyid Rabey:

> I was present in that speech. I was amazed to hear Shaykh Nadwi deliver such a scholarly and enlightening speech. I felt that it was merely due to Allah's special help which came down due to his sincerity and burning desire for *da'wah*. I have witnessed it happen on so many other occasions also. There were instances when he addressed very powerful people and it appeared that they might feel offended and retaliate. But it never happened so. Instead, his position got further elevated in their eyes as it happened in Morocco. The king came up to the door to see him off and lamented that he was invited to visit Morocco so many times, but did not come. The king asked him to come to Morocco more often.[19]

There was a similar situation with the king of Jordan. Shaykh Nadwi got an opportunity to meet the king. While advising the king, he pointed out to the weaknesses that were prevailing in the country. The king listened to Shaykh Nadwi's advice patiently and appreciated it.

Towards a New World

At the invitation of the Muslim Students Association (MSA) to attend its annual conference at Bloomington in Indiana (USA) in the summer of 1977, Shaykh Nadwi responded with much enthusiasm. After the conference, programs were organised by the MSA which took Shaykh Nadwi to the important cities as well as educational and cultural centres of North America (US and Canada). Muslim communities who hailed from India, Pakistan and the Arab world were settled in the major cities of North America. Shaykh Nadwi's extensive itinerary included New York City, Chicago, Washington, Montreal and Toronto.

---

[18] *Ibid.*, 90-1.
[19] Sayyid Muhammad Rabey Nadwi, *Syed Abul Hasan Ali Nadwi: An Eminent Scholar, Thinker and Reformer* (New Delhi, 2014), 100.

Shaykh Nadwi addressed twenty gatherings, half of them in Arabic and half in Urdu. He also had the opportunity to speak at five leading American universities - Columbia University at New York, Harvard University at Cambridge, Detroit University at Ann Arbor, South California University at Los Angeles, and Utah University at Salt Lake City. Furthermore, he was asked to deliver the Friday *khutbah* (sermon) in the Prayer Hall of the United Nations' headquarters and in the central mosques of Toronto and Detroit. A striking theme of these lectures, in the words of Shaykh Nadwi, [was] to speak straight from the heart, without mincing words, and offer some sincere suggestions to the Muslim brothers and sisters who have settled in the West, particularly in the US.[20]

Message to the West

Two distinct themes emerge from Shaykh Nadwi's Lectures in the US:

- Critique of Western civilisation so that humanity may not fall into the perils of materialism and godlessness.

- Muslim responsibility in terms of *da'wah* so that they may be ambassadors of the Prophetic teachings.

Before we attempt to examine the unifying themes of Shaykh Nadwi's lectures, it is worth noting that the Qur'anic recitation in a session or event generally guided him to deliver a specific message. His extempore speeches were precise and relevant; anecdotal accounts were presented to appeal to the minds and hearts of the audience. This forceful approach had a profound effect on his audience. Shaykh Nadwi's introductory comments at the Islamic Centre of Washington clearly reinforces this point:

> I was wondering what you would like to hear from me] when suddenly the Quranic recitation rescued me as it always does. I felt a wonderful portrait of the modern age, which has come to the extreme pinnacle of material development drawn in these verses:
> *There were two men of whom We bestowed one of the two vineyards,*

---

[20] Adapted from the Foreword to *From the Depth of the Heart in America* (Lucknow, 1978), 2.

Chapter IX
East and West: Cultural Encounters

surrounding both of them with date palms and putting a tillage in between. Both the vineyards yielded abundant produce without failure and We caused a stream to flow in their midst so that the owner had fruits in abundance and said to his neighbour, while conversing with him: "I have greater wealth than you and I am stronger than you in numbers." (18: 32-4)

Referring to the above parable, Shaykh Nadwi maintains that the possessor of the gardens "is a plain materialist, the soul of rebellious ingratitude, an egoist, while the other is a truthful believer; he is weak, he does not possess gardens of grapevines, but he is a believer and Allah has blessed him with faith."[21]

In a similar vein, Shaykh Nadwi's speech at Harvard University made a clear distinction between faith and material progress. Two conflicting portraits of American life have disrupted the balance that Islam advocates. There is no doubt that the US is fortunate, because Nature has endowed it with material prosperity. This is the result of pragmatic and robust imagination and admirable ethics of the American people.

Shaykh Nadwi ungrudgingly acknowledges its strides in science and technology. However, he equates the US as a land of misfortune. Material progress is no substitute to achieving spiritual equilibrium. Americans have not looked within themselves (*anfus*), but outside the realms of the horizon and the results have been tragic. The true worth of humanity has been forgotten. As a result, endless conflicts provoked by superpowers against weaker nations for exploiting natural resources or establishing their hegemony have become the norm. Conflict zones like Palestine have escalated into bloodshed with the US working in complicit with Israel. Also, many Muslim countries have been supported by the US to establish dictatorial regimes.

As discussed elsewhere in the volume, the East and the West relations have not demonstrated any semblance of goodwill and genuine dialogue from either Europe or the US. The trust deficit, Shaykh Nadwi argues, needs to be remedied. Therefore, Muslims have the great responsibility of engaging constructively with other faith communities to bring about meaningful changes in the religious landscapes of Europe and the US.

The thematic message contained in Shaykh Nadwi's public lectures at the Muslim Community Centre in Chicago (and other cities) is two-fold: Muslims are urged to preserve their religious heritage, and shun varieties of Islam, because these are detrimental on the American soil and other countries where

---

[21] Nadwi, *Muslims in the West: The Mission and Message* (Leicester, 1983), 67.

Muslims reside as minorities.

Two factors, economic and political, accounted for Muslim migration to the West in the early twentieth century. Economic opportunities were a catalyst because of the need for skills and labour in these countries. A parallel development was the volatile political situation in Muslim countries adopting repressive policies against their respective populations. In the wake of these persecutions, the West offered safe havens to Muslim refugees.

In the light of these underlying circumstances, Shaykh Nadwi's address to the emergent Muslim communities has a contemporary significance. He observes:

> I declare unequivocally that if your life and your stay in the West are beneficial to Islam, your migration is not only justifiable, but also an act of worship. But if your faith and the religious life of your children are not assured, I shudder at it. I shudder at the thought in what state death might come, and then, should we tell Allah that we came here only to earn our livelihood. Such a motive is not in the Islamic character; it does not befit a Muslim. If you had taken due care that your faith remains unblemished, and you are associated with some religious fervour, and have built up an Islamic environment or founded a circle (*halaqah*) in which religious activities are promoted... then you have my sincere good wishes.[22]

Need for an Islamic Environment

Shaykh Nadwi provides a framework for establishing and nurturing the Islamic environment, in the following words:

> Islam and the Quran demand of Muslims that they be the standard bearers of truth and virtue. They should possess a genuine Islamic disposition so that the Americans (and Europeans) here can distinguish clearly between their own society, which is being driven mercilessly by materialism, and an Islamic society which is pure, healthy and dignified. Observing it they will remark that the real joy of living is in the Islamic society.

---

[22] *Ibid.*, 129.

Chapter IX
East and West: Cultural Encounters

If we disconnect from the fountainhead of Islam... [then] American, Japanese, Iranian, Indian and Pakistani Islam will emerge. Such Islamic societies will appear whose mental attitudes and natural inclinations and values are widely apart.

Shaykh Nadwi is critical of the cultural accretions resulting from local versions of Islam. This did not imply that variations of culture vitiated the composite character of Islam. In response to the noted scholar Dr Suleyman Dunya's views on Islam as a universal religion, Shaykh Nadwi makes the following comment:

I wholly agree that Islam is not a territorial faith, yet, it also needs a distinctive environment to establish Islamic institutions, a congenial climate ... that may transcend cultural and intellectual standards and give forth, as one would say, the fragrance of Islam. It requires an Islamic homeland for it is neither a mystical doctrine nor a philosophy nor a collection of soulless beliefs and rituals, but a real, living and all-embracing faith[23].

The all-embracing faith, to which Shaykh Nadwi refers can be adapted to local conditions. However, Shaykh Nadwi makes a cautious appeal to Muslim communities who establish Islamic institutions on nation-based sentiments or on ethnic lines to desist from such practices as these are detrimental to the cause of da'wah. In this respect, he points out to the youth who may be alienated from mainstream Islamic education due to the rigid approaches and conflicting presentation of Islamic teachings. The prospects of them embracing atheism are the real concerns.

United Nations: Forum of Muslim Aspirations

Alongside his perceptive analysis of Western civilisation, Shaykh Nadwi reminded the Muslim countries' representatives about their pivotal role at the United Nations. His Friday *khutba* at the Assembly room was an impassioned appeal for Muslims to realign their vision to the universal message of Islam. The following extracts reveal Shaykh Nadwi's concern for the *ummah*:

---

[23] *Ibid.*, 129.

The Muslim countries carry a weight in the world and even in the United Nations. Were the people whom we have the honour to represent possessed of a living faith, the Muslims would even now be honourable in the world and commanding a position of strength and importance.

Brothers, do not look up to anyone for aid or support. Avoid being a hanger-on of others. Borrowed strength is ephemeral. It does not endure. Also let it not be that your name shine in the comity of nations, and numerically, you are strong in the population statistics, but have no weight in the scales of Allah. Believers, the spark of faith is present in our hearts and we are not only the bearer of the message of Islam, but proud of it here in the US, the citadel of Western power. We are no parasites or spongers, but possess our own culture and civilisation and we are not going to accept any grafting upon it.[24]

Lectures in Chicago

Shaykh Nadwi's visit to Chicago brought him into contact with a cross-section of community leaders and public figures who represented several strands of Islamic thought. The Nation of Islam[25] is a case in point. Under the charismatic leadership of Warith Deen Muhammad, the organisation severed ties with its founder Elijah Muhammad (d.1975) and committed itself to the Sunni interpretation of Islam. This was a dramatic changeover from the rhetoric of Elijah Muhammad claiming Islamic legitimacy as a Messenger of God.

The lecture series of Shaykh Nadwi focused on the perennial truths of Islam that cut across racial and geographical barriers. His reference to Malcom X (Malik Shahbaz) who gave a moving account of his *hajj* experience was a reaffirmation of the Islamic concept of brotherhood. The *hajj* for Malcom X stood in stark contrast with the deep-rooted racist attitudes he developed under the influence of Elijah. He recounts his own experience:

> During the past eleven days in the Muslim world, I have eaten from the same plate, drunk from the same glass, and slept in the same bed

---

[24] *Ibid.*, 123.
[25] See Edward Curtis, *Black Muslim Religion in the Nation of Islam, 1960- 1975* (Chapel Hill, 2006).

Chapter IX
East and West: Cultural Encounters

(or on the same rug)- while praying to the *same* God - with fellow Muslims, whose eyes were bluest of the blue, whose hair was blondest of the blond, and whose skin was the whitest of the white. And in the *words* and in the *actions* and in the *deeds* of the 'white' Muslims, I felt the same sincerity that I felt among the black African Muslims of Nigeria, Sudan and Ghana.

I could see from this, that perhaps if white Americans could accept the Oneness of God, then, perhaps, they could accept *in reality* the Oneness of man - and cease to measure, and hinder, and harm others in terms of their 'differences' in colour.[26]

Farewell Address to American Muslims

A close associate of Shaykh Nadwi and translator of his books in English, Ibadur Rahman Nishat, gave his personal impressions about the former's farewell address to the American Muslims. It was a recapitulation of his lectures and speeches on the American soil. A point-form summary is given hereunder:

- Do not abandon the sources of Islamic teachings and traditions.
- Give preference to the protection of one's *imān* over worldly considerations.
- Introspection can be strengthened through affinity with spiritual guides.
- Do not undermine the *islāhī* contributions of the *salaf.*
- Religious arrogance stems from the misplaced belief that Islam can only be understood in a contemporary context.
- Avoid intermingling of sexes at Islamic functions and events.[27]

Da'wah to the Western Audience

The following synopsis is based largely on Shaykh Nadwi's work, *Muslims in the West.* He is unequivocal in his presentation of *da'wah.* For him, *da'wah*

---

[26] Alex Huxley, *The Autobiography of Malcolm X as Told to Alex Huxley* (New York, 1992), 215.
[27] Nadwi, *Muslims in the West*, 155-6.

implies that the Muslim presence in the West can have only one justification- to communicate the message of Islam to non-Muslims, both in word and deed. A Muslim cannot exist as a Muslim unless he fulfils the mission entrusted to him by Allah and His Prophet (SAAS).

Shaykh Nadwi's *da'wah* vision is rooted in the Prophets' (SAAS) mission which is epitomised by his noble conduct.

Prophetic Mission

Shaykh Nadwi reiterates his view that the Prophetic mission should serve as the reference point for a meaningful understanding of *da'wah*. All the Prophets that came and the last of the Prophets, Muhammad (SAAS), made the "making of a new man" their sole concern. They opened to man the infinite forces within. They awakened in him his hidden possibilities. They opened the eye of the heart that he could see the Creator of this great universe and receive the treasures of guidance. Citing the following *ayah*: *"The Lord of East and West; there is no God save Him; so, you should choose Him alone for your Guidance.—* (73:9). Shaykh Nadwi maintains that the Prophets liberated man from all forms of idolatry and dualism, from superstition and subservience to irrational tradition and from every submission except submission to the Creator of the universe.

Prophetic Methodology

Rooted in divine guidance, the Prophetic methodology, Shaykh Nadwi contends, did not touch on mundane matters, but sought to put before man the "right kind of objectives, to draw from him the highest desire, the highest commitment." Addressing the Western world, Shaykh Nadwi makes an impassioned appeal to turn to the Prophetic revelation exemplified by Islam for its salvation. What does Islam offer to the Western mind? His response is twofold: The Qur'anic teachings with its inexhaustible intellectual wealth can still put new life into the nations of the world and is capable of facing the problems of modern times. Prophet Muhammad's (SAAS) life and the wisdom of his teachings are applicable to all, covering a wide variety of situations and problems. However, Shaykh Nadwi states that for the Western nations to turn to Islam requires moral courage and admission of failure. This is not possible, Shaykh Nadwi argues, for the following reasons:

Chapter IX
East and West: Cultural Encounters

The man in power in the West would rather see nations destroyed, landscapes and resources devastated, the whole of humanity plunged into distress, than make the admission. A false sense of prestige and inflated pride in their scientific and material progress, prevents them turning to the life-enriching achievements of that unlettered Prophet (SAAS) who alone offers the hope of salvation. The result of this self-conceit is that generations of mankind face the possible destruction of all existence.[28]

Against this gloomy background, Shaykh Nadwi offers hope to mankind by articulating the need for world leadership to access its spiritual resources from the message of Prophet Muhammad (SAAS) which will "lead humanity to its rightful destiny." Shaykh Nadwi boldly states that such a step would require a revolution, a tremendous capacity for sacrifice, to move from one way of life to another - in short, a profound revolution that would make leaders the example of humanity. This clarion call, he insists, is explained by the following *ayah*:

And we wished to be Gracious to those who were being depressed in the land, to make them leaders (in faith) and make them heirs. (28: 5)

After a prolonged absence of sixteen years, Shaykh Nadwi visited the US again in 1993 to participate in the World Conference of Religions in Chicago. The conference attracted a multitude of leaders and scholars of different religious persuasions and reflected a "unity in diversity— theme. In other words, it was a forum for articulating universal spiritual values. In this context, it was deemed appropriate that Shaykh Nadwi's monograph *The Revolutionary Message of Islam* be circulated at the conference preceding his address. A time slot in the concluding session, which included devotional prayers, was allocated to Shaykh Nadwi to address the participants about Islam.

Sojourn in Pakistan

The Asian conference hosted by Rābitā Islami in Pakistan in 1978 gave Shaykh Nadwi the opportunity to visit this leading Muslim country. As the

---

[28] *Ibid.*, 51.

only country established in the name of Islam, Pakistan was expected to play a pioneering role in the affairs of the Muslim *ummah*. Unfortunately, it suffered a turbulent political crisis[29] under various regimes whose covert aims were to destabilise the Islamic identity of the country. Under the regime of General Zia-ul-Haq[30] some semblance of Islamic rule was introduced. The *shari'ah* was partially implemented by way of the *hudūd* (penal) laws and the interest-free banking institutions. By the same token, the Council of Islamic Ideology served as a think-tank to monitor the phasing in of the *shari'ah* at every level of society. It was, therefore, expected that a stable Pakistan would have a positive impact on the marginalised Muslim community in India, whose sacrifices were etched in the `ages of history. Likewise, Shaykh Nadwi's assessment of Zia-ul-Haq revealed his admiration for the latter's Islamisation policies. His interaction with Muslim leaders, kings, presidents was based on his view that Islam should reach the corridors of power rather than alienating them from Islam. This approach was earlier adopted by Shaykh Ahmad Sirhindi.

Shaykh Nadwi's *da'wah* vision was strongly reflected in his lectures. These focused mainly on the following issues:

- Pakistani society needs a reappraisal. Only commitment to Islamic values can remove its social ills.
- Islamic leadership requires tremendous courage which can be drawn from the exemplary lives of the *salaf*. This trait has the potential transformative power for the Pakistani nation.
- Intellectual apostasy can be eradicated only if an educational system rooted in an Islamic ethos is properly crafted.
- Contemporary challenges can be positively addressed if the *madāris* review their present curriculum and contextualise the dynamic spirit of Islamic learning and teaching.[31]

Shaykh Nadwi's visit to Pakistan was productive, especially in his meetings with leading scholars, *'ulama*, political figures, *madāris* and universities. One may cite two eminent personalities with divergent orientations, Hakim Muhammad Said and Mawlana Mawdudi with whom

---

[29] For a brief survey on the political history of Pakistan after the Partition in 1947, see Waheed-uz Zaman, *Islam in South Asia* (Islamabad, 1993).
[30] Nadwi, *Purāne Charāgh*, vol. 3, 127-38.
[31] See Nadwi, *Hadīth-i Pakistan* (Karachi, 1983)

Chapter IX
East and West: Cultural Encounters

Shaykh Nadwi maintained decades-long relations. Moreover, his spiritual connection with the country, despite an absence of almost sixteen years, continued to grow considerably. Thus, *Hadīth-i Pakistan*[32] is a priceless gift of shared experiences and advice towards self-growth and development. Its *islāhī* contents resonate in this important work of Shaykh Nadwi.

Tuhfah Series

Like his *ismaʿi* lectures which addressed the Arab world, the *Tuhfah* series is a collection of lectures addressed to a Muslim audience in the subcontinent. The *islāhī* features are discernible in the *Tuhfah* series. Shaykh Nadwi presented his published lectures as a "gift" to the Muslim communities he visited. He believed that the reconstruction of Muslim society was imperative to eradicate the shortcomings that had sapped its vitality and dynamic character. One thing emerges clearly from this genre: The universal values embodied in Islam are the only panacea for the ills affecting Muslim societies.

The following is a summary of the dominant themes that are woven into his lectures and public addresses which he delivered in countries as far afield as Kashmir and Bangladesh. The relevant extracts gleaned from these works are aimed at giving the readers a thematic understanding of Shaykh Nadwi's contributions to the reconstruction of Muslim society. As discussed elsewhere in the volume, the concerns raised by him are relevant to Muslim societies in any part of the world. Likewise, the solutions he offers are pragmatic and also reflect his *ummatic* vision.

Tuhfah-i Kashmir (1981)

The act of leading a good, useful and dignified life consists, basically, of Allah-consciousness, altruism, self-restraint and willingness to subordinate one's own advantage to the common goal. These also include unselfish interest in the welfare of the others, respect for mankind, the right to protect the life, property and honour of fellow men (which are positive traits). Similarly, preference to duties over rights, defence of the weak and the downtrodden and the strength to stand up against the oppressors, firmness in opposition to those who have nothing to be proud of save power and wealth and refusal to be

---

[32] The *hadīth tuhfah* series, like the *ismaʿī* series in the Arab world is a collection of lectures delivered in South Asian countries. The *Hadīth-i Pakistan* was reprinted in India under a new a new title, *Daʾwat-i Fikr wa ʿAmal* (Lucknow, 1999).

overawed by them - these are the essential conditions of a good and noble life. They serve as the fundamental requirements of a healthy society and a strong and honourable nation.[33]

Tuhfah-i Dakkan (1982)

The motivating factors of any language are its religious and spiritual characteristics. It lends weight to a thing and raises it from the ground to reach the highest pinnacle... Thus, when a speech is imbued with religious feelings it produces a strong effect when it is sustained with spiritual energy. If a student of the Quran wishes to understand its underlying spirit and makes a concerted effort (towards this goal) then I can assure you he will be ahead of reputed Arabs. Passion and commitment are the potential traits that can empower the *ummah*.[34]

Tuhfah-i Malwa (1983)

But there is an exceptional glare of love in man's eyes which is not found in any other creature. His heart is characterised with a softness and melting quality inspired by love and quivers with the touch of pain and suffering for others. Such a heart is not in the treasures of the angels and surely man alone can present to his Lord a heart full of sincere love for others... If such a drop of tear is put in a sea of transgression, it will cleanse it. If it falls on a forest of sins, it will burn it and fill the space again with the light of virtue. The angels can bring forward anything, but they cannot present this drop of tear. The angels do not sleep due to their awareness of Allah's being and attribute. But their vigil does not have the excellence of man's inability to sleep due to the sufferings of others.

The quality of love permeating through the human heart is a very precious gift of Allah. When something stirs it, it assumes a strange power. It rises above the considerations of religion, community, nation and motherland. It then only sees another man's heart and feels its suffering and is drawn instinctively to it.[35]

---

[33] Nadwi, *Tuhfah-i Kashmir* (Karachi, n.d.), 103-4.
[34] Nadwi, *Tuhfah-i Dakkan* (Lucknow, 2005), 20.
[35] Nadwi, *Tuhfah-i Malwa* (Lucknow, 1992), 34-6.

Chapter IX
East and West: Cultural Encounters

Hadīth-i Pakistan (1984)

The most urgent need is a concerted effort to reform its society. Society must be saved from the rivalry and obsession of amassing wealth. There can be no greater disaster after the dissolution of the Ottoman Empire than anarchy in Pakistan. I consider everything else in relation to this problem as secondary. The first imperative for Pakistan is to be firmly established and maintain its Islamic moral responsibility. Other matters are peripheral. For Pakistan to maintain its distinctive identity and be protected against anarchy, the reform of society is crucial. The moral decline which has rapidly crept in its society, bringing in its wake compounded problems and disastrous results must be halted. The vociferous call must be given through the mosques, at political gatherings, Islamic conferences and on platforms of organisations. Pakistan must be saved from two dangerous elements: First, it must be saved from sectarian conflicts and second it must be protected against political anarchy. History shows the best of democracies of the time succumbed to corruption when they put an end to [possibilities] of progress.[36]

A revised edition of *Hadīth-i Pakistan* was published under a new title *Da'wat-i Fikr wa 'Amal*. The following excerpts from this important work encapsulate Shaykh Nadwi's impassioned message to the Pakistani Muslims:

It is evident that no belief system or educational institution of a nation can function in a vacuum. It requires an environment of freedom and resources. The society needs to develop unhindered. Also the articulation of '*aqā'id* must be consistently maintained.

A language promoting superficial unity (of a nation) undermines the efforts of the Prophets. Furthermore, it has a debilitating effect on the *islāhī* work in any part of the world.[37]

This important work must be read together with Shaykh Nadwi's thought-provoking monograph, *Calamity of Cultural and Linguistic Chauvinism*, to assess his critique of Pakistan and Bangladesh.

---

[36] Nadwi, *Tuhfah-i Pakistan* (Karachi, 1984), 38-40.
[37] Nadwi, *Da'wat-i Fikr wa 'Amal*, 61-3.

Tuhfah-i Mashriq: Banglades (1984)

You should appreciate and value your nation. You should close the wedge that has widened and caused a chasm between the old and new generations. Embrace both these sections. Embrace the *'ulama'* fraternity from whom you gain help in *dīnī* issues. They can be your guide and familiarise you with the Quranic teachings. The educated class can be utilised to disseminate these Islamic teachings in the Bangladeshi language. Both these classes can strenghten the nation by virtue of Islam's pioneering spirit. Bangladesh constitutes the third largest family demographically in the community of Muslim nations... The Islamic renaissance may start here and you have the potential to do this. It is imperative that Islam be given preference over family ties and lineage. Therefore, no obstacles should be placed in the pursuit (of its goals). We should love all of mankind and should love all languages. Ensure that your language progresses. Love your language, but do not harbour animosity against any language. Linguistic prejudice has no historical relevance in Islam.

This point is further reiterated by Shaykh Nadwi:

> Muslims in the past learnt all languages and gained mastery over them and developed Islamic literature through them. The Persian language is an instance in point. As the language of fire-worshipers (Zoroastrians) it produced in its literary history poets like Sa'di, Rumi, etc.[38]

Signposts of Moral Decadence in Saudi Arabia

Shaykh Nadwi's association with the organisations and scholars in the Saudi kingdom gave him insight into the emergent Arab society whose culture was gradually eroded by Western influence. These disturbing trends could be felt in the *Haramayn*. He, therefore, felt duty-bound to raise his concerns to the Saudi kingdom in respect of their position as custodian of the *Haramayn*. However, the kingdom was not impervious to the outside influences, especially the American presence in the oil-rich regions. More alarmingly, the Saudi-American joint ventures exposed a new, if not alien, lifestyle to the Saudis that was indiscriminately adopted by the royalty, elite and

---

[38] Nadwi, *Tuhfah-i Mashriq* (Karachi, n.d.), 31-2.

Chapter IX
East and West: Cultural Encounters

youth alike.

A historic letter written by Shaykh Nadwi in 1979[39] to the Saudi monarchy highlighted the social vices that had crept into the Saudi society and threatened to dilute the pristine form of Islam. Some of the concerns were:

- The proliferation of programs and films screened on television impacted negatively the Saudi mindset. As a result, violence, promiscuity, thrillers and anti- social tendencies were condoned.
- Sporting fanaticism became more glaring among the youth. Manly sports like archery and swimming were not given due recognition.
- Self-indulgence, extravagance and a profligate lifestyle were operative words for the elite. Their consuming passion for material comforts was proverbial. Consumerism shaped their outlook concerning Islamic values. Owing to their self-centred lives, no efforts were made to alleviate the grinding poverty and the bleak future facing the Saudi populace.[40]

Shaykh Nadwi's critique of the Arab society illustrated his independent thinking and also his deep concern about the moral decadence in Muslim societies.

"Consultation above confrontation" was his guiding principle to the very end. His letter to royalty (mention has been made elsewhere in the chapter) reinforced Shaykh Nadwi's view that Islam should reach the "portals of power."

A parallel development to the unchecked materialism was the rise of Islamic extremism in the kingdom. The growing discontent among some *'ulama'* to the intrusive presence of Western culture gave rise to a number of extremists among Arab youth. An influential extremist of Salafi leaning, Muhammad 'Abdullāh al-Qahtāni, claiming to be the promised Mahdi besieged the *Haram Sharif* during the *hajj* period in 1979. For five days there was pandemonium in the sacred precincts as the Mahdi group held the *hujjaj* (pilgrims) hostage. Their denunciation of the Saudi monarchy continued unabated. The bloody clashes between the extremists and the troops brought

---

[39] These letters are contained in his Arabic work, *Kayfa Yanzur al- Muslimūn ila al-Hijāz wa Jazirah al-'Arab.*

[40] Nadwi, *Kārwān*, vol. 2, 278-81.

the siege to an end. Al-Qahtāni the ringleader was killed by the Saudi troops while the other extremists surrendered. After approximately two weeks normality returned to the *Haram*. This tragic event was reminiscent of the siege by the deviant sect, Qaramites in the early period of Islam. Shaykh Nadwi expressed his concern that the sanctity of the *Haram* was violated by deviant sects with political ambitions.[41]

Sirah Conference

The International *Sirah* Conference was hosted in several Muslim countries to bring into broad relief the multifaceted personality of the Prophet (SAAS). Its success was credited to the visionary spirit of Shaykh 'Abdullāh Ansārī. Shaykh Nadwi's recollection of the Ansārī's contributions is eloquently expressed in these words:

> My acquaintance with Shaykh Ansārī spanned over a period of thirty years. During this period, I was able to observe at various meetings and conferences his unassuming personality, sincerity of purpose and passion for *'ilm* (knowledge).
> A pioneering figure in the establishment of the *sirah* conferences, Shaykh Ansari demonstrated his profound love for the Prophet (SAAS). Through these conferences, he infused a dynamic spirit to the study of the noble personality of the Prophet (SAAS). I had participated in many international conferences and symposia, but none that could rival the *sirah* conference presided by Shaykh Ansārī. His presence radiated an aura of spirituality among all the delegates who represented leading institutions in their respective countries. His charismatic personality endeared him to me.[42]

The conference was attended by intellectuals, high- ranking dignitaries and royalty from the Arab world. In his inaugural speech, Shaykh Nadwi reminded the audience that the dominant theme of the conference should focus on the pernicious effects of *nifaq* (hypocrisy) in Muslim societies.

> Thanks to Allah that our disease is not *kufr* (rejection of faith) or *shirk* (polytheism). Our disease is *nifaq* (hypocrisy). We proclaim one thing

---

[41] *Ibid.*, 284-6.
[42] Nadwi, *Purāne Charāgh*, vol. 3, 51-60.

Chapter IX
East and West: Cultural Encounters

and do something else. This duplicity has made us and our society untrustworthy. As a result, Islam has now become unattractive to others though our character was the main reason for others to appreciate Islam in the past.[43]

King Faisal Award (1980)

The King Faisal Foundation was established in 1976 by the sons of King Faisal, the third king of Saudi Arabia, to perpetuate their father's humanitarian legacy. Central to the Foundation's broad mission was its commitment to the spirit of preserving and promoting Islamic culture.[44] The first King Faisal International Prize for service to Islam, was received by Mawlana Mawdudi in 1979 in recognition of his scholarly excellence. Shaykh Nadwi received this prestigious prize in 1980. His response in keeping with his tradition of independence also reveals his spirit of self-sacrifice. He explained:

> I was in Rae Bareli and as usual preoccupied with my writing schedule when my nephew Sayyid Muhammad Rabey who had arrived from Lucknow informed me that I was the recipient of the Faisal Award. An invitation to receive the award in Riyad was already dispatched. What followed was an inundation of congratulatory messages.
> The procedure for the Faisal Award is as follows: Nominees for the Award are solicited from Islamic organisations and distinguished personalities. After much deliberation, the name of the candidate is announced. Apart from the citation and gold medal, a substantial monetary amount[45] is also given.
> In a letter addressed to the Chairman of the Selection Committee, I expressed my appreciation for its decision although I felt there were other scholars who were more worthy to receive the award... The cash prize was to be distributed to the following recipients as announced by my representative, Dr 'Abdullāh 'Abbās Nadwi. Half the cash prize was to be allocated to the Afghan refugees with the two other institutions, Tahfiz al-Quran and *Madrasah* Sawlatiyyah (Makkah)

---

[43] Rabey Hasani, *An Eminent Scholar*, 89.
[44] *Saudi Aramco World* (September/October 2000), 37.
[45] The cash prize was two hundred thousand *riyals*.

receiving a quarter of the cash prize, respectively.[46]

The sense of independence (*istighnā*) characterised Shaykh Nadwi's attitude towards inducements of wealth and status. These were to him paraphernalia of the transient life and did not deflect him from his *da'wah* mission. The following incident related by the leading scholar of Islam, 'Allāmah Yūsuf al-Qardāwī is a testimony to Shaykh Nadwi's spirit of independence:

I recall an incident approximately thirty years ago when Shaykh Nadwi visited Qatar. This was a period of extreme financial difficulty for Nadwah.

There was a strong suggestion by his friends and well-wishers that he should approach the influential businessmen of Qatar and present before them the problems faced by Nadwah and thereby solicit their financial assistance. Shaykh Nadwi firmly rejected this proposal even under these trying circumstances and remarked: "These wealthy individuals are all sick because of their inordinate love for the world. We are their physicians. Does it behoove a medical practitioner to stretch out his hand to his patient in order to cure him?" I rejoined: "Shaykh, you will be assisting the Nadwah by enlisting their financial support.— To this the Shaykh replied: "They cannot distinguish between a sincere and questionable contribution. In their estimation, we are only opportunists."[47]

Centennial Celebration of Dār al-'Ulūm Deoband

After the First War of Independence in 1857 (pejoratively called Mutiny) eminent scholars like Mawlana Qāsim Nānautwi, established the Dār al-'Ulūm Deoband in 1867. From its humble beginnings it rose to be a prestigious seat of learning and was regarded as the Al-Azhar of South Asia. Over the years, the institution produced outstanding scholars in the disciplines of *hadīth, fiqh, tasawwuf* and *tafsir*.[48]

---

[46] Nadwi, *Kārwān*, vol. 2, 295-77.
[47] Yūsuf Qardāwī, "Rabbāni Ummat] Mawlana Sayyid Abul Hasan Ali Nadwi" in *Ta'mir-i Hayāt* (Special Number, 2000), 139.
[48] For the history of Deoband, see Sayyid Mahbub Rizwi, *Tārikh Dār al- 'Ulūm Deoband*, vol.1-2 (Deoband, 1994).

Chapter IX
East and West: Cultural Encounters

The Dār al-'Ulūm strongly maintained its links with the Waliyullah tradition and strictly followed the Hanafi *fiqh*. It represented a synthesis of the four strands that endowed it with a unique identity. First, it eschewed sectarian disputations and instead promoted *tawhīd* as the bedrock of its reform program. This approach was in line with the vision of Shah Waliyullah and other reformers. Second, it maintained an indissoluble link with the *sunnah* in theory and practice.

Scholarly writings and biographical accounts are a testimony to the institution's devotion to revive the content and spirit of the *sunnah*. Third, *tasawwuf* was encouraged so that the correct perspective and balanced approach reflected its real essence. Faith and self-introspection generated the zeal and fervour to earn Divine pleasure. Last, efforts to uphold the message of Islam in its pure form was its outstanding feature. Reformist movements like the TJ crystallised the Dār al-'Ulūm's trajectory of *tabligh* and *da'wah*.

Shaykh Nadwi's historic speech, originally written in Arabic to cater for Arab *'ulama'* and intellectuals, was a brilliant piece of oratory. However, he chose to speak in Urdu so that the hundreds of thousands of attendees could understand the core message he wished to deliver. In keeping with his unassuming personality, Shaykh Nadwi set aside formalities and was vocal in his view that the centennial proceedings did not require embellished accounts to advance the image of the internationally- recognised institution.

Shaykh Nadwi in his evaluation of the institution praised its efforts to revive the Islamic spirit among the Indian Muslims, love for the *shari'ah* and engendering the qualities of dedication and self-sacrifice.

Deoband became the forerunner of the new religious trends and the most important seat of traditional Islamic culture and theological learning in India.

Deoband served as the bulwark of Islam for about a century. Its centennial celebration was commemorated in March 1980. Shaykh Nadwi's participation added an international dimension to this celebration on account of his association with the Arab world.[49]

Shaykh Nadwi did not attend the inaugural session of the centennial celebration as he did not like the idea of Prime Minister Indira Gandhi's participation, who was invited without his knowledge. The celebration

---

[49] As a member of the *Shūra* committee of Deoband, Shaykh Nadwi was tasked with the responsibility to network with the scholars of the Arab world. Cf. Nadwi, *Kārwān*, vol. 2, 306-9.

which attracted hundreds of thousands of participants from the Muslim world resembled the atmosphere of 'Arafat. Shaykh Nadwi delivered his important speech which apart from placing the Dār al-'Ulūm's contribution in perspective, also outlined the Indian Muslims' attachment to Islam.

Only you (Indian Muslims) can save India (from its moral anarchy). You possess the (noble) words of Allah and the Prophet (SAAS), *tawhīd* and beliefs, and principles of brotherhood. You possess a complete system of social justice which is the end result of the Allah-consciousness (*'āqibat al-muttaqīn*).

On a positive note, Shaykh Nadwi offered the following advice to the attendees:

> Know your strength. Do justice to yourselves. The question for you is neither limited to the character of an Islamic institution nor to the validity of a school of thought... Today the main challenge for you is to protect your Islamic identity and the sources of Islamic knowledge which form your Islamic character. The question you have to answer relates to the leadership of this country. You have not been raised here to follow passively in the footsteps of others, to attend and wait on others, or to take a cue from others. Your responsibility, in fact, is to diagnose the ailments of the present society of this country and to offer remedies.[50]

It is unfortunate that the centennial celebration was marred by a conflict between the governing body and Qāri Muhammad Tayyib, Rector of Deoband. Several factors brought the family members of Qāri Tayyib in conflict with the Shūrā Council. Political intervention, nepotism and other circumstances contributed to the split of this internationally-recognised institution.

Shaykh Nadwi's involvement to resolve the crisis was on a personal level. He deplored the politicised situation that gripped Deoband. While he acknowledged the services rendered by Qāri Tayyib to its growth and development, he had cherished the hope that the crisis could have been averted had schismatic elements not exploited the volatile situation. This level-headed approach would perhaps have preserved his image. Qāri

---

[50] For Shaykh Nadwi's complete address at the centennial celebration, see "Dār al-'Ulūm Deoband ka Paighām— in *Bayyināt* (Karachi, 1980), 3-11.

Chapter IX
East and West: Cultural Encounters

Tayyib's demise in 1983 was a sad chapter in the history of Deoband.[51] The phenomenon of splinter *madāris* (also known as *waqf*) was a disturbing trend in India. Deoband was no exception: Two *madāris* under the aegis of the Dār al-'Ulūm were operating two parallel institutions. It militated against the vision of the founders of these respectable institutions whose respectable institutions whose sacrifices were based on the corporate unity of the Muslim *ummah*. Shaykh Nadwi's critique of sectarian orientations can be appreciated in the light of his close association with these religious institutions.

Towards a New Era

The fifteenth century *hijrah* heralded renewed hopes for the *ummah* which had experienced an all-time low in its political fortunes during the last decades. In many countries it marked the turning point in the Muslims' quest for independence from the pervasive influence of the West. The rhetoric of advancement in science and technology was a new slogan to build self-confidence among the Muslims. Already the Iranian revolution of 1979 was considered a harbinger of revolutionary ideas that openly challenged the supremacy of the West. Thus, the celebratory mood in 1979 created a wave of euphoria across the Muslim world. It was also a palpable expression about promises of sweeping changes and the potential leadership for the *ummah*.

At the request of Students Islamic Movement who hosted the seminar, Shaykh Nadwi delivered a paper in which he shared his thoughts about the future of the *ummah*. There was no doubt that his critical evaluation of the challenges facing the *ummah* underscored his deep understanding about the dynamics that shaped global events.

According to Shaykh Nadwi, the Muslim revivalist trends were unerring guides to restore Muslim dignity among the comity of nations. And it was the Godly souls (*mashā'ikh*) who could extricate them from the crises they faced. By the same token, Muslims should not be insulated from the mainstream activities as there existed the proverbial fault line of ineffectual leadership. He formulated a ten-point program which he maintained would energise Muslim countries to be proactive in bringing about meaningful transformation.

---

[51] Nadwi, *Kārwān*, vol. 2, 313-4.

Salient Features

Islamic consciousness is linked to the emotional and spiritual progress of Muslims and needs to be optimally harnessed to strengthen the cause of *da'wah*. This can only be realised if the universality of the Prophetic message filters through all facets of life. In a similar vein, the world of Islam needs intellectual leadership which draws its inspiration from its rich legacy. In fact, the Islamic civilisation during its heydays was a symbol of progress and prosperity. It sustained an intellectual tradition that was not restricted to countries or cultures. Its overarching vision was to spread the timeless message of the Qur'an as embodied in the *iqra'* paradigm.[52]

In the Valley of Kashmir

Barely a year had passed after Shaykh Nadwi received the King Faisal Award when he was conferred a D.Litt. (Doctor of Literature) in October 1981 by the University of Kashmir. Shaykh Nadwi's conditional acceptance of this prestigious award was unambiguous - no political agenda[53] was to be attached to this conferment. Furthermore, he had several scholars[54] before him who set the precedent by receiving honorary doctorates. The brief address[55] which he delivered at the Seventh Convocation of the University of Kashmir was widely appreciated. The audience which included critics, teachers and students and specialists in both the traditional (*qadīm*) and modern (*jadīd*) sciences were enthralled by his inspirational address. Shaykh Nadwi's preliminary remarks showed that knowledge was an organic unity, an integral whole, that could not be divided into parts. His reference to the *iqra'* verses set the tone to his important address; the fusion of knowledge and action.

According to Shaykh Nadwi, knowledge should strengthen character-building and the bond between man and his Creator, Allah. Man is, by

---

[52] Nadwi, *The Fifteenth Century* (Lucknow, 1982).
[53] The Indian-occupied Kashmir has witnessed the escalating conflicts over the past decades from the *mujāhidin* drawn of Kashmir and Pakistan against the Indian military presence.
[54] Reference to Mawlana Daryabadi and Mawlana Sayyid Sulayman Nadwi.
[55] Published as a monograph *The Place of Knowledge and the Role of Scholars* (Springs, 2018).

Chapter IX
East and West: Cultural Encounters

himself, not the origin or fountainhead of knowledge. He is simply the deputy or agent to actualise the Will of Allah on this earth. The most tragic and dangerous turn in the history of knowledge, or rather that of humanity, occurred when man forgot this basic fact that he is only an agent or representative of Allah, the Lord of the worlds. He has been given charge of the world, but not its ownership. He does not have the right to use the resources found over and within this earth according to his wish or caprice or for the promotion of his limited national, ethnic, tribal or racial benefit, nor for achieving political and personal domination over others. It was really a great calamity when knowledge became severed from its relationship with its Bestower. What an appalling spectacle this world presents today! Man has taken over knowledge, but the Giver of knowledge has slipped away from his mind. I declare with all the sense of responsibility and all the emphasis at my command that man will not be able to set right the affairs of this world unless he recognises that he is simply a creature sent by Someone and unto Him he shall return. He needs to acknowledge that he stands at the one end of the knowledge he possesses today, while Allah, the Bestower of knowledge, his Creator and Master, is at the other end.[56]

In a similar vein, Shaykh Nadwi's public lectures in Srinagar focused on the need for Kashmiri Muslims to articulate a strong and visible Islamic personality. His appraisal of the *dīnī* conditions was a candid observation of the weaknesses that had crept into their the Kashmiri society. Therefore, it was the Islāmiyāt that linked them to the comity of Muslim countries.

In his lectures Shaykh Nadwi evoked the image of the picturesque valley that personified Kashmir. Its breathtaking landscape and heavenly fragrance pervaded its surroundings. Several centuries ago, Sayyid 'Ali Hamdani (d. 1384) gave a clarion call for Kashmiris to embrace *tawhīd* and, in turn, renounce their polytheistic beliefs. His phenomenal success in planting the seeds of Islam on the Kashmiri soil can be attributed to his charismatic personality. His life was infused with the spirit of *tabligh* which he zealously carried out in the valley.[57]

Shaykh Nadwi reminded his Kashmiri audience that *tawhīd* gave them the inner strength to face the formidable challenges of the day. In view of the turbulent period that marked the Indian rule over occupied Kashmir, Shaykh Nadwi's focus on raising an Islamic consciousness assumed greater importance. He urged advocacy groups in the valley to foster a unity of

---

[56] *Ibid.*, 9-10.
[57] Nadwi, *Islam: Three Core Beliefs* (Kuala Lumpur, 2016), 39-41.

purpose and strengthen the Islamic cause amid the draconian laws imposed by the Indian government.

Kashmir, like Palestine, had an institutional memory of the violation of human rights. Their shared history of dispossession illustrated the impotence of UN to give an effective voice to the resolutions passed by the Assembly. To date, the situations have worsened with no prospects of autonomy for both Muslim states.

Apart from the political crisis facing the Kashmiris, Shaykh Nadwi touched on the intrinsic value of integrity (*ghayrat*) as the redeeming feature of their restricted lives. In essence, *tawhīd* was the powerhouse that illumined the pathway under these dark and dismal circumstances. His message was emphatic; no hostile elements could sway the positive course of events destined for Kashmiri Muslims if they were to follow the Prophetic ideal. This approach also resonated for Muslims residing as minorities and sharing a similar predicament.

Seminar: *Islam and Orientalists*

An International Seminar on "Islam and Orientalists" hosted by Dār al-Musannifin (Azamgarh)[58] in February 1982 was aimed at making a critical evaluation of the Orientalists' contributions to Islamic studies. Shaykh Nadwi prepared a paper on *Islamic Studies, Orientalists and Muslim Scholars*.[59] This period also saw the sad demise of his nephew Mawlana Muhammad Thānī (d. 1982) which took a heavy toll on him. Mawlana Thānī was a right-hand man to him and was also an accomplished author, especially on the *mashā'ikh* of India.[60] Likewise, another important figure, Shaykh Nadwi's nephew, Sayyid Muhammad al-Hasani was an adept translator and critic of Arabic literature. He replicated Shaykh Nadwi's intellectual horizon and showed his versatility on contemporary Islamic thought.

The thrust of Shaykh Nadwi's paper was about the Orientalists' penchant for distorting historical events to disparage the personality of the Prophet (SAAS). He stated that no original works in both scope and depth have been written for the universities in Islamic studies. Shaykh Nadwi's critique of

---

[58] Established by the illustrious scholar and historian Shibli Nu'mānī (d. 1914), the academy has published Islamic literary works of unsurpassed merit.
[59] Nadwi, *Islamic Studies, Orientalists and Muslim Scholars* (Lucknow, 1983).
[60] See Muhammad Hasani, *Sawanih Sayyid Muhammad Thani Hasani* (Rae Bareli, 2019).

Chapter IX
East and West: Cultural Encounters

Orientalism does not betray any strands of emotionalism. While acknowledging the remarkable contributions made by some Orientalists[61] in the field of *hadīth* studies and the *sirah* of the Prophet (SAAS) he remarks that the typical Orientalists claim "loud profession of objectivity and scholarly impartiality." They tend to present their findings in a dramatic manner in order to dislodge the faith of Muslims in the Prophet (SAAS). In contrast, the sources of *sirah* are based on historical authenticity and moral unassailability. In other words, the Orientalists' tendency to distort historical data is clear; character assassination of the Prophet (SAAS). Thus, Shaykh Nadwi's evaluation is to counter their hidden agendas, notwithstanding the invaluable contributions made by some sincere Orientalists.

A similar analysis of the prescribed works in Islamic studies is echoed by Shaykh Nadwi. He remarked:

It is regrettable that no original and in-depth work has been undertaken by our universities, which was expected of them. As far as English language is concerned, there has been no forceful literature (on Islamic Studies) after Syed Ameer Ali's *Spirit of Islam* which has provided an introduction to Islam in an eloquent manner.[62]

A critical study of the Orientalists' research by Azami is an excellent study that traces the Orientalists' motivations for studying the Qur'an. The common threads of distortion, spurious reports and insinuations are woven in their interpretation of Qur'anic and *hadīth* studies. This sentiment is shared by Shaykh Nadwi's critique on Orientalism.[63]

An appraisal of the Orientalists' research, according to Azami, is based on the ingrained prejudice towards the Qur'an and *sunnah* by perpetuating the colonialist psyche into the mainstream Islamic life. Edward Said in his brilliant study of Orientalism cogently proves that it views "Islam as an encroachment and a challenge to their (Orientalists') supposed authority on what constitutes Islamic tradition."[64]

---

[61] "Some of these scholars have employed themselves to the study of Islamic sciences not with any political, economic or missionary motive, but for the satisfaction of their scholarly passion with devotion and diligence." Nadwi, *Islamic Studies*, 7-8.
[62] Nadwi, *Kārwān*, vol. 3, 232.
[63] Muhammad Mustafa Azami] *The History of the Qur'anic Text: From Revelation to Compilation* (Kuala Lumpur, 2003), 303-33.
[64] See Edward Said, *Orientalism* (London, 1994).

At the heart of Orientalist studies are the centuries' old misconceptions about Islam. Their missionary fervour, political expediency and other devious agendas have influenced their writings under the guise of objectivity. Needless to add, the scholarly literature in recent years has filtered through Islamic Studies departments in Western institutions to present a somewhat diluted form of Orientalist prejudice. However, their hostility towards Islam continues unabated. Muzaffar Iqbal makes a pertinent observation:

It is clear that no matter what Muslims say, the prejudice built into the western academic circles will not go away until those who are in the academy choose to drastically change its entrenched attitudes. Unfortunately, such a change is not now on the horizon[65].

Isma'il Nawwab reiterates Shaykh Nadwi's assessment of the Orientalist project. Several factors account for its polarising attitudes: Colonialism, Christian missionary zeal and the political manifestations of imperialism. In the intellectual domain the Orientalists have harvested the prevailing political climate to pursue their task of maligning the Islamic tradition and the image of the Holy Prophet (SAAS).[66]

The future of Islamic Studies is summed up in a well- balanced analysis by Shaykh Nadwi. He writes:

A paramount need of the present times is to stand up against the onslaught of irreligiousness on the world of Islam which is threatening to destroy its intellectual and cultural bases. To bring back the confidence of educated Muslim young men in Islamic norms and values, and above all, in the prophethood of Muhammad (SAAS), would be the greatest act of Islamic resurgence. As this class is suffering today from intellectual confusion and alienation... the need of the hour is to combat the present *Jāhiliyyah* through cogent reasoning and wisdom.[67]

---

[65] A similar view is expressed in Abdur Raheem Kidwai, *Literary Orientalism: A Companion* (New Delhi, 2012), 36-39.
[66] For an overview of these scholarly critiques, see John Esposito (ed.)] *Muslims and the West: Encounter and Dialogue* (Islamabad, 2001).
[67] Nadwi, *Islamic Studies*, 63-4.

Chapter IX
East and West: Cultural Encounters

Literary Orientalism

Another emerging trend in the study of Orientalism is Literary Orientalism. Abdur Raheem Kidwai has contributed immensely to this genre. Tracing the growth and development of Orientalism in a specific setting, Kidwai provides an archive of valuable information about the Western writers' entrenched prejudice towards Islam. The spate of literature dealing with Islam/Muslims has seen a steady growth of scholarship in recent years indicating an outgrowth in some ways to the ingrained hostility, polemical zeal and negative representations of Islam. There are serious and focused scholarly studies undertaken at several universities that suggest that Literary Orientalism has assumed significant importance in analysing the cross-cultural encounters that shape the contours of Muslim-Christian relations. Too often, the binary opposition between Islam and Christianity dominates the discourse of scholarly tradition. On a positive note, Kidwai's comments serve as a reference point about the future course of Literary Orientalism:

[It] brings home the point that misperceptions arise, in the main, from lack of knowledge and communication which precludes any sound understanding. In a multi-faith, pluralistic world of ours we stand in need of a better understanding, fostered by knowledge and nurtured by the spirit of tolerance which can put an end to misperceptions about one another.[68]

Seminar in Algeria

The Sixth International Seminar was organised by the Ministry of Religious Affairs headed by Shaykh 'Abdur Rahmān Shaybān in 1982. This was Shaykh Nadwi's first visit to this Islamic country which had thrown off the yoke of French colonialism through the innumerable sacrifices made by its *'ulama'* and the masses. Among the "beacons of light" were Shaykh 'Abdul Hamid ibn Badis, Shaykh Muhammad Bashir al-Ibrahim whose personalities are synonymous with Algeria's independence.

Tilmisan, the historic city of Algeria hosted the seminar. Shaykh Nadwi's address "The Characteristics of Islam" was based on a chapter from his book

---

[68] Cf. Abdur Raheem Kidwai, *Orientalism in English Literature: Perception of Islam and Muslims* (New Delhi, 2016).

A Guidebook for Muslims.[69] The rationale for this lecture was to highlight before the Arab audience the proper spirit of Islamic beliefs and practice. This entailed the correct understanding and interpretation of credal beliefs (*'aqā'id*) around the twin issues of pleasing Allah (*ridā ilāhi*) and the preparation for the Afterlife.

A series of lectures was also organised in Algiers, the capital city, and the response from the audience, particularly the youth, was overwhelming. At the same time, Shaykh Nadwi also noted with concern how the state machinery suppressed religious expressions and frowned upon the youth's adoption of an Islamic identity. Moreover, the state's repressive policy was emblematic of its unconcealed hostility towards Islam.[70]

Sri Lanka

Sri Lanka (Ceylon) evokes images of the progenitor of mankind, Prophet Adam, whose descent to earth, according to several historians, took place in this country. The Adam's Peak has been venerated as a landmark in mankind's epoch- making history; the large footprint of Adam is commonly associated with this event.

Furthermore, historical ties existed between Sri Lanka and the Umayyad dynasty although Islam did not establish itself there as in other countries. Shaykh Nadwi was sent as a representative in 1982 to participate in the convocation activities of the renowned university, Jami'ah Nazimiyyah founded by a philanthropist, Muhammad Nazim. Professor Muhammad Shukri, an Edinburgh graduate served as the institute's vice-chancellor. He was responsible for including several of Shaykh Nadwi's books in the university's curriculum. Shaykh Nadwi's address at the graduation ceremony dwelt on the unity of mankind and its significance in the context of Sri Lanka's own history.[71]

Muslims in Sri Lanka with its Buddhist majority enjoyed religious freedom. Much later, the ethnic conflict between the Tamil minority and the Sinhalese majority escalated into a civil war claiming losses of innocent human lives.

In a similar vein, Shaykh Nadwi wrote extensively on the occupation of Afghanistan by the Russians as well as the civil war in Lebanon. The genocide

---

[69] Nadwi, *A Guidebook for Muslims* (Lucknow, 1985), 31-57.
[70] For a critique of Algeria's Western-oriented leanings, see Nadwi, *Western Civilisation, Islam and Muslims*, 142-5.
[71] Nadwi, *Kārwān*, vol 2, 360-4.

Chapter IX
East and West: Cultural Encounters

against Muslim refugees perpetuated by the Maronite Christians and the Felangist militia had a heart-rending effect on Shaykh Nadwi. To this end, his articles reflected the culpability of the Muslim countries (Arab world, in particular) for their acquiescence and passivity towards the tragic circumstances of the Palestinian refugees.[72]

Da'wah in Hyderabad

Shaykh Nadwi's *da'wah* had a wider scope and this is illustrated in the series of lectures he delivered in Hyderabad which was hosted by the Central Institute of English and Foreign Languages. Hyderabad with its rich cultural legacy possessed resilience and inner resources to realign its destiny. In comparison to its Muslim compatriots in north India, Hyderabad demonstrated a remarkable degree of progress and maintained a harmonious co-existence with its Hindu majority. Shaykh Nadwi, in his illuminating lectures, warned the Muslims against moral decline which preceded general political decline. He stressed on the importance of *insāniyat* (humanity) and the active role of Muslims in saving the country from the abyss of anarchy, corruption and violence.

The following excerpt is a poignant reminder for the Muslims to maintain their collective identity in relation to the realities confronting their lives:

If the *'ulama'* shirk in their duty to raise awareness among Muslims about the challenges they face, then a grave danger looms ahead of their lives. The absence of effective leadership has both intellectual and religious repercussions for the Muslim society. If there is no concern about where the country is heading towards, then the effects will be felt by one and all. A time will come when performing the prescribed prayers will become extremely difficult. A worse possible scenario is the obliteration of Islamic landmarks of which the mosque occupies a pivotal space. Any attempt to disconnect from the prevailing situation creates a sense of alienation and impacts directly on the collective identity of Muslims.[73]

Conclusion

Of much significance is Shaykh Nadwi's elaboration of *da'wah* in the

---

[72] *Ibid.*, 365-8.
[73] Nadwi, *Tuhfah-i Dakkan*, 59-60 (Adapted).

West. In his estimation, there exists great possibilities for the future of Islam in the non-Muslim countries. This can be accomplished only when Muslims acknowledge their vital role as *du'āt*. Apart from the economic opportunities, their presence should be motivated by a zeal to promote the universal message of Islam among the non-Muslims.

Chapter X

Trends in Transnational Institutions

Beyond his intellectual horizons there were other factors that crafted Shaykh Nadwi's role as the articulator of the Muslim community's concerns and aspirations. Of particular interest was his vision of establishing academic institutions that could communicate the message of Islam in a contemporary idiom. In addition, these could provide the forum for a better understanding between Islam and the West. In the Indian context, he addressed issues that were linked to the political developments in the country and had a direct bearing on the future of the Muslim community.

Hadīth Studies

Shaykh Nadwi's multifarious activities over the years assumed greater importance both in terms of his *da'wah* travels and his writing schedule. His teaching career at Nadwah was cut short owing to his other preoccupations. However, it was his passion for *tafsīr*, *adab* (literature) and history that were reflected in a number of his works. No different was his scholarly interest in *hadīth* studies which had not been clearly delineated for several reasons:

- Shaykh Nadwi's brief teaching career did not give him the opportunity to teach the *Sihāh Sittah* (six authoritative collections of *ahadīth*).
- His literary pursuits overshadowed his interest in *hadīth*.[1] Shaykh Ruh al-Quds Nadwi has discussed in detail Shaykh Nadwi's position as a *muhaddith* (traditionist).[2] Readers may refer to Shaykh Nadwi's three slim volumes[3] for his contributions to

---

[1] Abu Suhbān Ruh al-Quds, "Mawlana Ali Mian awr GIlm i-Hadith" in *Al-Qāsim Special Issue: Mufakkir-i Islam Mawlana Sayyid Abul Hasan Ali Nadwi*, 2002, 33-34.

[2] Shaykh Nadwi's comprehensive introduction to Shaykh Zakariyyah's *Awjaz al-Masālik*, a commentary on Imām Malik's *Muwattā* has been widely acclaimed in the Arab world. To a large extent, Shaykh Nadwi's *muqaddimāt* introduced the Indian *'ulama* to the Arab scholarship. See Ruh al-Quddus, "Mawlana Ali Miyan awr 'Ilm i-Hadith", 41-45.

[3] *Al-Madkhal ilā Dirāsāt al-Hadīth al-Nabawin al-Shari: Muhammad bin Ismā'il al-Bukhārī wa Kitābahu al-Jāmi'al-Sahīh*. This monograph was published after his visit to Samarqand with a delegation of the OCIS. For additional details about the above publications, see *Al-Qasim Monthly*, 334-35.

the hadīth studies. In many respects the key themes[4] were amplified in his prolific writings and until the last days of his life Sahīh Bukhārī and Tahzib al-Akhlāq[5] were avidly studied by him.

The scholarly profile of Shaykh Nadwi in hadīth studies may be gleaned from his sanad (authorisation) by his teachers whose academic pedigrees enjoy an enviable position.

The Role of Hadīth in the Promotion of Islamic Climate and Attitudes[6] is an important monograph that was read in Makkah in 1981 before the scholars of King 'Abdul Aziz University and the learned hujjaj (pilgrims) hailing from different parts of the world. Shaykh Nadwi outlined the significance of hadīth in the lives of Muslims:

> The hadīth provides the guiding light with which to judge social norms and practices in the Muslim community. It motivates Muslims to attend to their duty of enjoining right and preventing wrong, refuting deviation in religious matters and rejecting the blind imitation of Western civilisation. Indeed, it is only through the sunnah that the Muslim community can preserve its identity.[7]

Rābitā Adab al-'Alam al-Islami
(World League of Islamic Literature)

Since the publication of Mukhtārāt, the Islamic orientation of literature had been enthusiastically promoted by Shaykh Nadwi. His earlier writings[8] on Arabic literature articulated the Islamic component without which the various academic disciplines could be ineffectual or otherwise become forums for promoting irreligiosity and scepticism. According to Shaykh Nadwi, adab has the transformative power to create space for positive ideals. On the contrary, literary critics and academics who are delinked from the Islamic

---

[4] Ruh al-Quds, " Mawlana Ali Miyan awr Ilm-i-Hadith", 37.
[5] An Arabic compendium of hadīth written in Arabic by Sayyid 'Abdul Hayy al-Hasani.
[6] Nadwi, The Role of Hadīth in the Promotion of Islamic Climate and Attitudes (Lucknow, 1982).
[7] Ibid., 2.
[8] His Mukhtārāt, for example, contained literary masterpieces from the classical period of the 'ulama', mashā'ikh who have not been considered as udabā. Hassan Basri and his soul-stirring lectures have been included in Shaykh Nadwi's classification of adab.

Chapter X
Trends in Transnational Institutions

culture have the tendency to undermine its objectives. The Nasserist regime in the twentieth century is representative of this mindset.

Aims and Objectives of Rābitā Adab

- Compilation of literary criticism works based on the Islamic principles.
- Systematic reappraisal of literary genres with a strong Islamic ethos.
- Preparation of literature in various languages to reach out to both Muslim and non-Muslim readership.
- Refutation of deviant literary movements and promotion of institutions with strong Islamic values and ideals.[9]

Rābitā Adab was guided by the Islamic orientation for making constructive inputs in the world of *adab*. It was, therefore, not surprising that Shaykh Nadwi with his vast experience in Arabic literature would be instrumental in the establishment of Rābitā Adab. Here again it would be worthwhile to contextualise his early Arabic writings like *Mukhtārāt* to explore the norms of Islamic literary criticism as embodied in Rābitā's mission statement. Shaykh Nadwi argued that the merger between classical writings and contemporary trends was possible. Indeed, it was an appropriate forum to present the holistic interpretation of *adab*.[10] This approach was consistent with Shaykh Nadwi's belief that Islam does not recognise the cleavage between the old (*qadīm*) and new (*jadīd*). A contributing factor to this dichotomy was Kipling's famous poetic expression.[11] It had caused irreparable harm to the good of humanity and to the concept of the unity of mankind. Thus, the production of knowledge with an Islamisation bias[12] (albeit with its variant interpretation and conceptual framework) has not been a very recent phenomenon. In fact, Shaykh Nadwi's writings reflect a vision that had been largely influenced by

---

[9] *Kārwān-i-Adab*, vol. 8, April 2001-March 2002. The aims listed have been selected to give a synopsis of Rābitā's global outreach program.
[10] Amin Hussain, "Rābitā Adab Islamī: Mawlana Shaykh Nadwi ki Fikri Qiyādat awr Tahrik Adab i-Islam ki Samara— in *Kārwān i-Adab*, vol. 8, pp. 115-124.
[11] Nadwi, *Speaking Plainly to the West*. Cf. Nadwi's *Islam and Civilisation*, 61-69 (Chapter 8, Alliance between Religion and Knowledge, for a full appreciation of his views on this theme.
[12] See Wan Daud, *The Educational Philosophy and Practice of Syed Muhammad Naquib Al-Attas*, 371-422.

scholars who were his contemporaries.[13] The production of writings related to the concept of Islamisation has been largely done by the International Institute of Islamic Thought (Washington). Professor Isma'il al-Faruqi is considered to be the founder of the Islamisation of Knowledge Project (1982). However, Wan Daud contends that the Malaysian scholar, Syed Naquib Al-Attās was the leading figure in the original exposition of the Islamisation concept.

For a brief overview of Shaykh Nadwi's pioneering influence on Rābitā, a special issue of *Al-Manhāl*, a monthly journal devoted to literature, arts and culture, was published. A number of articles were presented in Rābitā sessions which were held in several countries to honour Shaykh Nadwi's contributions. The *takrim* (eulogy) sessions also brought out important citations to recognise his singular services to this discipline. It would be no exaggeration to state that he had contributed immensely to a new interpretive reading of *adab*.[14]

Shaykh Nadwi envisaged the convergence of Muslim scholars, intellectuals and literary critics from around world whose contributions would influence the new generation of Muslims and create a new school of thought.[15] Nadwah, which mooted this idea, hosted an international seminar in 1981 which drew a large number of scholars from universities and other institutions. The role of Arabic literature and other languages with specific reference to their Islamic relevance was deliberated in this seminar. By 1984, Rābitā Adab was established with Shaykh Nadwi elected as its President. Its first international seminar was held in 1986. Representatives from Rābitā's various regions were elected to coordinate its activities. In sum, its global network facilitated the growing success of workshops and created a niche market in literary circles.

In Shaykh Nadwi's estimation, values and commitment are embedded in literature and, therefore, enhance the aesthetic appreciation of writings that are free from embellishments. Like our natural instincts, literature is not confined to external factors. Its expanse is as wide as the universe and its oceans of knowledge cannot be compressed into a small vessel.

Shaykh Nadwi deplores the trends that have defined literature in our present times. It is assumed that progressive thinking and freedom of

---

[13] Mention may be made of Muhammad Asad (1992) and his famous work, *Islam at the Crossroads* (1934).
[14] See Zayed Abdul, "Athār al-Shaykh Al-Nadwā fi al-Adab al-Islamī in *Al-Manhal* (Riyadh, 1421), 122-25.
[15] See Bilal Hasani, *Nadwi: Thought and Mission*, 168-72.

expression are markers of genuine literature. In other words, the old traditions and religious ideas have no place in the reconfigured world of literature. According to Shaykh Nadwi, literature originated in the divine scriptures and it is the Qur'an that "inscribed the everlasting seal of perfection on it."

A telling example of the universal tenor of literature, based on moral values is expressed in the following words:

"Should a flower not be appreciated if it blooms in the courtyard of a mosque?"

The secretary of Rābitā, 'Abdul Quddus Abu Salih made some important comments about Shaykh Nadwi's cherished hope of broadening its scope and function. Great strides were made under his chairmanship in terms of Rābitā becoming "[an] Islamic safe haven... a symbol of moderation, far removed from fanaticism and fully prepared to achieve its guidelines..."

A salient feature of Rābitā's literary output was the forceful production of children's Islamic literature. The precocious minds of children were easily receptive to Islamic values. Belonging to this genre, the *Qasas* series served as the alternative to storytelling, which was far removed from the ideals and realities of Islam. Many contemporary scholars and the *'ulama'* paid glowing tributes to his Arabic and Urdu works for their originality and fluency. We reproduce selected extracts to restate Shaykh Nadwi's celebrated status in the field of literature.

Shaikh Muhammad al-Majzub: Writer and Intellectual Figure

A reader of Shaykh Nadwi's works will feel that he is an immensely powerful author. This quality is rare. His writings spellbind you. He is one of the very few writers who can convey effectively their innermost feelings and fervour to their readers. This quality is special to only the spiritually alive writers.

Dr 'Abdul Bāsit: Distinguished Author and Poet

Your vision and familiarity with all the relevant issues baffle us. That day you spoke on the Westernised Arabic literature. For long we have been in the clutches of Western civilisation. Only when you spoke did we realise that a true writer is he whose writings are permeated with Islam and he thus, preserves the Arabic literary heritage.

Professor Rashid Ahmad Siddiqui

As I went reading *The Pathway to Medina* I thought this section was the best of all. When I reached the next, I found it better than the last one. The next was even better than both. I then moved onto the heights of literary excellence. I have such tremendous praise for you that words fail me in expressing the same. What a treasure of insights and truths you have encompassed in its few pages. Besides, it was the elegance of your thought-provoking and persuasive style.

Māhir al-Qādiri: Eminent Urdu Poet

The learned author deserves huge praise for his sensitive and insightful interpretation of Iqbal's poetry in *Glory of Iqbal*. His book has all the charms of Shibli's style. Ghazali's thought and Ibn Taimiyyah's sincerity and fervour. Some good critical studies are no doubt there. However, this is a work by a *mujahid* scholar who represents Iqbal's *Mard-i Mu'min* (the ideal Muslim).

Shaykh Nadwi's Major Contributions

Shaykh Nadwi accomplished three revivalist objectives: First, he imbued writers who were polarised from Islam with its true content and spirit. Second, he articulated the Islamic ideals with such literary grace that it impressed everyone. Last, he instilled a literary taste among the *'ulama'* for the purpose of *da'wah*.

An attempt is made to highlight three seminars of the Rābitā to offer readers some idea of their scope and content:

Azamgarh (India): 1995
Theme: Biographical Writings

The seminar focused on biographical writings at two levels:

- *Sirah writing*: This genre was significant as 'Allāmah Shibli Nu'māni (d. 1914)] founder of Dār al-Musannifin (Azamgarh) was a pioneer in *sirah* writing. His multivolume *Sirat al-Nabi (SAAS)* is a significant contribution to this genre.
- *Elements of biographical writing*: The conspicuous features of this

Chapter X
Trends in Transnational Institutions

genre were elaborated. The various sessions focused on the multidisciplinary approaches to this form of writing. From a different angle, a negative feature' embellishment of persona which tended to obscure the true contributions of these Islamic personalities was also highlighted.

Istanbul (Turkey): 1996
Theme: Contributions of Sayyid Abul Hasan Ali Nadwi: Honorary Session

In recognition of Shaykh Nadwi's literary contributions, Rābitā organised this esteemed session. Notable scholars who included 'Allāmah Yūsuf Qardāwī and Professor Muhammad Qutb (brother of Sayyid Qutb) eulogised the services of Shaykh Nadwi. Sixteen papers were read by prominent scholars from the Muslim world who paid glowing tributes to his unique approach to *da'wah*, literary contributions and outstanding scholarship in contemporary Islamic thought.

Lahore (Pakistan): 1997
Theme: Travelogues to Makka and Madina

Shaykh Nadwi's keynote address was based on Iqbal's soul-stirring verses about the *Haramayn*. The poet's literary contributions to the genre were also highlighted. Interestingly, international figures to this seminar illustrated the variety of travelogues drawn from the Muslim world. The focal point, however, was the *Haramayn* around which literary styles were explored.[16]

Oxford Centre for Islamic Studies (OCIS)

Shaykh Nadwi's travels to the West had mellowed his understanding about the dynamics of Western culture. He had hoped that the appreciation of the rich Islamic cultural traditions could be sustained through the establishment of an institution for this purpose. A letter from Professor Khaliq Ahmad Nizami (d. 1997)[17] stressed the urgency of such an institution. Its

---

[16] A detailed report on this seminar was published in *Ta'mir-i Hayāt*, 1995: 33, 27-30. For a detailed discussion of Shaykh Nadwi's impressions about this seminar organised in his honour, see *Kārwān*, vol. 6, 280-95.
[17] See Mohammad Ahmad, *Literary Contributions of Professor K.A. Nizami* (Delhi, 2000) for a comprehensive list of Nizami's literary contributions.

feasibility was supported by leading non-Muslim intellectuals among whom was the eminent British academic, Dr D.G. Browning. An erudite scholar and leading authority on the history of Muslim India, Professor Nizami was closely associated with the Aligarh Muslim University as a lecturer and vice-chancellor. His list of books includes a critical reading of the Mughal emperor, Akbar and the life and times series on the Chishti saints in Muslim India.

Shaykh Nadwi was requested to present a paper on "Islam and the West." The Oxford University with its proud tradition of seven hundred years of academic learning was the ideal location for the proposed institution. For Shaykh Nadwi, it was the materialisation of a cherished hope that someday he might address an audience where he could freely express his thoughts on Western culture which has been holding the reins in the political, scientific and intellectual spheres.

Shaykh Nadwi read his paper "Islam and the West" in the seminar held at Oxford University on 22 July 1983. The seminar, presided over by Dr D.G. Browning of St. Cross College, Oxford, was attended by a large number of professors, academics, besides several scholars from Pakistan and several Arab countries who had been invited to express their views on the subject. As the seminar was convened to consider the establishment of an Islamic Centre in Oxford, his paper focused on the importance of such an institution in the heartland of the proud academic tradition of scholarship. Also, he made appreciative comments about Dr Farhan Nizami who served as the Director of the Centre since its inception.[18]

The thrust of Shaykh Nadwi's message to the West is succinctly brought out in the following extracts of his insightful paper:

> The world today would have been altogether different if the progress in science and technology had been accompanied by Allah-consciousness and respect for human values. Then its powerful and unlimited resources would have been guided by loftier aims and ideals. In a similar vein, it would have promoted co-operative endeavour between different nations instead of generating the spirit of contest, collision and conflict. When we would have found ourselves living as members of a civilised and enlightened family. Unfortunately, we are being divided into the present power blocs of East and West, whose rivalry is threatening the very existence of human civilisation or rather, the human race itself.

---

[18] Nadwi, *Islam and the West* (Lucknow, 1983).

Chapter X
Trends in Transnational Institutions

A revolutionary leadership is now required to save human civilisation, especially in the West (of which Britain forms a part and also has a glorious history). Such leadership needs to be realistic, noble-minded, courageous and accommodating for instilling a new life into the dying frame of modern civilisation and even humanity. The educational and intellectual centres, littérateurs and writers of this country can play a leading role in this noble endeavour. I hope that the proposed Islamic Centre which is being set up by you here at the most appropriate time will prove to be the first step in that direction. This is the hope and desire that has brought me here despite ill-health and heavy engagements.[19]

The following information gleaned from the *OCIS Newsletter* deals briefly with Shaykh Nadwi's important role in the Islamic Centre:

Throughout the early years of the Centre's development Sayyid Abul Hasan Ali Nadwi was tireless in promoting the mobilisation of moral and material support for the Centre. As Chairman of the Board of Trustees he rarely allowed the frailty of advancing years to prevent his regular visits to Oxford and remained in constant contact with fellow Trustees and the Centre's growing number of well-wishers and supporters.
Shaykh Nadwi maintained an active interest in and steadfast support for the careful preparation of the Centre's academic activities. He supported the early priority given to the direct sponsorship of research on the intellectual and social history of the Muslim world. He encouraged the commitment to scholarly publication and, in particular, involvement by leading scholars from the Islamic and Western worlds of learning, through the successful production of the *Journal of Islamic Studies* published by the Oxford University Press for the Centre since 1990. He was active in the steady recruitment of a core group of scholars to contribute and to complement teaching about the Islamic world at Oxford.[20]

On the occasion of the tenth anniversary of the establishment of the Centre, though unable to attend the celebrations in person, Shaykh Nadwi delivered a message which re-emphasised that early sense of vision and

---

[19] Nadwi, *Islam and the West*, 6-16.
[20] *OCIS Newsletter Special Issue*, 2000, 1.

commitment upon which the Centre had been founded:

> World events during the past decade emphasise the need for an academic institution in the West dedicated to the dispassionate and objective study of the Islamic world - its religious beliefs, social and moral values, cultural traditions, and contemporary challenges and opportunities. In its first decade the Oxford Centre for Islamic Studies has made good progress towards this worthy objective. I am confident that, having been welcomed by the University of Oxford and having engaged the interest and support of many throughout the world, *In sha'Allah* the Centre will continue to make an intellectual and educational contribution to the benefit of all.[21]

During his visit to Oxford in 1987, Shaykh Nadwi presented a public lecture, "Islam and Knowledge" in which he developed themes having a contemporary relevance. He maintained that the eternal values of revealed guidance can inform the Islamic interpretations in modern scholarship.

Shaykh Nadwi's 1989 lecture at Oxford on "Mankind's Debt to the Prophet Muhammad (SAAS)" contributed further to the wider appreciation of the contemporary relevance of the life and teachings of the Prophet (SAAS).[22]

The Islamic Foundation: Leicester

A premier institute with a strong publishing network, the Islamic Foundation has played a significant role in disseminating the message of Islam in the West. Its publishing output is admirable, and it has over the years complemented its interfaith dialogues and seminars to promote a better understanding of Islam in Europe. Although the Foundation has a strong Jamā'at-i Islami affiliation, Shaykh Nadwi maintained a cordial relationship with its core leadership.[23] His regular visits and lectures, some of which were published by the Foundation, demonstrated a mutual respect and affection. His analytical writings about the West and Muslim responsibility in communicating the message of Islam reflect his shared interest and concerns with the Foundation to this important field.

---

[21] *Ibid.*, 4.
[22] *Ibid.*, 3.
[23] Mention may be made of Professor Khurshid Ahmad, Khurram Murad, authors of books contributing to the "Islam and the West" theme.

Chapter X
Trends in Transnational Institutions

Da'wah in the West: The Qur'anic Paradigm[24] outlines the Qur'anic model of conducting *da'wah* together with its requisites and challenges. This perceptive study offers practical guidance on how to invite mankind to Islam, particularly in the West.

The Role and Responsibilities of Muslims in the West[25] drawing upon the Qur'an and Islamic history, suggests to Muslims in the West how they should face the challenges confronting them and carrying out their duty of *da'wah*.

Kingdom of Jordan

The Al-i Bayt Foundation under the chairmanship of Crown Prince Hasan bin Talāl, of which Shaykh Nadwi was a member, organised a conference in Amman in April 1984. The theme was based on the intellectual and historical activities of Muslim countries. Shaykh Nadwi acceded to the personal request of Prince Hasan to attend the conference.[26]

As a leading historian, Shaykh Nadwi's address dwelt on the Islamic culture in India and the unremitting efforts made by the scholars, *'ulama'* to promote it. He referred to the *tajdīdi* efforts of Shah Waliyullah, particularly to the propagation of Islamic culture in an alien society. This aspect was comprehensively covered by Sayyid 'Abdul Hayy in his excellent publications.[27] Overall, these are a summative account of the intellectual and cultural activities during Muslim rule in the country.

At a state dinner hosted by Prince Hasan of Jordan, Shaykh Nadwi was requested to address the guests. He addressed them thus:

> After a long time today, I have the privilege of addressing a select gathering of the Arab elite. Let me tell you that Arabs were a non-entity before they embraced Islam. In future, too, you will be nobody, without Islam. You had been wandering in the desert. Allah selected a pious servant of His for conveying the eternal message of truth. He being the recipient of the Book of Allah familiarised the backward, illiterate Arabs with knowledge and intuition. The Romans and Persians of the day used to look down upon Arabs as nomads and

---

[24] Nadwi, *Da'wah in the West: The Qur'anic Paradigm* (Leicester, 1992). Several of Shaykh Nadwi's books have been translated into English by Abdur Raheem Kidwai.
[25] Nadwi, *The Role and Responsibilities of Muslims in the West* (Leicester, 1993).
[26] Nadwi, *Kārwān*, vol. 3, 12.
[27] Sayyid 'Abdul Hayy, *Al-Thaqāfat al-Islamiyyat fi al-Hind* (Damascus, n.d.).

shepherds. Yet they lost their empires to the same Arabs and placed at their feet all that they had. More importantly, they followed those Arabs, drawing heavily upon them. Today history repeats itself. We are faced with a similar scenario. The greedy ones are desperately trying to push the Arabs back to the desert, by depriving them of their faith and wealth.

You had been blessed with honour and power in the past by Islam alone. Today the same source can overpower you. This is not my observation; the Caliph 'Umar asserted the above truth. Arab nationalism did you no good in the past. Nor will it help you today.[28]

Prince Hasan was impressed by Shaykh Nadwi's candid assessment about the conditions prevailing in Jordan. His respect for Shaykh Nadwi increased considerably judging by his keen interest in the former's writings. It was at his behest that the government facilitated Shaykh Nadwi's lectures in several universities. Thus, he was treated as a state guest.

Shaykh Nadwi's busy schedule included an important lecture at Yarmuk University where he delivered an inspirational talk to thousands of university students. His visit to the *Ashāb-i Kahf* (People of the Cave), a historical site, was a particularly moving account for him. His book *Faith versus Materialism* is a comparative and analytical study of this important event mentioned in detail in the Qur'an.

In fact, *Surah Al-Kahf* was revealed at Makkah at a time when the small band of helpless Muslims, Shaykh Nadwi observed, was facing almost the same type of religious persecution which had led the Companions of the Cave to hide themselves in a cave from the fury of the Roman Empire. A picturesque description of the conditions then obtaining in Makkah preserved in the Quran, illustrates the perilous situation of the Makkan Muslims.[29]

Another dimension linked to the *surahs* is elaborated by Imran Hosein. His research suggests the unholy alliance between the Euro-Jewish and Euro-Christian world orders. The conspiracy of these civilisations embodies the secularisation of knowledge resulting in the "[rejection] of spiritual insight as a source of knowledge."[30] Thus, the consequences are inevitable as

---

[28] Cf. Akram Nadwi, *Shaykh Abu Al-Hasan Ali Nadwi*, 152-3.
[29] Nadwi, *Faith versus Materialism: The Message of Surat al-Kahf* (Lucknow, 1976), pp. 17-53. The parallel between the Companions of the Cave and the Companions of the Prophet (SAAS) is recorded by Shaykh Nadwi.
[30] Imran N. Hosein, *Surah Al-Kahf and the Modern Age* (San Fernando, 2007).

the world continues to plunge into corruption and godlessness.

Congress Rule: An Assessment

Political fortunes and loyalist tendencies marked the electoral victory of the Congress against the then ruling Janata Party. It was expected that the Congress Party would reassess its past policies for which it suffered a humiliating defeat. Hence future strategies would be judiciously implemented bearing in mind the constitutional rights of the citizens. However, subsequent events under Congress rule revealed the entrenched forms of political expediency over good governance. According to Shaykh Nadwi, despotic rule robbed the masses of their democratic rights and exposed them to a new kind of enslavement that was no different from the brutality of the 1857 uprising against British rule.[31] It is in this context that Shaykh Nadwi considered it his moral duty to address Indira Gandhi personally on the crisis engulfing the country. His letter preceding the meeting with the Prime Minister focused on the following issues:

- Indiscriminate imprisonment of innocent civilians against whom abuses had been committed.
- State machinery committed grave excesses against the public.
- Family-planning schemes violated the basic human rights and had eroded public confidence in the government.
- Dilution of moral values resulting from the state's despotic measures.[32]

Shaykh Nadwi's impassioned appeal for the restoration of law and order and the return of normalcy in society was indicative of his concern as an Indian citizen, a Muslim scholar and a well-wisher (*qadrdān*) of humanity.

The shifting political realities in India also saw the rise of the Hindu extremist organisations advancing the "saffronisation" programme in the country. During the Congress electoral victory in 1980, these movements bravely pursued their militant goals; a Hindutva state with no protection of minority rights as enshrined in the Constitution. Muslims, who formed the largest minority, became the target of the RSS and other like-minded extremist outfits.

---

[31] Nadwi, *Kārwān*, vol. 2, 209.
[32] A detailed account appears in the *Kārwān*, vol. 2, 215-21.

The rise of Hindu fundamentalism and aggressive Hindu revivalism[33] during Indira Gandhi's rule unleashed the potential for a Hindu-Muslim conflict with tragic consequences. In fact, the Moradabad tragedy, as Shaykh Nadwi noted, was also aimed at destroying the economic base[34] of the prosperous Muslim community. There existed a consistent pattern of destroying lives and property of Muslims by these movements supported by the police force. The litany of economic woes and senseless loss of human lives assumed alarming proportions[35] in the years to follow. Other minority communities were not spared from the wave of communal tension. The desecration of the Sikh Temple in Amritsar in 1984 by the army to quell the demand for an independent state gave rise to counter- insurgent movements. Worse still, the assassination of Prime Minister Indira Gandhi in 1984 by her Sikh security guards reopened a bloody chapter against minorities, in this case the Sikh community. It was almost a case of ethnic cleansing for which the Congress Party was largely culpable. Indiscriminate killing was just a beginning to the mayhem that engulfed the country in a relatively short period of time. The following graphic details provided by Shaykh Nadwi illustrates his concern for humanity:

> The (tragedy) was evident in the capital, Delhi, where it was reported that approximately five hundred Sikhs were killed... many were set alight with petrol while many were tied to pillars and burnt alive. Their properties were looted and invariably this carnage was conducted in cahoots with the police. In many places, Muslims were also involved in looting which revealed their lack of moral training and avarice... In my gatherings I stated that whoever had these stolen goods in their homes would be struck by sickness and affliction. The result was that many Muslims feared my statements as ominous and returned the goods. When the Sikhs were informed of this, they arrived at my home individually as well as collectively and expressed their appreciation. I informed them that it was my moral and religious duty. Moreover, Muslims were taught this important lesson in Islam as categorically stated in the Quran:

---

[33] The RSS and Shiv Sena are aggressive Hindu movements pursuing their notoriously utopian Hindu state and the forcible re-conversion of Muslims/Christians to the Hindu *dharma*.
[34] Nadwi, *Kārwān*, vol. 2, 318.
[35] The Gujarat genocide (2002) where thousands of Muslims were killed in Ahmedabad and its outlying areas reinforced fears of Muslim vulnerability to Hindu militancy.

Chapter X
Trends in Transnational Institutions

O you who believe! Be faithful witnesses for Allah in justice, and do not let hatred of any people incite you so that you cannot deal justly. Deal justly, that is closer to your piety. Fear Allah. Allah knows what you do. (5:8).[36]

Shaykh Nadwi's active involvement was much appreciated by the Sikh community. In a particular sense, it further enhanced the status of the *Payām* movement to reach out to other faith-based communities.

We now make a brief mention of another scion of the Gandhi dynasty, Rajiv Gandhi (d. 1991). Shaykh Nadwi's interaction with the Prime Minister was much evident in the Shah Bano case and the tragic Babri Masjid incident (which are discussed in the next chapter). His courageous stance defused the tension that bordered on national crisis. At the heart of his correspondence with Rajiv Gandhi were issues that affected the nation at sociopolitical levels.

Shaykh Nadwi's love for his country and its people personified his patriotism 'unalloyed and unwavering' and he made it his practice to write to every Prime Minister regardless of their political affiliation with the sole purpose of *nasīhah* (counsel).[37]

Malaysia: A New Experience

Shaykh Nadwi's journey to Malaysia in April 1987 was an important milestone to his *da'wah* outreach activities. The Malay archipelago before the imposition of British rule in the nineteenth century was made up of traditional Malay states under the control of hereditary Malay sultans. Malaysia and Indonesia, two predominantly Muslim countries in the archipelago, supported the reformist (*islāh*) trends in this part of the Muslim world. In a similar move, their nationalist aspirations combined with their *da'wah* vision provided markers for their distinctive Islamic identity. Traits of brotherhood and commitment to the Islamic ideals were most prominent in their lives.

Shaykh Nadwi's program was organised by ABIM under the charismatic leadership of the intellectual activist Anwar Ibrahim.[38] ABIM is the Malay

---

[36] Nadwi, *Kārwān*, vol. 3, 91-92.
[37] Nadwi, *Kārwān*, vol. 5, 100-101.
[38] Anwar Ibrahim's chequered history from an intellectual activist to a Deputy Minister in Prime Minister Muhammad Mahathir's cabinet in 1998, ending with extended periods of imprisonment on charges of corruption and sexual

acronym for Malyasian Islamic Youth Organisation, which was officially registered in 1972. Its major objective, *inter alia*, was:

[to] establish and propagate Islamic tenets and principles as enshrined in the Quran in a progressive manner and the Islamic message in its universal dimension.[39]

The thrust of Shaykh Nadwi's addresses at universities and institutions was thematic in its significance. Muslims had to be reformed at societal level so that the Islamic values could infiltrate into their lives. An important talk guided by the story of the youth in Surah Al-Kahf[40] had a direct bearing on the Malaysians in terms of their responsibilities and their obligations to Islam.

Shaykh Nadwi's impressions of some of the Malaysian sultanates highlighted the pervasive Islamic presence over the centuries. He also visited the International Islamic University of Malaysia (IIUM), an international Islamic institution drawing scholars and its teaching personnel from all over the world. The Islamisatiōn of knowledge which the distinguished scholar, Professor Isma'il Raji al-Faruqi envisioned, was designed and developed at the university. It opened new pathways to contemporary Islamic thought. Interestingly, his meeting with Professor al-Faruqi took place in 1986 at the Institute of Islamic Research in Luxemburg.

It must be noted that Nadwah's international prestige had attracted a substantial number of students from both Malaysia and Indonesia. Their contributions and influence in their respective countries have been considerable.

During Shaykh Nadwi's visit to the country an unfortunate incident occurred that provoked a series of violent reactions among Muslims. Someone had posted a distorted version of the Quran on the internet. Many naive Muslims believed this act to be a sign of the end times and the world was going to perish soon. Shaykh Nadwi repudiated this claim with the Qur'anic declaration that its sanctity and protection against the devious schemes is a Divine providence. Muslim opposition across the world against this sacrilegious act resulted in its swift removal from the internet.

---

misconduct, have been extensively covered in John Esposito and John Voll, *Makers of Contemporary Islam* (New York, 2001), 177-98.
[39] For details on the organization, see *The Oxford Encyclopedia of the Modern Islamic World* under the entry *ABIM*, vol. 1, 15-16.
[40] Nadwi, *Kārwān*, vol. 3, 246-49.

Chapter X
Trends in Transnational Institutions

Two Conflicting Portraits

The Iranian Revolution of 1979 in Iran that to led the tyrannical rule of the Pahlavi dynasty was inspired by the charismatic personality of Ayatollah Khomeini. When he gave the call for the Islamic revolution as expressed in the slogan, *Neither East nor West, Islam is the Best,* the response was overwhelming. It was expected that, as Shaykh Nadwi argued, it would not reopen the pages of history of bitter disputes and controversies between Sunnis and Shi'ahs. If Khomeini, due to some local or political reasons, could not dissociate himself from the views and beliefs of the *Ithnā' 'Ashariyyah* (the dominant Shi'ite sect to which Khomeini belonged), he would at least not proclaim them. These hopes cherished by Shaykh Nadwi did not materialise as the events after the revolution revealed. The Iranian Islamic Revolution launched a relentless campaign to promote its brand of Islam with its entrenched anti-Sunni rhetoric.

In response to the growing presence of Shi'ism in the Muslim countries and its uncritical acceptance among many Muslim organisations for which a number of reasons may be mentioned, the noted Indian scholar, Mawlana Manzur Nu'māni wrote a comprehensive book *Khomeini: Iranian Revolution and the Shi'ite Faith* to repudiate their deviant beliefs. According to Nu'māni:

> [it] was my religious duty as well as moral obligation to my co-religionists to try, to the best of my ability, to acquaint them with the real position with regard to Khomeini. It was intended to highlight the revolution engineered by him and the Shi'ite faith with special reference to the doctrine of Imamate, for it forms the religious and intellectual foundation of the Iranian Revolution.[41]

When Shaykh Nadwi prepared his views and analysis of Shi'ism,[42] he chose a different approach. This was in line with his literary style. The book, *Islam and the Earliest Muslims: Two Conflicting Portraits,*

> [is] an attempt to present a sketch of the earliest, ideal era of Islam and compared with beliefs and deeds of the *'Ithnā 'Ashari* sect (from its first protagonist to Ayatollah Khomeini) as presented in the authentic works. It has been left to the discretion, common sense,

---

[41] Mohammad Manzoor Nomani, *Iranian Revolution and the Shi'ite Faith* (1986), 16.
[42] Nadwi, *Islam and the Earliest Muslims: Two Conflicting Portraits* (Lucknow, 1984).

prudence and better judgement of the readers to form their own opinion as to which of the two portrayals is upheld by the Quran as well as accepted by historians, Muslim and non-Muslim.[43]

Shaykh Nadwi's critical evaluation of Shi'ism is free from the sophistry of polemics and sensationalism. This does not suggest that his writings are defensive or an elaborate apologia. Rather, it is a forceful exposition of facts anchored on historical objectivity and academic sobriety. Shaykh Nadwi eschewed all forms of personal or sectarian prejudice that tended to mar a scholarly treatment of such works.

It is interesting to note that Shaykh Nadwi's reference to the classical works on Shi'ism, especially the writings of Ibn Taimiyyah, reinforces the critique of this sect over the centuries. His work, which is a major contribution to this important study, was received with mixed reactions by a handful of Muslim scholars and organisations. Their emotional outburst was based on Khomeini's Sunni-Shi'ah unity call. Paradoxically, it was a veneer for exporting the Iranian Revolution with its strong sectarian bias. However, later events only confirmed Shaykh Nadwi's intuitive insight. The virulent demonstrations and sinister campaigns by Iranians to destablise the Saudi monarchy during the *hajj* period in 1987 was a testimony to the Revolution's political propaganda strategies.

In the context of these political happenings, Shaykh Nadwi's keynote address in 1987 at Rābitā's international conference about the sanctity of the *Haramayn* (Makkah and Madinah) was a timeous reminder to the the delegates concerning the Shi'ite movement's sinister moves in this regard.

An equally important work, *Al-Murtadā* (1989) should be read in tandem with *Two Conflicting Portraits* to assess Shaykh Nadwi's stature as a literary critic. He says:

> One of these victimised personalities, whose real worth was never appreciated, was 'Ali bin Abi Talib. Peculiar circumstances during his lifetime, curious creeds and some psychological impulses have combined to blur his life and character. Let alone impartial scholars, even those who had based their creed on his greatness never thought it worthwhile to undertake an objective study of his life and achievements. The demands of the age in which he had lived and the difficulties he had to face were never dispassionately analysed...

---

[43] *Ibid.*, 2.

Chapter X
Trends in Transnational Institutions

[Likewise] his underlying policy in dealing with the political and administrative affairs are some of the essential aspects of his life that need to be explored and studied judiciously. Any attempt that ignores these features of his life and character is bound to be unjust and incomplete besides being liable to lead us to a wrong and misleading conclusion.[44]

The blame for the distorted portrayal of the life and times of Caliph 'Ali lies squarely with historians and biographers who conflate eulogy with historiography. This serious shortcoming exists in the works of Muslim biographers and historians of 'Ali. Shaykh Nadwi maintains that any work which employs modern analytical tools in bringing out the multifaceted life of Caliph 'Ali requires a breadth of vision and catholicity of views. It is an indisputable fact that the controversy surrounding his personality has eclipsed his real contributions, with the result that the brilliance of his character has been lost in the mists of time.

Al-Murtadā, originally written in Arabic and translated into English as *The Life of Caliph 'Ali*, not only recounts the historical circumstances which brought out the versatile genius of 'Ali, but also refutes the distortions and misconceptions that came to be woven around his charismatic personality.

Shaykh Nadwi's presentation of biographical writings mirrors his critical approach to the genre. He cautions writers to avoid the pitfalls of eulogy in recounting the life and times of scholars, *mashā'ikh* and *'ulama'*. According to him, historical criticism requires an affinity to the personality on whom a biography is written. A detached approach makes the writing a dull prosaic and soulless account. In direct contrast are the embellished accounts that project a personality who holds an unrivalled position among his peers and represents the epitome of perfection. Through the misty lens their achievements are blurred making it difficult for readers to separate fact from fiction. Shaykh Nadwi urges biographers to be careful in their choice of words and engage constructively while making historical assessments.

Conclusion

The versatility of Shaykh Nadwi's intellectual life began to unfold largely on account of his active association with the institutions abroad. Likewise, his writings also defined the maturity of his outlook. More often than not

---

[44] Nadwi, *The Life of Caliph 'Ali* (Lucknow, 1990), 2.

sensationalism, an ideological tool to foment religious conflict, is discernible in polemical works related to the contributions of eminent Islamic personalities. In contrast, Shaykh Nadwi's objectivity is illustrated in his series of biographical accounts of Islamic personalities and their contributions to Islamic revival rather than the embellished portraits belonging to the eulogy genre.

Chapter XI

Revival of Islamic Authenticity

This chapter seeks to highlight the important contributions of Shaykh Nadwi to the preservation of the corporate identity of Muslims in India. Although mention is made of important events which are central to his *da'wah*, two incidents of national importance reinforced his position as an eminent religious figure, a leader with consummate skills and an outstanding visionary. His Islamic fervour was tempered with pragmatism, an enduring quality that sustained him during the turbulent period of political crisis and religious fanaticism in the country.

Muslim Personal Law

The establishment of the Muslim Personal Law Board in India was not an arbitrary phenomenon. Indeed, the loss of Muslim rule after the 1857 uprising brought to a tragic end the implementation of the *shari'ah*, albeit in its fragmented forms, by various Muslim dynasties over the centuries. In the political context, the Muslim Personal Law was the residual expression of the *'ulama's* efforts to retain the *shari'ah* at a crucial period when British imperialism[1] crushed the last vestige of Muslim rule. There was no doubt that the Partition of India in 1947 altered the demographic character of the Muslims; now a marginalised community relegated to a minority status. Efforts were thus made to preserve the Muslim Personal Law as a rebuttal to the Uniform Civil Code. For example, the Shari'ah Act of 1937 was adopted, implemented to safeguard the independent charter of Muslim law. In fact, the curtailment of the *shari'ah* under British rule invariably led to the promulgation of the *Shari'ah* Act of 1937 - a grim reminder of the limited power and authority of the *qazdis* (judges). In this case, access was restricted to the family personal laws. This included *waqf*, divorce, inheritance, etc.[2]

However, there was an orchestrated attempt by both secularist and modernist Muslims to tamper with issues affecting Muslim life that were embedded in the *shari'ah*. In response to these rising threats against the *shari'ah*, the *'ulama'* of divergent backgrounds convened a special meeting at

---

[1] For a detailed account on the changing fortunes of the *shari'ah* with special reference to the diminishing roles of the *qazdis*, see Dietrich Reetz, *Islam in the Public Sphere* (New Delhi, 2006).
[2] Mahmood Tahir, "Muslim Personal Law in India: A Historical Footnote" in S.A.H.A. Rizwi, *Supreme Court and the Muslim Personal Law* (Delhi, 1985), 1-5.

Dār al-'Ulūm Deoband. It was a collective voice to articulate the innate dynamism and quality of adaptability of the shari'ah to the changing circumstances in the country. Thus, the All India Muslim Personal Law Board[3] was established in 1972. Its objectives were clear: To preserve and safeguard the shari'ah in India. Qāri Muhammad Tayyib (d.1983)[4] was the first president of AIMPLB who played a significant role in promoting the autonomous character of the shari'ah.

After Qāri Tayyib's demise in 1983, Shaykh Nadwi was unanimously elected as president, a position which he held until his death in 1999. At an important gathering in Kolkata in 1985, an estimated 500,000 Muslims attended to listen to the inspiring address of Shaykh Nadwi. He called upon the Muslims to do some soul-searching, an introspection in the light of scathing campaigns against the shari'ah. These were proliferated with anti-Islamic slogans as well as the establishment of quasi-courts to apply customary laws over the shari'ah. The civil court did not reflect the role of the Imarāt, an officially mandated Muslim court vested with complete powers to adjudicate over matters that fell within the purview of Muslim Personal Law. In contrast, the court was an amalgam of customs with no shar'i sanction. It condoned bid'ah in societal matters, and undermined the clear-cut Qur'anic injunctions with regard to women's inheritance, rights of orphans, etc. In short, it was antithetical to the spirit of Islam. On the other hand, Muslim antipathy to change was based largely on the perceived loss of authority. The patriarchal society influenced by the rigid Hindu caste system influenced their response to pertinent Islamic issues. It was, therefore, hardly surprising that opposition or the subtle rejection of the shari'ah was in line with their mindset.[5]

Shaykh Nadwi's critique of the Muslim society's declining norms and values was taken seriously at a resolution passed to accept the Board as the sole arbiter of the shari'ah, which consolidated its position as the voice of the Muslim masses.

During that year (1986), the Board was faced with a formidable challenge to its credibility as the guardian of the shari'ah. The blatant interference of the Supreme Court to amend the Qur'anic stipulations pertaining to nafaqah

---

[3] Syed Habibul Haq Nadvi, *Islamic Legal Philosophy and the Qur'anic Origins of the Islamic Law*, 365.
[4] Qāri Tayyib's contribution to the growth and development of Dār-ul-'Ulūm Deoband is discussed in Syed Mahbub Rizwi, *Tārikh Dār al-'Ulūm, Deoband*, vol. 1 (Deoband, 1992).
[5] See Nadwi, *Kārwān*, vol. 3, 113-15.

Chapter XI
Revival of Islamic Authenticity

(maintenance) for a divorced woman provoked an unprecedented series of protests and demonstrations, compelling the state to rescind its decision. Here the Qur'anic usage of *matā'* had been wrongly translated by the Supreme Court as maintenance instead of provision. The court's arbitrary translation breached the content of the Islamic law. Maintenance implies a fixed amount which a husband is made to pay to his divorced wife. Also, the due process in respect of *talāq* (divorce) has to be followed. Moreover, all the *mufassirin* (commentators) are unanimous that *matā'* in this context has no bearing to the English equivalent of the term 'maintenance.'[6]

Under the charismatic leadership of Shaykh Nadwi, leaders from the diverse spectrum of Muslim thought worked tirelessly to stem the tide of political manipulation and religious extremism. Shaykh Nadwi's preoccupation during this crucial period was to defend the *shari'ah* against the hostile elements hell-bent on destroying the fabric of Islamic identity. As Syed Shahabuddin (ex. MP) noted:

> (Shaykh Nadwi) clearly saw the historic process of assimilation at work as the long-term objective of Hindu nationalism to absorb the Muslim Indians into the Hindu fold. That explains his firm stand on the question of Muslim Personal Law against any interference through legislation or through judicial pronouncement.[7]

A major challenge in the Shah Bano case was the Qur'anic elaboration of *nafaqah* which pitted the Muslim *ummah* against the state bureaucracy. Against the *ijma'* (consensus) of the *fuqahā'* (jurists) the deliberate distortion and interpolation of Qur'anic verses by the judges in the Supreme court was a blatant attempt to enforce the Uniform Civil Code. There was no gainsaying that such a move was clearly the dissolution of Muslim Personal Law, loss of corporate Muslim identity and its assimilation into the Hindutva ideology.[8]

It was a perilous situation, a *Fitna* that could have radically altered the destiny of Muslims if it had went unchallenged. Shaykh Nadwi's role must be understood in the background of these volatile happenings. From the protracted meetings to his correspondence[9] with Prime Minister Rajiv

---

[6] On the Quranic interpretation of *nafaqah* vis-a-vis the Supreme Court ruling, see Rizvi, *Supreme Court and the Muslim Personal Law*, 28-32.
[7] *The Fragrance of the East* (January- June 2000), 88-89.
[8] Nadwi, *Kārwān*, vol. 3, 116-17.
[9] *Ibid.*, 31-40.

221

Gandhi, he stood like the proverbial solid rock against the currents of hostility and disparagement. The Board, through its sustained campaign of mobilising support across the sectarian divide, forced the government to change its position with regard to the enactment of the Muslim Divorce Bill (1986). Habibul Haq Nadvi's comments about the Shah Bano case are pertinent:

> The Shah Bano case showed that under the leadership of Shaykh Nadwi the struggle against the Supreme Court verdict mirrored the precarious situation of a beleaguered minority whose corporate Muslim identity was threatened by secularist forces that ironically was meant to protect their constitutional rights.[10]

The Board refuted claims of perpetuating patriarchy in the light of the plight faced by divorced women. It argued that the reforms were underway provided there were no State interference vociferously advocating a uniform civil code for all its citizens. Another matter of grave concern was the perceived gender inequality relating to divorce. Thus, the provisions of Muslim law were misinterpreted for political expediency. However, legal experts were of the opinion that the proposed civil code negated the religious diversity of the country. In view of the negative reception received by the State and Muslim fringe groups, the Board embarked on campaigns across the country to educate the Muslim masses about the *shari'ah* injunctions. By the same token, the Board opposed legislations that tampered with the Muslim Personal Law. Therefore, a clear distinction had to be made between reform as envisaged by the Board and abolition demanded by the advocacy groups comprising both Muslims and non- Muslims. In this respect, the *shari'ah* courts played a leading role in the protection of women's rights by crafting contracts to ensure that due processes were followed should divorce be the only option.[11]

Reform implied instituting corrective measures adopted by the Board over customary laws that perpetuated gender violence and family honour killings. Notwithstanding the Board's continued efforts to project the correct image of *shari'ah* laws, debates about imposing the civil code reappeared 'like a

---

[10] Nadwi, *Islamic Legal Philosophy*, 367.
[11] For a detailed *discussion* on the Shah Bano case, See Rizvi, *Supreme Court and the Muslim Personal Law,* 67-87.

Chapter XI
Revival of Islamic Authenticity

malignant growth'. The recent ordinance (2018) invalidating triple *talāq* is illustrative of the state interference.

In sum, the Board continues to face a barrage of criticisms for creating an alleged parallel legal system, privatising justice and undermining the Constitution. Regrettably, the cogent response by the Board which serves as an arbitration council for dispute resolution on Muslim Personal Law matters has been manipulated by politicians to polarise Muslims and other faith-based communities.

Babri Masjid: A Tragedy

Another intrusion on the Muslim autonomy were threats to mosques, purportedly claimed to be originally Hindu temples. The timeline of events from 1986 in Shaykh Nadwi's busy schedule was overshadowed by the Babri Masjid dispute, which culminated in its tragic demolition in 1992. Again, the Board under the leadership of Shaykh Nadwi launched a vigorous campaign to stop the encroachment of the sacred precinct by the fanatical movement of the Bharatiya Janata Party (BJP).[12] Not surprisingly, the state collusion with the Hindutva movement was decried by the Muslim masses who saw this as a betrayal of the values that Gandhi and other pioneers of the freedom struggle had fought for. A predictable pattern emerged - the bedrock of democracy and secularism was weakened by Hindu nationalism and religious bigotry.

The history of the Babri Masjid in Ayodhya in Uttar Pradesh which dates back to the rule of Emperor Babur (1526-1530),[13] founder of Mughal dynasty in India, has always maintained a Muslim presence on this disputed site. Claims that it has been the birthplace of the Hindu god Rama were refuted by historians with conclusive evidence of exclusive Muslim rights[14] over the Babri Masjid from 1528.

It would be an oversimplification to assume that the *'ulama* and leaders who were actively involved in the conflict simply capitulated to the

---

[12] Cf. Thomas Blom Hansen, *The Saffron Wave: Democracy and Hindu Nationalism in Modern India* (Delhi, 1999). There were exceptions who were sympathetic to the Muslim cause: Shaykh Nadwi mentions the Minister of Railways, Laloo Prasad Yadav, who introduced strong measures to stop or at least control the provocative procession under militant opposition leaders and religious figures.
[13] It was Mir Bāqi, a distinguished noble of Babur's imperial flotilla, who laid the foundation of the mosque in 1528 and dedicated it to the name of Emperor Babur. Se Arshad Islam, "The Hindu-Muslim Conflict Over the Babri Mosque: A Historical Analysis" in *Hamdard Islamicus*, July-September 2003 (Karachi, 2003), 35-36.
[14] *Ibid.*, 49-53.

extremist Hindu groups' brazen attempts to demolish the mosque. As much as Shaykh Nadwi eschewed agitational politics, he adopted practical strategies to engage the government as well as moderate Hindu religious figures[15] to resolve the dispute. He feared that the potential for communal riots was as volatile as ever and the inflamed passions of the Muslims could have serious consequences for their future.

In response to the Muslim pressure the government intervened to prevent the Vishwa Hindu Parishad (World Hindu Council) fanatics from converting the mosque into a *mandir* (temple), but achieved limited success. In Shaykh Nadwi's words:

> The opening of locks in the *darshana* (ritual offerings) are dangerous steps that are likely to inflame Muslims' emotions... the perceptions are that the government is biased towards one faction only.

Critics like Zoya Hasan have claimed that Shaykh Nadwi struck a deal with the Prime Minister Rajiv Gandhi to have the verdict on the Shah Bano case revoked through Parliament while Hindus would be allowed to offer rituals on the disputed site by unlocking the gate of this mosque. This accusation has been refuted by Shaykh Nadwi in his letter to Professor David Ludden.[16]

Muslims were disillusioned at the pace of negotiations which slowed down meaningful resolutions to the crisis. The Babri Masjid conflict was a traumatic period for Muslims in India. Shaykh Nadwi recounted the unwavering efforts of the Board[17] to secure a settlement with the government to protect the Babri Masjid. He himself worked tirelessly towards finding an acceptable formula that would in no way jeopardise the peace and insecurity of the country.

Muslim response to the Hindutva encroachment saw the emergence of

---

[15] Shaykh Nadwi mentions Shankaracharya of Kanchipuram (Tamil Nadu), an eminent Hindu priest who widely respected for his erudition and religious charisma. See Nadwi, *Kārwān*, vol. 4, 285-90 to understand his role in the Ayodhya conflict.

[16] See Zoya Hasan, "Communal Mobilisation and Changing Majority", in David Ludden *Making India Hind* (New Delhi, 1998). For a rebuttal of Zoya Hasan's article see Shaykh Nadwi's letter to David Ludden in *The Fragrance of the East*, (2003), 219-20.

[17] On the role fo the AIMPLB in the conflict, a detailed account appears in Nadwi, *Kārwān*, vol. 4, 335-408.

Chapter XI
Revival of Islamic Authenticity

the Babri Action Committee.[18] It sought to mobilise the Muslim masses to protest against such draconian measures. Shaykh Nadwi counselled self-restraint under these trying circumstances and it was not always that his advice was heeded to by the Muslim organisations. Outrage, agitational politics, according to him, were detrimental to the Muslim cause, because the Hindutva followers exploited disunity in the Muslim ranks to achieve their sinister goals. However, this did not imply that Shaykh Nadwi opted for passive resistance. Rather, he demonstrated that through consultation with state bureaucracy some measure of success could be achieved. His direct communication with the Prime Ministers[19] and other influential politicians was meant to highlight the Muslim position against the menacing onslaught of the Hindu militants.

As events unfolded, the Babri Masjid conflict redefined Shaykh Nadwi's leadership role. It was a mammoth task for him and his associates to prepare detailed resolutions for an interactive dialogue with important stakeholders. A looming crisis was an ominous sign of the imminent confrontation between Muslims and Hindus, a confrontation that Shaykh Nadwi believed had to be averted at all cost.

The series of shortlived and weak central governments, following the assassination of Rajiv Gandhi in 1991, finally opened the doors of open communal politics. The BJP increasingly used communal symbols in its electoral propaganda, under the presidency of its later Union Home Minister Lal Krishna Advani. The Babri Masjid issue was transformed from a regional issue to a national question. The ideal Hindu nation (read as Hindutva) was symbolic in Advani's *ratha-yātrā* (march) in September 1990. He led a campaign towards Ayodhya in an open Toyota jeep as an allegory of the epic battles of the *Ramayana* and *Mahabharata*, the march of fervent Hindus against evil powers (Muslims). The BJP government in the state of Uttar Pradesh finally provided the political framework for the demolition of the mosque in 1992. On 6 December 1992, the religious work (*kārasevā*) commenced and the 464-year-old Babri Masjid was completely razed to the ground by Hindu zealots. State authorities and other law-enforcing agencies stood helpless while thousands of people were

---

[18] Established by the Lucknow-based advocate, Zafaryab Jilani, the Babri Masjid Action Committee (BMAC), initially a regionally based organisation, assumed a national status during this turbulent period.

[19] See Nadwi, *Kārwān*, vol. 4, 372-74 for these high-profile meetings with Indian Prime Ministers.

summarily butchered throughout the country. Attempts to rebuild the mosque were futile as state protection was just another attempt to cover the barbaric acts of the Hindu zealots.

After a protracted legal battle, the Supreme Court delivered its verdict on 9 November 2019. Hindus were granted rights over the disputed land to build a temple. In a similar vein the court was unanimous in its judgement that the demolition of the mosque was a violation of the Muslim rights for which restitution was provided. The government was required to allocate five acres of land as an alternative for a mosque to be built. Thus ended the decades-long dispute which saw thousands of innocent lives lost during this politically charged period.

For Shaykh Nadwi the rule of law surpassed the reactions from the disaffected communities. In this respect, mobocracy or the spike in communal violence was counterproductive to maintain peace and order in the country. The rule of law was applicable to all citizens irrespective of their reservations. Again, Shaykh Nadwi maintained that a secular state like India should advance the cause of democracy. However, not all the Muslim organisations and parties endorsed his approach to this volatile issue. In many instances, Shaykh Nadwi's efforts at finding a practical solution were ridiculed by Muslim hardliners. He was vilified and worse accused of complicity with the Hindu groups demanding the 'usurped' site be returned to them. The verdict (2019) after 17 years perhaps vindicated his stance.

In retrospect, the secular image of India was seriously tarnished by successive governments failing dismally to find a just solution to this conflict.[20]

The Gulf Crisis

As a transnational scholar whose early popularity struck roots in the Arab world, it was no coincidence that Shaykh Nadwi's reaction to the Gulf crisis would resonate across this part of the Muslim world. Iraq's invasion of Kuwait in August 2000 was a fateful event with calamitous consequences. Shaykh Nadwi's analysis of the Iraqi occupation (briefly recounted hereunder) suggested that it was like the war of attrition between Iraq and Iran. Iraq's occupation of Kuwait, a small kingdom with no military resources to match the firepower of the former, was plain brigandage (*qazzāqī*)[21] that militated against the universal principles of morality and human dignity. According to

---

[20] Arshad Islam, *The Hindu and Muslim Conflict*, 45-47.
[21] Nadwi, *Kārwān*, vol. 4, 274-92.

Chapter XI
Revival of Islamic Authenticity

Shaykh Nadwi:

- Iraqi occupation brought in its wake the predictable desecration of property and humiliation of the subjugated nation.[22]
- Saddam Hussein's military superiority created a euphoria that under his leadership the Arab world would once again be a dynamic nation reminiscent of the rule of Salahuddin Ayyubi.[23]
- Instead of directing his military might against Israel, Saddam made the Arab countries his prime targets, thus creating a climate of vulnerability for the Muslim *ummah*.[24]
- Under such circumstances, Saudi Arabia solicited the military aid of its allies, the US and Britain to protect the kingdom.

According to Shaykh Nadwi, the Saudi action provoked widespread reaction from the Muslim world. As a prolific writer with his *da'wah* focused largely on the Arab world, Shaykh Nadwi lamented their apathy towards establishing a model Islamic society. Tracing the history of the *Haramayn* (Makkah and Madinah), Shaykh Nadwi noted that under its various rulers, despite their shortcomings, the kingdom always defended the sanctity of the holy sites. It was, therefore, a regrettable move to co-opt non-Muslim allies for its security.

Saddam's disregard for the security of the *Haramayn* only confirmed his sinister political motive. In an important monograph[25] which was read at a seminar on the Gulf War in Cairo, Shaykh Nadwi argued that hysteria[26] among Muslim individuals and organisations overwhelmed their sense of objectivity with the result that they would object to any criticism of Saddam. In other words, they were willing to exonerate Saddam from his tarnished record of human rights abuse and genocide simply because he challenged the might of the imperialist American military.

After the Gulf War, the geopolitics of the Muslim world changed rapidly.

---

[22] The following Quranic *āyah* attested to the violation of human rights, ironically perpetrated by Iraqi soldiers against the helpless Kuwaiti victims. (Surah Naml: 34.).
[23] See Stanley Lane Poole, *Salahuddin and the Fall of the Kingdom of Jerusalem* (Lahore, 1979).
[24] Nadwi, *Kārwān*, vol. 4, 274.
[25] Nadwi, *Ummat i-Islama kā Mustaqbil: Khaliji Jang ke Ba'd* (Karachi, n.d.); cf. Nadwi, *'Ālam-i Arabi ke Liye sab se Bada Khatra* (Lucknow, 1991).
[26] *Ibid.*, 5.

Just two years after Shaykh Nadwi's demise (d. 1999), the invasion of Afghanistan by the US and the coalition forces brought another tragic chapter in Muslim history. Likewise, the invasion of Iraq for the second time (2003) by the American forces brought the downfall of Saddam Hussein. Worse, the invasion exposed the Iraqi nation to a brutality that was incomparable to the bloody massacre perpetrated by the Tatars[27] in 1253.

The rise of the Islamist movements to counteract the menace of American imperialism under the notorious rule of George Bush brought in its wake the phenomenon of Islamophobia. A relentless campaign of Islam/Muslim bashing in the West was the outcome of discrediting everything that was Islamic in character. Much earlier, Shaykh Nadwi saw the urgent need for a dynamic Islamic movement which could instill confidence in the Muslim society and be a source of inspiration by virtue of its valour, courage and vision.[28] By the same token, Shaykh Nadwi's call for self-introspection for Muslims was in line with his *Payām* movement. It was committed to the universal values of mutual respect and compassion without compromising its Islamic identity.

Tragic Loss

Two important figures complementing Shaykh Nadwi's personal and academic life are discussed. Although he was reticent to provide a comprehensive profile of his domestic life, readers have a glimpse of a relationship reflecting the Islamic ideal. Similarly, his enduring relationship with the scholar, Asif Kidwai mirrors his own academic pursuits.

Tayyib al-Nisā'

A companionship spanning over fifty years, Sayyidah Tayyib al-Nisā' was the epitome of a devoted wife who shared the hopes and aspirations of Shaykh Nadwi. Belonging to the scion of the Qutbiyyah nobility[29] she possessed winsome qualities of compassion, meticulous observance of the *shari'ah* and likewise, detached from worldly possessions. Her generosity was proverbial towards her relatives, indigent and destitute families. Sayyidah was a heart

---

[27] See, Nadwi, *Saviours of Islamic Spirit*, vol. 1, 277-311.
[28] Nadwi, *Ummat-i Islam ka Mustaqbil*, 18.
[29] Sayyid Tufayl Madani, *Sirat-i Sādāt-i Qutbiyyah* (Delhi, n.d.).

Chapter XI
Revival of Islamic Authenticity

patient and suffered multiple ailments.[30] In her last years she suffered from a fractured hip due to a fall. The pain was excruciating for almost three weeks. Furthermore, specialists advised against a hip replacement operation. Sayyidah passed away on 15 December 1989. The plethora of letters of condolence to Shaykh Nadwi indicated the respect she enjoyed in many parts of the country.

Muhammad Asif Kidwai

A detailed discussion on this erudite scholar of Islam will not be inappropriate with special reference to his translation of Shaykh Nadwi's major works.

Mawlana Nu'māni, a noted Islamic scholar was largely responsible for the introductory meetings with Dr Asif Kidwai. Shaykh Nadwi was most impressed by his academic profile: A PhD in politics from London University (his dissertation received favourable comments from his supervisor), and an accomplished writer in both English and Urdu. After the establishment of the Academy of Islamic Research and Publications in 1959, Kidwai's collection of articles entitled *Maqālāt-i Sirah* was published in 1960 and well received in literary circles.

After the Arabic publication of *Mādhā Khasir al-'Ālam* there was a strong urge to have this book translated into English. The original work in Arabic had seen numerous editions and its translation had to be undertaken by an accomplished writer. Shaykh Nadwi's choice naturally fell on Kidwai who executed this task with such dexterity that after this important publication his (Nadwi's) fame spread in many parts of the world. According to Professor Zafar Ishaq Ansari, a distinguished scholar and translator, Kidwai's English translation was flawless and unsurpassed in its literary style. This was confirmed by Professor Seyyed Hossein Nasr, a scholar of international repute whose works are widely read in the Muslim world.

The popularity of the English translation titled *Islam and the World* (first translation) served as an impetus to utilise Kidwai's consummate skills for translating Mawlana Nu'māni's and Shaykh Nadwi's well-known works into English. His enthusiastic response to comply with their requests was overwhelming. It must be remembered that Kidwai's chronic illness had confined him to bed. His immobility prevented him from assuming onerous

---

[30] *Kārwān*, vol. 4, 163-64.

responsibilities. The severity of his illness can be gauged from the fact that a hardbound volume placed on his chest would inconvenience him. Therefore, he had to take recourse to loose pages for his translation work.

Shaykh Nadwi's book *The Four Pillars of Islam* was also favourably received in the English-speaking world for its lucid style in presenting the pillars of Islam. It must be borne in mind that each work has its own peculiarities in terms of terminology and content. To this end, Kidwai fully conscious of this responsibility never deviates from the parameters of the *shari'ah*. His translations are conspicuously free from traces of bias, misrepresentation and distortion. In a similar vein, *Glory of Iqbal* and *Pathway to Medina* are masterpieces reinforcing the translator's literary versatility. Sadly, after a prolonged illness Kidwai passed away on 29 February 1989.[31]

Da'wah Journeys

Although the timeline has not been rigidly followed in this section, the following *da'wah* journeys by Shaykh Nadwi are a pointed reference to his global contributions.

Turkey: A Reappraisal

During September 1989 a seminar organised by Rābitā Adab on children's Islamic literature was chaired by Shaykh Nadwi in Istanbul. The concept of *adab* was discussed in detail to demonstrate its organic link to *akhlaq* (morality).

At the request of Rābitā an important lecture was delivered by Shaykh Nadwi. Tracing the glorious past of Turkey's contribution to Islamic culture, Shaykh Nadwi pointed out to the factors that deepened the country's tragic decline. There was a need for introspection, he insisted, to restore confidence and pride about its Islamic legacy. To this end, he warned the Turks about the imperialist forces working against Islam.

Shaykh Nadwi outlined a three-pronged strategy for Turkey's Islamic renaissance:

- To strengthen the *dīnī* consciousness among the Turkish masses.
- To create the Islamic ambience so that their faith (*imān*) served as a bulwark against the un-Islamic movements.[32]

---

[31] *Al-Ahsan Magazine*, vol. 2, 20-21.
[32] *Kārwān*, vol. 4, 101.

Chapter XI
Revival of Islamic Authenticity

- To ensure that the future generation of Turkish Muslims, especially the children were familiar with Islamic doctrines and teachings without which the understanding of the true content and spirit of 'ibādah (worship) might whittle away.

Several of Shaykh Nadwi's major works have been translated into Turkish by Shaykh Yusuf Caraca (d.2021). Common to these translations is the revivalist theme elaborated by Shaykh Nadwi.

Signs of Islamic resurgence have been perceptible over the few decades in Turkey. The Naqshbandi order has been influential in spreading the message of the Quran and sunnah. In the same vein, the ruling party has made bold attempts to establish the mainstream Islamic identity that had been undermined after the abolition of the Ottoman Caliphate in 1923. Turning the tide has been a formidable challenge for the ruling party to restore the Islamic practices in the country as it faces opposition from politicians and activists wedded to secularism.

Islamic identity is another key theme addressed to the Turkish nation. Here Shaykh Nadwi refers to the question the Prophet Ya'qūb posed to his sons and grandsons: *"What will you worship after me?"* This Qur'anic statement has a universal relevance. It reinforces the need for introspection in terms of one's relationship with Allah, and the degree of commitment that this relationship entails. It would be of interest to note that Shaykh Nadwi also contextualised this Qur'anic statement to the Indian Muslims against the backdrop of the Hindutva ideology. This message also has resonance for countries with a Muslim majority whose faith unfortunately has tilted towards isms like Socialism and Communism. These ideologies are in stark contrast to the unconditional obedience, worship and devotion to Allah.[33]

The publication of forceful Islamic literature was needed to meet the needs of the intellectual Muslims trained in Western institutions. These Muslims continue to influence educational and political institutions in Muslim countries. In many instances, they possess the *de facto* legislative power to implement a hybrid system in violation of the Islamic ideals. Shaykh Nadwi made an impassioned plea to reach out to this rising generation to instill

---

[33] For an elaboration on this theme:
- Nadwi, *Inviting to the Way of Allah* (London, 1996).
- Khurram Murad, *In the Early Hours: Reflections on Spiritual and Self Development* (Leicestershire, 2001), 57-84.
- Khalid Baig, *First Things First* (Stanton, 2004), 18-22.

"both in their hearts and minds an *imāni* (faith-inspired) and mature approach to the permanence of Islam, the relevance of its teachings and its leadership at all times." According to Shaykh Nadwi, the Muslim elites of Western orientation cling to the notion of liberal and political democracy as the panacea for the ills affecting Muslim countries. Their fixation on democracy as opposed to the *shari'ah* is a reflection of their ignorance or antipathy towards the *shūrā* system. Straddling from Malaysia to Mali this system was developed, refined and successfully implemented during Muslim rule over the centuries.[34]

Satanic Verses

The Indian-born British writer, Salman Rushdie earned notoriety for his sacrilegeous novel *Satanic Verses* (1989) in which he caricatured the illustrious personality of the Prophet (SAAS). The Muslim reaction in the United Kingdom and second parts of the Muslim world was vocal: Protest marches, demands for the banning of the infamous novel and withdrawal of all copies from the shelves of bookshops set the mood for a long-drawn campaign against Rushdie.[35] The *fatwā* of death sentence against Rushdie issued by Khomeini was the solitary exception of a Muslim country taking this step amid worldwide protests. It provoked a series of debates and academic discussions about the *shari'ah* position concerning the validity of the *fatwā*. Kharroufah's analysis of the leading scholars' (particularly the four Imams) views is a balanced approach on this issue.[36]

Amid the volatile situation, Shaykh Nadwi deplored the apathetic attitude[37] of the Arab world for their conspiracy of silence against Rushdie's *kufr*. A more disturbing trend was the protection extended to Rushdie by the British government, ostensibly to promote freedom of the press and in blatant defiance of Muslim sensibilities.

In sum, the vilification of the Prophet (SAAS) continues unabated by the West. In recent past the cartoons of the Holy Prophet (SAAS) published by a Danish newspaper, Jyllands-Posten sparked protests from Muslims across

---

[34] Amartya Sen, *South Africa and a Global Democracy in Discourse*, (Auckland Park, 2004), 30-32; cf. Nadwi, *Turki ki Mujāhid-i Millat-i Islam* (Lucknow, 1989).
[35] For a dispassionate account of the Rushdie affair see Akbar Ahmed, *Postmodernism and Islam* (London, 1992), pp. 169-77.
[36] Ala-al-Dān Kharroufah, *The Judgement of Islam on the Crisis of Salman Rushdie* (Kuala Lumpur, n.d.).
[37] Nadwi, *Kārwān*, vol. 4, p. 107.

Chapter XI
Revival of Islamic Authenticity

the globe. The failure of the Danish authorities to censure newspapers publishing such blasphemous cartoons must be seen in a broader context. In 2015 the French satirical magazine *Charlie Hebdo* featured caricatures portraying the Prophet (SAAS) in derogatory ways. Re-runs of the cartoons in major European newspapers reinforced the stereotyping of the Muslims. The parody of the Prophet (SAAS) as a terrorist is among the latest slanderous attempts to ridicule his noble personality. These caricatures reveal a particularly grotesque trend in a Europe that "manifests increasing Islamophobia and xenophobia, where Muslims are scapegoats for deepening social misery."

In a facile attempt to give credence to his notorious work, Rushdie's memoir[38] is nothing short of an unrepentant writer treading the slippery ground of self-destruction. Not surprising, therefore, are the media houses of Europe extending their unconditional support to his diatribe. Likewise, under the veneer of freedom of expression, the cartoonists offer no apology to their lampooning of Prophet Muhammad's (SAAS) character. Muzaffar Iqbal gives a rare insight about the different and often conflicting attitudes on the cartoon affair:

> And there are others to whom the love of profit is dearer than the love of the Prophet (SAAS) and who harvest a rich crop of dollars from the protests that follow the publication of cartoons - but what a bitter harvest they reap! And there are those who are confounded by the uproar when the hearts of the believers are rent asunder with pain and suffering and they ask in astonishment: why all the fuss? And then there are those who silently pray in the dead of the night for these terrible times to come to an end. And then there are those who see the coming of the Hour when each soul will stand before a Just Ruler, with a record containing all the deeds, a record hanging from their necks, omitting nothing, and on that Day they will be truly astounded. But alas, then there will be no return, no way to come back to this temporary abode where they would wish to erase the deeds committed in the terrible recesses of their caprice[39].

In response to Rushdie's offensive publication, Shaykh Nadwi prepared a

---

[38] Salman Rushdie, *Joseph Anton: A Memoir* (London, 2012).
[39] Muzaffar Iqbal critiques the Islamophobic tendencies in the light of Muslim belief in the Afterlife where the justice of Allah will prevail. See Zafar Ishaq Ansari, *Muslims and the West: Encounter and Dialogue* (Islamabad, 2002), 271-2.

monograph which was read at the OCIS Oxford University Hall. The public lecture "Mankind's Debt to the Prophet Muhammad (SAAS)" was an obvious choice- it was an intellectual refutation of Rushdie's vilification of the Prophet (SAAS). Given the context and content of the lecture, it attracted a large audience. The response was overwhelming and the lecture published as a monograph was read at various venues to Arabic, English and Urdu audience. Quoting extensively from non-Muslim scholars, Shaykh Nadwi attempted to show the universal impact of the Prophet (SAAS) to the growth and development of human culture and civilisation:

Now, at the time when mankind and human civilisation were on the edge of destruction, the Lord and Creator of the world caused a man to be born in Arabia who was entrusted the most difficult task: Not only to rescue mankind from imminent destruction, but also to raise it to heights sublime beyond the knowledge of historians and the imagination of poets. If there were not incontrovertible historical evidence to demonstrate his achievements, it would be difficult to believe his greatness. This man was Muhammad (peace be upon him) who was born in the sixth century. He saved mankind from the threatened and imminent danger and gave them new life, new ambition, fresh energy, a revitalised sense of human dignity and intellect and idealism. It was because of him that a new era came about, of spirituality, in art and literature, of personal sincerity and selfless service of others, which produced an ordered, graceful and sublime culture.[40]

Again, Shaykh Nadwi recounted the precious gifts which played a pivotal role in the advancement of human values and culture. These represent a synthesis of mundane and spiritual values. Their influences have now become integral to the life and culture of different nations. The universal gifts of Islam to human civilisation are presented hereunder:

- The clear and unambiguous creed of the Oneness of Allah.
- The concept of human equality and brotherhood.
- The concept of human dignity and man being the masterpiece of Allah's creation.
- Acknowledgement of the proper status of women and

---

[40] Nadwi, *Mankind's Debt to the Prophet Muhammad* (Oxford, 1992), 3-4.

Chapter XI
Revival of Islamic Authenticity

restoration of their legitimate rights.
- Rejection of despair and infusion of hope in human beings.
- Fusion of secular and religious knowledge.
- Integration of religion and knowledge as a means of earning divine pleasure.
- Emphasis on the use of intellectual faculties in religious and spiritual domains for the study and contemplation of natural phenomena.
- Entrusting Muslims to promote virtue in the world, and restoring truth and justice.
- Establishment of a universal creed and culture.[41]

Seminar: Abul Kalam Azad

Under the auspices of the Mawlana Azad Memorial Academy (Lucknow), Shaykh Nadwi delivered a public lecture on Azad's multifaceted contributions. His centennial celebration was marked by the Hindi translation of his *Tarjumān al-Qur'ān* (vol. 1). Shaykh Nadwi dwelt at length on the outstanding qualities that embodied Azad's unique personality. A scholar, politician, *mujahid*, Azad expended all his energies and talents to the freedom of India. His sacrifices were exemplary; his services were unblemished and he was steadfast to the ideals which he stood for. No political expediency or the vagaries of time and circumstances could change his mission and to this end he endured hardships with admirable courage.

Azad maintained that an independent India should respect the distinctive status of its minorities. This inalienable right was enshrined in the Constitution. However, Azad accepted the realities and challenges facing the Indian Muslims after Partition. The following comments reinforce his Islamic Indian identity:

I am a Muslim and profoundly conscious of the fact that I have inherited Islam's glorious traditions of the last thirteen hundred years. I am not prepared to lose even a small part of that legacy... As a Muslim, I have a special identity within the field of religion and culture and I cannot tolerate any undue interference with it. But with these feelings, I have another deep realisation born out of my life's

---
[41] Nadwi, *Islam and Civilisation* (Lucknow, 1986), 5-6.

experience, which is strengthened, not hindered by the spirit of Islam. I am equally proud of the fact that I am an Indian, an essential part of that indivisible unity of Indian nationhood. It is a vital factor in its total make-up without which this noble structure will remain incomplete. I can never give up this sincere claim.[42]

The Russian Revolution: A Reappraisal

The year 1990 was an important milestone in world history when two countries USSR and South Africa dismantled their existing political structures and opted for a democratic system that guaranteed the Freedom Charter to its citizens. Our focus is on the Russian Revolution. Indeed, it was the collapse of an imperial power with stained records of oppression, persecution and despotic rule. USSR was no more than an imposition of the Slavic rule on large segments of independent Muslim countries and dynasties in Central Asia. Their forced integration into the Russian Federation meant an abject surrender to Communism, abolition of Islam from their lives and adoption of a life that negated their own corporate identity.

It was the assimilation policies of the Soviet regime that had grave consequences for the Muslims in the Central Asian regions. The Russification of their Islamic identity had one sinister goal - obliteration of Islam from their lives. Punitive measures were instituted against Muslims. The closure of mosques and *maktabs*, symbols of Islamic activism, was a death-knell to their articulation of Islam. About the *maktab* system, Adeeb Khalid has shown that these Islamic schools were adopted by the *jadīds* as repositories of change and cultural regeneration.[43] The *jadīds*' reformist approach was in response to the outdated Islamic curriculum and the political decadence in the *khanates* (prinicipalities). In addition, they opposed customary rites erroneously associated with the *sunnah*. Muslim countries like Uzbekistan, Kyrgystan and Kazakhstan with an unbroken and established tradition of Islamic culture and civilisation were cut off from the Muslim world. Likewise, Bukhara,[44] the pride of Islam, was subjugated by Soviet imperialism and became a relic of the past. Other important centres of Islamic learning were

---

[42] Syed Saiyidain Hameed, *Islamic Seal on India's Independence*, (Karachi, 1998), 190.
[43] Adeeb Khalid, *The Politics of Muslim Cultural Reform: Jadidism in Central Asia* (Berkeley, 1998), 89-113.
[44] Mention may be made of Imām Bukhārī, whose collection of the *ahadīth* is regarded as the most reliable after the Quran.

Chapter XI
Revival of Islamic Authenticity

overshadowed by the presence of an alien system that espoused atheism, imposed the Cyrillic script that severed their glorious Islamic past.[45] As a result of these repressive measures a diaspora of displaced Muslims was created - a grim reminder of the brutality of the Soviet regime.

The dissolution of the Soviet Union was preceded by a series of dramatic events in Europe. East and West Germany was reunified after the dismantling of the notorious Berlin Wall. Likewise, Socialism and Communism became appendages of the past following the rise of democracy in these former republics. Moreover, internal disunity within the Soviet political hierarchy, and dissenting voices about the dismal failure of Marxism resonated across the corridors of power. The then Soviet President, Mikhail Gorbachev adopted a policy called *Perestroika*, which opened the doors of dialogue with other countries. His bold statement was that the socialist policy of enforced equality was a major cause for the Soviet collapse.

Shaykh Nadwi compared Marxism to a jail where prisoners received their rations, while work, effort and the spirit of competition were shut out to them. The whole country resembled machines operating perfunctorily in factories.[46] Against this backdrop, the changing tides in the post-Soviet era swept across countries where Communism was still zealously followed. The iron-handed policies in certain countries began to weaken with the result that Socialism; gave way to a greater measure of political freedom. Even South Yemen,[47] a strong ally of Communism, having suffered defeat in a protracted war against north Yemen was finally reunited with the latter by forming the Republic of Yemen.

The turbulent period for Muslims under Soviet rule did not exterminate Islam forever. On the contrary, the clandestine activities in the form of *maktabs* and orders infiltrated the lives of the Muslim masses, albeit in a restricted way. The Naqshbandi order,[48] an indigenous sufi movement was a dominant

---

[45] The parallel may be drawn between Turkey and the Central Asian nations. The abolition of the Arabic script effectively cut the Turkish Muslims from direct access to the sources of Islam. Likewise, Soviet Muslims suffered a similar fate under the Soviet regime.

[46] See Nadwi, *Western Civilisation, Islam and Muslims*, 116-19.

[47] *Ibid.*, 24-26.

[48] The Naqshbandi Order has been extensively studied. See K.A. Nizami] "The Naqshbandi Order" in S.H. Nasr, *Islamic Spirituality: Manifestations*, vol. 2 (New York, 1991), 162-93.

force that provided spiritual solace to the oppressed masses. As the *shari'ah*-oriented movement, it eschewed practices deemed as customary expressions and censured *bid'ah* (innovation). The sufi activists mobilised the masses to adhere strictly to the teachings of Islam. They also provided social cohesion for the dispossessed Muslims under the tyrannical Soviet rule.

Conclusion

Muslim tendency to interpret events subjectively posed a grave danger when political figures raised the dubious slogans of Islamic solidarity. On the contrary, Muslim quest for meaningful dialogue was possible in a climate of tolerance. This could be achieved by emphasising the universal values of Islam in the context of changing geopolitical settings.

Chapter XII

Da'wah Paradigms: Translocal Trends

Shaykh Nadwi's *da'wah* presentation extended beyond the traditional *nasīhah* (counsel) approach. Although the *islāhī* elements informed his relationship with royalty, political leaders and intellectuals, his *majālis* (sessions) also mirrored his concern for a wider audience in respect of the Islam and West discourse. In a broader sense, his *da'wah* outreach was a constructive understanding of the challenges Muslims in the West faced in their daily lives. A case in point are the views given in Tariq Ramadān's prolific writings about Muslims in the West. Both he and Shaykh Nadwi share a commonality: Muslim presence should reflect an Islamic identity built around the principles of *da'wah* and *islāh*.

Letter to King Fahd bin 'Abdul 'Aziz: Islāhi Concerns

The letter focuses on the pertinent issues affecting the Muslim world in the aftermath of the Gulf War (1991). Shaykh Nadwi emphasised the need to follow the teachings of the Qur'an and *sunnah*, eschewing vices that had crept into the Muslim society and reconfiguring the *ummah*'s vision of Allah-consciousness.

In view of the incursion of Western culture in the kingdom, the reform of Muslim society at all levels was, therefore, imperative. Apart from the challenges faced by the kingdom there was an urgency for Muslim nations to reassess their present predicament. It was only *imān* combined with the spirit of courage, sacrifice, fortitude that could thwart the political ideologies on the rise. These baneful influences were widespread and held sway over the Muslim world. Thus, only a formidable force like Islam could counteract their ungodly tendencies.

The Muslim world was facing a crisis of confidence in emulating the visionary outlook of eminent leaders like 'Umar bin 'Abdul 'Aziz and Salāhuddin Ayyubi who could have defused the prevailing political impasse.[1]

Shaykh Nadwi's candour and wise counsels to King Fahd were dictated by his *ummatic* concerns. More importantly, it was in response to the tragic turn of events in the Gulf. Iraq's invasion of Kuwait in 1991, according to Shaykh Nadwi, was a huge tragedy that caused incalculable harm to the moral

---

[1] Nadwi, *Kārwān*, vol. 5, 24-27.

integrity of Islam.[2] It was no secret that Saddam espoused the vision of the Ba'thist Party whose goals of Arab nationalism were aimed at undermining the universal values of Islam. His penchant for dubious Islamic slogans were embedded in his anti-West rhetoric.[3] Indeed, the populist sentiments had the viral effect among sections of Muslims. In this instance, Shaykh Nadwi was unambiguous in his assessment:

> There is a glaring shortcoming in our subcontinent that whenever a person makes a strident call against a strong Western power then he becomes a hero. His record of misdeeds is (conveniently) forgotten. The big tragedy is that it brings much harm to Islam's efforts in the *da'wah* sphere.[4]

Subsequent to Iraq's invasion of Kuwait, a series of tumultuous events followed which caused a deep divide in the Muslim *ummah*. The Gulf War in 1991 against Iraq by the US-led coalition, including several Arab countries, brought untold misery to the Iraqi nation. Sanctions and oil embargo were part of the punitive measures imposed by the United Nations working in complicit with the US.

Shaykh Nadwi's perceptive analysis of the volatile Gulf region showed unmissable signs of a major conflict.[5] Another debilitating factor was the prevailing mood of apathy in the Arab world. Shaykh Nadwi maintained that it was Islam alone which would give impetus to the moral regeneration of the Arab nation. He remarked:

> Today the Arab nations can defeat their enemies (through strength of *imān*) and protect themselves. Without Islam and *imān* the Arabs enjoy no distinction, prestige, integrity...[6]

---

[2] *Ibid.*, 18.
[3] Shaykh Nadwi's critique of the West is discernible in his diffuse writings. See his *Western Civilisation, Islam and Muslims* (1974) which provides a detailed discussion on the West.
[4] Nadwi, *Kārwān*, vol. 5, 18.
[5] The American invasion of Iraq in 2003 highlighted once again the brutality against the Iraqi nation.
[6] Nadwi, *Unmmat-i Islamiya ka Mustaqbil*, 20.

Chapter XII
Da'wah Paradigms: Translocal Trends

Political Developments in India: Muslim Response

We now shift to the Indian scene in which Shaykh Nadwi's involvement was two-fold:

- To promote the interests of the Indian Muslims through existing organisations.
- To participate in forums that aimed at the reconstruction of the Indian society.

Barely had the Gulf crisis ended when Shaykh Nadwi had to face a tragic event in India; the assassination of Prime Minister Rajiv Gandhi on 21 May 1991. A backlash was what Shaykh Nadwi dreaded the most. The specter of communal violence after the assassination of Indira Gandhi in 1984 against the Sikhs sparked fears in his mind that a Muslim involvement would break down the efforts of communal harmony. Ethnic tension during this period was surcharged with clamorous demands for the independent states. The Separatist Tamil Tiger group of Sri Lanka were suspected of assassinating Rajiv Gandhi.[7]

Shaykh Nadwi's interaction with Rajiv Gandhi also occurred during the critical period when a legislation was enacted for the Uniform Civil Code.[8] This move was a direct challenge to the Muslim Personal Law which enjoyed an autonomy unhindered by the state authorities. Rajiv's intervention, largely due to Muslim pressure, halted the proposed implementation of legislation pertaining to this sensitive issue.

Shaykh Nadwi's involvement in the political developments of the country prompted him to maintain direct contact with Rajiv's successor, Narasimha Rao who became Prime Minister of India in 1992. The series of meetings and correspondence with Rao focused on the Babri Masjid issue and in the broader context the socio-political problems bedevilling the country. On the political front, the emergence of the Bharatiya Janata Party (BJP) promoting the Hindutva (fascist) policy threatened to destroy the fragile communal harmony between Muslims and Hindus. Its electoral victory in several states raised alarms for the ruling Congress and also did not augur well for the

---

[7] Nadwi, Kārwān, vol. 5, 32-33.
[8] For a detailed account of the All India Muslim Personal Board's involvement in preventing the implementation of the Uniform Civil Code, see Syed Habibul Haq Nadvi, Islamic Legal Philosophy and the Qur'anic Origins of the Islamic Law, 360-67.

Muslims. Moreover, the party's "saffronisation" outlined its vision in no uncertain terms: India was a Hindu country. This meant that there were no safeguards for minorities as enshrined in the Constitution.[9]

The wave of unrest that followed wreaked havoc in Mumbai, Surat and other parts of Maharashtra. Shaykh Nadwi described the indiscriminate killing of Muslims, rape and looting as a "volcanic" eruption. Following this gruesome violence, Muslims suffered irreparable loss. The rising death toll of Muslims implicated police forces working in collusion with the rioters. Businesses were looted, which created an economic crisis for the once-prosperous community. Media reports covering the carnage described the bleak prospects of restoring peace in these affected areas.[10]

In response to the growing unrest in the country, Shaykh Nadwi addressed several gatherings consisting of Muslim and non-Muslim audience in Lucknow and Rae Bareli. His theme was based on the extremely harmful effects of injustice on the Indian society. Injustice (*zulm*), Shaykh Nadwi concluded, was an affront to humanity and incurred divine wrath. He was unsparing in his criticism of agitational politics. In his view, political exploitation and parochial interest undermined the fabric of a stable society. These tendencies violated the ideals of democracy, secularism and non-violence. By virtue of the country's pluralistic composition and democratic safeguards Muslims and non-Muslims could live in harmony. Shaykh Nadwi emphasised the need to appreciate cultural diversity and made an impassioned plea for the promotion of the values of love, mutual respect and cooperation. Several monographs[11] were written by him identifying communal harmony as the basis for the reconstruction of the Indian society. This approach was in line with the *Payām*'s vision of forging better relations with other faith groups. With no political affiliation, Shaykh Nadwi was able to express his views independently, a trait that he shared with Mawlana Madani:

> He (Madani) undertook extensive tours of the country, preaching the *gospel of unity* (emphasis added) from town to town and village to

---

[9] Nadwi, *Kārwān*, vol. 5, 109-117.
[10] *Ibid.*, 113-16; 132-33.
[11] The following writings by Shaykh Nadwi provided a synopsis of this theme:
- *Tuhfah Insāniyat* (Lucknow, 1992).
- *Ta'mir-i Insāniyat* (Karachi, n.d).
- *Islāhīyat* (Karachi] 1987).
- *Millat i-Islamia Hind ka Tārikhi Kirdar* (Lucknow, 2000).

village. Morally and religiously, his commitment remained absolutely stainless and above suspicion throughout that period of trial and crisis. He sought no favours for himself, so much that he politely declined the title of *Padma Vibushan* (civilian honour) in 1954 saying that it was against the traditions of his precursors to receive honours from the government.[12]

Likewise, Shaykh Nadwi declined this coveted honour in 1992 from Prime Minister Rao stating that it was against his principles and the traditions of his predecessors. He was able to restate the ideals of the *salaf* in a contemporary setting. In a specific sense, he was able to realign the Islamic teachings in response the demands of present realities.

Da'wah in England

Shaykh Nadwi's travels to Britain during 1963-96 broadened his intellectual horizon and gave him an in- depth understanding of the conflictual relationship between Islam and the West. Even in his critique of the West, he saw opportunities of the sustained Islamic presence in Europe, particularly Britain, which owing to its colonial past played a significant role in its interaction with Muslim immigrants from South Asia. His *majālis* and correspondence are contained in Akram Nadwi's *Armughān-i Farang*. These resonate in contemporary idiom; the spiritual discourses are distinctly South Asian.

A few extracts illustrate Shaykh Nadwi's belief that Islamic culture can prevail over the Western mind. Implicit in his discussion is the persuasive reminder to Muslims residing in the West that their commitment to Islam should be unconditional.

In our Muslim countries there is supposedly much confusion which I regard as irrelevant and avoidable. The reason is simple; our leaders are living in a world of the West. Their physical presence is in the East while their mind and soul are oriented to the West. Their norms and frame of reference are distinctly Western.

Today, too, our Muslims continue to possess the innate power of *imān*. Unfortunately, our leaders do not know the language of faith. Their intellect is familiar with a language which verbalises their personal aspirations and expressions [that are distinctly un-Islamic]. However, they are not familiar

---

[12] Nadwi, *Muslims in India*, pp. 121-22; cf. *Kārwān*, vol. 5, 66.

with the language of the heart whose spontaneous and direct message has the [desired effect]. This language is linked to *imān* (faith), Qur'an and the *Sahābah*.[13]

Shaykh Nadwi's close association with the Islamic institutions in England had a two-fold purpose:

- To create a forum for a better understanding of Islam in the West.
- To promote *da'wah* in the West by supporting the publication of literature reflecting this aim.

The Islamic Foundation (Leicester), a premier institution was representative of this trend. Several of his writings dealing with Muslim interaction with the West[14] were published by the Foundation. Shaykh Nadwi's speech elucidated the requisites and challenges of *da'wah* in the West. He says:

[The] basic requisite for a message to succeed is that it should comprise good words (*kalimah tayyibah*), leading to good objectives. The language should not only be couched in linguistic finesse. If one writes about that which one feels the most and from the depths of one's heart, it may have the desired effect on the audience. So by taking into account these constituents of *da'wah*, be it oral or written, it will yield fruits in the West in the ever-changing times and on speakers of different languages.[15]'

According to Shaykh Nadwi, linguistic competence and sincerity are effective communicators of *da'wah*. Therefore, these distinctive features should be articulated well and also keeping in mind the intellectual temperament of non-Muslims in the West. This approach has been explained by the noted *'ālim*, 'Allāmah Qardāwī. He comments:

[Shaykh Nadwi] had a profound understanding of the gulf that existed between Western and Islamic civilisation, in particular the educational, cultural and moral crisis that set them apart. [He] adopted the third approach which was neither a blind imitation (of

---

[13] Muhammad Akram Nadwi, *Armaghān-i Farang* (London, 2004), 90-92.
[14] Nadwi, *Muslims in the West: The Message and Mission* (Leicester, 1983).
[15] Nadwi, *Da'wah in the West: The Qur'anic Paradigm* (Leicester, 1992), 10-17.

Chapter XII
Da'wah Paradigms: Translocal Trends

the West) nor remained insulated from the benefits that it offered in terms of science and technology. Thus, he steered away from a polemical approach towards the West and adopted a course that would serve as a signpost for both civilisations.[16]

For Shaykh Nadwi, the presence of Muslim communities should reflect the totality of Islam in a Western environment. The following extracts are pertinent reminders about the importance of expressing an Islamic identity:

> You must earn your recognition in this country (UK). You should earn your place and leave an imprint on the host community of your value and significance. You must show that your exemplary conduct is far nobler than other people. You must impart to them the lessons of humanity. You should demonstrate such commitment and noble virtues that there cannot be found more upright humans elsewhere besides you. You need to establish your worth, showing what blessing and mercy you are for the country.
> If, however, you decide to live in an enclosed environment simply content with your prayers and fasting, apathetic to the people and society you live in, never introducing them to the high Islamic values and your personal qualities, then beware lest any religious or sectarian violence flares up. In such a situation, you will not find safety or protection.[17]

Fundamentalism: An Assessment

It would not be out of place to highlight the geopolitical developments that had a direct bearing on the Muslim world. The emergence of Muslim states in Central Asia after the dissolution of the Soviet Empire saw the gradual realignment of these Muslim states towards the Islamic world. Not surprisingly, Islamic renaissance would not go unchallenged in the West. An armoury of semantics was coined to undermine the reawakening among Muslims about their faith and practices. Shaykh Nadwi's first-hand

---

[16] Yūsuf Qardāwī, "Mufakkir-i-Islam Hadrat Mawlana Shaykh Nadwi ke Da'wati Usul" in *Fikri Islami*, (Basti 2000-1), 211.
[17] See Nadwi, *Islamic Studies, Orientalists and Muslim Scholars* (Lucknow, 1983).

experience and critical writings about the West's stereotypical representation of Islam are illustrated by the phenomenon of fundamentalism (*usūliyyah*). According to the West's definition, fundamentalism is associated with Islam's rigidity and bigotry. Shaykh Nadwi's acute analysis of fundamentalism is summed up as follows:

The West sought to redefine the term fundamentalism as a propaganda tool to justify its hostility towards the Muslims' entrenched belief in the divinely revealed scripture (Qur'an) and its teachings. Even in the Arab world its connotation has been expanded in a negative sense for their ideological discourse. The West's campaign to challenge fundamentalism has its resonance in ancient Greece where Epicureanism was considered an ideal. A free lifestyle with no accountability to the Hereafter was the criterion for materialistic success. Arab countries like Algeria, Tunisia and Libya launched a crusade against the Muslim fundamentalists who believed in Islamic teachings in their pristine form and the primacy of the *shari'ah* in the collective Muslim life. Therefore, a collective will was required from the *'ulama'* and Muslim intelligentsia to counteract this growing menace.[18] In contrast, Epicurean ideals, Shaykh Nadwi argued, have espoused a "materialistic viewpoint and selfish outlook towards life."[19] Fundamentalism, on the contrary, negates this belief. In an address to an Arab audience, Shaykh Nadwi categorically stated:

If you want, O Arabs, to help us any way or wish any success to us (Indian Muslims) know that it is not any material or monetary assistance that we need. We only ask one thing of you: That you be an example of steadfastness in faith and act as you did in the past - as the bearers of the eternal message of Allah... If you did this, you would have given us all the help [we need].[20]

Shaykh Nadwi's commitment to Islamic authenticity is also articulated in his *da'wah* travels which are discussed in the next section.

---

[18] Nadwi, *Kārwān*, vol. 5, 161-67.
[19] Nadwi, *Religion and Civilisation* (Lucknow, 1975), 63-64.
[20] Muhammad Qasim Zaman, *The 'Ulamā' in Contemporary Islam*, 165.

Chapter XII
Da'wah Paradigms: Translocal Trends

The Long Journey

The long Journey (1993) to the US was Shaykh Nadwi's second visit. In 1977 he was invited by Muslim Students Association (MSA) for a series of lectures. It was in Chicago (1993) that a Parliament of World Religions had organised a conference and Shaykh Nadwi was invited to deliver a paper. Shaykh Nadwi's frank assessment about this conference was a clear expression of his uncompromising attitude to things that were un-Islamic. Instead, he attended a conference hosted by the Muslims at the Malcolm X hall on the theme "The State of Ummah." A monograph entitled *Islam and the West* was Shaykh Nadwi's contribution to the critique of Western civilisation. The following passage reveals the impasse between Islam and the West:

[The] West which had produced in the past such giants in the field of social and physical sciences as well as in politics, who changed the map of the world, whose brilliance was acknowledged and whose discoveries were utilised with advantage by all, is now passing through a phase of intellectual stagnation. The West now needs a new and revolutionary leadership possessing Prophetic courage to alter radically the goal of science and technology from destruction to re-construction. [It] needs to infuse a sense of equilibrium and self-restraint and to bring about a readjustment between the rival political camps for saving human society from impending decay and decline. The West has been lacking in such a leadership for a long time.[21]

This journey also revived old acquaintances for Shaykh Nadwi, especially his meeting with Dr Sa'īd Ramadān while in transit in Geneva, Switzerland. The son in law of Ikhwān's founder, Hasan Al-Banna, Sa'īd Ramadān founded the Islamic Centre of Geneva in 1969 with the support of intellectual figures from across the Muslim world, of which Shaykh Nadwi was an influential member. His prestigious magazine *Al-Muslimīn* contained articles of outstanding merit to which Shaykh Nadwi contributed regularly. According to Tariq Ramadān,

[the] scholar Abu-al-Hasan al-Nadwi showed him (Sa'īd Ramadān) the signs of infinite respect, and during a visit to Lucknow in India,

---

[21] Nadwi, *Islam and the West* (Lucknow, 1982).

where is found the Nadwat al-'Ulamā', al-Nadwi recalled with deep emotion one of his visits and the impressions it left on him.[22]

Sa'īd Ramadān passed away in 1995. Another significant journey was undertaken by Shaykh Nadwi with the OCIS delegation to the historic cities of Samarqand and Bukhara. These citadels of Islamic culture evoked images of scholarship: Hadīth, fiqh, philosophy, science and other related branches of knowledge. The most outstanding personality that towered above all the 'ulama' and scholars was the illustrious muhaddith, Imām Bukhari. During the Communist rule[23] the centres of Islamic learning were shut down with the result that fears were raised that they would become relics of the past. It was under President Gorbachev that the predominantly Islamic states of the Soviet empire were granted autonomy, albeit in a limited way, to practise their faith. The OCIS, of which Shaykh Nadwi was the chairman, earmarked the restoration project of Imām Bukhārī's mausoleum with plans of setting up a research centre. According to Sayyid Rabey Nadwi, the proposed plans were aimed at rekindling the spirit and fervour of Imām Bukhārī's contribution to Islamic scholarship.[24] Shaykh Nadwi's lecture was based on Imām Bukhārī's Al-Sahīh and its position in the history of Islam as well as its universal relevance. Its outstanding features together with the Imam's unique contribution to the hadīth studies were also discussed.[25] Also, a visit to the historic cities of Samarqand, Bukhara, Tashkent and Farghana in Uzbekistan brought in full the splendour of Islamic civilisation.[26] Bukhara in particular was the seat of the Naqshbandi sufi[27] order and served as a nexus of the Mujaddidi order[28] of Shaykh Ahmad Sirhindi and the islāhī movement of Sayyid Shah

---

[22] Tariq Ramadan, *Islam, the West and the Challenges of Modernity* (Leicester, 2001), xi.
[23] Nadwi, *Kārwān*, vol. 5, 295-96.
[24] Sayyid Muhammad Rabey Nadwi, *Samarqand wa Bukhāra ki Bazyāft* (Lucknow, 1996).
[25] Published as a monograph with the title *Al-Imam Muhammad bin Ismā'il al-Bukhārī wa Kitābahu Sahīh al-Bukhārī* (Lucknow, 1996).
[26] Ibid., 30-38.
[27] On the Naqshbandiyyah the following books may be consulted: Muhammad Hisham Kabbani, *The Naqshabandi Sufis Way* (Chicago, 1995), K.A. Nizami, "The Naqshbandiyyah Order" in Seyyed Hossein Nasr, *Islamic Spirituality: Manifestations* (New York, 1991), pp. 162-93.
[28] See Muhammad Abdul Haq Ansari, *Sufism and Shari'ah* (Leicester, 1986), Nadwi, *Saviours of Islamic Spirit*, vol. 3 (Lucknow, 1983).

'Alamullah.[29] A brief description of Uzbekistan by Shaykh Nadwi showed the challenges the country faced to restore its former position in the comity of Muslim nations. It was an indisputable fact that the anomaly that existed was created by the Communist rule and even after Independence there was no significant change that suggested a transformative Islamic identity.[30]

Divine Intervention

Back in India, Shaykh Nadwi continued with his two- pronged mission of promoting the *Payām* and Muslims' concerns over the Babri Masjid demolition. The communal riots were disavowed by him and instead constructive efforts were made by AIMPLB to find amicable ways to defuse the rising tensions between Muslims and extremist Hindu groups. However, the ensuing crisis took a different turn when a massive earthquake struck a place called Latur. It earned notoriety for sending volunteers to participate in the destruction of the Babri Mosque. It was from this place that a gold brick was sent to Ayodhya for the construction of the proposed Ram temple on the same site of the demolished Masjid. The whole area was reduced to rubble except a Masjid which remained safe from the effects of the earthquake. About 77, 000 people lost their lives in this natural disaster. Strangely enough, Muslims suffered marginal loss.[31] Based on reliable reports, Shaykh Nadwi observed that this unnatural occurrence was considered an ominous sign of Divine retribution against a community hell-bent on destroying the Babri Masjid. Thus, some reports suggested that there were credible reasons to connect the earthquake with the destruction of the mosque.[32]

---

[29] Muhammad al-Hasani, *Tadhkirah Hadrat Sayyid Shah Alam-ullah Hasani Rae Bareli*.
[30] Nadwi, *Kārwān*, vol. 5, 296.
[31] Syed Iqbal Zaheer, *Abul Hasan Ali Nadwi: A Man of Hope through a Century of Turmoil* (Bengaluru, 2005), 75-76.
[32] Nadwi, *Kārwān*, vol. 5, 297-98.

Conclusion

From Babri Masjid to the Imām Bukhārī mausoleum, the recurrent theme for preserving Islamic legacy was clear. There was no disconnect to the *turāth* discernible in Muslim countries over the centuries. Despite political turmoil and the loss of Muslim power, the potential for Islamic resurgence was promising as the emergent trends in these countries showed. Again, Shaykh Nadwi's practical approach pointed the way that consultation rather than confrontation was a viable option in searching for solutions affecting Muslims in their determination to retain their distinctive identity and culture.

Chapter XIII

Honours Beyond Borders: Shaykh Nadwi's Contributions

The dramatic developments in India and the Muslim world had a direct impact on Shaykh Nadwi's intellectual formulation of Islamic authenticity. Across the spectrum of his busy schedule were the challenges to which he had to respond with unwavering commitment. Another pressing challenge was related to the Muslim corporate identity. As a scholar of international repute, Shaykh Nadwi's association with leading institutions involved multiple audiences with different backgrounds and concerns. In fact, the years under review in the chapter (1994-97) represented the threshold of Shaykh Nadwi's intellectual career. Notwithstanding his advancing age and deteriorating health, Shaykh Nadwi pursued a course of action which highlighted his qualities of resilience and tenacity. This was evident in the leadership he had to provide in respect of his Islamic authenticity formulation.

Aligarh Muslim University

Shaykh Nadwi's association with the Aligarh Muslim University (AMU)[1] commenced in the 1940s with the Islamic Theology Department. His contribution lay in his efforts to establish a rapprochement between the traditional and academic institutions.[2] AMU was one such example which championed the cause of Muslim education during a period of crisis when their political fortunes were at their lowest ebb. Sir Sayyid Ahmad Khan's pioneering role as a reformer[3] drew both admiration and criticism for his controversial views regarding the reconstruction of Muslim society.[4] Islamic modernism[5] was a term coined to describe scholars like Sir Sayyid who advanced the theory that Islam's destiny was based on the progressive

---

[1] On the early history of AMU, see Hadi Hussain, *Syed Ahmed Khan: Pioneer of Muslim Resurgence* (Lahore, 1970), 113-64.
[2] This approach is highlighted in his multivolume *Kārwān*.
[3] See XMS Baljon, *The Reforms and Religious Ideas of Sir Sayyid Ahmad Khan* (Lahore, 1970).
[4] *Ibid.*, 105-43
[5] The growth and development of Islamic modernism is analysed in Mazheruddin Siddiqi, *Modern Reformist Thought in the Muslim World* (Islamabad, 1982).

and rational interpretation of its belief system.[6] Thus, a new *kalām* (theology)[7] evolved with clearly' defined goals. In this regard, Sir Sayyid attempted to recast the Islamic intellectual legacy against the backdrop of changing political realities. The frame of reference was his rational exposition of Islamic thought that clearly pointed out to the uncritical adoption of Western civilisation. Recent studies about the life and thought of Sir Sayyid have reconstructed a balanced account of this 'pioneering modernist.' The refreshing perspectives about his multidimensional contributions are indicators of his lasting legacy for the Muslim cause and communal harmony.[8]

Shaykh Nadwi's critique of the AMU showed his impartial assessment of the prestigious institution. He observed:

> Sir Sayyid was unique in many respects among all the Muslim leaders of his time. He had the most powerful personality and waged his struggle on a very wide front. The success his movement achieved and the amount of influence it exercised on the rising generations of Muslims were unparalleled in the social and educational history of Muslim India. Sir Sayyid left his mark on language and literature and laid the foundation of a new intellectual and literary school which proved very fertile and original.
>
> But, on the whole the Aligarh movement fell much short of expectations in providing a suitable answer to the cultural and intellectual needs of Muslims at that fateful juncture of their history. The task that lay before it was the harnessing of the mental and material experiences of the West to the requirements of Muslim society and the production of a new Islamic generation, firm of faith and strong of conviction and alive to the role it had to play in the cultural leadership of the world. [It] could take from the Western civilisation what was good and useful in it and reject what was false and harmful...[9]

During the course of its crucial period when state interference threatened its Islamic character, relentless efforts were made to give it a minority status,

---

[6] Baljon, *The Reform and Religious Ideas...138-40*. Cf. Hafeez Malik, *Political Profile of Sir Sayyid Ahmad Khan* (Islamabad, 1982), 336-38.
[7] Baljon, *The Reform and Religious Ideas*, 132-42.
[8] Nadwi, *Western Civilisation, Islam and Muslims* (Lucknow, 1974), 70- 71.
[9] *Ibid.*, 74-75.

Chapter XIII
Honours Beyond Borders: Shaykh Nadwi's Contributions

much against the collective will of the Muslim community. Shaykh Nadwi was in the forefront to defend its autonomous position. The following extract reveals his concerns about the repercussions of state legislation in regard to AMU's Muslim character:

It is a great tragedy of modern politics that the springhead of thought and morality, the laboratories of personality and character and the watch-towers of life are being exploited for ruthless political ends and electoral expediencies. Notwithstanding the fact that a national government is expected to be nearer and more sympathetic to popular needs and urges than an alien government, now the functions of the government are confined only to the maintenance of law and order, defence against foreign aggression and collection of taxes. I say without hesitation that to make judgements about educational institutions on the basis of mills and factories, to destroy their autonomy and to sever their bonds with the community or group that founded and maintained them is wrong, unjust and prejudiced[10].

In an important address at the AMU during 1994, Shaykh Nadwi emphasised the need for raising a generation of intellectuals whose academic excellence and moral conduct could serve as an example to the rest of the community.[11] The vision which he espoused was also extended to Dār al-'Ulūms, where the Islamic sciences could be harmoniously integrated with contemporary knowledge. Holistic education rooted in Islamic spirituality[12] could successfully maintain the equilibrium between worldly and otherworldly pursuits. This view is also reinforced by the noted scholar, Muhammad Asad who says that the Muslim world needs the building up of "an equitable, progressive society in which the Islamic way of life could find its cultural expression."[13]

---

[10] Sheikh Jameil 'Ali, *Islamic Thought and Movement in the Subcontinent* (New Delhi, 2010), 334-35.
[11] Nadwi, *Kārwān*, vol. 6, 23-24.
[12] Nadwi, *Western Civilisation, Islam and Muslims*, 31-32.
[13] *Ibid.*, 32.

Rābitā Adab

Since its inception in 1981, Rābitā Adab made steady progress in terms of its vision and expansionist ambitions. Arab littérateurs in particular joined ranks with Rābitā to promote its objectives. To this end, the production of forceful Islamic literature could effectively stem the tide of "literary apostasy."[14] In a similar vein, Shaykh Nadwi's earlier work *The New Menace and Its Answer*[15] reinforced this vision:

> The cure of the ills of the Muslim world lies in our capacity to produce a band of dedicated activists who may be above all personal considerations and have no worldly motives for themselves. Their entire effort should be directed towards loosening the intellectual and psychological knots of the ruling classes of the society through establishing personal contacts with them. It would require effective religious literature for them, and reforming them by personal example. Positive traits like piety, sincerity, self-sacrifice and the Prophetic conduct serve as markers for such a reform.

Egypt: Reforms

Shaykh Nadwi's academic preoccupations were not confined to the *madrasah* institutions. As an executive member of Federation of Muslim Universities (Morocco) his contributions were very much appreciated by its office- bearers. In 1995 an international conference was organised in Cairo. Owing to his poor health and busy schedule he could not attend the conference. However, he was represented by Mawlana Nazrul Hafeez Azhari, a lecturer at Nadwah who read the Former's paper about the training of the 'ulama and da'wah workers. The conference also deliberated on the feasibility of a uniform curriculum for institutions affiliated to the Federation. Based on Mawlana Azhari's report, it was noted that significant changes were discernible in the lives of the Egyptian masses. The second half of the twentieth century saw the religious decline on account of the Nasserist policies. Likewise, the successive regimes adopted a hardline approach to quell

---

[14] *Kārwān-i Adab* (Lucknow, 2001-02), pp. 122-24. Cf. Nadwi, Muhammad Rabey, *Mawlana Sayyid Abul Hasan Ali Nadwi, 'Ahd-Saz Shakhsiyyat* (Lucknow, 2001), 185-99.

[15] Nadwi, *The New Menace and its Answer* (Lucknow, n.d.).

Chapter XIII
Honours Beyond Borders: Shaykh Nadwi's Contributions

the surge of Islamic activism. Voices of opposition were stifled and major Islamic movements were banned from the mainstream political participation. Even so, the Islamic revival became more pronounced as the youth became more religiously inclined. There was a noteworthy interest in Islamic literature, in particular the works of contemporary scholars. A course in Islamic studies was designed by 'Abdul Karim Sulaymān, a student of Shaykh Nadwi. Included in the curriculum were *Rise and Fall of Muslims* and *Saviours of Islamic Spirit*. Another highly acclaimed work, *Al-Murtadā* detailing the life and times of Caliph 'Ali was much appreciated by the Egyptian *'ulama'* and littérateurs. The book was broadcast on air in a well-documented series. In the context of the religiosity that emerged during this period, Shaykh Nadwi's notable contributions could not be ignored.[16]

Corporate Islamic Identity: The Road Ahead

It was no coincidence that Shaykh Nadwi was motivated to review the challenges the Indian Muslims faced in terms of their collective identity. In the evolution of the Muslim society, religious and cultural traditions with a distinct Hindu influence were deemed as acceptable norms. While lavishing praises about the community's rich Islamic legacy developed over the centuries during the various periods of Muslim rule, Shaykh Nadwi adopted a practical stance. For him, the syncretic practices weakened the moral fibre of the vibrant Muslim society. These practices were also elevated to the status of meritorious acts worthy of divine reward. In the light of these alarming developments, he considered it his moral duty to expose these social vices. Weddings in particular assumed a hue that were not dissimilar from their Hindu counterparts. These functions vitiated the simplicity of the Prophet's (SAAS) *sunnah*.[17] Ostentation and vulgar opulence were entrenched traits of the elites while the assimilation of customary rites accentuated the gulf between Islamic ideals and *bid'ah* (innovation). In sum, the reform of the Muslim society was a priority against the backdrop of the rise of Hindu revivalism. Furthermore, political maturity was required to preserve the Muslim cultural identity.

The response to challenges facing the Muslim community, Shaykh Nadwi asserted, was only possible through unity of thought and action rather than sectarian interest. India could proudly boast of reformers of the calibre of

---

[16] *Ibid.*, 20-21.
[17] See Nadwi, *Western Civilisation, Islam and Muslims*, 112-14.

Shah Waliyullah, Sayyid Ahmad Shahid and Shah Isma'il Shahid for their exemplary contributions. Their enduring influence saw the establishment of institutions like Nadwah and the transnational movement like the Tablighī Jamā'at.[18]

In the realm of action Shaykh Nadwi provided two strategies for the Indian Muslims. First, a *da'wah* programme was essential to acquaint non-Muslims about the Islamic teachings and the universal values of brotherhood and equality. The Muslim community had over the centuries imparted these life-enriching experiences on the Indian soil. Second, the educated class in the community could make a positive contribution by preparing Islamic literature with a global appeal.

In a similar vein, Shaykh Nadwi's analysis of Islamic movements in the Indian context is elaborated in his multivolume *Saviours of Islamic Spirit*. He says:

> History bears a testimony to the fact that there has never been a spell, however brief, during the past one and a half thousand years when the message of Islam was eclipsed. Neither were its teachings engulfed by heresy nor did the Islamic conscience became dormant enough to accept a contaminated faith. Whenever an effort was made from any quarter to distort the tenets of Islam, pervert or falsify its teachings, or it was attacked by materialistic tendencies, someone invariably came forward to accept the challenge. History records many a powerful movement in its day, which posed a danger for Islam, but now it is difficult to find out even the true impact of its thought. [It] was Islam which gained ascendancy over these contending forces. These powerful movements are known today as simply different schools of thought and are to be found now in philosophical and theological works only. This tradition of struggle against un-Islam, the spirit to preserve and renovate the pristine teachings of the faith and the effort to infuse people with a revolutionary spirit to reassert the divine message are as old as Islam itself[19].

The continuity of *islāh* and *tajdīd* have enabled Islam to "respond to challenges of the day and stem the tide of interpolation and deviation from

---

[18] Nadwi, *The Life of Caliph 'Ali* (Lucknow, 1991). Cf. 'Abbās Nadwi, *Mir Kārwān*, 446-47.
[19] Nadwi, *Kārwān*, vol. 6, 87-101.

its perennial sources." In Shaykh Nadwi's view, the *dīnī* institutions should take cognisance of changing circumstances affecting the *ummah* and provide realistic solutions that offer a promising future. He pointed out to the ghetto mentality in which Muslims were mired. Inferiority complex and self-defeatism were thus, counterproductive to the role of *da'wah* in the Indian society.

The *Payām* movement reaffirmed Shaykh Nadwi's vision of interfaith dialogue at a time when the climate of religious bigotry made co-existence between Muslims and other faith groups a daunting challenge. Likewise, he advocated Muslim participation in the political activities of the country. His patriotism was admirable; he made it his practice to write to every Prime Minister of the country as part of his *da'wah* and present his frank views about ways to ameliorate the deteriorating conditions in the country. Syed Shihabuddin had correctly observed:

> [Shaykh Nadwi] saw clearly that the destiny of Indian Muslims was intertwined with that of the Indian people as a whole. Moreover, in the age of democratic pluralism, an Islamic revolution or the restoration of the Islamic power was out of the realm of possibility. However, it was possible for the Indian Muslims to lead an Islamic life and at the same time participate in managing the affairs of the country and contribute to its progress and development.[20]

Police Raid in Nadwah

In the context of Shaykh Nadwi's established personality and religious credentials, it came as a shock when Nadwah was raided on the pretext that it harboured militant students. The police raid was arbitrary and had strong political overtones. Several students were injured while others were arrested. It was clear that the police action was blatantly provocative and a deliberate attempt to bring into disrepute the patriotic character of the institution. Muslim outrage across the country was understandable. Islamic institutions were targeted as dens of terrorist networks on baseless grounds. In response to the wave of unrest among Muslims, Shaykh Nadwi pursued the democratic process to highlight the fiasco in Nadwah. A press conference was organised which was attended by politicians, social activists and journalists from the leading media houses. Shaykh Nadwi's reappraisal of

---

[20] Nadwi, *Muslims in India*, 7-21.

the tragic events pointed out to the non-discretionary measures adopted by the police. Again, he reminded the attendees of Nadwah's international status and the Indian *'ulama's* pioneering role in the freedom struggle. It was, therefore, ironic that the *madrasah* image should be tarnished and charges of conspiracy be laid against them. The intervening periods (1994-95) saw a flurry of activities in support of Nadwah by institutions like Rābitā ʿĀlam al-Islami from the Arab world, which expressed its solidarity to the Nadwah's cause and made representations at state level on this matter.[21] There was no gainsaying that Shaykh Nadwi's international profile and mediating role was acknowledged in the higher echelons of politics.

Literary Seminars

Since its establishment in 1981, Rābitā Adab expanded its footprints in South Asia and the Arab world. It also drew an appreciable number of scholars with impeccable credentials. Journals devoted to the study of literature as an Islamic genre[22] in both Arabic and Urdu were noted for their rigorous scholarship and literary appeal. In many respects, they excelled prestigious publications in other Islamic disciplines. Shaykh Nadwi's visionary leadership saw Rābitā extending its reach to other Muslim countries like Turkey and Malaysia. Its success rate was appreciable. Additionally, the number of conferences across the Muslim world served to enhance its important role over the years.

An international seminar was held in Turkey in August 1996 to recognise Shaykh Nadwi's *dīnī* and literary contributions. Pre-eminent scholars like Qardāwī and Professor Muhammad Qutb,[23] contemporaries of Shaykh Nadwi delivered the keynote addresses regarding his outstanding contributions to Islamic thought. The sessions (*haflat al-takrīm*) focused on his versatility and was a fitting tribute to his pioneering role in the Islamic resurgence.[24]

The main address of the sessions was on Shaykh Nadwi himself which was prepared and read out by Qardāwī entitled "Da'wah Methodology in Shaykh Nadwi's Writings." During his stay in Istanbul, Shaykh Nadwi thought it fit to send his customary letter to the Prime Minister of Turkey, Najmuddin Erbakan whom he met in previous meetings. The letter discussed the need for

---

[21] Nadwi, *Kārwān*, vol. 6, 150-51.
[22] *Ibid.*, 153.
[23] Nadwi, *Ahm Dīnī Da'wat* (Karachi, n.d.).
[24] Nadwi, *Kārwān*, vol. 6, 156-58.

Chapter XIII
Honours Beyond Borders: Shaykh Nadwi's Contributions

creating an Islamic environment, particularly among the Turkish youth. He had entertained high hopes for an Islamic resurgence in the country which was once the bastion of Islamic culture and civilisation.[25]

Honour: Keys to the Ka'bah

Another honour was given to Shaykh Nadwi on 18 December 1996 when his name was included among the throngs of aspirants to enter the Ka'bah. In the words of Shaykh Nadwi:

> I stood a distance away from the House of Allah and wondered if I would be honoured to (enter the Ka'bah). Suddenly the revered Shaykh Shaybi whose family was the key bearer since the Prophet's (SAAS) time handed over the keys to me and beckoned me to open the door... In this way I was the first person who was blessed to enter the House of Allah. I was requested by Prince Mash'al bin Muhammad bin Saud to make *du'ā*... There was no greater honour in this world than this blessed act.[26]

During his second *hajj* in 1950 Shaykh Nadwi was given the singular honour to enter the Ka'bah and take with him whomsoever he wished. According to Shaykh Rabey, Shaykh Nadwi attributed this special blessing to Mawlana Rāipūrī's special grace and supplications. His intuitive insight into and mentoring of Shaykh Nadwi opened the pathways of scholarly recognition in the Arab world. The *hajj* in many ways "planted the seeds and their fruits continued appearing for years to come."

Sectarianism: An Overview

Shaykh Nadwi's association with scholars and organisations of diverse orientations in India had important implications for his Islamic resurgence presentation. According to him, *islāh* and *tajdīd* were rooted in multiple discourses and there was no singular and monolithic expression to this effect. Of central concern to Shaykh Nadwi was the cumulative expression of the Muslim identity and the overarching need to preserve it. The distinctive Indo-Islamic culture, which took centuries to evolve is a case in point. Its religious

---

[25] Nadwi, *Saviours of Islamic Spirit*, vol. 1, 11-13.
[26] Nadwi, *Kārwān*, vol. 6, 206-7.

institutions were built around a vast network of transnational scholarship. In this connection, Islamic movements and institutions served as the bulwark against *shirk* (idolatry) and *bid'ah* (innovation). More importantly, two schools of *fiqh* (Hanafi and Shafi'i) were established in the country's geographical regions and their dominance was influenced by political events ever since Islam made its presence in the subcontinent. The Hanafi *fiqh* became dominant in India largely through the efforts of immigrant scholars from Central Asia and the patronage of political dynasties over the centuries.

During the nineteenth century the emergence of the Ahl-i Hadīth movement[27] brought into sharp relief the sectarian conflict that embroiled the country for the next century. Polemical writings of a peripheral (*furu'*) nature turned into ideological battles. Furthermore, during the later part of the twentieth century the Ahl-i Hadīth allied themselves with the Salafis of the Gulf region. Ideological support funded by petrodollars enabled the movement to launch a vitriolic campaign against the Islamic reformist movements and *madāris*. These well-established institutions maintained a harmonious balance between *taqlīd* and *tasawwuf*. Shaykh Nadwi refuted the condemnatory stance of the Ahl-i Hadīth highlighting the unique role of the reformers and *madāris* of the country. His own academic pedigree included *hadīth* training from erudite scholars like 'Allāmah 'Abdur Rahmān Mubārakpuri, an Ahl-i Hadīth *'ālim*. By all accounts, his respect among Arab *'ulama'* made him the ideal choice to present an unbiased appraisal of the country's *turāth* (legacy). In this respect, the monograph *Al-Adwā* had a two-fold purpose:

- To inform the Arab *'ulama'* of the primacy of the Quran and *sunnah* that permeated the vision and mission of *tajdīdi* movements and the *madāris* in the country.
- To highlight the challenges of Indian Muslims against the Hindutva menace and the proposed implementation of a uniform civil law.

The monograph[28] written in a positive and lucid style contained a factual account of the *da'wah* activities in the country and their role in imparting the true contents of *tawhīd*. In reply, the Arab *'ulama'* gave a tacit

---

[27] Ibid., 90.
[28] Nadwi, *Al-Adwā* (Lucknow, 2000).

endorsement of *taqlīd*, which also reinforced Shaykh Nadwi's position as a spokesman (*tarjumān*) of the Indian Muslims. Shaykh 'Abdul 'Aziz bin Bāz, the Grand Mufti of Saudi Arabia issued a ruling (*fatwā*) on behalf of the Council of Fiqh and the World Muslim League that following any four of the well-known schools of *fiqh* was perfectly valid. Thus, the Salafi campaign in India, to some extent, was curbed largely through the concerted efforts of Shaykh Nadwi.

Strands of *Salafiyyah* have not always followed a uniform pattern. This variation is due to the ideological contents it espouses. For example, the *'ulama'* of moderate *Salafiyyah* adopt a cautious approach in relation to the four established juristic schools of thought (*fiqh*). By contrast, the hardliners brand Muslims as heretics for adhering to *fiqh*-based practices. Simply put, they oppose all forms of *taqlīd*. Their obsession with creeds and 'deviant sects' is reminiscent of the *Khawarij* mindset of early Islamic history. Intellectual sterility and salvific exclusivity are traits of their Islamic discourse. In a specific sense, the critical engagement of the Islamic tradition is totally rejected. Additionally, their confrontational approach reinforces their intolerant attitude to the healthy evolution of Islamic thought.

Another aspect that merits serious attention is the spate of polemical literature produced by the *Salafiyyah*. The disproportionate focus on abstract and dogmatic issues come to the fore. Their reference to Ibn Taimiyyah as their ideologue is untenable in view of his vast learning. In sum, invoking Ibn Taimiyyah's credentials to bolster their *fatwā* bashing against mainstream Muslims betray their lack of scholarly decorum.[29]

These disturbing trends point out to their stifling production of Islamic works through social media and publishing houses. Needless to add, Islamic scholars and institutions funded by the Saudi and Gulf states are also responsible for the dissemination of their doctrines.

International Conference: Qadianism

In the previous years the Muslim world was exposed to a barrage of religious labels associated with the term fundamentalism. Islam in its pristine form was an anathema in the West and Muslim modernists saw this phenomenon as an obstacle to their progressive understanding of the Islamic faith and practice. The battle of ideological ideas launched by the West

---

[29] See 'Abbās Nadwi, *Mir Kārwān*, 428-30.

conveniently overlooked deviant sects that sought to erode the immutable tenets of Islam. Qadianism, for example, with a notorious history of heresy gained ground under the devious patronage of British colonialism whose political ambitions they carried out with unabated fervour. In its early years of evolution as a parallel religion to Islam, Mirza Ghulam Ahmad made bizarre claims of his prophethood, which were vehemently challenged by the 'ulama'. Mawlana Muhammad 'Ali Mongiri, founder of Nadwah, spent the last years of his life to combat the menace of Qadianism. Other leading 'ulama' like Anwar Shah Kashmiri wrote important works to counter the heretical movement. Iqbal's *Islam and Ahmadism* exposed the "grave nature of misbelief both religious and cultural to the body politic of Islam."

Resistance to Qadianism gained momentum in the last few decades with Islamic organisations, particularly in Pakistan, mobilising their energies to raise awareness of Qadianism's sinister ambitions in countries around the world. An international conference was convened at Nadwah in November 1997, which was presided by Shaykh Muhammad bin 'Abdullāh al-Subayyal, Chairman of the Imām Council in Makkah. Other leading dignitaries and Islamic institutions participated in the Conference. The theme of the sessions was clear: Qadianism was a clandestine revolt and an orchestrated conspiracy against the Finality of Prophethood and solidarity of Islam. In a similar vein, Shaykh Nadwi articulated the pithy remark of Iqbal in his address:

> It is obvious that Islam which claims to unite its different sects on the basis of a uniform creed for all, cannot show any sympathy to a movement which presently endangers its own solidarity and is fraught with the danger of dissension to humanity in future.

The "danger of dissension" was a cause of concern for the Muslim *ummah* and in Shaykh Nadwi's view, Indian Muslims could contribute positively to works combating the onslaught of heretical movements like Qadianism.[30]

Onslaught against Islam

As an executive member of Rābitā (World Muslim League), Shaykh Nadwi's regular visits to the *Haramayn* (Makkah and Madinah) also involved a series of lectures before an audience of representatives of international Islamic movements and institutions. This lecture encapsulated Islam's universal

---

[30] Nadwi, *Kārwān*, vol. 7, 53-7.

role against the adversarial campaign by the West. The following excerpts reiterate Shaykh Nadwi's pertinent observations about the West's entrenched hostility towards Islam:

[The] conspiracy viewed from different angles is a disingenuous attempt to divert Muslims from their credal and cultural moorings. Thus, Islam should be another nominal faith preserving religious artefacts in a museum. In this way, there will be no practical manifestation of the Islamic faith and practice and thus, will lose its global character. The reins of this conspiracy lie with the US and its cohort, Israel.

Today's challenge is to demonstrate to the present- day Muslims the intrinsic power of Islam which will remain forever and is amenable to every part of the globe. Humanity's salvation lies in its universal message. Islam has hitherto not been exposed to such great danger as it is today, when superpowers are making sustained efforts to control the resources of the world..... Islam continues to be regarded as a potential danger and is moving headlong towards this precipice [of hostility] brought about by the superpowers. This perilous period should reawaken Muslims to face the challenges ahead.[31]

These above comments reveal Shaykh Nadwi's profound understanding of world events which were beginning to reconfigure along civilisational lines. Another tragic drama that began to unfold was the Clash of Civilisations discourse in the West.

Conclusion

Organisations as divergent in their orientation as Rābitā Adab symbolised Shaykh Nadwi's versatility in addressing concerns that were germane to the collective aspirations of the Muslim *ummah*. More important was the uncertain future of Muslim countries brought about by globalisation and geopolitical developments.

---

[31] Nadwi, *Kārwān*, vol.7, 66-8.

Chapter XIV

Towards Journey's End

Shaykh Nadwi's long career spanning over sixty years was largely eventful. With mounting pressures and taxing schedules which required extensive travels abroad, his preoccupation with urgent issues at home also reflected his ambitions for the *Payām*. By now, way past the proverbial eighty years, his health began to deteriorate and he was required to rest following his doctors' orders. However, Shaykh Nadwi could not remain aloof from developments in the country in relation to the future destiny of Muslims as a viable political force. This period (1998-99) may be regarded as the culmination phase in his life on account of his major contributions towards his formulation of an Islamic order and the international recognition of his literary accomplishments.

Dīnī Taʻlīmī Council: Challenges and Opportunities

The *Takbir-i Musalsal*,[1] a collection of presidential addresses by Shaykh Nadwi is a pioneering work reflecting the progress of the Council over a period of fifty years. The following extract by Shaykh Nadwi succinctly captures the spirit of the Dīnī Taʻlīmī Council:

> We are completely successful in our endeavours. The non-religious form of the educational system which is encouraged [by the state] will not overshadow the need to impart to our children *dīnī* (religious) education and moral training. The existence of the Muslim community is anchored on sound and established beliefs (*'aqā'id*).[2] Muslims should consider it their obligatory duty to spread the message of the Dīnī Taʻlīmī Council in every village. The [tendency] by state authorities is to impose their own will on the masses by expressing their parochial views. This trend was evident in the Muslim Personal Law debacle. Thus, Muslims could take a collective stand to strengthen [the aims] of the Council and make a firm resolution to overcome obstacles and protect their culture, *shariʻah* and their faith.[3]

---

[1] Masud ul-Hasan 'Uthmāni, *Takbir-i Musalsal* (Lucknow, 2002).
[2] Nadwi, *Kārwān*, vol. 1, 434.
[3] Uthmāni, *Takbir-i Musalsal*, 621.

The orchestrated attempt by the state to align religious education to a syncretic curriculum was fraught with danger. The outcomes were predictable; the new generation would be alienated from their *'aqīdah* and compulsory learning of the mythology-based history was calculated to mislead Muslims in general.[4] Shaykh Nadwi's concern for the *ummah* was also derived from the life of the Prophet Ya'qūb (A.S.) whose words are eloquently expressed in the Qur'an:

> *Or were your present when death came to Ya'qūb when he said to his sons: What will you worship after me? They said: We shall worship your God, the God of your fathers, Ibrahim and Isma'il.*[5]

The parallel between Indian Muslims and the Prophet Ya'qūb's advice to his sons has important implications. Islam can survive only when an unquestioning loyalty is maintained with the faith as a way of life rather than as a motley collection of rites and customs.[6] If no corrective action was taken to address the serious concerns then a grave danger existed for the *ummah* to suffer the same fate as the Muslims in Spain. In this way, the Andalusian syndrome,[7] a metaphor for Muslim decline would be inevitable.

Vande Mataram: An Assessment

A clarification is required about the national song *Vande Mataram* in order to understand Shaykh Nadwi's opposition to it on religious grounds. Following the 1999 election when the Bharatiya Janata Party (BJP) was able to form a coalition government, it made the singing of the national song compulsory in all schools. Every classroom was required to hang a map of India and the image of the goddess Sarasvati and sing also *Vande Mataram*.[8]

It was clear that the polytheistic contents were antithetical to *tawhīd* and Muslim opposition to its compulsory introduction was not motivated by political agendas. Members of the Hindutva party, however, perceived Shaykh Nadwi's stance as unpatriotic and launched smear campaigns to

---

[4] *Ibid.*, 624.
[5] *Qur'an*, 2:133.
[6] Nadwi, *Kārwān*, vol. 7, 126-27.
[7] For details, see Phiilip Hitti, *History of the Arabs* (London, 1986), 537- 56.
[8] Cited in Zaheer, *Abul Hasan 'Ali Nadwi*, 85.

Chapter XIV
Towards Journey's End

discredit his contributions to communal harmony. Representatives of local and overseas media inundated Nadwah to interview him regarding the *Vande Mataram* controversy. Shaykh Nadwi's response reaffirmed the Islamic creed of *tawhīd*.

During this politically-charged period another incident impacted on Shaykh Nadwi's credibility as a spokesman for Indian Muslims. Security agents chose the early hours of the morning to conduct an unwarranted search for subversive material at his home in Takya Kalān. Shaykh Nadwi was in Lucknow when the search took place. It was not surprising, given his reputation, that prominent politicians converged on Nadwah to express their outrage to this illegal search. In political circles Sonia Gandhi, President of the Congress Party, showed her deep concern in a letter addressed to Shaykh Nadwi. The contents of the letter revealed her profound reverence for him as an Islamic scholar of global fame.[9] Another development in Rae Bareli showed the esteem he was held in by both Hindus and Sikhs after news reached them regarding the unwarranted search. A wave of protests swept the entire Rae Bareli district. All businesses were shut down to express solidarity with Shaykh Nadwi. This action was unprecedented, because it was initiated by a leading Hindu activist[10] and became a symbolic representation of the communal harmony between Muslims and Hindus. A positive outcome of the events following Shaykh Nadwi's uncompromising approach and the subsequent protests by Muslims prompted the then Prime Minister Vajpayee and his Home Minister to restore normality in the country. An order was promulgated effectively rescinding the compulsory singing of *Vande Mataram*.

Shaykh Nadwi's concern for the amelioration of society was linked to his patriotic spirit. If there were any natural disasters, political upheavels or religious clashes in India he raised his voice to address these concerns. According to Shaykh Nadwi, humanity transcends racial and religious classification; therefore, there can be no variance between the unity of ideals and religious tolerance. He lamented the moral decline that impacted negatively on the country's quest for peace and harmony. Instead, its telltale signs of corruption and casteism were ingrained vices and a blight to this great civilisation.

---

[9] Nadwi, *Kārwān*, vol. 7, 211-12.
[10] *Ibid.*

Muslims in a Pluralist Society

The authoritative voice of Shaykh Nadwi went beyond the Muslim cause. At high profile gatherings whose numbers sometimes exceeded hundreds of thousands from different religious groups, he emphasised the correlation between progress and stability for the country's success. On the contrary, an unwarranted tilt in the pendulum would be likely to cause conflict of interest and unrest. Under these adverse circumstances it would be impossible to envision a society where peace and mutual respect could prosper. In Shaykh Nadwi's view, the manifestation of injustice (*zulm*) would rear its ugly head and pose a grave danger to society. Thus, a multicultural and pluralist society like India could achieve real success if it pursued the ideals of democracy, secularism and non-violence.[11]

Islam and the Indian constitution shared complementary ideals to the promotion of universal values. In the Indian context, this paradox could be reconciled, because the constitution enshrined the inalienable religious rights of the Muslim community. Moreover, since its first contact with India the religion of Islam had left a lasting imprint on Indian thought and culture. The proclamation of human dignity and the concept of unity and equality were distinguishing Islamic features[12] incorporated in the Indian Constitution. In this regard, Shaykh Nadwi says:

> It is also for the well-being of this country that when we have decided to make India our home along with our religious beliefs and other cultural and Islamic characteristics, we also naturally took upon ourselves the responsibility that goes with it. Therefore, we have to not only safeguard our religious future and religious survival of our future generations, but also to leave a permanent mark of our contributions and our selfless patriotism... We have to participate wholeheartedly in the making of a new India with all the potentialities granted to us by Allah and nurtured by Islam... We have to raise India high in the esteem of the world and furnish an irrefutable proof of its secular and democratic character which allows us to prosper with our faith and culture intact.[13]

---

[11] Excerpted from the article *"Zulm kā Mizāj and Samāj ke liye Sabse Barā Khatra."* Cited in Nadwah, *Kārwān*, vol. 7, 198-201.
[12] On the Islamic contribution to Indian thought and culture, see Nadwi, *Islam and Civilisation* (Lucknow, 1986), 19-34.
[13] Nadwi, *Presidential Address*, 4-5 June 1961, 14.

Chapter XIV
Towards Journey's End

Honorary Awards

Almost eighteen years earlier (in 1980) Shaykh Nadwi was awarded the King Faisal Award in recognition of his service to Islam. As much as he shunned publicity, a number of accolades were conferred on him locally and abroad. He received two coveted awards during 1998-99, while two others were conferred on him posthumously.

Dubai Award

The International Islamic Personality Award organised under the aegis of the *Amir* of Dubai, Shaykh Rāshid al- Maktoum, was hosted annually during the month of Ramadān. Notable scholars from leading Islamic institutions were appointed to the selection committee. The year 1998 was memorable for Shaykh Nadwi when he was unanimously nominated for the prestigious award. He accepted it after much persuasion from the committee and his close associates. In view of his failing health a special charter was arranged to fly him from Lucknow. A series of interviews from several television channels were also done aboard the flight.

At the Conference, Shaykh Nadwi's presence almost assumed an iconic status. Following the announcement of the prize money, he, too, made an announcement concerning its distribution to various Islamic institutions. It was, however, his keynote address which contained his *da'wah* message to the Arab world. Referring to Iqbal's inspirational verses about the Prophet (SAAS) as the soul of the Arab world,[14] Shaykh Nadwi reminded them of their commitment to Islam. A rousing applause from the audience was a clear indication of his impactful contribution to *da'wah*.

Sultan of Brunei Prize: 1999

The 1999 Sultan of Brunei Prize was awarded to scholars in recognition of their academic excellence in the biographical studies of major figures in Islamic thought. The purpose of the Prize, which was awarded in collaboration with Oxford Centre for Islamic Studies (OCIS), was to encourage

---

[14] On the proceedings of the Awards function see Taqiuddin Nadwi, "Mawlana Nadwi kā 'Ālami Award ki Munāsibat se Dubai ka Safr" in *Ta'mir-i Hayāt*, 2000, 157-260.

academic excellence in the fields of arts, social sciences and humanities associated with the study of Islamic civilisation. Previously, it was awarded in Qur'anic Studies, *hadīth* studies and *fiqh*. The choice of Shaykh Nadwi's nomination was based on his *Saviours of Islamic Spirit*, a detailed study of the revivalist figures from the earlier period of Islam to Indian scholars in the eighteenth century. A high-powered delegation led by a senior minister of Brunei announced its decision to personally hand over the Award to Shaykh Nadwi in Lucknow. However, the government refused permission on grounds that it was unable to provide the necessary security to the foreign delegation. Finally, the Brunei High Commissioner resolved to hold the function in Delhi where Sayyid Rabey Nadwi represented Shaykh Nadwi to receive two shields and a cash award.

The security concerns raised by the state authorities was indeed a political move. Politically, Malaysia maintained strong bilateral relations with India. It was ironic, Shaykh Nadwi argued, that political smear campaigns against him by bigoted politicians and university students with extremist leanings should be the real cause for thwarting Islamic functions of this nature.[15]

Posthumous Awards

After Shaykh Nadwi)'s death in 1999, the following awards were conferred on him:

- The Shah Waliyullah Award by the Institute of Objective Studies (IOS), New Delhi in 2000. The Award was in the form of cash and a scroll of honour containing a citation to recognise scholars with outstanding contribution in social science, humanities, law and Islamic studies.
- The Islamic Educational, Scientific and Cultural Organisation (ISESCO) Award in recognition of Shaykh Nadwi's invaluable services to Islamic and Arabic culture.[16]

Health Concerns

Shaykh Nadwi's association with various organisations, which involved extensive travelling across the country and abroad began to take its toll on

---

[15] Nadwi, *Kārwān*, vol. 7, 276-81.
[16] Cited in Ali, *Islamic Thought and Movement*, 417.

Chapter XIV
Towards Journey's End

his failing health. His heavy schedule in south India included keynote addresses for the *Payām* and Rābitā Adab in Bengaluru and Bhatkal. When he returned to Lucknow in March 1999 he was extremely exhausted. A stroke paralysed the right side of his body. On the doctors' recommendations, relatives and friends agreed that he be taken to Delhi by a chartered flight arranged by the government for special medical treatment. However, they were apprehensive of Shaykh Nadwi's disapproval since he was uncompromising in his principle of accepting patronage from the government. (His refusal in the past to accept the highest civilian award was well known.) As expected, Shaykh Nadwi protested strongly at the proposal and was unequivocal in expressing his reliance on Allah instead. Weeks later, several doctors attending to him were amazed at his rapid recovery. From almost complete paralysis, Shaykh Nadwi began to show positive signs of improvement. During his convalescence Nadwah was inundated with visitors as well as correspondence from the Muslim world. Among the influential visitors was Prime Minister Vajpayee. Shaykh Nadwi's patriotic sentiments were forcefully conveyed to him: India's heterogeneous character could be united only by the principles of democracy, secularism and non-violence.[17]

Political figures, influential personalities and well-wishers were among the teeming visitors concerned about Shaykh Nadwi's health. Telephonic calls and faxes from across the world were received during his convalescence. It was not uncommon for the *mashā'ikh* to be engaged in *du'ās* for his speedy recovery. The following incident of Shaykh Muhammad Farouq (Sukkur, Pakistan) is illustrative of Shaykh Nadwi's rapport with spiritual masters. A prominent shaykh himself, Shaykh Farouq had not met Shaykh Nadwi. However, he expressed his wish to undertake a special trip solely for the purpose of meeting him. While performing *hajj*, he was informed about Shaykh Nadwi's stroke. A collective *du'ā* was made at `Arafat for his recovery. This spiritual bond between them was strengthened through divine grace *(fayd)*.

Another dimension of Allah's special grace on Shaykh Nadwi was his extraordinary levels of endurance. Shaykh Nadwi suffered from severe ailments particularly the excruciating attacks of gout. These drained him physically. In the last years of his life he used the wheelchair for mobility. Notwithstanding these obstacles, Shaykh Nadwi possessed the indomitable energy that spurred him to undertake *da'wah* travels abroad. Bangladesh was

---

[17] Nadwi, *Kārwān*, vol. 7, 242-48.

one of the destinations to which he committed despite his frail health. At a function in Dhaka, it was suggested by the organisers that Shaykh Nadwi be carried on a chair to the dais to spare him any inconvenience. He politely refused and instead mustered enough energy to walk to the dais. He witnessed the excitement and great expectation from his audience. Overwhelmed by such a huge attendance Shaykh Nadwi "spoke with the energy of an excited child delivering the message from a heart full of suffering about the plight of the Muslim *ummah.*"

Likewise, his strong willpower was demonstrated at the Samarqand airport (Uzbekistan) where no wheelchair was available. In fact, the airport did not provide travel-friendly services causing hardship to many travellers. As the plane was parked at a distance from the arrival lounge Shaykh Nadwi had to walk with much difficulty to reach it. In sum, *da'wah* was his priority and no obstacles were insurmountable for him.[18]

Tablīghī Ijtimā: 1999

Shaykh Nadwi's improved health emboldened him to address the Tablīghī gathering at Nadwah. According to reliable sources the *Ijtima* exceeded 100,000 attendees. Shaykh Nadwi mustered enough strength to deliver an important speech based on the theme of *furqān* (distinctive characteristics) of a Muslim.

The following extracts reveal his intuitive insight into the Qur'anic message of hope for Muslims living under different political situations in the world:

> *Taqwā* is usually translated as fear or piety. However, in the Quranic terminology it is much more comprehensive and revolutionary in its content. It covers beliefs and practices, aims and a complete way of life sanctioned by Allah. If a believer is infused with the true spirit of *taqwā* then Allah grants him *furqān* (distinctive characteristics) that permeate his whole being... By his exemplary conduct, he obeys the dictates of Allah and his beloved Prophet (SAAS). He is a well-wisher of humanity; he is a disseminator of guidance; he is a perfect human being who is virtuous, who keeps his eyes lowered, his tongue guarded and his mind pure of evil plots and schemes - in short, such a person possesses these distincitive characteristics (*furqān*).

---

[18] Bilāl Hasani, *Nadwi: Mission and Thought,* 180-4.

Chapter XIV
Towards Journey's End

Shaykh Nadwi referred to the earlier generations of Muslims who were the true embodiment of *furqān*. Their distinctive character won the hearts of non-Muslims and their impact was such that entire cities embraced Islam. Present-day Muslims also possess this inherent characteristic to change the world. They have survived despite the fact that the world has witnessed indescribable brutality, violence and tyranny. Yet these distinctive characteristics are able to weather the storm and make an Islamic presence felt throughout the world. The history of Islam is replete with examples of those pure - hearted souls who were able to change the religious settings of countries. Their inspiring conduct rooted in the Islamic ethos succeeded in establishing vibrant Muslim communities in a short period of time. Their example can be replicated even today if they follow the Qur'anic message contained in the following *ayah: O you who believe enter into Islam completely...*[19]

Embodiment of Patriotism

Shaykh Nadwi strongly censured any Muslim action that compromised the integrity of Islam. In his last public statement (December 1999) he condemned the hijacking of the Indian Airlines by the Taliban and made an impassioned appeal for the safety of the hijacked passengers. In his appeal, Shaykh Nadwi said:

> The information about the hijacking of the aeroplane flying from Kathmandu to Delhi reached me late... It is brutal to detain innocent passengers under compulsion and also a threat to life. Nobody having respect and love for a human being can ever approve of such action.
> I strongly appeal to all those who are involved in solving this problem to accelerate their efforts for obtaining safe release of all innocent passengers involved in this tragedy as soon as possible. All responsible persons should see to it that these problems are solved peacefully and in the best interest of human beings with sympathy and love.[20]

---

[19] For a detailed discussion of his soul-stirring speech, see Nadwi, *Kārwān,* vol. 7, 259-64.
[20] *The Fragrance of the East*, 2000, 74.

Last Days

When Ramadān approached it was Shaykh Nadwi's routine to spend the last days in *i'tikāf* (seclusion) at Takya Kalān. However, that year (1999) he was advised by doctors to stay at Nadwah, because travelling would have an adverse effect on his health. Against the advice of doctors, Shaykh Nadwi started observing all the fasts. His routine remained unchanged; *tarāwīh salāh* and his *majālis* were rigorously upheld.

It was on 29 December 1999 when Shaykh Nadwi left for Rae Bareli to spend the last ten days of Ramadān at his ancestral home. During these days his personality exuded much radiance (*ruhāniyat*) and it was common knowledge that his generosity knew no bounds. His life mirrored the *sunnah* of Prophet (SAAS) and it appeared that he was in readiness to meet his Lord, Allah.

It was Friday, 22 Ramadān 1422H (31 December 1999) when Shaykh Nadwi breathed his last. Contrary to his practice of reciting *Surah Al-Kahf*, he began reciting audibly, several *ayat* (verses) of *Surah Yāsin* and in this condition his epoch-making life came to a sad end. In life and in death, Takya Kalān was his final homecoming.

Shaykh Nadwi was buried in the family cemetery at Takya Kalān. It was estimated that more than 200,000 mourners participated in his funeral (*janāzah*) service. Prayers in absentia were held in several Muslim countries. On 27 Ramadān 1422 the Saudi monarch King Fahd ordered prayers to be held for him in the *Haramayn*. This was a fitting tribute to an illustrious scholar revered by millions around the world.

The lucid comments by Akram Nadwi about Al-Azhar's communique deserve mention. It praised Shaykh Nadwi as "an energetic Imām from among the leaders of *da'wah* and revival. The *shaykh* of the *ummah*...who spoke the truth, and was the one who called towards good."

The aura of spirituality pervaded the environs of Takya Kalān. Shaykh Nadwi's last two days captured the essence of his life-enriching career; *da'wah*, counsel and worship. There was no change in the Ramadān schedule as he believed that consistency took precedence over individual interest.[21]

Shaykh Nadwi's poor health did not deter him from expressing his intention to perform *hajj* the following year. Like his ancestor Shah 'Alamullah, he, too, emphasised the importance of *tawhīd*. Moral regeneration of the *ummah* and humanity were the theme that Shaykh

---

[21] Details of Shaykh Nadwi's final days are succinctly described in *Ta'mir-i Hayāt*, 2000, 235-40.

Chapter XIV
Towards Journey's End

Nadwi reinforced in his talks.
Iqbal's poignant couplet mirrored the life and times of Shaykh Nadwi:

Either isolate yourself in the cave of the earth to remember and glorify Him.
Or, continue proclaiming His greatness in the vastness of the universe.[22]

---

[22] Cited in Rabey Hasani, *An Eminent Scholar*, 93

Chapter XV

Shaykh Nadwi's Personality: Impressions

Shaykh Yūsuf Qardāwī's assessment of Shaykh Nadwi's personal attributes is a testimony to his multifaceted personality. He says:

> Whatever merits Allah had bestowed on you are from among the salient qualities of the heirs of the Prophets... and the revivalists of Islam. These merits are portrayed in your clear thinking, eloquent speech, ardent *da'wah* and forceful *tasawwuf*.
> A balanced temperament is your distinctive characteristic which is well known among Islamic organisations. This attribute has had a great impact on your speech and writing and is a clear indication of your acceptance among Muslims and the Islamic organisations of different backgrounds.[1]

Salient Features of Shaykh Nadwi's Multifaceted Personality
Unassuming personality

Shaykh Nadwi personified the *salaf* outlook on life. Ahmad Shirbāsi who wrote the Arabic Introduction to *Rise and Fall of Muslims* made the following comments about Shaykh Nadwi's lifestyle:

> [Shaykh Nadwi] was against all forms of ostentation. He was very simple in his clothing, food and bedding. He disliked excessive formalities and flatteries. He never attached any value to wealth throughout his life. His perseverance for whatever he believed in was proverbial and his deep sincerity was the secret of his success where others failed.[2]

'Abdul Quddus Abu Sālih echoed a similar sentiment:

> [Shaykh Nadwi] possessed an inclination towards humility which at times was misconstrued for submissiveness and timidity. The following verse, however, belied his perceived weakness: *But when there was a serious situation, he was like a ferocious lion.*[3]

---

[1] Nadwi, *Rasā'il 'Alam*, 78-9 (Adapted).
[2] Akram Nadwi, *Shaykh Nadwi: Life and Works*, 279.
[3] Ibid., 278-9.

Humility was the hallmark of his character; self-importance was an anathema to him. In a similar vein, he eschewed all forms of vanity and ostentation. On the positive note, he nurtured qualities that were intrinsic to his family legacy. Reference may be made to his forebear, Sayyid 'Alamullah Hasani.

Courage and valour, perseverance and commitment, generosity and hospitality, these were the family traits that were linked to his Hasani lineage.

Love for Humanity

Empathy and compassion defined his interaction with people across the spectrum of society. His charismatic personality attracted royalty and laity alike. There was no distinction in his relation with friends, relatives and aristocratic families and common people. Mention may be made of the Sultan of Sharjah, Shaykh Muhammad al-Qasimi who visited Shaykh Nadwi in Lucknow. Shaykh Nadwi's pithy statement embodied his independent spirit:"It is a blessing for the *amīr* to visit the home of the *faqīr*."

The *amīr* representing power did not overwhelm the *faqīr* who was detached from worldly possessions. The kings and sultans recognised this distinctive quality of Shaykh Nadwi. He cherished no favours from them nor was he inclined to accept any monetary inducement.

The Prime Ministers of India from different political parties tried unsuccessfully to win over his trust. However, Shaykh Nadwi kept in regular contact with them to raise awareness of the social and political dilemmas affecting the country. The polarisation between the state and its citizens was of primary concern to him. Therefore, it was natural for citizens to harbour distrust in the state institutions. Instead, they demanded transformation - a qualitative change in their lives. Worse, the vicious cycle of poverty among the large chunks of the down-trodden people was a grim reminder that the country was sliding away from its moral compass. Under these bleak circumstances, Shaykh Nadwi reinforced the *Payām* message that cut across racial and religious lines. For him, love was synonymous with humanity and it possessed the innate quality to reactivate the dormant feelings in man. He explains:

> The excellence of man is his love and mercy for others. One person is pricked with a thorn, but another person feels the pain. Man is gifted with tears which fall from his eyes when he sees a widow's

Chapter XV
Shaykh Nadwi's Personality Impressions

head uncovered in helplessness, a poor man's kitchen unlit and a sick man in distress. If such a drop of tear is put in a sea of transgression it will cleanse it. The quality of love permeating through the human heart is a very precious gift of Allah. When something stirs it, it assumes a strange power. It rises above the consideration of religion, community, nation and motherland. It then only sees another man's heart and feels its suffering and is drawn to it like a magnet.[4]

Shaykh Nadwi's life personified the above ideal.

Embodiment of generosity

The Prophet's (SAAS) generosity was matchless; no needs of people were left unfulfilled. Shaykh Nadwi, too, made every effort to emulate the Prophetic teachings. He shunned worldly pursuits and spent large amounts of cash he received from the international awards on needy persons and cash-strapped Islamic organisations. During the month of Ramadān the number of people breaking their fast (*iftār*) swelled into more than a thousand. This was a daily routine during the blessed month. Ever mindful of the straitened financial circumstances of family members, friends and well-wishers, Shaykh Nadwi took upon himself the responsibility of alleviating their plight. According to his close associates, money orders were sent regularly to recipients whose identities were not disclosed to anyone except his confidantes.[5]

Forbearance

Da'wah in many ways represented the battleground of ideologies and it was not unoften that individuals and organisations were pitted against each other for a triumphant victory. The losses were counted in terms of character assassination and demonisation of individuals working for *da'wah*. There was the pervasive intolerance to those who held different views on peripheral (*furū'ī*) matters. Polemical literature, public lectures and the media were vehicles through which the integrity of individuals and organisations were disparaged. Labels of *takfīr* (declaration of disbelief for

---

[4] Nadwi, *Islam: An Introduction* (Lucknow, 1998), 151-2.
[5] Several incident are related by Burhānuddin Sambhali about Shaykh Nadwi's generosity in *Athār wa Afkār* (2000), 443.

those holding dissenting views)[6] were a salience of sectarian groups that caused untold harm to the image of Islam.

Shaykh Nadwi, too, had to endure a barrage of criticism for his tolerant approach to issues on Muslim unity. By all accounts, the *Payām* movement was inclusive, because it addressed the concerns of the Indian society. His appeal to restore moral values among all faith-based groups was censured by hardliners who deemed his movement as totally un-Islamic.

Likewise, the modernist Muslims saw his stance against the Uniform Civil Code as a betrayal of progressive Islamic values. For the media it was a field day to challenge his patriotism regarding contentious religious issues against which Shaykh Nadwi maintained an uncompromising stance. According to Shaykh Nadwi, truth and justice were firmly rooted in the collective consciousness of Muslims. Rather, injustice and corruption had to be resisted for the sake of a stable society.[7] However, this approach did not imply that Shaykh Nadwi was vindictive towards hostile elements. On the contrary, he was predisposed to forbearance and maintained an exemplary decorum under these circumstances. If the media made scathing attacks on his personality, he responded with civility. The tone of harshness was alien to his amiable personality.

There were many critics and enemies of Shaykh Nadwi. He bore their verbal abuse with equanimity. At the same time, he forbade his close circle of associates to counter their criticisms. Silence was a fitting response to his detractors.[8] Shaykh Nadwi's deep-seated love and concern for mankind empowered him to face hostile situations with a calm disposition. This approach was in essence the personal conduct of the Prophet (SAAS) towards his enemies.

Towards moral regeneration

In his *majālis* Shaykh Nadwi reminded the attendees about the importance of self-reformation. These spiritual assemblies were nurturing environments to cleanse aspirants of unwholesome qualities. In a specific sense, these provided therapeutic healing. To this end, Shaykh Nadwi disallowed frivolous talks, backbiting and worldly engagements. For him,

---

[6] On the *takfīr* movement, See Habibul Haq Nadwi, *Islamic Resurgent Movement*.
[7] Nadwi, *Reconstruction of Indian Society: What Muslims Can Do?* (Lucknow] n.d). 26-8.
[8] *Afkār wa Athār*, 444.

Chapter XV
Shaykh Nadwi's Personality Impressions

spiritual assemblies were the conduits of character refinement and, therefore, actions had to be aligned to the Prophetic teachings.

In his *majālis*, Shaykh Nadwi dispensed with the technicalities relating to *tasawwuf* and instead focused on moral regeneration as an integral link to his *islāhī* endeavours.

Nobility of character

Shaykh Nadwi loved the *mashā'ikh* and appreciated their comprehensive effort for the cause of Islam. His books about their *islāhī* contributions were articulated with an open mind and free from sectarian bias. Even when he disagreed with their views these were based on the Qur'an and *sunnah*. Shaykh Nadwi's critical appraisal of their writings was marked by objectivity and professional decorum. His critique was free from malice, diatribe and above all vindictiveness. Unlike certain *'ulama'* of sectarian leanings who have a penchant for declaring scholars or intellectuals with dissenting views as deviants, Shaykh Nadwi adopted a cautious approach. This is evident in his critique of specific writings of Sayyid Qutb and Mawdudi.[9]

Shaykh Qardāwī makes a thoughtful comment about Shaykh Nadwi's balanced approach. He says:

> [Shaykh Nadwi] possessed integrity in his speech and writings ... I have never heard him insult anyone by his speech or speak ill of anyone... However, this did not stop him from criticising ideas and opinions which he felt were incorrect... But he did this with absolute decorum, kind words and with the language of a loving and trustworthy adviser.[10]

Perspectives of *Da'wah*

The Qur'an is replete with references to the scope and function of *da'wah*. Consider the following verse:

Invite to the way of your Lord with wisdom and fair exhortation (16:125)

---

[9] Choughley, *Islamic Resurgence: Sayyid Abul Hasan Ali Nadwi and His Contemporaries* (New Delhi, 2011), 199-240.
[10] Akram Nadwi, *Shaykh Nadwi: Life and works,* 166.

According to Shaykh Nadwi these words of the above verse "open new horizons of thought and action for they are not limited. The Qur'an has left it to the discretion and better judgement of one who invites (to work within this framework). It is the fervour of Allah-consciousness dominating his personality that will guide him to the way in a particular situation."[11]

Overview of Shaykh Nadwi's Qualities as a Dā'i

Qardāwī gives his personal impressions regarding Shaykh Nadwi's da'wah activities in his insightful assessment:

Shaykh Nadwi was a *Rabbānī*; his *taqwā* was a living experience of his total commitment in word and deed to Islam in its broadest sense. He was *Qur'ānī*; his primary source and constant companion was the Book of Allah. He was a student of the Qur'an and practised its teachings throughout his life.

He reminded Muslims that the study of the Qur'an is beyond academic exercise. It is the Book of eternal guidance. Everyone can easily relate to the Qur'an when one approaches it "as a living Book meant for one's own reform ... and self development."[12]

Shaykh Nadwi was a *Muhammadī*; he made the Prophet (SAAS) his model in manners, conduct and lifestyle. Abstinence and aversion to the allurements of the world - qualities of the Prophet's (SAAS) outlook and life were embedded in Shaykh Nadwi's personality.

Pure *Tawhīd*

Shaykh Nadwi made *tawhīd* the frame of reference for his *da'wah* efforts. It was absolute monotheism that was the first call and objective of the Prophets in every era and environment. This was an epoch-making declaration that challenged the prevailing notions of polytheism (*shirk*). Thus, the Islamic concept of *tawhīd* "dispensed with all intermediaries between man and his Creator in respect of prayer and supplication."[13]

In a similar vein, the brief comments by Shaykh Nadwi on *Taqwiyat al-Īmān* endorse his presentation of *shirk*. It manifests itself in different forms and in

---

[11] Nadwi, *Inviting to the Way of Allah*, 10-11.
[12] Nadwi, *Guidance from the Qur'an*, 9.
[13] Cf. Nadwi, *Three Core Beliefs*, 46-7.

Chapter XV
Shaykh Nadwi's Personality Impressions

different ages. Therefore, its unintended consequences have posed a grave danger to the correct beliefs (*'aqā'id*) of Muslims. In Shaykh Nadwi's view, *shirk* entails "attributing to another, qualities and actions that Allah has reserved for Himself and making them a feature of worship of that other." In other words, entertaining beliefs and performing actions that are censured in the Qur'an and *sunnah*.

Ritualistic Islam was greatly influenced by Hinduism and this was evident in the public veneration of shrines (*mazārs*) and intercessory supplications through the *awliyā'* (saints). Shaykh Nadwi highlighted the religious decline among the masses on these counts. His writings and lectures are reflective of this theme. Moreover, in the Indian setting] the role of the *mashā'ikh* has been emphasised to show their unbroken link to the *sunnah*.

Purification of the Soul (*Tazkiyah*)

Tazkiyah or the Islamic path to self-development is based on two ideals: To achieve Allah's pleasure and gain success in the Afterlife. Shaykh Nadwi's writings on self-purification (*tazkiyah*) are not restrictive; they point out to the maladies that afflict individuals, religious leaders, social and political organisations. For him, the starting point to this journey is self-evaluation, an acknowledgement of the moral vices that act as the barrier towards controlling the egotistical promptings of the self. Therefore, mentorship (*tarbiyah*) is essential to develop a nurturing soul by making every effort to overcome the "heavy veils which prevent one from deriving benefit from the Prophetic teachings and absorbing the dye (*sibghat*) of Allah."

Character development is not the product of a training manual, but a sincere and meaningful commitment to steer away from vices that are impediments to achieving the perfection of faith (*ihsān*). According to Shaykh Nadwi, vices assume different forms and permeate the individual and collective life of society. These are reflected in the culture of pessimism that envelop them. In fact, the social fibre gradually weakens and then things fall apart. Greed, opulence, ostentation, hypocrisy, rivalry are moral vices that affect all sections of life. Against this doom and gloom syndrome, Shaykh Nadwi offers an effective remedy; self-purification (*tazkiyah*) which the Qur'an speaks about and for which the Prophet (SAAS) was sent.[14]

---

[14] For a detailed discussion on *tazkiyah* in a contemporary setting, see Nadwi, *Message of Humanity: Reflections* (Springs, 2021).

The Unity and Comprehensiveness of Islam

Shaykh Nadwi was of the view that the differences of opinion (*ikhtilāf*) are a natural phenomenon for Islamic organisations. In this connection, he did not oppose Islamic movements seeking to build an Islamic society. Likewise, in the political sphere he was clear about the scope and function of the Islamic state. There was a general tendency to project a political dimension to this concept and to disregard the comprehensive vision that Islam advocated. Shaykh Nadwi set out clear guidelines to the establishment of an Islamic state which he believed was viable only if it reflected the moral regeneration of society. He prioritised *tazkiyah* to achieve this ideal.

Elsewhere in the volume the baneful effects of nationalism and materialism elaborated by Shaykh Nadwi have been examined. Nationalism is an ideology which opposes the universal character of Islam. Shaykh Nadwi designated it as a rebranded form of *Jāhiliyyah* in modern times. It is steeped in materialism and has a direct bearing on factionalism flourishing in Muslim countries.

Shaykh Nadwi made an incisive study about these ideologies and alerted the Muslim world regarding their intrusive presence. In his critique of these ideological trends, Shaykh Nadwi provided a balanced approach to Western civilisation. Muslims were urged to benefit from West's technological advancements without compromising their Islamic legacy.[15] Likewise, his rejection of Arab nationalism did not imply a total onslaught of the Arab world. Rather, he recognised their invaluable contribution to the promotion of Islamic culture and civilisation.

Universality of Islamic Message

In several of his writings on *tajdīd*, Shaykh Nadwi makes pointed reference to a particular historical incident that underpins the universal message of Islam. Before the Battle of Qādisiyyah, Sa'd bin Waqqās sent Rab'ī ibn Āmir as an envoy to Rustum, the commander-in-chief of the Persian army. Rab'ī ibn Āmir appeared in Rustum's court. His dress was marred with patches and darning marks. He was carrying an ordinary sword and shield. He entered the Persian camp riding an ordinary horse. Dressed in his unimpressive outfit he entered the court, crushing its plush carpets. He tied his horse and approached Rustum. As he was armed with his shield and sword, guards at

---

[15] Nadwi, *Da'wah in the West*, 16-9.

Chapter XV
Shaykh Nadwi's Personality Impressions

the entrance objected and asked him to lay down his weapons. Rab'ī ibn Āmir refused, saying that he had not approached Rustum on his own, rather Rustum had invited him. If the guards did not let him enter in his armed state, he would return to his camp. Rustum allowed him to retain his arms. Unaffected or unawed by the grandiose setting of the court, Rab'ī ibn Āmir approached him with great confidence. Rustum asked him what had brought the Arabs to Persia? With his indomitable courage and conviction which owed its origin to the Divine Scripture and the Prophet's (SAAS) message he curtly said: "Allah has sent us so that we may liberate fellow human beings from subservience to fellow human beings and bring them to obedience to the One True God. We are here to take them from the narrowness of the world to its spaciousness. Our aim is to free them of the persecution perpetrated against them by other religions. We want to bless them with the justice and equity of Islam."[16]

Rab'ī ibn Āmir conveyed the message of Islam in direct and forceful language. He was guided by the inner light and conviction in Islam which had rippling effects in the court of Rustum.

Challenges to *Da'wah*

In Shaykh Nadwi's view, the template of *da'wah* can be adapted according to the needs of changing conditions. He outlines the criteria for the success of *da'wah*:

- One should be fully cognisant with human psychology and hold a good command of the language. Linguistic competence is of the utmost importance for the purpose of *da'wah*.
- Apart from knowledge and scholarship one should also be well equipped with a powerful and effective language. And the most important ingredient is sincerity and an earnest urge to persuade others. If one writes about that which one feels the most and from the depth of one's heart, it may have the desired effect on the audience.
- As a student of Islam, I (Shaykh Nadwi) would nonetheless urge you not to make a *da'wah* or educational centre a medium or platform for presenting the views of a particular school of thought or for publicising a particular organisation. All of us should be

---

[16] Nadwi, *The Role and Responsibilities of Muslims in the West* (Leicester, 1993), 16-7.

prompted only by the ideal of seeking Allah's pleasure and preaching the message of Islam in its pristine form to others. Allah will guide them and those who directed them to the message of Islam and provide them with resources. They will be rewarded by Allah.

- We must present Islam in its totality and as the message of truth. Islam is not anyone's monopoly.[17]

Tributes to Shaykh Nadwi

As a global personality in the *tajdīd* discourse, Shaykh Nadwi's interaction with the *'ulama'*, intellectuals and Islamic organisations was significant. Through the lens of his diverse activities, he was able to make his contribution to Islamic reformist thought. These aspects are examined in the volume.

After his demise, tributes poured in from the Arab world and other Muslim countries. In many ways, the tributes were a testimony to his multidimensional personality and his commitment to raise religious consciousness among the different sections of the *ummah*. His popularity was not confined to the Arab world or the subcontinent as it is assumed by his critics. In fact, his writings engaged Islamists and intellectuals who played a pivotal role to the issues of *tajdīd*. By the same token, Shaykh Nadwi's patriotism drew him into the mainstream activities of the day. He exchanged views with Prime Ministers, political and religious figures about India's destiny. Letters of condolences from influential figures and institutions reinforced his position as an Islamic scholar of distinction.

The following tributes are gleaned from journals and magazines published in 2000.

Shaykh Muhammad bin 'Abdullāh Al-Subayyal: Imām of the *Haram* (Makkah)

The international scholar and *dā'ī* devoted his life through his lectures and writings to promote *da'wah* and work unremittingly to Allah's cause. In this field Shaykh Nadwi's contributions are undeniable.

---

[17] Cf. Nadwi, *Muslims in the West: The Message and Mission.*

Chapter XV
Shaykh Nadwi's Personality Impressions

Dr. 'Abdullāh Sālih 'Ubad: General Secretary, World Muslim League (Rābitā 'Ālam)

Shaykh Nadwi undertook the onerous task of guiding the Muslim *ummah* over a long period. He enlightened the world with the authentic message and spirit of Islam and employed wisdom in its comprehensive sense to promote *da'wah*. He adopted the noble conduct of the *salaf* to illumine the path of his *da'wah* efforts. He urged the *ummah* to hold steadfast to the Quran and *sunnah* - a counsel which he carried out until his last days of this mortal life.

Dr 'Abdul Quddus Abu Sālih: Vice President, World Muslim League of Islamic Literature (Rābitā Adab)

Obituaries are not sufficient to express our profound grief at the loss of our patron and mentor, Shaykh Nadwi. The Indian Muslims are deprived of a leadership and have now become orphans. Even Rābitā Adab will sorely miss its founder and chairman through whose guidance and *du'ās* its activities were sustained by his aura and charismatic personality.

Dr Anwar al-Jundi

A noteworthy contribution of Shaykh Nadwi was to focus on the Arab world and create an Islamic reawakening so that they could undertake the great responsibility of *da'wah*. He reminded the Arab Muslims of the glorious position Allah had granted them in the comity of nations and the leadership the Quran had blessed them with.

Khalifa Jāsim Al-Kawāri: Director, Institute of Islamic Affairs, Qatar

After receiving the news of Shaykh Nadwi's demise our grief increased. The Muslim world has suffered an irreparable loss of this internationally acclaimed personality.

'Abdul Rahmān bin Nasir Al-Awhali: Saudi Ambassador to India

Shaykh Nadwi utilised every moment of his life to raise an Islamic awareness of the *ummah*. He was amongst the leaders who worked tirelessly towards the unity of Muslims and established on sound Islamic basis educational and cultural institutions. There are no words to describe his true worth.

Dr Zaki Badawi: Chairman of Islamic University (London)

Shaykh Nadwi was an international scholar and *'ālim* who represented in his personality, a teacher, writer and *dā'ī*. He left behind a scholarly legacy of more than eighty works which have been translated into major European languages. In recognition of his *taqwā* and spiritual eminence, the Saudi Kingdom gave him the honour to open the Ka'bah with its keys. When the Oxford Islamic Centre was formally established, its founding executive nominated Shaykh Nadwi as chairman of this prestigious institution. He was a peerless scholar and a pride for the contemporary Muslim world.

Shaykh Sālih Mahdi Samarai: Director, Islamic Centre (Japan)

Shaykh Nadwi's services to Islam were established in his unique approach to *da'wah* and guidance. His influence is not only confined to the subcontinent or the Arab world, but extends across the world. His contribution touched the lives of Muslims and non-Muslims alike.

'Abdullāh al-Tantāwī (Gordan)

Shaykh Nadwi enjoyed a prominent status by virtue of his exemplary *taqwā* and abstinence. Unlike other religious leaders whose words and deeds are devoid of the sublimity of character, Shaykh Nadwi was an *'ālim* who practised what he preached. He was a priceless gem preserved in the treasure trove of Islam.

Chapter XV
Shaykh Nadwi's Personality Impressions

Impressions of the *'Ulama'* and Intellectuals from the Subcontinent

Mufti Taqi Uthmānī (A leading scholar of Pakistan and expert in the field of Islamic finance)

Shaykh Nadwi was such a gifted personality of our time who left his indelible and glorious mark on many fields of Islamic studies and activities with his brilliant contributions. He blended in his personality knowledge, visionary spirit, *taqwā* and a balanced outlook on Islamic matters. By his personal example, he touched the lives of millions of Muslims across the world. His impact on contemporary Islamic thought was significant. It was his commitment to Islamic ideals represented by the *salaf* that he formulated his *islāhī* efforts in response to contemporary challenges. His busy schedule for the cause of Islam personifies his exemplary levels of sacrifice and indominable courage. His multivolume autobiography is a remarkable work that details his multifarious activities. His imprints are visible across the world and he may be rightfully regarded as a personality of the Muslim world.

Mawlana Muhammad Sālim Qāsmī: Rector, Dār al-'Ulūm Waqf (Deoband)

In the field of history Shaykh Nadwi's orientation examined the impact of *Tabligh* in reconfiguring Muslim societies during its epoch-making periods. He avoided the stereotypical representation presented by past and modern historians and instead focused on the relevance of Islamic culture, learning and spirituality that shaped the destinies of the Muslim societies. His was an authoritative voice about Islamic history which integrated contemporary historical trends with an Islamic ethos.

Shaykh Nadwi mastered the various disciplines in Quran and *hadīth* and presented a correct approach to analysing contemporary issues in the light of his profound Quranic studies.

Sayyid Abul Hasan Nadwi: Life and Legacy
Chapter XV

Khurshid Ahmad: Eminent Scholar and Amir of the Jamā'at-i Islāmī (Pakistan)

Shaykh Nadwi combined in his unique personality an *'ālim*, historian, reformer, mentor and *dā'i*. His contributions were a bouquet of varied creative thinkers in the Islamic legacy. He was an amalgam of a sufi-shaykh of preeminence. The spiritual retreat and revolutionary spirit and self- purification were complementary ideals. His seminal work on Sayyid Ahmad Shahid interiorised the above ideals. Shaykh Nadwi, too, internalised the *salaf* model in his writings and personal life. If Mawlana Mawdudi had a rational approach to formulating Islamic revival, Shaykh Nadwi stirred the hearts of people to reawaken the dormant aspirations for reform.

Khawājah Hasan Thānī Nizāmi

The multivolume *Saviours of Islamic Spirit* is not only a historical account of *islāh* and *tajdīd*, but a projection of Shaykh Nadwi's life and works. It has a bearing on modern day realities in which the Muslim world is exposed to trials of a different kind. Shaykh Nadwi's writings diagnosed the malaise affecting Muslims and provided an appropriate remedy.

A disturbing trend discernible in Islamic institutions is the absence of spirituality. Shaykh Nadwi filled the void by infusing the genuine spirit that inspired the lives of the influential sufi figures. He was associated with the Naqshbandiyyah and supported through his writings and lectures the outstanding contributions of the Chishti order.

Impressions: Islamic Scholars and Associates
Mahmud al-Hasan Arif

It is inevitable that everyone has to experience death and the effect of such a loss brings tears to the eyes. Shaykh Nadwi's demise brought to a sad end the era reminiscent of the *salaf*. He was a versatile scholar, a spiritual luminary and possessed an unrivalled personality. Pakistani Muslims have mourned the loss of a great Islamic scholar and *dā'i*.

Chapter XV
Shaykh Nadwi's Personality Impressions

Dr Jameile Shawkat: Dean, Islamic Knowledge and Culture, University of Punjab

If we consider the multifaceted personality of Shaykh Nadwi a characteristic emerges; a sincere and upright man. I regard Shaykh Nadwi's writing imbued with a missionary vision; *islāh* was not limited in its conventional sense. His writings, however, were a critique of Western civilisation and Muslim intelligens a who were captivated by its trappings. Shaykh Nadwi devoted his energies to this objective.

Dr. Muhammad Akram Chaudhry: Chairman, Oriental College, Lahore

The Arabic Department prides itself in having lecturers on its staff who have been recognised internationally. Iqbal, Poet of the East, taught here. Shaykh Nadwi mentioned that his uncle Sayyid Muhammad Talha was a lecturer of Arabic grammar literature. During his stay at Lahore Shaykh Nadwi, too, studied grammar under his revered uncle. About the literature genre, it is assumed that literature embodies the whole gamut of life. However, Shaykh Nadwi added a new perspective that faith and the Prophetic teachings are the surest guides to appreciating Islamic literature. Thus, a reorientation was given to the concept of literature. Rābitā Adab is a tribute to Shaykh Nadwi's singular contribution.

Dr. Qāri Muhammad Tāhir: Vice Chairman, Rābitā Adab, Faisalabad

The end of the second millennium saw the demise of that great scholar who devoted over seventy years to the cause of Islam. I had several opportunities to meet him. Shaykh Nadwi's unassuming personality can be elicited from his shaykh, Mawlana 'Abdul Qādir Rāipūrī's estimation of him. He mentioned that on the day of Qiyāmat if Allah asked him what he brought from this world, he would state that he brought two eminent personalities: Shaykh Nadwi and Mawlana Nu'māni.

Mujibur Rahmān Shāmī: Editor, Qawmi Digest

Shaykh Nadwi was above the sectarian divide that characterised the Muslim community. He maintained cordial relations with all schools of thought. A distinctive quality of Shaykh Nadwi's lectures was the absence of criticism. He was cautious even when he disagreed on issues with other Islamic groups.

Dr. Sarfaraz Naeemi: Principal, Jām'iah Naeemia, Lahore

We have gathered to pay tribute to an outstanding personality who faithfully carried out the message of Islam. In his writings and lectures to the Arab world he represented the subcontinent Muslims and proved an important point that non-Arabs, too, possessed a galaxy of Islamic scholars who have left imprints on Arabic literature and other disciplines of Islamic thought. He graciously accepted our invitation to visit our institution and expressed his love, affection and brotherhood. His appreciative comments about the institute will be etched in our memories.[18]

Impressions by Contemporary Scholars

The following information is gleaned from the authoritative works of Akram Nadwi about the life and legacy of Shaykh Nadwi.

Mufti 'Amin al-Husayni said: "A sincere believer who is able to diagnose the illness and prescribe the appropriate medication."

Shaykh Muhammad Bahjat al-Baytar al-Dimashqi said in a letter to him: "O noble friend and loyal confidante, whenever I think of you or speak about you among my people, I think of your extensive knowledge, your noble character, the gracefulness of your speech, and the pleasure you impart to your companions through your open-heartedness, and your humorous and enjoyable anecdotes."

Dr. Mustafa al-Sibā'ī said in his Introduction to the book, *Saviours of Islamic*

---

[18] Cf. Muhammad As'ad Qāsimi, *Abul Hasan Ali Nadwi Number*, (Basti, 2001), 635-86.

Chapter XV
Shaykh Nadwi's Personality Impressions

Spirit: "From among the leading figures of this blessed movement is Ustādh Abul Hasan Nadwi, the author of this book. He is a scholar who is a reformer and a devoted *dā'i*. Ever since God blessed him with knowledge, he has continued calling to God with his pen and tongue, through his numerous journeys to the Arab lands and Islamic countries, and his tours which were specifically for the work of *da'wah*.

He continued with all this and is today considered to be the most distinguished Islamic reformer from India. He has students spread in every country, and his books and writings are known for their academic accuracy, in-depth understanding of the wisdom of the *shari'ah*, accurate diagnosis of the problems of the Islamic world, and the means of treating these problems.

In addition to all this, he distinguished himself by an illustrious soul, noble Prophetic character, and a way of life which reminds you of the scholars of the virtuous past, in his abstinence, asceticism, worship and noble-mindedness."

Shahid Sayyid Qutb said of him: "I got to know him personally and through his writings. I recognised in him the heart and intellect of a believer. I recognised in him a person who lives by Islam, for the sake of Islam, and has an excellent understanding of Islam... This is the testimony which I give for the sake of Allah."

Shaykh Muhammad al-Gazāli said, in appreciation of the sentiments, zeal and spirit evident in the writings of Shaykh Abul Hasan: "This is the Islam which none but a perceptive and soaring spirit can serve. As for the spirits that are senseless and ruined, they have no share whatsoever in this."

Shaykh Ahmad ibn 'Abd al-'Aziz al-Mubārak commented: "He is a *dā'i* for Islam and comes to its defence through his speeches and writings. He combines sound understanding with wisdom. He is from a branch of the Prophet's (SAAS) family tree and a member of the family of al-Mustafa."

Shaykh 'Abd al-Fattāh Abu Ghuddah described him in his book *Safahat min Sabr al-'Ulama'* in the following words:

He is one of the senior figures of the era of divinely guided scholars and a righteous role-model. He is one of the most famous scholars, *du'āt* and thinkers. He is the great scholar, outstanding proponent of Islam, and inviter towards Allah through his very words and actions. When he writes or speaks, he provides food to the hearts and souls, and illuminates the intellect and mind. He is our Mawlana, a man of virtue and excellence,

Shaykh Abul Hasan Ali Nadwi.
He also said in a letter to him:
You were and still are - by the grace of Allah - that lofty example who reminds us of those personalities whom Allah blessed with his love in their hearts and the love of people for them by virtue of their love for Allah and His Messenger. There is nothing strange in your being such, because a noble tree continues having flourishing branches, attractive colours and a wonderful fragrance in every era and every place. All praise is due to Allah.

Shaykh 'Abd al-Fattah also said about him: "He is the blessing of this era."

Shaykh Mustafā al-Zarqā said: "He is the proof of Islam and Muslims in India... He is from our righteous predecessors whom Allah willed to live in our present age."

Dr Mani ibn Hammād al-Juhāni, the General Secretary of the International Islamic Federation of Student Organisations, sent the following message to Nadwah: "He bore the responsibility of *da'wah* and reform and travelled the world inviting to Allah and conveying the glad tidings of Islam."

Shaykh 'Abd al-Halim Uways remarked: "A man who never compromised his principles for a single day, who never begged at the door of anyone for a single day and who never hankered after the world for a single day."

Shaykh Yūsuf al-Qardāwī wrote the following lines about him:
I testify that I love him, and I hope that is for the sake of Allah. I love him for his abstinence, sincerity and devotion. I love him for his balance and moderation. I loved him for the fact that he was free from all falsehood. His heart was free from jealousy. His beliefs were free from all forms of polytheism, his worship was free from all forms of innovation. And his tongue was free from accusations and insinuations.[19]

---

[19] Akram Nadwi, *Shaykh Nadwi: Life and Works*, 273-7 (Adapted).

Chapter XVI

Conversations from the Heart

Shaykh Nadwi's Contributions to the *Malfūzāt* Literature

The tradition of recording the *malfūzāt* which relate to the question-and-answer sessions of notable scholars or sufis can be traced back to the early period of Islamic history. Compilations of the sayings of outstanding personalities like Abu Yazīd Bistāmī were posthumously collected in monograph forms in Arabic. Similar compilations in Persian featured the works of illustrious sufis like Abu Sa'īd Abu Khair (d. 1049).

In the subcontinent *tasawwuf* gained a firm footing and attained its fullest development. It became "a revitalising force and a flowing current of socio-religious and religious-ethical progress as a result of the teachings of a group of intellectuals." The *malfūzāt* literature in its seminal period revolved around the exhaustive discussion about the nature and function of *tasawwuf*. It was during the thirteenth century that this form of literature witnessed the emergence of the *maktūbāt* genre.[1]

A cursory view of the *malfūzāt* literature shows two important categorisations; content and function. In its literal sense, it denotes words, utterances or discourses, but it has a specific connotation that takes into account the table talks of sufi saints or proceedings of their regular and periodic meetings, assemblies and audiences given to their disciples and admirers. In a similar vein, its function was aimed at spreading the inner dimensions of Islam by combining anecdotes with the teachings of the Qur'an, *sunnah* and sufi masters. The language of the anecdotes was kept simple so that everyone with average intelligence could understand the meanings.

The style of the conversation was informal and generally included a variety of subjects. From a historical perspective, it was a fragment of informal conversation and a useful approach for reconstructing the social milieu of the period.

---

[1] See, Akhtarul Wasey, *Roshnī ka Safar* (New Delhi, 2008), 11-20.

Shaykh Nadwi's Reappraisal of the *Malfūzāt*

In his *Saviours of Islamic Spirit* Shaykh Nadwi correctly analysed the *islāhī* component of the *malfūzāt*.[2] For example, Shaykh Nizāmuddin Awliyā (d. 1324) was a towering spiritual figure who "transformed the (sufi) discipline from the individual culture into a mass movement for the moral and spiritual uplift of humanity." His teachings transcended racial and religious barriers and created new pathways about the unity of mankind theme. Shaykh Nadwi's *Payām* movement resonated with similar teachings concerning the moral regeneration of society. Shaykh Nizāmuddin was a firm believer in non-violence and reiterated the need for forgiveness and large-heartedness. "If a man places a thorn in your way", he said, "and you place another thorn in his way, it will be thorns everywhere." His advice is eloquently expressed in the following line:

May every flower that blossoms in the garden of his life be without thorns.

The above discourse was frequently used by Shaykh Nadwi to demonstrate the link between *tasawwuf* and service to humanity. This does not suggest that the eclectic elements of mysticism defined Shaykh Nadwi's formulation of *Payām*. On the contrary, his presentation is brought to the fore through the universality of the Prophetic teachings and the fusion between faith and practice. In his personal life Shaykh Nadwi embodied this vision.[3]

In *Morals for the Heart* Shaykh Nizāmuddin makes reference to anecdotes of saints, *'ulama'* to reinforce the lessons he succinctly presents to his disciples. It would be worth-noting that the attachment to the Qur'an and *sunnah* is the key theme in his conversations. Contrary to the assumption that Shaykh Nizāmuddin condoned practices deemed un-Islamic by the *'ulama'*, he was meticulous in the observance of the *sunnah*. His methodology may have varied, but his promotion of *islāhī* values is his abiding legacy. The following extract is a synopsis of his profound understanding of the Qur'an.

---

[2] In fact, *Saviours of Islamic Spirit* (vol. 2) cover these aspects of sufis like Yahya Maneri and Nizāmuddin Awliyā'.
[3] Cf. Khaliq Ahmad Nizāmuddin, *The Life and Times of Shaykh Nizāmuddin Auliyā* (Delhi, 1991), 91-102; 103-9.

Chapter XVI
Conversation from the Heart

Levels of Preparation for Reciting the Quran

The first is that at the time of reciting the Quran the heart of the reciter becomes only attached to Allah. If that is not possible then the meaning of that which he is reading should persuade his heart. And if that is not possible, the experience of Allah's majesty and awe should pervade his heart.

[Another dimension] occurs at the time of reciting the Quran when the reciter feels overcome with humility and repeatedly asks himself: "How am I worthy of this benefit? How did I merit such a high station of honour?" And if that level is not attainable then, at least, he recollects that Allah Himself has promised to reward those who recite the Qur'an and, therefore, he will be rewarded for each moment that he recites it.[4]

The following 'conversations' deal with spiritual maladies that by and large tend to blur out the distinction between truth and fiction. Take the example of ostentation. It gets ingrained in the righteous actions and like a termite it eats away all forms of sincerity. In many instances, it is like the ant that creeps through the darkness of night into the crevice of a rock. Its effects are harmful, to say the least. In the course of time, ostentation seeks to find gratification in the company of those whose hearts are infested with this malignant growth. Man turns away his gaze from Allah and patronises power and authority. As opposed to this vice, spiritual prescription is required from the *mashā'ikh*.[5]

Environment has a peculiar characteristic and can easily affect the disposition of man. It has its own colour and texture and penetrates his mind and soul. Take, for example, a tannery. The skins of the carcasses emanate a dreadful odour and it is unbearable to remain in that place. Even the best perfumes cannot remove the stain of filth. Likewise, an environment which is defiled with immorality is not conducive to a healthy and productive lifestyle.[6]

In the Company of the *Mashā'ikh*

The evolution of the *malfūzāt* in the twentieth century encapsulated distinctive characteristics and the unbroken link to the methodology of the earlier sufis. As our focus is on the subcontinent the *malfūzāt* grew out

---

[4] Nizam-Ad-Dīn Awliyā', *Morals of the Heart* (New York, 1992), 162-3.
[5] *Ibid.*, 140.
[6] *Ibid.*, 333.

of political developments, and in response to the growing influence of Hinduism among the masses. Since the upheavels of 1857 the *'ulama'* and *mashā'ikh* looked inwardly to stem the tide of ritualistic forms of Islam and at the same time located *islāh* within the *tasawwuf* paradigm.

The Dār al-'Ulūm Deoband, for example, played a pioneering role in promoting the synthesis of the *sharī'ah* and *tasawwuf*. However, the *tasawwuf* tradition reflected a sober interpretation which took into account the changing realities impacted by colonialism. At the same time, *tasawwuf* was revisited to make it more compatible to the temperament of the masses.[7] Again, the emergence of the sufi-shaykh sought to authenticate *tasawwuf* practices within the *sharī'ah* framework.

Belonging to the *malfūzāt* genre is an important work by Shaykh Nadwi about the eminent Shaykh Ya'qūb Mujaddidī.

A few extracts recorded by Shaykh Nadwi reveal the changing patterns of *tasawwuf*:

During my youth I spent a considerable period of time in Hyderabad in the company of the *mashā'ikh*. Unsurprisingly, the *tasawwuf* literature dominated their discussion and it was not uncommon to find the *majlis* (assembly) assiduously preoccupied with the intricate concepts contained in the writings of the great sufi, ibn 'Arabi.

Rumi's *Mathnawi* was a must-read in these assemblies. However, my thoughts were focused on the study of the Qur'an and *sunnah*. Sadly, the glaring absence of the Islamic textual sources in such *majālis* made me agitated. The least I expected from these *mashā'ikh* was some study of the Qur'an with reference to the authentic *tafāsir*. Again there was no sign to remotely connect an interest to the study of the Glorious Qur'an.[8]

The explanation for this indifference to the study of the Qur'an is simple: The Book dismantles any semblance of shaykh-based superiority and blurs out lines of religious distinction. Thus, there exists no monopoly over spirituality. During the Prophet's (SAAS) time a bedouin could approach his *majlis* and without any formality ask who was the Messenger of Allah (SAAS).[9]

It is difficult to give an analogy for the Hereafter. For the purpose of

---

[7] *Tasawwuf* became a bugbear for the Islamists who have labelled it a 'deviant sect Shaykh Nadwi's *Rabbāniyah* is a cogent response to this misperception.
[8] Nadwi, *Suhbate bā Ahl-i Dil* (Karachi, 1982), 62.
[9] *Ibid.*, 152.

Chapter XVI
Conversation from the Heart

simplifying its unfathomable nature the following example will suffice. If a single star of the cosmos can illuminate our world, then why is it difficult to accept the *hadīth* that promises the reward of a hundred martyrs for a *sunnah* that has been abandoned?

This problem lies in our indifferent attitude, because we disregard the rewards attached to the revival (*tajdīd*) of a *sunnah*. In this way we devalue matters relating to Islam and consider practice to be impossible. Hardly surprising, therefore, is our neglect towards *fiqh* issues pertaining to *salāh* or the *sunan* acts. Our inclinations are steeped in worldly benefits only. Additionally, the world becomes a veil and screens off its harsh realities. As a result, the consequence is serious attachment to worldly possession cannot escape the harsh reality of the grave.[10]

Shaykh Nadwi's Discourse: New Pespectives
Takya Kalān

Shaykh Nadwi's ancestral village had always resonated with *tawhīd* and the sober interpretation of *tasawwuf* aligned to the Qur'an and *sunnah*. No ceremonial or ritual practices associated with shrine-based Islam were in evidence. The illustrious *mujāhid*, Sayyid Ahmad Shahid, vigorously campaigned against all religious accretions that undermined the spirit of Islam.[11]

It is a truism that *tasawwuf* dominated the lives of the Hasani lineage. It produced innumerable *mashā'ikh* who made their mark in restoring the true content of *tasawwuf*. Shaykh Nadwi was fortunate to be in the company of Shaykh 'Abdul Qadir Rāipūrī whose spiritual eminence and enlightened mind shaped his understanding about *tazkiyah*. Furthermore, Shaykh Nadwi's exposure to the different strands of Islamic reformist thought deepened his understanding of *tasawwuf* that was not cluttered with technicalities.

As discussed in the previous chapters, *tasawwuf* was a much-maligned term on account of its regimen of disciplines undertaken by an aspirant (*sālik*) for his spiritual growth. It appeared to be eclectic and defined by the semblance of syncretic practices. This was not the *tasawwuf* Shaykh Nadwi espoused. Following the Naqshbandi order, he drew a line between *tasawwuf*-laden practices and the promotion of *tazkiyah* supported by the

---

[10] *Ibid.*, 196.
[11] The sweeping reformers initiated by Sayyid Ahmad Shahid are succinctly discussed in Nadwi, *A Misunderstood Reformer* (Lucknow, 1979), 9-16.

Qur'an and exemplified by the Prophet (SAAS).
There are three sources that deal with Shaykh Nadwi's *malfūzāt*. These have been recorded by compilers who have been actively involved with Shaykh Nadwi's *islāhī* activities. His *malfūzāt* differ from others on the following counts:

- Anecdotes are kept to a bare minimum. Reference to the *mashā'ikh* is intended to highlight their spirituality (*ruhāniyat*) on account of their strict adherence to the *sunnah*. Embellished or overcontrived accounts are not included in his discourse.
- The discourse of the West is thoroughly examined in the light of Shaykh Nadwi's multiple journeys and experiences. His is an authoritative voice that guides the attendees to develop a balanced attitude towards the West. In sum, the themes are around the clash of civilisations and materialism versus spirituality.
- As a mentor, Shaykh Nadwi urges the attendees to reform their lives based on the Prophetic teachings. He refers to anecdotes gleaned from Islamic history to demonstrate the continuity of *islāh* as an essential component of character development (*tarbiyah*).

Rae Bareli: Hub of Spirituality

Shaykh Nadwi's brilliant grasp of history and current affairs as well as his association with *dīnī* organisations gave him thoughtful insights to connect these to *tarbiyah*.
The *malfūzāt* compiled by Muhammad Hasan Ansari in Rae Bareli, contain the essence of Shaykh Nadwi's thoughts and responses to questions.

Timeline: 1974-99

The basis of my career is the Qur'an, *sīrah* and Islamic history. I have also benefited immensely from Islamic *adab* in several languages. In my view, the Qur'an should be your album through which the portraits of your life may be seen.
About the universal character of Arabic, Shaykh Nadwi says: "The educated Arab prefers to speak to Indians in English. I had met an Arab youth and our conversation commenced in English. After a while I requested that we both

Chapter XVI
Conversation from the Heart

speak in Arabic. He was speechless when he realised my proficiency in the language. On a lighter note, there is a misconception that the Nadwi title belongs to a distinguished family whose mother tongue is Arabic."[12]

During one of my *da'wah* travels to Madinah, I was requested to deliver a lecture in the Masjid al-Nabawī. I expressed my reluctance because of the time constraint between *Maghrib* and *'Ishā'*. I had to take into consideration that many *musallīs* were usually engrossed in *dhikr*. It would thus be a breach of decorum to deliver a lengthy lecture. Instead, I related the following incident of 'Allāmah Iqbal and its relevance to the *dhikr* of the Prophet (SAAS):

> A *rajah* (king) of a princely state requested Iqbal to translate several Persian documents into English. The *rajah* ensured that the comforts behoving the status of Iqbal were arranged. Late at night, a royal courtier entered Iqbal's room and found him sleeping on the floor. He was concerned about Iqbal's state of restlessness and enquired about it. Iqbal replied: "Our Prophet (SAAS) used to sleep on the floor. This thought flashed across my mind and, thereafter, I could not bear the thought of sleeping on the bed. It is a matter of pride that I could observe a *sunnah* of the Prophet (SAAS)."

This incident formed the essence of my brief lecture. Iqbal expressed his profound love for the Prophet (SAAS) in majestic language through his poetical works.

In a television interview Shaykh Nadwi was asked what was his beloved place. As the plane was about to disembark on the runway, Shaykh Nadwi mentioned his book *Pathway to Medina*. This was the destination that connected Muslims to the love of the Prophet (SAAS). This is *'ishq* which has no English equivalent to describe their deep-seated love for the Prophet (SAAS).[13]

The following *āyah* (verse) poignantly describes the importance of *tawhīd* in our lives. Prophet Ya'qūb (AS) asked his children a pertinent question: "*What will you worship after me?*" This question was asked by Ya'qūb in the last moments of his life. Muslim parents, too, need to ask the same question to their children when the articles of faith are exposed to danger. In this way

---

[12] Muhammad Hasan Ansari, *Sayyid Abul Hasan Ali Nadwi: Hayāt wa Kārnāme* (Lucknow, 1999), 102.
[13] *Ibid.*, 141-2.

the importance of *dīnī* education can be clarified. If this positive attitude is maintained then we will ensure that appropriate measures are taken to secure our children's education. It is my wish that a poster containing this *āyah* with its translation be distributed on a wider scale.

A country cannot sustain itself regardless of its available resources and military power if it does not possess peace and harmony. This quality is reflected in the indomitable spirit of endurance and self-discipline. It has a positive influence on character-building and social dealings.

The value of things varies with people. If a priceless item is given to someone, he disdainfully treats it as a mediocre item. The following anecdote is taken from *The Arabian Nights* to illustrate this point:

A person was on a journey and entrusted with a bag of gold coins to give to his acquaintance. After some time, he returned from the journey and requested the person to return his bag of gold coins. The latter replied that he had no knowledge of it.

The person was in dire straits and overwhelmed with anxiety. He approached the judge of the town and related the incident to him. The judge reassured him that he would retrieve his money after five days. Immediately, he made the announcement that the person who abused the trust was appointed governor of a certain area. After five days, the aggrieved person approached the judge again who directed him to the governor.

When the governor spotted the person from at a distance, he called out to him: "Where have you been? I have waiting for days to return your *amānat* (bag of gold coins)." The person was astonished at the governor's concern and immediately reported the matter to the judge. He had a simple question: "What spell did the judge cast on the governor?"

The judge replied: "When a person receives a big thing then the value of the small thing is insignificant."

Chapter XVI
Conversation from the Heart

This anecdote is applicable to Muslims living across the world.[14]

Locale: Nadwat al-'Ulama Guesthouse
Compiler: Mawlana Faisal Bhatkali
Compilation: Majālis-i Hasanah
Timeline: 1995-99

Mawlana Bhatkali relates the reasons for compiling the *Majālis*:

During my student years (1995-99) I was blessed with the opportunity to observe Shaykh Nadwi closely. As long as he stayed at Nadwah there were two *majālis* sessions; after *'Asr* and *'Ishā'*. It was the *'Ishā' majlis* which drew hundreds of students and teachers in the dining hall of the guesthouse. Shaykh Nadwi's *majlis* was somewhat different from the traditional *majālis*. He would often remain silent and reply to questions posed to him by the audience. Otherwise, Shaykh Nadwi would recount an incident from the *salaf* and contextualise its significance for students. Incidental topics dominated the *majālis* as Shaykh Nadwi sought to instil qualities of reverence for the *mashā'ikh*. Invariably, the message of *da'wah* dominated the discussion. It was the link that connected Islamic legacy of the past to present realities.

As the *majālis* progressed it dawned upon me that if these priceless counsels were not preserved, then it would be a real loss for the *ummah*. The *majālis* are in essence Shaykh Nadwi's presentation of *da'wah*. They encapsulate an array of topics about *tasawwuf*, anecdotes from the *mashā'ikh*, horizons of knowledge, historical accounts and literature. As far as possible the transcription of each *majlis* is a faithful rendering of Shaykh Nadwi's *malfūzāt*.[15]

The reconstruction of the *malfūzāt* within the social milieu is emblematic of the currents of Islamic thought and activities sweeping across the Muslim world. Also, globalisation features prominently in Shaykh Nadwi's discourse due to the proliferation of technology in our lives. The following observations are illustrative of his multidimensional personality:

Practical conduct brings practical results for a *dā'i*. The first condition is detachment from worldly pursuits. A spirit of independence has greater

---

[14] *Ibid.*, 131-2.
[15] Faisal Bhatkali, *Mājalis-i Hasanah* (Lucknow, 2011), 49-51.

impact on the addressee. The Quran and the *sīrah* of Prophet (SAAS) are infallible guides to promote *da'wah* among non-Muslims. The Qur'anic dictum of success is based on an important factor; *taqwā* which creates an ambience for nurturing positive qualities. If a Muslim internalises the true content and spirit of *taqwā* then his personal conduct will be appealing to non-Muslims. It must be borne in mind that anything new has an effect on people. Likewise, if non-Muslims observe Muslims carrying out simple chores like opening and closing taps for others, this act will be favourably received. One simple, ordinary act can draw the attention of hundreds of non-Muslims.[16]

(The humanitarian initiative must be sustained for earning the Pleasure of Allah).

Some time ago, a Palestinian delegation visited me. In the course of our conversation, I pointed to the contradiction in Jewish thought. As much as they claim to have received the Divine Scripture, they are devoid of its message and teachings. Instead, their claims hinge on parochialism and their lineage to the major Messengers. For these reasons they consider themselves to be the chosen people anointed with the noble blood of Allah's Messengers. From the Islamic perspective, noble descent and blood ties have no significance. Rather, adherence to Allah's orders is the criterion that is important (for one's success in the Hereafter).

The Islamic renaissance has had its impact on Turkey, a secular state. Interestingly, there has been a groundswell of interest in my books. Several of my major works have been translated into Turkish. A conservative estimate (in 1999) mentions that over thirty of my works have been translated by Yusuf Caraca and other expert translators. The Islamic renaissance that we witness today shows definite traces from my multivolume *Saviours of Islamic Spirit*. In fact, an intelligence report by Turkish authorities has been monitoring the impact of my books on the Turkish nation.

Humility and gratitude were shared quality of the *mashā'ikh*. Their lifestyle epitomised an earth-rooted humility. Gratitude assumes different forms: Reverence, appreciation, reciprocity and acknowledgement. Regrettably, these attributes are slowly diminishing from our lives.

I had written a monograph *Prophet Muhammad (SAAS) in the Mirror of His Supplications* which sheds light about the revitalising power of *du'ā*. The impact of the Prophet's (SAAS) supplications was emphasised. These pointed out to

---

[16] *Ibid.*, 205.

Chapter XVI
Conversation from the Heart

his Prophetic wisdom and moral excellence. Another dimension to his supplications was their literary elegance and indirectly poignant expression of his elevated status. To date, no writings have detailed the varied aspects of *du'ās*.

I would like to relate one incident. I cannot thank Allah enough that during *tawāf*, an Arab of Wahhabi persuasion held my hands and remarked that I had presented an accurate picture about the demise of Ibrahim, son of the Prophet (SAAS). I asked him about his knowledge of this incident. He replied that my book on the *sīrah* was a prescribed reading at a college in Saudi Arabia. This incident referred to the coincidence between Ibrahim's passing away and the solar eclipse. The Prophet's (SAAS) prompt action was meant to dispel any misconception that the solar eclipse resulted from any person's death. It was a natural phenomenon and a sign of Allah's majesty and power.

Shaykh Nadwi continued:

> Compare this Prophet's (SAAS) standpoint to political leaders. If such occurrence does take place, they exploit the situation for their political interest. Their pretentious sympathy, empathy and solidarity are a veneer to conceal their hidden agendas. In more ways than one political expediency takes precedence over the genuine concerns of the masses.[17]

Heart of the Matter

The *malfūzāt* have been paraphrased in the volume for readers who are not familiar with technical terms or historical references in the texts. The compilation of the *malfūzāt* in Oxford is gleaned from Akram Nadwi's *Armughān-i Farang*. The book covers the lectures, discourses and correspondence of Shaykh Nadwi with scholars from UK. Akram Nadwi's illustrious career captures the versatility of his mentor, Shaykh Nadwi. An erudite *hadīth* scholar, he has completed a monumental compilation about the lives of *Muhaddithāt* (female *hadīth* scholars in Islam) in Arabic.[18] Indeed, it is a major undertaking to this discipline.

Shaykh Nadwi was the chairman of Oxford Centre for Islamic Studies and

---

[17] *Ibid.*, 333.
[18] Akram Nadwi is the author of *Al-Muhaddithāt*, a 43-volume biographical dictionary which documents the significant contributions made by female *hadīth* scholars over the past 1400 years.

visited the Centre annually for its executive council meetings. For the period under discussion (28 August-1 September 1991), the *majālis* were held regularly in London and Oxford. Shaykh Nadwi provided insightful comments into the varied aspects of Islamic history and culture. Among the distinguished guests was Professor Khaliq Ahmad Nizami, an eminent historian of Muslim history in the subcontinent.

Iqbal's love for the Prophet (SAAS) was remarkable. Any mention of Madinah spontaneously brought tears to his eyes. According to Professor Nizami, Iqbal's system worked differently. On the one hand, he was engaged in conversation and at the same time his tongue was engaged in the recitation of *durūd* to the Prophet (SAAS). Although he was a student of Philosophy, his deep-seated love for the Prophet (SAAS) was a manifestation of the power that gave him inner strength (even during his bouts of severe illness).

Once a person spoke to Iqbal about languages and made a critical comment about Arabic. Iqbal was infuriated and remarked: "You have made a mockery at my leader's language." Immediately he asked his attendant to expel the man from his house.[19]

The teachings contained in the *hadīth* literature have a beneficial effect on society. In our society, the wasteful expenditure on weddings is glaring. An incident recorded in the *hadīth* illustrates the simplicity of *nikāh*. 'Abdur Rahmān bin 'Awf, a leading Companion (*Sahābi*) did *nikāh*. There were visible stain marks on his clothing. The Prophet (SAAS) enquired from him and he replied that he did *nikāh*. The Prophet (SAAS) remarked that he was not invited for the reception. 'Abdur Rahmān replied that he did not want to inconvenience the Prophet (SAAS).[20]

If only Muslims could devote more time to functions that are *da'wah*-oriented, the benefits accrued would be immensely rewarding.

There has been no rupture in the continuity of *da'wah* and *tabligh*. If any *fitna* (trial) reared its ugly head, the reformers of the time challenged it. For example, hypocrisy was rife during Hasan Basri's times. The bureaucrats and officials were steeped in the vice of hypocrisy. Hasan Basri stood up courageously against this *fitna* and exposed its nefarious designs.

He made an important remark which showed how hypocrisy was ingrained in the fabric of society. "If hypocrites left the alleys of Basra then the city would be deserted."

It is among the distinguishing characteristics of Islam that *da'wah* enjoys a

---

[19] Akram, *Armaghān-i Farang*, 130.
[20] *Ibid.*, 132.

Chapter XVI
Conversation from the Heart

universal status. By contrast, Christianity and Judaism are devoid of this enduring characteristic. In fact, Christianity has no ties to the original message brought by 'Īsā (AS). Islam, on the other hand, is uniquely endowed with *da'wah* as it protects it against the distortion and interpolation of its universal message.

On the Palestinian question, Mufti Amin Husayni's position was clearly expressed. 'Abdul Quddus Abu Salih recounted the Mufti's concern about the Palestine's future during his meeting with Shaykh Nadwi. The conversation struck an unexpressed foreboding that Mufti Amin was going to be separated from them forever. His parting advice was unambiguous: "Do not have any truce with Israel even if its [illegal occupation] continues to expand. Regardless of Israel's superiority over us (Palestinians), it cannot overcome us."

Hindus have expressed alarm at the increasing Muslim population in the country. Professor Nizami related the following incident: "A Hindu political leader complained to Mawlana Abul Kalam Azad about the rapid growth of the Muslim population. He sarcastically replied that Muslims were prepared to assist the Hindu birth rate!"[21]

The British attitude towards India in Pre-Partition days can be summed up in one word; contempt. The noted Urdu litterateur, Professor Rashid Ahmad Siddiqui, recounted a personal experience. In those days Indians were required to travel in the third class. He, however, was sleeping in the second- class compartment. An English person saw him and expressed his displeasure by remarking that this was not the third class allocated to Indians. The Professor asked him where he was going. The English disdainfully replied: "To hell!" Professor's wit was unmatched: "I am also going there, but I do have a return ticket."[22]

Sayyid Ahmad Shahid went to Gwalior which was a princely state of a Hindu *rajah*. He gave *'adhān* and performed *salah* with the congregation (*jamā'ah*). This was the first time that *salah* was offered in his mansion. He requested the Sayyid to focus his spiritual energy so that he could derive benefit. (The reverence shown to the Sayyid was immense). Sayyid Ahmad curtly replied that such a spiritual exercise was only possible if it was accompanied by faith (*imān*). However, he acceded to his request. Likewise, Maharajah Sandhiya, a lineal descendent of the *rajah* showed great respect to Shaykh Nadwi.

His wife visited the home of Sayyid Ahmad in Rae Bareli and took a mound

---

[21] *Ibid.*, 50.
[22] *Ibid.*, 142.

of sand as a token of blessing (barakah).[23]

As an executive member of OCIS, Shaykh Yūsuf Qardāwī used to meet Shaykh Nadwi regularly. He gave his impressions about the Egyptian government's deliberate attempts to prevent students wearing hijāb at the universities. Al-Azhar issued a bold statement declaring that such a move was un-Islamic. Following the strongly-worded communique, the Minister of Education bowed to pressure and rescinded his decision. Interestingly, the students observing purdah in Egypt produced exceptional results in the examinations. Their performance contradicted the misperception that the hijāb was an impediment to academic success.[24]

Qardāwī expressed his concern about the disturbing trends spawned by the anti-taqlīd movement. Its proponents influenced by Nāsiruddin Albānī (d. 1999) sought to put an end to the established fiqh schools and thus, initiate a new fiqh movement. Imam Hasan al-Banna was of the view that if people did not possess the requisite understanding of the sharī'ah they should observe taqlīd.

Shaykh Nadwi gave a telling example with regards to the scope and function of ijtihād. Had the 'ulama' not expended their energies to resolve the problems of the day, the Muslims would have taken recourse to the Roman law.

The Imāms possessed civility and a culture of adab (courtesy) regardless of their fiqhi differences (ikhtilāf). They applied their minds to formulate a coherent Islamic legal system that reflected the higher objectives of the sharī'ah (maqāsid). In this regard, eminent scholars like Sa'īd bin Musayyib undertook arduous journeys in search of a single hadīth. (Such were the meticulous and exacting standards adopted by scholars).

Assessment

The malfūzāt is a rich literary legacy highlighting the primacy of islāh in Muslim society. Its format and style have varied over the period of time in view of sociopolitical factors. Central to its core vision is the transforming element of being connected to the unbroken chain of the islāhī traditions. In line with Shaykh Nadwi's overall presentation of tajdīd, this genre has extended its footprints in largely South Asian Muslim communities residing in Europe and the US.

---

[23] Ibid., 144-5.
[24] Ibid., 145-6.

Chapter XVII

Key Themes in Shaykh Nadwi's Writings

The following extracts which are drawn from Shaykh Nadwi's prolific writings encapsulate his contribution to contemporary Islamic thought. They form an organic link to his *iṣlāḥ* and *tajdīd* formulation and are representative of his *da'wah* mission which has an appeal to an audience, Muslim and non-Muslim, of diverse ideological backgrounds.

Our study has shown the multiple influences that shaped Shaykh Nadwi's versatility. It must also be borne in mind that this broad range of interaction opened up vistas of understanding the dynamics of challenges facing the Muslim world. Thus, the thrust of his academic and *da'wah* contributions was in response to the sociopolitical developments, which was characterised by the Islam and West discourse, reformist movements espousing the *salf al-sālih* ideal and Muslims in search of a collective identity. These core issues are addressed by Shaykh Nadwi in his major writings.

Qur'ānic Horizons

The first revelation was a remarkable event: It was the first contact between the earth and the Heaven after 600 years when Jesus Christ had preached the Gospel to the world. Now, these initial verses did not command obedience to Allah nor his glorification, nor attaining His nearness, nor even forsaking idolatry or the rites and customs of paganism. These were left for later occasions and the holy Prophet (SAAS) was just told that:

> *Read: In the name of your Lord who created, created man from a clot of blood. Read: Your Lord is the most Bounteous, Who has taught the use of the pen, Has taught man, that which he did not know. (96: 1-5)*

This was an event of immense significance which had an important bearing on the life of humanity. This was the beginning of an era, which saw the most concerted efforts being made for the promotion of learning never attempted earlier. It was the era in which faith and knowledge joined hands for creating a new civilisation. It was an age of faith as well as of reason.

The command to read and acquire knowledge was to be executed under the guidance of a divine messenger and in the name of the Lord so that man proceeded ahead in his journey in the light of Allah's knowledge and certitude of faith. The reference to the creation of man from the clot of blood was meant to point out that man should not exceed his limits, nor feel exultant on capturing the forces of nature, since this was to come about with the acquisition of knowledge.

The pen then got the honour of being mentioned in the revelation since it has always been the most important means of learning. However, little of its significance and use was known to the then Arabs. The few men versed in the arts of reading and writing were known as *kātibs* or the writers. Thereafter, the revelation referred to teaching of man by saying: "Allah taught man that which he did not know", for Allah is the ultimate source of all knowledge which could enable man to know what is unknown. All the discoveries made in any field have come from this ability of man to learn and extend the horizon of his knowledge.

This was the starting point of revelation to the Prophet of Islam (SAAS), which had a deep impact on the subsequent course of attaining knowledge, preaching Allah's message and the modes of thought. It made knowledge a fellow and ally of religion that always helped man in solving new social and cultural problems. Religion, on the other hand, was thereafter never frightened and timid in the face of knowledge.[1]

Islamic Concept of Life

The prophethood of Muhammad (SAAS) converted the entire life of man into devotion to Allah by making the announcement that a search for the basis of all actions, religious or worldly, was what was needed to determine their worth and value. This in the terminology of *shari'ah* was called *niyyah* (intention), which meant that every man will be judged by what he had intended. Every act performed by man sincerely with the intention of abiding by the commands of Allah can be a means for attaining nearness to Him. Everything done for the pleasure of Allah, whether it be fighting or administration, satisfaction of the demands of human nature or earning one's living, marriage or innocent amusement was included in the ambit of religion. Conversely, all these and even the acts of devotion and worship to Allah became irreligious if they were devoid of the intention to win the pleasure of Allah and to attain salvation through them in the Hereafter.[2]

---

[1] Nadwi, *Islam and Civilisation*, 62-4.
[2] *Ibid.*, 59-60.

Chapter XVII
Key Themes in Shaykh Nadwi's Writings

Hadīth: A Censor of Morals

The actions and sayings of the Prophet (SAAS) are life-giving, effective and weighty, which have always helped the people to exercise self-criticism and urged them to fight against iniquity and evil, deviation and innovation in the religious norms and usages of the private and public life. They have given birth to virtuous persons in every age and country who have taken upon themselves the task of reform and revivalism, relentlessly fought superstitious beliefs and erroneous doctrines and invited the people back to the Islamic way of life. The *ahadīth* of the Prophet (SAAS) have for that reason, always remained the sheet-anchor of every Muslim community; their diligent preservation, propagation and study is a prerequisite for the continuity of the social, cultural, intellectual, moral and spiritual standards of Islamic way of life.

The truth of the matter is that the *sunnah* of the Prophet (SAAS) preserved in numerous collections of *ahadīth* has always been the fountain of genuine Islamic thought and the passionate desire to reform and renovate the Muslim society. It was the *hadīth* from which the reformers born from time to time were able to get an accurate knowledge of Islamic faith and thought; from it they acquired their thesis and arguments and on it they have always relied upon for the defence of their stand. It has also been the inspirational force behind their fervid enthusiasm to invite the people back to the true faith and fight every unsound norm and usage. And so it shall remain till the end of time for anyone desiring to take up a reformatory undertaking in order to forge a link between the lives of the people today and the perfect example of the Holy Prophet (SAAS). He shall have to take recourse to *hadīth* if he wants to cater to the changing needs of society in accordance with the principles of faith and morality as enunciated by Islam.[3]

Islam and the Revival of Humanity

The rise of the Muslim power and the coming of age of the Islamic civilisation during the first century of the Hijra were events of unequalled significance in man's moral and social development. These events

---

[3] Nadwi, *Role of the Hadīth in the Promotion of Islamic Character and Attitude*, 302.

confronted the "World of Ignorance" with a crisis of an unprecedented magnitude. So far Islam was no more than a religious movement, but henceforth it emerged as a complete civilization refined, progressive and full of life and energy.

The superior society of Islamic ideology was envisaged and brought to life on solid spiritual foundations. The real emphasis in it was not on material prosperity, but on the development of moral stamina in man and on the metaphysical orientation of life. The soul of man was, as such, free from contradictions within its framework. It was contented. There was no greed, no insatiable longing for worldly power or riches. The government stood firmly for equity and equality and held itself as much responsible for the moral and spiritual prosperity of its people as for the protection of their lives and property. Its governors and administrators were also the finest citizens of the Islamic state; the most exalted ascetics were not unoften found among those who had the greatest opportunities of indulging in comfort and luxury of all kinds.

The people who had entered the fold of Islam could now exert themselves more effectively for the moral and spiritual revival of humanity. They could perform the duty of establishing right and prohibiting wrong with much greater success. The rejuvenating currents of Islam ran through the world, infusing man everywhere with a new life and an unparalleled enthusiasm for progress. The lost values of life had been discovered. Paganism became a sign of reaction, while it was considered progressive to be associated with Islam. Even nations that did not come directly under the influence of Islam, profoundly, though unconsciously, benefitted by the freshness and vitality of the new creative impulses released by its impact on large parts of the world. Numerous aspects of their thought and culture bear evidence to the magic touch of Islam. All the reform movements that arose in their midst, owed their origin to Islamic influences.

A universal gift of Islam to humanity was the re-establishment of man's belief in the Unity of Allah. So uncompromisingly and so energetically did the Muslims espouse the doctrine of monotheism (*tawhīd*) that even the Trinitarians and the worshippers of idols had to offer apologies and excuses for their ideas on religion and for their modes of worship.[4]

---

[4] Nadwi, *Islam and the World*, 85-7.

Chapter XVII
Key Themes in Shaykh Nadwi's Writings

Renaissance of Faith

To attain this objective the world of Islam will have to find its spiritual roots. It will have to re-dedicate itself to Islam. There is absolutely no need of a new religion, a new Canonical Law or a new set of moral teachings for the Muslims. Like the sun, Islam was, is and will never be old. The Prophethood of Muhammad (SAAS) is endowed with the quality of timelessness. No other Messenger of Allah is to be raised now. His religion is everlasting and his teachings are immortal. But the Muslims do require a renaissance of faith. One cannot face new hazards and meet new challenges with a dilapidated faith and unauthorised practices. A decaying building cannot withstand a flood. One must have a living, glowing and unbending faith in the cause one seeks to uphold. If the Islamic world aspires to inject a new enthusiasm and a new life into humanity, to give it the courage to resist and revert the torrents of materialism and religious disbelief, it will first have to produce that enthusiasm and that life in itself.

The Muslims will have to regenerate themselves internally. They cannot brave the onslaught of the ungodly West by imitating its empty cultural forms, customs and social concepts, for these things have no place in the growth and rise of nations. All cultural imitations are bound to make a people small. The Muslims can exert themselves only by means of that inner force, in respect of which the West is growing insolvent day after day.

The secret of a Muslim's strength lies in his faith in the divine recompense and reward in the Afterlife. If the Muslim world, too, sets up the same worldly ideals before itself and gets caught in the same web of material desires as the West, the latter with its larger fund of material knowledge and power evidently has a prior claim to superiority.

History speaks of times when Muslims grew indifferent to the value of the inner force and the wells of spiritual vigour within them ran dry owing to disuse. Then arose occasions calling for great feats of faith and the Muslims tried to draw upon that force, but to their dismay they learnt that it had deserted them long ago. It then dawned upon them that they had done themselves great injury by neglecting it, and they made frantic efforts to work it up artificially, but it proved futile.

During such times there also occurred events in the course of which the honour of Islam seemed to be at stake, and it was hoped that the entire Muslim world would be set ablaze with fury and Muslims would rush forth from every quarter to defend their sacred rights, but nothing happened beyond a ripple here and a wavelet there. Under the surface, everything remained dead and motionless.

The major task before Muslim leaders and thinkers today is to rekindle the flame of faith in the heart of Muslims. In this respect, they should do all that the early preachers of Islam did, and at the same time avail themselves fully of all the opportunities the modern age has put into their hands.[5]

Divine Blessings

Allah's attitude towards the human race is just opposite to man's attitude toward it. Allah is not disappointed with man. His divine blessings and favours are constantly descending upon human beings. Each new-born baby proclaims that Allah has not lost hope in mankind. Each drop of rain falling from the sky and each grain of crop coming out from the earth reflects that Allah is not disappointed with man. The sun rises every morning without fail to provide light and heat to mankind; the moon shines in the sky at night with regularity and spreads its cool and soothing light over the world. Among the myriad majestic and elegant creations of Allah, man remains the most wonderful and is the dearest to Allah. It is he for whom the whole world is created and for whom it is maintained.

But nowadays man shows from his behaviour that the human race, the best creation of Allah, deserves no respect. Man hates man, exploits him, oppresses him, and kills him as if there is no good in him. It seems that man wishes to plead in the court of Allah himself that the human race deserves annihilation. It seems that man wishes to prove that the angels were right in submitting to Allah at the time of his creation that he would cause destruction on earth and shed blood.[6]

Indo-Islamic Culture

The cultural structure of Muslims everywhere is determined by two major factors: (i) Islamic belief, way of life and system of ethics; and (ii) the indigenous civilisation and local customs which are bound to make their influence felt as a result of living and mixing with the original elements of the population.

The first constituent of Islamic faith, way of life and code of ethics is the common attribute of the cultural make-up of Muslims all over the world.

---

[5] *Ibid.*, 188-9.
[6] Nadwi, *Introduction to Islam*, 151.

Chapter XVII
Key Themes in Shaykh Nadwi's Writings

Wherever they may be living; and whatever their language or dress, this attribute is shared by them universally and, by virtue of it, they impress as members of a single brotherhood in spite of so many other things that differentiate them locally. The other component signifies that part of their culture which distinguishes them from their co-religionists living in other parts of the world and imparts to them their individual national character.

From the point of view of Islamic belief, morality and way of life, Indian Muslims, along with Muslims of all other lands, possess a distinctive civilisation for which there can be no more appropriate and comprehensive title than Ibrahimi civilisation. This civilisation has three essential attributes which have fixed their stamp on its entire spiritual, intellectual and social design and given it a flavour and a character that are manifestly its own. The three attributes are Allah-consciousness, monotheism (which has been taught ceaselessly by all the Prophets belonging to the line of Prophet Ibrahim and a complete elaboration of which is contained in the Qur'an), and a permanent and natural awareness of human dignity and equality that never deserts the mind of a Muslim. It is these characteristics which lend a distinctive personality to the Ibrahimi civilisation. As far as we can say, in no other system of civilisation are these features so strikingly in evidence.[7]

Muslim Corporate Identity

We the Muslims of India have firmly decided that we shall not forsake our motherland. No power on earth except Allah can change our resolve. We have reached this decision neither as a matter of expediency nor owing to any helplessness or weakness. On the contrary, our decision reflects our firm resolve reached after giving full thought to the matter.

Another decision is that we shall in our motherland as Muslims uphold our distinctive creed and culture, our religious precepts, observances and way of life. We are not prepared and shall never give up the smallest portion of our faith, come what may.

As citizens of this country, we have a right to live in this land of ours with complete freedom and self-respect. The Constitution of India and the democratic and secular ideals adopted by us guarantee these rights to us. It is absolutely wrong and a misconception if someone thinks that we would ever agree to live in this country at the cost of our faith and traditions,

---

[7] Nadwi, *Muslims in India*, 67-8.

language and culture; for, the country would then not be a motherland, but a vast prison for the entire community, where it is condemned to a life of indignity and humiliation. We are undoubtedly children of this land and we are second to none in our love and respect for it, but we subscribe at the same time to the Ibrahimi view of life and the world. And whatever be the land of birth and the nationality of a Muslim, he cannot forsake his Ibrahimi culture. Thus, let there be no doubt that we want to live in this land as free and respectable citizens of a free country, demanding our share and shouldering our responsibilities in the administration and development of our motherland. There is absolutely no question of our being second-class citizens. Freedom and dignity are two inalienable rights of man; guaranteed by human, moral and legal values of the civilised society, and their denial to a people has never produced a happy result.[8]

Islam and the West

There is now only one way for the salvation of the Western world and that is to acknowledge its moral and intellectual failure as far as the ultimate issues of life and the guiding framework for social and corporate existence are concerned, and to turn to religion and prophetic revelation for the necessary guidance. Only a religion that gives the Western nations a right conception of Allah, of His attributes and His names; that inspires the Western mind with love and fear of Him; that awakens the soul without weakening intellect; that creates strong faith in the Afterlife when man will be held to account for all his deeds, secret or open, that provides in the example of the Prophet's (SAAS) life and works, a substantial and practical guidance in every area of life - only such a religion can prevent the collapse from within of Western civilisation.

But perhaps this will not be religion in the Western sense of the word. Rather, it will be a complete social order whose actual working has been exemplified in the lives of millions of human beings belonging to different periods of history and in conformity with which the administration and government of many countries and empires have been run. This religion will be free from the monasticism of Christianity, the materialism of the modern West, the yogic beliefs and practices of ancient India, the luxurious living of the ancient Persians, the softness and aesthetic excesses of the Greeks and

---

[8] Nadwi, *Islam: The Perfect Religion and Way of Life*, 17-9.

the harsh rigours of the Stoic philosophers. It should repudiate nationalism and stress the essential duty of all nations, races and classes. It should make man less selfish and free him from the domination of desire and thereby harness his energies to the constructive tasks of civilisation.

This kind of teaching with all the qualities I have enumerated is still extant in the Qur'an, the only religious book free from human interpolation and alive in all its first purity. It can still put new life into the nations of the world, its inexhaustible intellectual wealth is still capable of facing the problems of modern times. The Qur'an's profundity of thought remains accessible to general human understanding without the aid of laboured interpretations.

Likewise, the Prophet's (SAAS) life and the wisdom of his teachings are applicable to all, covering a variety of situations and problems. For rich or poor, for young and old, for husbands or fathers, for wives or daughters, for the rulers and the ruled, for the treaty-maker or the sovereign at war - the Qur'an and the life of Muhammad (SAAS) provide a store of principles and norms by which even the vastly altered conditions of modern life can be enriched and guided towards an equitable social order that really does permit to all men opportunity for fulfilment.

For the Western nations to turn to Islam requires enormous moral courage; it requires an admission of failure - and this precisely stands in the way of their taking the right path. The men in power in the West would rather see nations destroyed, landscapes and resources devastated, the whole of humanity plunged into distress, than make the admission. A false sense of prestige and inflated pride in their scientific and material progress prevents them from turning to the life-work of that unlettered Prophet (SAAS) who alone offers hope of salvation. The result of this self-conceit is that generations of mankind face the possible destruction of all existence.[9]

Challenges to Da'wah

One should be fully cognisant with human psychology and hold a good command of the language. Linguistic competence is of the utmost importance for the purpose of *da'wah*. The Islamic Foundation (Leicester) deserves credit, for it has taken every possible step to present the message of Islam in the best idiom. Its production of standard works on Islam in

---

[9] Nadwi, *Muslims in the West*, 50-52.

chaste English will undoubtedly go a long way in disseminating the message of Islam. Apart from common sense and an awareness of the mental make-up of the audience, da'wah should also be articulated well. Some people tend to think that language is irrelevant to da'wah. For them, da'wah consists in making one's views known in whatever form. However, on reading the sermons of Sayyid 'Abdul Qadir Jilani and Imām Hasan al-Basri one realises the importance they attached to an effective presentation of their views. These sermons reflect their mastery over the nuances of language in order to reach their audiences. The rhetorical and oratory skills of Hajjaj and Hasan al-Basri are almost unique. Hasan al-Basri excelled Hajjaj in these skills. 'Ali Murtada was undoubtedly the master of rhetoric and oratory. Apart from him, Ibn al-Jawzi too, maintained very high standards of linguistic competence in his works. Being a student of the Arabic language and literature and a compiler of Arabic masterpieces, I came across the passages containing excellent literary qualities in the works of Ibn Taimiyyah and Shaykh Muhyi al-din Ibn al-'Arabi. Though they are not generally considered as masters of the Arabic language, they are alive to the importance of the language in putting across their views. Sayyid 'Abdul Qadir Jilani led a life of asceticism and renunciation, yet his sermons reflect his concern for the niceties of the language. Generally speaking, these sermons are more reliable and authentic than the royal decrees of literary works of the day, for people held these sermons in greater esteem and exercised the utmost care and caution in transmitting them. They are, therefore, a truthful reproduction of the actual words used by saints. On reading collections of these sermons one marvels at their eloquence, fiery rhetorical powers and the effectiveness of their language.

Thus, apart from knowledge and scholarship one should also be well equipped with a powerful and effective language. And the most important ingredient is sincerity and an earnest urge to persuade others. If one writes about that which one feels the most and from the depths of one's heart, it may have the desired effect on the audience. So by taking into account these constituents of da'wah, be it oral or written, it will yield fruits in the West, in the ever-changing times and on speakers of different languages. Allah will grant the best results for da'wah.[10]

---

[10] Nadwi, Da'wah in the West, 16-8.

Chapter XVII
Key Themes in Shaykh Nadwi's Writings

Da'wah : Muslim Responsibility

Brothers and sisters, you are not here merely to earn and spend. Any community can do that. You are here to earn according to your need, but you must also know your mission and present before the Americans a new way of life. You should call the *'adhān* to stir their minds and offer *salāh* that they may see and ponder over it. Lead a pure life in order that a revulsion is created in them for their own degenerate ways of living. Practise moderation so that a realisation may come to them of the foulness and folly of excessive self-indulgence. Free yourselves from the ruthless domination of machines, live in a cool, calm and collected manner in order that they may know where peace lies. Rediscover the world that lies within you and develop the spirituality which might be felt by those who come into contact with you. I wish that the devout bondsmen of the Lord, men with illumined hearts, may come to live here and teach these people who are disgusted with life that "*Verily in the remembrance of Allah do hearts find rest*" (Al-Ra'd, 13:28).

Today, only the Muslims can give this message, but where are they? Has any Muslim country or community the face to tell the Americans that "in the remembrance of Allah do hearts find rest"? They no longer believe in it themselves. How can they convey the message of Divine Unity to others who have themselves lost faith in the efficacy of *salāh*, in the ultimate power of Allah over all gains and losses, and in the pre-ordination of good and evil? How can they, who revere the Americans as the great providers of the daily bread, tell them that there is no giver of sustenance save Allah?

First, try to create faith within yourselves; observe *salāh* and spend some time everyday in meditation; generate the sensitiveness that has been dried out by the smoke of the factories; refresh your souls, set right the aim of your life; read the Qur'an daily, study the life of the Prophet (SAAS) and seek light from it; and then convey the message of Islam to the Americans.

Islam alone is the religion that does not frown upon human nature, but declares it to be essentially pure and flawless. Allah gave a clean slate to man, a guiltless nature, an inclination towards goodness; we have debased it. Man is by nature upright; left to his natural instincts, he will follow the correct path. First, realise these truths, effect them within yourselves, in your hearts as well as in your minds, and then put them to the Americans.

You are people of preaching and instruction; a community with a purpose, and the bearers of the Message. It does not become you to live like two-legged animals, filling your stomachs and procreating.[11]

Supplication: Evidence of Prophethood

The Prophet (SAAS) taught us how to supplicate to Allah and enriched the treasure-house of humanity and the archives of world literature with those gems of supplications, which are second only to the Holy Qur'an in lustre and brilliance. He addressed his Lord in words so moving and meaningful, so apt and suitable that they can never be surpassed by human eloquence. These supplications live as the Prophet's (SAAS) lasting miracle and as a monumental testimony to his prophethood. The words of these supplications connote that they are from the tongue of a Prophet. They reflect the light of prophecy and the faith of a prophet. They breathe the humility of a perfect bondsman and the confidence and pride of one who is beloved of the Lord of the worlds. They are informed with the simplicity of the prophetic nature, and the straightforwardness of an anguished and restless heart. These supplications are charged with the impassioned prayers and anxieties of one in need and want, and with sensitive care and profound reverence as shown by one who is well aware of the august decorum of the court of the Lord of Lords. They throb with the distress of the bleeding heart and the agony of the suffering with blissful faith in the All-Healing, All-Relieving.

In addition to their spiritual and expressive values, the supplications of the Prophet (SAAS) are of the highest literary standard. As literary rarities and masterpieces, they stand unparalleled in the whole history of man's literature. Many critics have given a high literary place to personal letters on the ground that they are spontaneous and informal, and contain a frank expression of emotions. But they do not know that, in the words of an Urdu poet: "There exist worlds even beyond the stars."

There is another form of literature which far excels personal letters in frankness and spontaneousness, and in which all disguises and formalities of communication disappear, and the speaker lays his heart bare in the utmost sincerity, his tongue becoming truly representative of his heart. When supplicating to Allah the speaker rises above the considerations of ovation and applause and "plays" not to the "gallery", but addresses his Maker, urged by the dictates of his own heart. This sublime form of

---

[11] Nadwi, *Muslims in the West*, 112-3.

literature is called devotional prayers (munājāt).[12]

---

[12] Nadwi, *Prophet Muhammad in the Mirror of His Supplications*, 11-3.

Conclusion

A holistic presentation of Shaykh Nadwi's multi- dimensional personality reveals interesting insights into the various strands of Islamic thought that have helped shape the destiny of the Muslim *ummah*. It was the emergent patterns of transnational scholarship that had a direct influence on his perception of an *ummah* undergoing major changes in response to globalisation, modernity and geo-political developments.

No scholar could ignore the winds of change in defining the fundamental shift of *iṣlāh* and *tajdīd*. This twin concept elaborated by Shaykh Nadwi in his major works bore the imprints of the *salaf al-sālih* and the existing realities the *'ulama'* faced in meeting the challenges of the day.

Our study is a modest attempt to identify the prominent features which contributed to Shaykh Nadwi's *tajdīdi* profile. The timeline of his life provides snapshots of an *'ālim* contributing significantly to contemporary Islamic thought. His versatility in Arabic and Urdu with focus on its rich literary genres, combined with his competence in English, opened up vistas of opportunities to understand the Islamic renaissance and its impact on the Muslim world.

Any biographical writing has to take into account the set of multiple discourses that shape the life and times of personalities. Shaykh Nadwi is no exception to this norm. As the study shows, his association with personalities and organisations of different backgrounds would naturally have led to divergent interpretations. In fact, it would be an exaggerated claim that Shaykh Nadwi enjoyed the admiration and respect of all his co-religionists. This naivety stems from the *'ismat 'alā al-khatā* (infallibility) concept which rejects all forms of critical evaluation of Islamic figures, in this case, an *'ālim*. This is discussed in the study where embellished accounts that are hagiographical in nature preclude any form of objective and impartial research.

It would, therefore, not be surprising that critiques on core issues reflected in Shaykh Nadwi's prolific writings are rigorously examined. According to some scholars, a threadbare minority, his study of *hadīth* was superficial in relation to the contributions of other eminent *'ulama'*. This view is untenable when one considers his scholarly *muqaddimāt* (Introductions) to major Arabic commentaries. Likewise, his study of the Qur'an was profound as is evident from his famous works. However, his scholarly output is downplayed by the assertions that his historical expertise overshadowed his knowledge of *tafsīr*. Viewed from another angle it is suggested that Shaykh Nadwi's proficiency in *tafsīr* was peripheral in comparison to the vast corpus of Qur'anic studies written by his contemporaries. This view also is erroneous, because his tutors were illustrious *mufassirīn* who left indelible impressions on his *tafsīr* experience. In the South Asian context, Shaykh Nadwi's association with the Tablighī Jamā'at was considered reactionary largely because of its puritanically reformist vision. When the *Payām* was established with specific goals of realigning moral issues affecting the citizens of the country he was criticised for promoting *wahdat al-adyān* (unity of religions) reminiscent of Emperor Akbar's religious syncretism. Yet Shaykh Nadwi's interfaith dialogue was a bold attempt to seek common grounds for the harmonious co-existence among the different faith-groups. In a similar vein, the *Salafis* vehemently opposed his declarative association with *tasawwuf* in all its manifestations. On the Indian soil, the Ahl-i Hadith condemned his promotion of a *tasawwuf* that expressed the *salaf al-sālih* perspective. Paradoxically, Shaykh Nadwi's sufi leanings were distorted to project the Nadwah's tenuous links with *Salafiyyah*, largely because of his close ties to the Arab world. These contradictory relationships clearly express the ambivalence that characterised his intellectual life.

India after Partition in 1947 offered a symbiotic relationship between an ideal steeped in the medieval past and a present where democratic ideals could safeguard the Indian Muslims' corporate identity. It is in this broader setting that we should see the multiple Islamic discourses and Shaykh Nadwi's contributions, which provided him with an authoritative voice to articulate his Islamic authenticity paradigm. His pioneering work *Rise and Fall of Muslims* was a bold attempt to locate the role of Islam in world events. This view showed the primacy of the Qur'an and *sunnah* exemplified within the distinctive *salaf* framework. The projection of this vision finds fuller expression in his multivolume *Saviours of Islamic Spirit* which delineates the characteristics of *tajdīd* from the early years of Islam to the eighteenth century.

According to Shaykh Nadwi's thesis, there has never been a rupture in Islamic history in terms of *mujaddid*s and for a radical interpretation of Islam. On the other hand, Islam possesses the dynamic spirit to be able to retain its distinctive character in meeting the challenges of the times. In the specific historical setting, he refers to the emergent trends of Western civilisation and its pervasive influence on the Muslim world. He offers a pragmatic solution: Muslims should benefit from the scientific and technological contributions of the West while extending the scope of *da'wah* to these countries. Another dimension of *da'wah* is Islamic *adab* (literature). It has the potential to stem the tide of irreligiousness and immorality that is very much conspicuous in Western literature. The admirable role of Rābitā Adab under Shaykh Nadwi's visionary leadership created a forum for scholars of diverse backgrounds to build bridges for promoting the Islamic ethos in literature.

Consultation rather than confrontation was his guiding principle and this was evident in the crucial decisions he together with leading delegates had to make in order to defuse the many crises that would otherwise have tragic consequences for the Indian Muslims. Shaykh Nadwi's singular contribution was his practical approach to situations of sociopolitical importance. He cautioned Muslims against excessive emotionalism and advocated democratic means through which the inalienable rights of every Indian citizen could be achieved. This explained his abstention from party politics and his independence to express his views that would have otherwise demanded a patronising attitude.

A reluctant activist, Shaykh Nadwi was drawn into the mainstream politics largely because of Muslim concerns. He eschewed self-importance as much as he abhorred corruption. In his view an Islamic society could only prosper if the Qur'an and *sunnah* became its infallible guides. Therefore, it was imperative for Muslims to show constancy and shun practices that were inimical to the spirit of Islam. The repositories of Islamic *turāth* were the Islamic institutions, *'ulama'* and *mashā'ikh* who contributed significantly to the Islamic resurgence in India. Shaykh Nadwi paid glowing tributes to them and was able to show how a Dār al-'Ulūm like Nadwah was warmly received in the Arab world as a prestigious institution of Islamic higher learning. His *Muslims in India* reinforced his view that Indian Muslims were an integral part of the intellectual developments in the Muslim world.

Much as the political fortunes of the Indian Muslims underwent a dramatic transformation after 1947, there was a pressing need to safeguard the corporate Muslim identity in relation to their dominant Hindu counterparts. Apart from the *islāhī* efforts of the Tablighī Jāma'at, Shaykh Nadwi was able to expand the base of his *da'wah* initiative through his *Payām*. The movement envisaged a *wahdat al-akhlāq* (unity of morality), which promoted the core values shared by humanity. Shaykh Nadwi approached the *Payām* from the Islamic perspective; the *da'wah* envisaged was based on the Prophetic model which had its relevance for humanity at all times. Likewise, his critique of nationalism in the Arab world which he equated with *Jāhiliyyah* was not randomly

applied to Indian nationalism. Shaykh Nadwi argued that an Islamic society could prosper under an Indian Constitution which espoused the principles of democracy, secularism and non-violence. It was his patriotic spirit that paved the way for the broader acceptance by the Hindus of the Muslim community's devotion and commitment to their homeland. A secular country like India offered safeguards to Muslim religious practices and Shaykh Nadwi through institutions like the AIMPLB and Dīnī Ta'līmī Council resisted attempts by the government to undermine the *tashakhkhus* (corporate identity) of Indian Muslims. His association with kings and *amirs* was *islāh*-based; the coveted awards he received did not sway him from expressing his candour when Islam was compromised. This approach was in line with the Mujaddid's preference of reaching out to nobility to effect meaningful reforms.

It is clear that Shaykh Nadwi was inspired by a concern that rooted itself in a contextual reading of the primary sources of Islam, stressing realism and pragmatism. Yet as the growing interest in his writings in both India and elsewhere suggests, his appeals on a broad range of issues seem to be striking a receptive chord among Muslims as regards the challenges of globalisation and modernity.

Glossary

Āyah (pl: *āyat*)	-	A verse of the Quran
Āyatullah	-	"Sign of God—; an honorific title reserved for leading members of the Shi'ite religious hierarchy
Bid'ah	-	Reprehensible innovation
Bay'ah	-	Spiritual allegiance
Dār al-'Ulūm	-	An institution of Islamic learning
Da'wah	-	The act of inviting others to Islam, reminding Muslims of their religious obligations.
Dhikr	-	Remembrance of Allah
Dīn	-	Religion, faith
Fiqh	-	Islamic Law and jurisprudence
Hadīth	-	A report concerning the words and deeds of the Prophet *(SAAS)* (plural: *ahadīth*).
Hanafī	-	A school of Sunni law named after Abu Hanifa (d. 767)
'Ibādah	-	A ritual practice
'Ilm	-	Religious knowledge
Iman	-	Belief, faith
Jāhiliyyah	-	A common Islamic designation for the "age of pagan ignorance" before the advent of Islam
Khalīfah	-	spiritual deputy of a sufi order
Kufr	-	the act of solemnly declaring one's disbelief
Madhab	-	school of Islamic law

Madrasah	-	Institution of higher Islamic learning
Masjid	-	Mosque
Muftī	-	Jurisconsult
Mujaddid	-	Renewer
Murīd	-	Spiritual novice/initiate
Murshid	-	Spiritual master
Salafis	-	Those professing the practices of the earlier representatives of Islam
Shā'fi'ī	-	A school of Sunni law named after Muhammad bin Idris-al-Shā'fi'ī (d. 820)
Shari'ah	-	The sacred law of Islam
Shaykh	-	A notable *'ālim*
Shirk	-	Associating partners with Allah
Sufi	-	Muslim mystic
Sunnah	-	The normative example of the Prophet (SAAS)
Tafsīr	-	Commentary on the Quran
Taqlīd	-	Following the legal rulings of the earlier scholars
Taqwā	-	Piety, faith and Allah-consciousness
Tarbiyah	-	Moral upbringing
Tarīqah	-	Sufi order
Tawhīd	-	Oneness of Allah
'Ulama'	-	People of religious knowledge
Ummah	-	Muslim community

Bibliography

Abdul Hai, *India During Muslim Rule*, Lucknow, 1977.

Ahmed, Akbar, *Discovering Islam: Making Sense of Muslim History and Society*, London, 1988.

———, *Postmodernism and Islam*, London, 1992.

Al-Hasani, Muhammad, *Rudād-i-Chaman*, Lucknow, 1976.

———, *Payām-Nadwat al-'Ulamā'*, Karachi, n.d.

———, *Sīrat Mawlana Muhammad 'Ali Mongīri Bānī Nadwat-al 'Ulamā'*, Karachi, 1980.

———, *Tadhkirah Sayyid Shah 'Alamullah Hasani Rae Bareli*, Karachi, n.d.

Ali, Sheikh Jameil, *Islamic Thought and Movement in the Subcontinent*, New Delhi, 2010.

Andrabi, Abroo, *Muhammad Asad His Contribution to Islamic Learning*, New Delhi, 2007.

Ansari, Muhammad Abdul Haq, *Sufism and Shari'ah*, Leicester, 1986.

Azad, Abul Kalam, *India Wins Freedom*, Calcutta, 1962.

Azami, Muhammad Mustafa, *Studies in Hadīth Methodology and Literature*, Indiana, 1977.

Badawi, Zaki, *The Reformers of Egypt*, London, 1978.

Baig, Khalid, *First Things First*, Stanton, 2004.

Baljon, JMS, *The Reforms and Religious Ideas of Sir Sayyid Ahmad Khan*, Lahore, 1970.

Al-Bannā, Hasan, *Mudhakkirāt al-Da'wat wa al-Dā'iyah*, Beirut, 1984.

Bijnori, Azizur Rahmān, *Tadhkirah Mawlana Muhammad Yusuf Amir-i Tabligh*, Bijnor, 1996.

Chughtā'ī, Ikram, *Muhammad Asad: Europe's Gift to Islam*, Lahore, 2006.

Doi, 'Abdur Rahmān, *'Ulum Al-Qur'ān: A Study in Methodology and Approach,* Pretoria, 1997.

Douglas, I.H., *Mawlana Abul Kalam Azad: An Intellectual and Religious Biography,* Oxford, 1988.

Esposito, John (ed.), *Makers of Contemporary Islam,* New York, 2001.

Faridi, Nasim Ahmad, *Hadhrat Shah Abu Sa'id Hasani,* Lucknow, 1989.

Faruqi, Ismail and Faruqi, Lois Lamya, *The Cultural Atlas of Islam,* New York, 1986.

Ghazali, Muhammad, *The Socio-Political Thought of Shah Wali Allah,* Islamabad, 2001.

Gilani, S.M. Yunus, *The Socio-Political Role of Ulama in Egypt: 1798-1870,* New Delhi, 2007.

Hadi, Husain, *Syed Ahmed Khan: Pioneer of Muslim Resurgence,* Lahore, 1970.

Hameed, Syeda, *Islamic Seal on India's Independence,* New Delhi, 1999.

Hansen, Thomas Blom, *The Saffron Wave: Democracy and Hindu Nationalism in Modern India,* Delhi, 1999.

Hasani, Abdul Hayy, *Nuzhat al-Khawātir,* Rae Bareli, 1991.

———, *Al-Thaqāfat al Islamiyyah fi al-Hind,* Damascus, n.d.

Hermansen, Marcia, *The Conclusive Argument of God,* Islamabad, 2003.

Hitti, Philip, *History of the Arabs,* London, 1986.

Hourani, Albert, *Arabic Thought in the Liberal Age 1798- 1939,* Cambridge, 1983.

Iqbal, Muhammad, *The Achievement of Love: The Spiritual Dimension of Islam,* Vermont, 1987.

Islahi, Zafar-al-Islam, *Fatawa Literature of the Delhi Sultanate Period,* New Delhi, 2005.

Bibliography

Ismaʻil, Abu Rabi, *Intellectual Origins of Islamic Resurgence in the Arab World,* New York, 1996.

Kharroufah, Alā-ud-Din, *The Judgement of Islam and the Crisis of Salman Rushdie,* Kuala Lumpur, n.d.

Khalid, Adeeb, *The Politics of Muslim Cultural Reform: Jadidism in Central Asia,* Berkeley, 1998.

Khan, Masihullah, *Strike,* Port Elizabeth, n.d.

Khan, Shams Tabriz, *Tārikh Nadwat al-'Ulamā,* Lucknow, 1984.

Kidwai, 'Abdus Salām, *85 Years of Nadwat al-'Ulamā',* Lucknow, n.d.

Kidwai, Abdur Raheem (ed.), *Sir Syed Ahmad Khan: Muslim Renaissance Man of India,* New Delhi, 2017.

Lawrence, Bruce, *Nizāmuddin Awliyā: Morals of the Heart,* New York, 1992.

Ludden, David, *Making India Hind,* New Delhi, 1998.

Madani, Sayyid Tufayl, *Sirat-i Sādāt-i Qutbiyyah,* Delhi, n.d.

Maneri, Sharfuddin, *The Hundred Letters,* New York, 1980.

Masud, Muhammad Khalid, *Travellers in Faith,* Leiden, 2000.

Masʻūdi, Muhammad Anzar, *Naqsh-i Dawām: Hayāt-i Muhaddith-i Kashmiri,* Multan, 2006.

Mawdudi, Sayyid Abul Aʻla, *A Short History of the Revivalist Movement in Islam,* Lahore, 1972.

———, *The Qadiani Problem,* Lahore, n.d.

———, *Towards Understanding the Qur'an,* vol. V, Leicester, 1995.

Metcalf, Barbara, *Islamic Contestations,* New Delhi, 2004.

———, *Islamic Revival in British India: Deoband, 1860-1900,* Princeton, 1982.

Miftahi, Muhammad Zafiruddin, *Hayāt-i-Mawlānā Gilāni,* Karachi, 1994.

Murad, Khurram, *In the Early Hours: Reflections on Spiritual and Self-Development,* Leicester, 2001.

Nadvi, Syed Habibul Haq, *Islamic Legal Philosophy and the Qur'anic Origins of the Islamic Law,* Durban, 1989.

———, *Islamic Resurgent Movements in the Indo-Pak Subcontinent,* Durban, 1987.

———, *The Dynamics of Islam,* Durban, 1982.

Nadwi, 'Abdullāh 'Abbās, *Mīr-i Kārwān,* New Delhi, 1999.

———, Abu Suhbān Ruh al-Quds, *Mawlānā Shaykh Nadwi awr 'Ilm-i Hadīth,* Lucknow, 2000.

Nadwi, Muhammad Akram, *Armughān-I Farang,* London, 2004.

Nadwi, Muhammad Imran Khan, *Mashāhīr Ahl-i 'ilm kī Muhsin Kitāben,* Lucknow, 2004.

Nadwi, Muhammad Rabey, *Samarqand wa Bukhārā kī Bāzyaft,* Lucknow, 1998.

Nadwi, Sayyid Abul Hasan Ali, *A Misunderstood Reformer,* Lucknow, 1979.

———, *'Ālam-i Arabiyyah ka Almiyah,* Karachi, 1980.

———, *Al-Imām Muhammad bin Isma'il al Bukhārī wa Kitabahu Sahīh al-Bukhārī,* Lucknow, 1996.

———, *Al-Muslimūn wa Qadiyat al-Filistīn,* Lucknow, n.d.

———, *Appreciation and Interpretation of Religion in the Modern Age,* Lucknow, 1982.

———, *Da'wah in the West: Qur'anic Paradigm,* Leicester, 1992.

———, *Do Hafte Maghrib Aqsa Men,* Lucknow, n.d.

———, *Do Hafte Turkey Men,* Karachi, 1992.

———, *Faith versus Materialism,* Lucknow, 1976.

———, *From the Depth of the Heart in America,* Lucknow, 1978.

Bibliography

———, *Glory of Iqbal*, Lucknow, 1973.
———, *Guidance from the Holy Qur'an*, Leicester, 2005.
———, *Hayāt i-'Abdul Hayy*, Karachi, 1989.
———, *Inviting to the Way of Allah*, London, 1996.
———, *Islam and Civilisation*, Lucknow, 1986.
———, *Islam and the Earliest Muslims: Two Conflicting Portraits*, Lucknow, 1984.
———, *Islam and the World*, Lucknow, 1974.
———, *Kārwān-i Zindagi*, 7 vols., Lucknow, 1999.
———, *Life and Mission of Maulana Mohammad Ilyās*, 1979.
———, *Mankind's Debt to the Prophet Muhammad*, Oxford, 1992.
———, *Meri 'Ilmi wa Mutāla'āti Zindagi*, Rae Bareli, n.d.
———, *Muslims in India*, Lucknow, 1972.
———, *Pathway to Medina*, Lucknow, 1982.
———, *Purāne Charāgh*, Lucknow, 1984.
———, *Rabbāniyah lā Rahbāniyah*, Karachi, n.d.
———, *Riddatun wa lā Abā Bakr lahā*, Lucknow, 1959.
———, *Reconstruction of Indian Society*, Lucknow, 1976.
———, *Religion and Civilisation*, Lucknow, 1975.
———, *Saviours of Islamic Spirit*, 4 vols., Lucknow, 1990.
———, *Sawānih Mawlana Abdul Qādir Rāipūrī*, Lahore, 1977.
———, *Stories of the Prophets*, Lucknow, 1976.
———, *Studying the Glorious Qur'an: Principles and Methodology*, Leicester, 2003
———, *Suhbate bā Ahl-i Dil*, Karachi, 1982.
———, *Ta'mīr-i Insāniyat*, Karachi, n.d.
———, *Tārikh Da'wat wa 'Azīmat*, Karachi, n.d.
———, *The Life of Caliph 'Ali*, Lucknow, 1991.

―――, *The Role and Responsibility of Muslims in the West*, Leicester, 1993.

―――, *Ummat-i Islāmī ka Mustaqbil Khalijā Jang ke Ba'd*, Karachi, n.d.

―――, *Western Civilisation, Islam and Muslims*, Lucknow, 1974.

Nadwi, Sayyid Muhammad Hamza, *Maktūbāt-i Hadhrat Mawlana Sayyid Abul Hasan Ali Nadwi*, 2 vols., Rae Bareli, 2004.

Nadwi, Sulaymān, *Hayāt-i Shibli*, Azamgarh, n.d.

Nasr, S.H., *Islamic Spirituality*, vol. 2, New York, 1991.

Nasr, Seyyed Vali Reza, *The Vanguard of the Islamic Revolution: The Jamā 'at-i-Islāmī of Pakistan*, Berkeley, 1995.

Nizami, Khaliq Ahmad, *Secular Tradition at Aligarh Muslim University*, Delhi, 1999.

―――, *Some Aspects of Religion and Politics in India during the Thirteenth Century*, Delhi, 1974.

―――, *On Sources and Source Materials*, New Delhi, 1995.

Nomani, M.M., *Khomeini, Iranian Revolution and the Shi'ite Faith*, Lucknow, 1986.

Poole, S.L., *Salahuddin and the Fall of the Kingdom of Jerusalem*, Lahore, 1979.

Qāsimi, Mamshad Ali, *Sayyid Abul Hasan 'Ali Nadwi, Akābir ki Nazar men*, Phulat, 1998.

Qāsimi, Muhammad Asjad, *Mufakkir-i Islam Mawlana Sayyid Abul Hasan Ali Nadwi*, Deoband, 2000.

Qureshi, Ishtiaq Husain, *Ulema in Politics*, Karachi, 1974.

Rahnema, Ali, *The Pioneers of Islamic Revival*, London, 1994.

Rahman, Fazlur, *Selected Letters of Shaykh Ahmad Sirhindi*, Lahore, 1984.

Ramadān, Tariq, *Islam, The West and the Challenges of Modernity*, Leicester,

Bibliography

2001.

Reetz, Dietrich, *Islam and the Public Sphere*, New Delhi, 2006.

Rizwi, S.A.H.A., Supreme Court and the *Muslim Personal Law*, Delhi, 1985.

Robert, Hefner, *Schooling Islam*, Princeton, 2007.

Robinson, Francis, *Islam and Modern History in South Asia*, Delhi, 2001.

———, *Islam and Muslim History in South Asia*, New Delhi, 2001.

———, *The Ulama of Farangi Mahal and Islamic Culture in South Asia*, Lucknow, 2001.

Schimmel, Annemarie, *Mystical Dimensions of Islam*, Chapel Hill, 1975.

Shafi, Muhammad, *Ma'arif-ul Qur'ān*, vol. 5, Karachi, 2001.

Shahid, Muhammad Isma'il, *Taqwiyat al-Imān*, Lucknow, 1991.

Siddiqi, Mazheruddin, *Modern Reformist Thought in the Muslim World*, Islamabad, 1982.

Siddique, Abdur Rashid, *Tazkiyah: The Path to Self- Development*, Leicester, 2004.

Siddiqui, Muhammad Na'im, *'Allāmah Sayyid Sulaymān Nadwi: Shakhsiyyat wa Adabī Khidmāt*, Lucknow, 1985.

Sikand, Yoginder, *Muslims in India since 1947: Islamic Pespectives on Inter-Faith Relations*, London, 2004.

———, *The Origins and Development of the Tablighī Jamā'at: 1920-2000*, New Delhi, 2002.

Uthama, Thamccm, *Methodologies of the Qur'anic Exegesis*, Kuala Lumpur, 1995.

'Uthmāni, Masud-ul Hasan, *Takbir-i-Musalsal*, Lucknow, 2002.

Wan Daud, Wan Mohammad Nor, *The Educational Philosophy and Practice of Syed Muhammed Naquib Al-Attas*, Kuala Lumpur, 1998.

Watt, Mont., *Muslim Intellectual: A Study of Al- Ghazali*, Edinburgh, 1963.

Zaheer, Syed Iqbal, *Abul Hasan Ali Nadwi, A Man of Hope Through a Century of Turmoil*, Bangalore, 2005.

Zakariyyah, Muhammad, *Āp Bītī: Autobiography*, 6 vol., Lenasia, 2007.

Zaman, Muhammad Qasim, *The Ulama in Contemporary Islam: Custodians of Change*, Princeton, 2002.

Zebiri, K., *Mahmud Shaltut and Islamic Modernism*, Oxford, 1996.

Journals

Ta'mīr-i Hayāt, Special Issue (Lucknow, 2000).

The Fragrance of the East, Special Issue (Lucknow, 2000.)

Islamic Studies (Islamabad 1993, 32: 4).

OCIS Newsletter (January, 2000).

International Journal of Middle Eastern Studies (2003).

Al-Ahsan, (2001 vol. 1-2).

Al-Qāsim, Special Issue (Lahore, 2001).

Kārwān-i Adab (Lucknow, 2001).

Al-Mimbar Monthly (Faisalabad, 1993).

Al Furqan Digest (Lucknow, 1976).

Bayyināt (Karachi, 1980).

Al-Manhal (Riyad, 1421).

Hamdard Islamicus (Karachi, 2003).

Discourse (Auckland Park, 2004).

Fikri-i Islami (Basti, 2001).

SAYYID ABUL HASAN ALI NADWI: LIFE AND LEGACY, by Abdul Kader Choughley. Aligarh, India: K.A.N. Centre for Quranic Studies in association with Springs, South Africa: Ahsan Academy of Research, 2022, 416pp. ISBN: 9789391601256.

Students of South Asian Islam, particularly *Da'wah*, Islamic revivalism and the identity issue of Indian Muslims in post-1947 independent India shouldbe grateful to the renowned South African Muslim scholar Dr Abdul Kader Choughley for having produced an authoritative and analytical work on the entire oeuvre of a towering Islamic scholar and revivalist of our times, Syed Abu'l-Hasan 'Ali Nadwi (1913–1999). Nadwi's highly motivating and eloquent writings, originally written in chaste, idiomatic Arabic and translated into major languages, represent a clarion call for the return to pristine Islam. He devoted himself, heart and soul, to Islamic revivalism, particularly in the Arab lands. As a devout and pious scholar who led an ascetic life, he commanded respect across the Muslim world. Choughley has done well to present his inspiring, enviable life and accomplishments.

This work is derived, in the main, from Nadwi's seven-volume autobiography, *Kāravān-i Zindagī* in Urdu (1984–1999), though the author has also drawn upon the following seminal, thought-provoking works of Nadwi: (i) *The Rise and Fall of Muslims: Its Impact on the World* (originally written in Arabic entitled *Mādhā Khasira al- 'Ālam bi'Inhitāt al- Muslimīn*) and (2) *Muslim in the West: The Message and Mission* (1983).

Nadwi's multivolume autobiography running into thousands of pages stands out also as a well-documented chronicle of his times, acquainting readers with the intellectual, religious, socio-cultural and ideological currents and crosscurrents of the day. In penning this wide-ranging chronicle, Nadwi seems to be following in the footsteps of his father, a renowned Islamic scholar, 'Abdal-Hayy al-Hasani, whose *Nuzhat al- Khawatīr* stands out as an encyclopaedic work on the intellectual history of Muslim India. This latter work in eight volumes in Arabic serves as an excellent biographical dictionary of eminent Muslims down the ages from the 1st to 14th *Hijrī* century. In his prefatory note, Nadwi refers to three Urdu autobiographies of his predecessors, who were also his mentors in varying degrees, which inspired him to embark on this venture: Husayn Ahmad Madani's *Naqsh-i Hayāt*, Muhammad Zakariyya's *Āp Biti* and Abdul Majid Daryabadi's *Āp Biti*.

Common to these works and Nadwi's own is the intellectual history of Indian Muslims, with a focus on their religious life in 20th century India. All the four works grapple with the issue of the Islamic identity of Indian Muslims in the face of the threats and challenges posed by colonialism, westernization and, of late, the right-wing Hindu aggressiveness directed at Indian Muslims. Not only has Choughley discerningly condensed Nadwi's tome, he has also packaged it well with his brilliant editorial and presentational skills. The speaking titles of sixteen chapters of the book, the extensive time line of Nadwi's life and legacy (pp. xx-xxix), and exhaustive bibliography, with a focus on Nadwi's writings (pp. 395–397) are some of the commendable features of Choughley's book, which have rendered it quite reader-friendly.

In his introduction (pp. xxxi-xxxvii) Choughley offers a conspectus of Nadwi's contributions which consist in according primacy to the Qur'an and Sunnah, reinvigorating *Da'wah* and *tajdīd* (Islamic revivalism), mounting an incisive critique on westernization, materialism and un-Islamic practices throughout the Muslim world, particularly in Arab lands, and preserving and reinforcing Islamic identity among the beleaguered Muslim minority of India. It is noteworthy that Nadwi's striving on the above crucial fronts was not confined to producing stirring and engaging works, for he was also an activist, as he visited many countries and towns to deliver inspiring and motivating lectures and established a number of institutions, organizations, academies and networks. Little wonder then that several academies across the world, set up as a memorial to him, have been actively carrying out his mission for the last two decades, since his demise. The co-publisher of the book under review, Ahsan Academy is also named after him and has brought out more than a dozen quality books in English on Islam in South Asia and Islamic resurgence.

Sayyid Abu'l-Hasan Nadwi was born into a family of pious Muslim scholars and had the perfect Islamic upbringing. Apart from his pious parents, in his formative years he was influenced by Arab teachers at his school, *Nadwat al-'Ulamā'*, Lucknow, Shaykh Khalil and Shaykh Taqi al-Din al-Hilali, and his occasional meetings with the widely acclaimed Islamic revivalist poet and thinker, Muhammad Iqbal. This interaction went a long way in honing his enviable mastery of the Arabic language and literature, his immersion in the cause of *Da'wah* and Islamic revivalism and his life-long devotion to academic pursuits wedded unflinchingly to Islam. Amid his early writings, a series of his textbooks *Qasas al-Nabīyyīn* deserves special mention. While intended for Arabic readers, these stories are profusely interspersed with Qur'ānic verses which familiarize young students with both the literary marvels of the Qur'an as well as its inspiriting and didactic message. In his early career as an Islamist in 1941, he was drawn towards Sayyid Mawdudi's writings and vision of Islam. Choughley has deftly analysed this companionship which ended with Sayyid Nadwi moving away from *Jamā'at-i Islāmī* to the *Tablighi Jamā'at*, another highly popular Islamic revivalist movement, set in motion by Muhammad Ilyās (pp. 53-57 and 69-70). *The Rise and Fall of Muslims,* another of his

Book Review

major works originally written in Arabic in 1947, which is a brilliant critique of modern, secular liberalism, established his credentials as a profound Muslim thinker. His religio-political activism took him frequently to Arab lands, particularly Saudi Arabia. In his impassioned speeches, he exhorted Muslims to return to the original Islam and emulate the Prophet's role model. Vigorously he carried out the same *Da'wah* work in the West. Scores of his books, based on his speeches in both the Muslim world and the West, bear out his unstinting commitment to *Da'wah*.

Sayyid Nadwi also excelled as a pragmatic activist who set up institutions for the wider dissemination of the ideals dear to his heart. Apart from consolidating *Nadwat al-'Ulamā'*, Lucknow, he was instrumental in establishing the following institutions: *Dīnī Ta'līmī* Council, *Majlīs-i Mushāwarah*, *Payām-i Insāniyat*, *Rābitat Adab al-'Ālam al-Islāmī* and Muslim Personal Law Board. The *Payām-i Insāniyat* movement aimed at forging cordial Hindu-Muslim relations, particularly in the wake of horrendous communal riots in post-1947 Independent India, in which thousands of Muslims had been brutally killed by both state police and Hindutva forces. He strove to rally Hindus and Muslims under the banner of their common moral and spiritual values.

Choughley has perceptively identified the following key themes in Sayyid Nadwi's writings: the elucidation of the meaning and message of the Qur'an as a guide for Muslims in today's world; the elaboration of the Islamic way of life, encompassing both faith and practices; the relevance of Islam not only for Muslims but for humanity at large; the preservation of the Indo-Islamic culture; maintaining and reinforcing Muslim identity, particularly the identity of the Indian Muslim minority community; the critique of westernization and materialism; devising new strategies for *Da'wah*; promoting Islamic literature, and ensuring *tarbiyyah* (education) for the young and striving for Islamic revivalism.

Appended to the work are a helpful glossary, a comprehensive bibliography and some photos. Choughley is to be applauded for having made Sayyid Nadwi's voluminous autobiographical work available in a neatly condensed form in English. It will be read with much profit by all those interested in 20th century Islamic revivalism and the Indian Muslim community. This well-documented work encompasses almost all there is to know about Sayyid Nadwi's accomplishments, and 20th century Islamic revivalism.

Aligarh Muslim University
Abdur Raheem Kidwai
Aligarh, India